D1599973

# Improving Children's Lives

# Primary Prevention of Psychopathology

George W. Albee and Justin M. Joffe
*General Editors*

## *VOLUMES IN THIS SERIES:*

Prevention of Delinquent Behavior, 1987
John D. Burchard and Sara N. Burchard, *Editors*
VOLUME X

Families in Transition, 1988
Lynne A. Bond and Barry M. Wagner, *Editors*
VOLUME XI

Primary Prevention and Promotion in the Schools, 1989
Lynne A. Bond and Bruce E. Compas, *Editors*
VOLUME XII

Primary Prevention of AIDS, 1989
Vickie M. Mays, George W. Albee, and Stanley F. Schneider, *Editors*
VOLUME XIII

Improving Children's Lives, 1992
George W. Albee, Lynne A. Bond, and Toni V. Cook Monsey, *Editors*
VOLUME XIV

Volumes I-IX are available from
University Press of New England
3 Lebanon Street, Hanover, New Hampshire 03755

# Improving Children's
# Children's
# Lives Global Perspectives on Prevention

EDITORS
GEORGE W. ALBEE
LYNNE A. BOND
TONI V. COOK MONSEY

**SAGE** PUBLICATIONS
*The International Professional Publishers*
Newbury Park   London   New Delhi

*For information address*:

SAGE Publications, Inc.
2455 Teller Road
Newbury Park, California 91320

SAGE Publications Ltd.
6 Bonhill Street
London EC2A 4PU
United Kingdom

SAGE Publications India Pvt. Ltd.
M-32 Market
Greater Kailash I
New Delhi 110 048 India

Printed in the United States of America

**Library of Congress Cataloging-in-Publication Data**

Main entry under title:

Improving children's lives: global perspectives on prevention /
    editors, George W. Albee, Lynne A. Bond, Toni V. C. Monsey.
        p.    cm.—(Primary prevention of psychopathology; v. 14)
    Outgrowth of the Fifteenth Vermont Conference on the Primary
Prevention of Psychopathology, held June 1990 at the University of Vermont.
    Includes bibliographical references and indexes.
    ISBN 0-8039-4610-4 (cl)
    1. Child psychiatry—Congresses.   2. Community mental health
services for children—Congresses.   3. Mental illness—Prevention—
Congresses.   I. Albee, George W.   II. Bond, Lynne A., 1949-   .
III. Monsey, Toni V. C.   IV. Vermont Conference on the Primary
Prevention of Psychopathology (15th: 1990: University of Vermont)
V. Series
RC454.P683   vol. 14
[RJ499]
616.89'05 s—dc20
[618.92'8905]                                                                91-35916

92  93  94  95   10  9  8  7  6  5  4  3  2  1

Sage Production Editor:  Diane S. Foster

# Contents

# Preface

This book grew, in large part, from the fifteenth Vermont Conference on the Primary Prevention of Psychopathology, convened in June 1990, and part of a series of annual meetings at the University of Vermont since 1975. This conference was cohosted by the World Federation for Mental Health, with generous support from the National Institute of Mental Health, the John D. and Catherine T. MacArthur Foundation, and the Division of Continuing Education at the University of Vermont.

The 1990 meetings focused on efforts to improve children's lives around the world. Scholars, practitioners, educators, and policymakers from multiple and diverse nations came together to consider both common and unique problems facing youth around the world. They analyzed successes, failures, obstacles, and possibilities for promoting healthier development and well-being among our children.

Nowhere is there clearer evidence of the need for social and political changes to bring about successful efforts at prevention than in the massive problems facing children throughout the world. The problems, both physical and psychological, afflicting the world's children are so vast as to numb the mind. It is impossible to absorb the fact that 12-14 million children die unnecessarily each year of easily curable infant diarrhea and common infectious childhood diseases, or that millions of others die of diseases such as kwashiorkor (a term originating in the Ashanti languages of West Africa, describing protein deficiency and wasting away) or simple starvation—and the list goes on and on. All of these conditions are easily treatable and clearly preventable. A modest investment of a few cents per child could reverse critical cases of infant diarrhea; further modest investment of available technology could bring pure water to replace the contaminated water that causes infant diarrhea. Sharing our vast resources of protein and grains, or restoring parched and unproductive farmlands with irrigation, could save millions from misery, starvation, and developmental delays and disabilities.

Technology for family planning could be used to reduce high birthrates in impoverished nations, while dealing with the religious, cultural, and political resistance. The frequently heard argument that the millions of unnecessary childhood deaths are a necessary part of population control is simply untrue. Reducing infant mortality has been shown, in country after country, to be associated with a reduction in the number of conceptions. If parents can have reasonable expectations for the survival of their infants and young children, there follows a significant reduction in the number of babies born. With a smaller number of pregnancies, births are more optimally spaced and infants are more likely to be nourished and nurtured adequately.

For a number of social, cultural, and political reasons, nations have invested fewer of their economic resources in programs to ensure healthy babies and children than in a large number of other areas that have greater appeal to politicians in male-dominated governments. The needs of women and children, particularly female children, have had a low priority in the less developed, so-called Third World nations, as well as in those of the so-called Second and First Worlds, where we also find significant numbers of children at high risk for physical and mental difficulties. In the United States the problems of oppressed multicultural children, homeless children, and children of undereducated, underserved, and other exploited groups are so numerous as to command a significant share of our attention. Too many U.S. and Canadian inhabitants point to the problems of less developed countries and avoid acknowledgment of the serious injustices on their own doorsteps.

We have been struck by how difficult it seems to be to recognize that each of the millions of children who are suffering around the world are *individuals*. While we hear of the large numbers of children affected by serious problems of health, education, and development, it is difficult to grasp the meaning of these mass statistics. Featured individually and in detail, each one of these millions of children presents a dramatic illustration of the severity of the issues at hand. It is ironic that the more common and widespread problems typically draw less focused attention and response from the media and the public than the more idiosyncratic and singular instances of child distress and pain. We are challenged to construct strategies for retaining an appreciation of the many individuals who make up the masses, and for acting on their behalf.

To examine these and related issues, the Vermont Conference on Primary Prevention and its cohost, the World Federation for Mental Health, invited nominations for conference speakers from a variety of national and international groups and from organizations and individuals active in efforts at improving children's lives around the world. What emerged was a talented, diverse, and committed group of individuals, a number of whom have contributed to the present volume.

The Vermont Conference on the Primary Prevention of Psychopathology (VCPPP) is a nonprofit educational foundation incorporated in the state of Vermont and based at the Department of Psychology, University of Vermont. Its board members include George W. Albee, Ph.D., professor of psychology; Lynne A. Bond, Ph.D., professor of psychology and dean of the Graduate College; John D. Burchard, Ph.D., professor of psychology; Marc Kessler, Ph.D., associate professor of psychology; Justin M. Joffe, Ph.D., professor of psychology; and Barbara York, a historian currently employed at the Smithsonian Institute, Washington, DC.

Special recognition and thanks go to the staff of VCPPP. During the planning and organizing of the 1990 conference, Toni V. C. Monsey, a doctoral candidate in developmental psychology at the University of Vermont, served as conference coordinator, assisted by Mary Pyle, a recent graduate of the University of Rhode Island, and Pat Burgmeier, a graduate student in developmental psychology. Gisele Lizewski and Samantha Austin in the Psychology Department and Anne Buley in the Graduate College made major contributions to conference organization, operations, correspondence, and information management.

Three members of the World Federation for Mental Health were particularly important in contributing to the planning, publicity, and convening of the conference: Max Abbott, president-elect; Beverly Benson Long, vice president for North America; and Hilda Robbins, board member at large. Their dedication and enthusiasm throughout the conference activities were extraordinary.

Support from several organizations was critical to both the success of the 1990 conference and the completion of this book. As in years past, the National Institute of Mental Health (NIMH) provided significant funding as well as technical and scholarly input to the conference. We are particularly grateful to Juan Ramos, deputy director of Prevention and Special Projects at NIMH; Joyce Lazar, former chief of the Prevention Research Branch at NIMH; Doreen Koretz, assistant chief of the Prevention Research Branch; and Edward J. Kelty, staff director, International Programs, Office of the Director NIMH, all of whom were instrumental in supporting the conference and book activities.

We also appreciate the generous support of the John D. and Catherine T. MacArthur Foundation, which provided significant funding to transport and accommodate our international speakers as well as to ensure the dissemination of this volume to nations around the world, supporting an ever-growing international prevention network.

Special thanks go to the University of Vermont for providing a home and base of support to the VCPPP, Inc., over the last 15 years, and we thank the university's Division of Continuing Education for generously contributing its services in order to make this year's conference possible.

—George W. Albee
—Lynne A. Bond
—Toni V. C. Monsey

# PART I
# Epidemiology of Distress and Risk

As everyone in the field of public health knows, effective prevention programs only begin following a clear understanding of the distribution of the condition or conditions to be prevented. A study of the distribution and size of groups at risk is one of the cornerstones of the field of epidemiology. Our book begins with an overview of epidemiological considerations from several varied and quite distinct levels and perspectives, ranging from broad-based statistical and conceptual representation to an individual case study. The complement of these varied perspectives offers a richer understanding of the task we face in trying to improve the lives of children around the world.

The first chapter is authored by Professor Emeritus Morton Kramer of the Johns Hopkins University School of Hygiene and Public Health. Dr. Kramer was for many years head of the Biostatistics Research Branch of the National Institute of Mental Health. In recent years he has continued to be a major observer of the worldwide patterns of demographic and related factors associated with the incidence and prevalence of physical illness and mental disorders. Kramer provides us with detailed figures to use in the development of an accurate perception of different regions of the world and their demography, including such things as population growth, age distributions, life expectancy, HIV infection (AIDS), and comparative rates of poverty.

Often factual tables, while essential for planning and for giving perspective, do not convey the human anguish and suffering associated with overcrowding, overpopulation, family disruption, and exploitation. Allen Durning's chapter, reprinted from *World Watch* magazine, illustrates graphically and at a human level the growing division between the world of the wealthy and the world of the poverty-stricken. He pictures vividly the lives of the poor and the landless, the exploitation of women who often are powerless to change their lives, and the savage toll measured in the lives of children. He gives some hopeful examples of innovative grass-roots programs, but warns about those who block progress. Durning is senior researcher at the Worldwatch Institute in Washington, D.C., and he specializes in issues of the relationship between inequality and environmental degradation. One of his Worldwatch papers on poverty was awarded First Prize for Periodical Coverage in the 1989 World Hunger Media Awards.

In Chapter 3, a group of psychologists and psychiatrists from the Soviet Union report an epidemiological study of the rate of mental/emotional disorders

1

among children in Moscow. Interestingly, the rates turn out to be very similar to those in the United States and Canada. This chapter provides an interesting perspective on the recent emergence of prevention programs affecting children in the Soviet Union during a time of major social change. The authors, all working at the All-Union Mental Health Research Center of the USSR Academy of Medical Sciences in Moscow, note the enormous current social changes occurring in their country and suggest examples of how these changes are reflected in new approaches to prevention work with children and families.

During the 1990 Vermont Conference on Primary Prevention, participants heard about the horrors that befell a young girl, Fatima, from Bangladesh. One of the conference attendees, Barry Jay, Ph.D., provided information he had collected, and he also reported on the efforts of a New Haven attorney, Debra W. Weecks, and the law firm with which she is associated, to obtain the release of Fatima. Since the conference, Jay and Weecks have provided additional information about this little girl and the problems of child trafficking and child/woman slavery. The story of Fatima provides a real case study of what happens to hundreds of thousands of children. We decided to include it in this section so the reader will be reminded that behind the epidemiological data there are real individuals who are truly suffering.

# 1

# Barriers to the Primary Prevention of Mental, Neurological, and Psychosocial Disorders of Children: A Global Perspective

**Morton Kramer**

The 39th World Health Assembly in May 1986 adopted a resolution calling on all member states to apply the preventive measures identified in the World Health Organization's Director General's report *Prevention of Mental, Neurological and Psychosocial Disorders* (WHO, 1986a) and to include these activities in their strategies to achieve Health for All by the Year 2000 (WHO, 1987). The report referred to in this resolution summarized the magnitude of the worldwide public health burden resulting from the following mental, neurological, and psychosocial disorders and problems (WHO, 1986a, 1986c):

- mental retardation
- acquired lesions of the central nervous system
- peripheral neuropathy
- psychosis
- epilepsy
- emotional and conduct disorders
- psychoactive substance abuse
- conditions of life that lead to disease
- violence
- excessive risk-taking behaviors among youth
- family breakdown

I will not go into the details of the epidemiologic data on the incidence and prevalence of these disorders and the burdens they create for individuals affected by one or more of these conditions, their families, children, friends, and

3

the communities in which they live. It is sufficient to say that these disorders and problems—to be referred to here as MNP disorders—take a heavy toll in each period of the life span. What I will dwell on are selected phenomena that I perceive to be major barriers to carrying out preventive activities, indeed, to applying knowledge that could prevent certain mental disorders from occurring, particularly those of organic etiology (e.g., organic brain syndromes associated with syphilis, pellagra, poisonings, infections, perinatal factors, accidents) and knowledge that, in other instances, could reduce considerably the disabling conditions resulting from disorders of unknown etiology that as yet cannot be prevented from occurring (e.g., schizophrenia, depressive disorders, Alzheimer's disease).

I will direct my comments principally to barriers to primary prevention. However, in my illustrations I will be using prevalence data to illustrate points I wish to make, as the types of incidence data I need for my illustrations are difficult or impossible to come by. As prevalence varies as the product of incidence and duration, the reduction of prevalence can be accomplished by reducing incidence, duration, or both.

## Population Growth, by Regions of the World

A major barrier to prevention is the rate of growth of the world's population. The rapid rate of total population growth will be adding large numbers of persons to populations already experiencing high prevalence rates of specific MNP disorders. These additions contain many persons with biological, social, and economic characteristics that place them at high risk of developing at least one MNP disorder. This means that the prevalence of these disorders will increase more rapidly than society can prevent their occurrence. This will happen *unless* programs are instituted rapidly, with sufficient personnel and resources, to prevent from occurring specific disorders that can be prevented, to terminate disorders that respond to specific treatments, and to reduce the duration of the disabling effects of those disorders that cannot be terminated or prevented.

The following data will illustrate these points. As of 1990 the population of the world was estimated to be 5.25 billion (medium variant estimate, United Nations, 1987). It is projected to be 6.12 billion by the year 2000, an increase of 17%. The corresponding estimates and projections for the more developed regions of the world are 1.21 billion for 1990 and 1.27 billion for 2000, an increase of 5.5%, and for the less developed regions, 4.03 billion in 1990 and 4.84 billion in 2000, an increase of 20.0%. Table 1.1 provides these estimates for the major regions and areas of the world, plus an additional set for the year 2010.

Although the annual rates of population growth of both the more and the less developed regions of the world have been decreasing steadily (Figure 1.1), the number of persons being added annually is and will continue to be considerable.

**Table 1.1** Estimated Population of the World (medium variant) by Regions and Areas of the World, Percentage Distributions 1990, 2000, and 2010, and Percentage Change 1990-2000, 2000-2010, 1990-2010

| Region and Areas of the World | 1990 | 2000 | 2010 |
|---|---|---|---|
| *Number in 000s* | | | |
| World | 5,246,209 | 6,121,813 | 6,989,128 |
| More Developed | 1,209,777 | 1,276,647 | 1,331,199 |
| Less Developed | 4,036,432 | 4,845,166 | 5,657,929 |
| World | 5,246,209 | 6,121,813 | 6,989,128 |
| South Asia | 1,733,500 | 2,073,960 | 2,393,805 |
| East Asia | 1,324,149 | 1,475,036 | 1,588,553 |
| Africa | 645,282 | 871,817 | 1,157,528 |
| Latin America | 451,072 | 546,395 | 641,978 |
| Europe | 498,592 | 512,474 | 519,520 |
| Soviet Union | 291,822 | 314,736 | 337,120 |
| North America | 275,325 | 297,335 | 317,222 |
| Oceania | 26,467 | 30,062 | 33,402 |
| *Percentage of Total* | | | |
| World | 100.0 | 100.0 | 100.0 |
| More Developed | 23.1 | 20.9 | 19.0 |
| Less Developed | 76.9 | 79.1 | 81.0 |
| World | 100.0 | 100.0 | 100.0 |
| South Asia | 33.0 | 33.9 | 34.3 |
| East Asia | 25.2 | 24.1 | 22.7 |
| Africa | 12.3 | 14.2 | 16.6 |
| Latin America | 8.6 | 8.9 | 9.2 |
| Europe | 9.5 | 8.4 | 7.4 |
| Soviet Union | 5.6 | 5.1 | 4.8 |
| North America | 5.2 | 4.9 | 4.5 |
| Oceania | .5 | .5 | .5 |
| *Percentage Change* | *1990 to 2000* | *2000 to 2010* | *1990 to 2010* |
| World | 16.7 | 14.2 | 33.2 |
| More Developed | 5.5 | 4.3 | 10.0 |
| Less Developed | 20.0 | 16.8 | 40.2 |
| World | 16.7 | 14.2 | 33.2 |
| South Asia | 19.6 | 15.4 | 38.1 |
| East Asia | 11.4 | 7.7 | 20.0 |
| Africa | 35.1 | 32.8 | 79.4 |
| Latin America | 21.1 | 17.5 | 42.3 |
| Europe | 2.8 | 1.4 | 4.2 |
| Soviet Union | 7.9 | 7.1 | 15.5 |
| North America | 8.0 | 6.7 | 15.2 |
| Oceania | 13.5 | 11.1 | 26.2 |

SOURCE: United Nations (1987). *Global Estimates and Projections of Population by Sex and Age.* Department of International Economic and Social Affairs. ST/ESA/SER.R/70. New York.

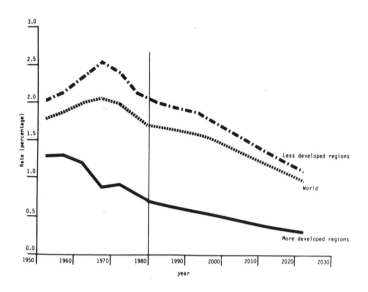

**Figure 1.1.** Average Annual Rate of Population Growth for the World, More Developed and Less Developed Regions, Medium Variant, 1950-2025
SOURCE: United Nations (1985). Reprinted by permission.

To illustrate, between 1990 and 2000 the average annual increment to the population of the world (medium variant) is expected to be about 87.6 million, with the annual increment in the more developed regions accounting for 6.7 million, 8% of this total, and that for the less developed regions accounting for 80.9 million, 92% of the total.

Table 1.1 shows the projected increase in the population of the world and the percentage distribution by region for the years 1990, 2000, and 2010. The world population will increase from 5.2 billion in 1990 to 6.1 billion in 2000 (17%) and is projected to increase to about 7.0 billion in 2010. The latter figure is an increase of 14% over the population of the year 2000 and 33% increase over that for 1990. The projected changes in the growth rates of the populations in the different regions and areas of the world are quite striking, particularly the growth rates between 1990 and 2010. These range from 79.4% for Africa to 4.2% for Europe (Table 1.1 and Figure 1.2).

The changes in percentages of the population of the world in the different areas have major implications for political, economic, social, and health policies facing the governments of the various countries in these regions, and for international collaboration among them.

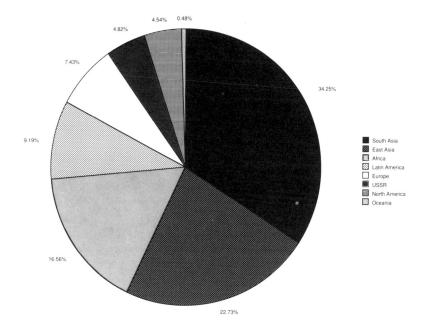

2010:    Population 7.0 Billion

**Figure 1.2.** Estimated Percentage of the Population of the World by Region, 2010
SOURCE: United Nations (1987). Reprinted by permission.
NOTE: See Table 1.1.

## Population Changes by Age

### All Ages

As background for changes in the age groups of specific interest to readers of this volume—the age groups under 15 years of age—I shall show the changes for the total range of age groups projected for the population of the world and its more and less developed regions between 1990 and 2000. For the world there will be a considerable increase in every age group, varying from a low of 4.8% in the age group 15-24 years to a high of 34.9% in the age group 45-54 years (Table 1.2 and Figure 1.3).

The age-specific increases of the population of the more developed regions are considerably lower in every age group than those of the less developed regions. To illustrate, the population in the age group 0-4 years in the more developed regions will decrease by 0.6%, while that in the less developed regions will increase by

**Table 1.2** Estimated Population of the World (medium variant), Numerical and Percentage Change for the World and Its More Developed and Less Developed Regions Specific for Age, 1990-2000

| Age (Years) | 1990 | | | 2000 | | |
|---|---|---|---|---|---|---|
| | Total | More Developed Regions | Less Developed Regions | Total | More Developed Regions | Less Developed Regions |
| *Population in 000s* | | | | | | |
| Total | 5,246,209 | 1,209,777 | 4,036,432 | 6,121,813 | 1,276,647 | 4,845,166 |
| 0-4 | 599,752 | 88,722 | 511,030 | 654,162 | 88,187 | 565,975 |
| 5-14 | 1,071,250 | 173,821 | 897,427 | 1,197,960 | 177,664 | 1,020,295 |
| 5-9 | 552,889 | 88,196 | 464,692 | 617,440 | 88,684 | 528,756 |
| 10-14 | 518,361 | 85,625 | 432,735 | 550,520 | 88,980 | 491,539 |
| 15-24 | 1,007,697 | 176,861 | 830,835 | 1,055,534 | 174,532 | 881,003 |
| 25-34 | 825,173 | 192,170 | 633,004 | 988,477 | 177,224 | 811,254 |
| 35-44 | 626,219 | 172,882 | 453,336 | 804,382 | 191,002 | 613,378 |
| 45-54 | 444,485 | 138,911 | 305,574 | 599,752 | 168,976 | 430,776 |
| 55-64 | 348,812 | 124,312 | 224,499 | 403,789 | 129,825 | 273,965 |
| 65-74 | 211,135 | 83,424 | 127,710 | 277,058 | 103,730 | 173,328 |
| 75+ | 111,688 | 58,673 | 53,015 | 140,700 | 65,506 | 75,192 |
| | *Change in Number of Persons, 1990-2000 (in 000s)* | | | *Percentage Change, 1990-2000* | | |
| Total | 875,604 | 66,870 | 808,734 | 16.69 | 5.53 | 20.04 |
| 0-4 | 54,410 | -535 | 54,945 | 9.17 | -0.60 | 10.75 |
| 5-14 | 126,710 | 3,843 | 122,868 | 11.83 | 2.21 | 13.69 |
| 5-9 | 64,551 | 488 | 64,064 | 11.68 | 0.55 | 13.79 |
| 10-14 | 62,159 | 3,355 | 58,804 | 11.99 | 3.91 | 13.59 |
| 15-24 | 47,837 | -2,329 | 50,168 | 4.75 | -1.32 | 6.04 |
| 25-34 | 163,304 | -14,946 | 178,250 | 19.79 | -7.78 | 28.16 |
| 35-44 | 178,163 | 18,120 | 160,042 | 28.45 | 10.48 | 35.30 |
| 45-54 | 155,267 | 30,065 | 125,202 | 34.93 | 21.64 | 40.97 |
| 55-64 | 54,977 | 5,513 | 49,466 | 15.76 | 4.43 | 22.03 |
| 65-74 | 65,923 | 20,306 | 45,618 | 31.22 | 24.34 | 35.72 |
| 75+ | 29,012 | 6,833 | 22,177 | 25.98 | 11.64 | 41.83 |

SOURCE: United Nations (1987). *Global Estimates and Projections of Population by Sex and Age.* Department of International Economic and Social Affairs. ST/ESA/SER.R/70. New York.
NOTE: More developed regions include North America, Japan, all regions of Europe, Australia-New Zealand, and the Soviet Union. Less developed regions include all regions of Africa, all regions of Latin America, China, other East Asia, all regions of South Asia, Melanesia, and Micronesia-Polynesia.

10.8%. The populations in the age groups 15-24 and 25-34 of the more developed regions will decrease by 1.3% and 7.8%, respectively, while in the less developed regions the corresponding age groups will increase by 6.0% and 28.1%.

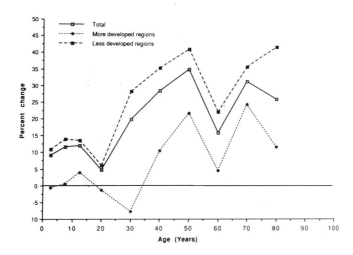

**Figure 1.3.** Percentage Change in Estimated Population for the World and More Developed and Less Developed Regions, Specific for Age, 1990-2000

SOURCE: United Nations (1987). Reprinted by permission.
NOTE: See Table 1.2.

The percentage increase expected in the populations of each of the other age groups of the less developed regions will exceed by considerable amounts the corresponding increases of the more developed regions.

### Ages 15 and Younger

As of 1990, the world population of children under 5 years of age is 599.8 million; of children 5-9 years, 552.9 million; and of those 10-14 years, 518.4 million (Table 1.2). Together, this makes a total population of 1.7 billion children under 15 years of age. In relation to the total population of the world, children 0-4 years account for 11.4% of this total; those 5-9 years, 10.5%; and those 10-14 years, 9.9%. Thus children under 15 years of age account for 31.8%, almost one-third, of the world's population.

By the year 2000 the number of children 0-4 years will increase by 9.2%; those 5-9 years by 11.7%; and those 10-14 years by 12.0%. The total number of children under 15 years of age in the year 2000 will be 1.9 billion, accounting for about 30% of the world's population in that year.

## Population Changes by Regions and Areas of the World

### Ages 4 Years and Younger

Table 1.3 shows the distribution of children in the age group under 5 years in the more and less developed regions of the world and in its major areas. Of the 599.8 million children in this age group as of 1990, about 15% are in the more developed and 85% in the less developed regions. The percentage distribution of these children by areas of the world ranges from 37.9% in South Asia, 18.8% in East Asia, 19.6% in Africa, and 9.9% in Latin America to 5.5% in Europe, 4.3% in the Soviet Union, 3.5% in North America, and 0.4% in Oceania.

### Ages 5-14

As of 1990, 1.07 billion of the world's children are in the 5-14 age group. This number will increase to 1.2 billion by the year 2000 (11.8% increase). The percentages of these children in the various regions and areas of the world are quite similar to those for children 0-4 years of age. The largest percentage of children 5-14 years are in the less developed regions of the world (83.8%); the smallest percentage is in more developed regions (16.2%). With respect to the specific areas of the world, the largest proportion is in South Asia (38.4%) and the smallest in Oceania (0.4%).

Projections to the year 2000 indicate that the largest percentage population increase will occur in Africa, from 174.6 million in 1990 to 237.3 million in 2000, an increase of 35.9%. The next largest increase during this decade will be in Latin America, from 105.2 million to 118.9 million, an increase of 13.0%. The other areas will experience smaller increases: 9.2% in South Asia, 4.0% in the Soviet Union, 3.5% in East Asia and a decrease of 1.7% in Europe. Table 1.4 also shows the effect of these changes on the percentage distribution of the number of children 5-14 in the regions and major areas of the world for the year 2000. Additional data are given to demonstrate the projections to the year 2010.

## Differential Growth Rates Within Areas

The preceding text and tables have described the differential growth rates of the populations in the major regions and areas of the world. There are equally important differences in the growth rates of countries within regions and among different ethnic and racial groups within countries. Data for the United States illustrate differences in the projected rates of growth between 1990 and 2000 of white non-Hispanics, blacks, Hispanics, and persons of other races specific for age (U.S. Bureau of the Census, 1986b) (Table 1.5).

During the decade 1990-2000, the total white non-Hispanic population of the United States will increase by 3.6%, the black population by 13.8%, the Hispanic

**Table 1.3** Estimated Number of Young Children 0-4 Years of Age by Regions and Areas of the World, Percentage Distributions 1990, 2000, and 2010, and Percentage Change 1990-2000, 2000-2010, and 1990-2010

| Regions and Areas of the World | 1990 | 2000 | 2010 |
|---|---|---|---|
| *Number in 000s* | | | |
| World | 599,752 | 654,162 | 670,436 |
| More Developed | 88,722 | 88,187 | 89,649 |
| Less Developed | 511,030 | 565,975 | 580,787 |
| World | 599,752 | 654,162 | 670,436 |
| South Asia | 227,594 | 236,287 | 230,894 |
| East Asia | 112,955 | 121,711 | 105,927 |
| Africa | 117,572 | 152,528 | 185,193 |
| Latin America | 59,459 | 62,932 | 65,829 |
| Europe | 33,018 | 32,826 | 31,399 |
| Soviet Union | 25,504 | 24,252 | 26,725 |
| North America | 21,169 | 21,026 | 21,846 |
| Oceania | 2,481 | 2,601 | 2,624 |
| *Percentage of Total* | | | |
| World | 100.0 | 100.0 | 100.0 |
| More Developed | 14.8 | 13.5 | 13.3 |
| Less Developed | 85.2 | 86.5 | 86.7 |
| World | 99.9 | 99.9 | 100.0 |
| South Asia | 37.9 | 36.1 | 34.4 |
| East Asia | 18.8 | 18.6 | 15.8 |
| Africa | 19.6 | 23.3 | 27.6 |
| Latin America | 9.9 | 9.6 | 9.8 |
| Europe | 5.5 | 5.0 | 4.7 |
| Soviet Union | 4.3 | 3.7 | 4.0 |
| North America | 3.5 | 3.2 | 3.3 |
| Oceania | 0.4 | 0.4 | 0.4 |
| *Percentage Change in Number of Persons* | | | |
| | *1990 to 2000* | *2000 to 2010* | *1990 to 2010* |
| World | 9.1 | 2.5 | 11.8 |
| More Developed | −0.6 | 1.7 | 1.0 |
| Less Developed | 10.8 | 2.6 | 13.7 |
| World | 9.1 | 2.5 | 11.8 |
| South Asia | 3.8 | −2.3 | 1.4 |
| East Asia | 7.8 | −13.0 | −6.2 |
| Africa | 29.7 | 21.4 | 57.5 |
| Latin America | 5.8 | 4.6 | 10.7 |
| Europe | −0.6 | −4.4 | −4.9 |
| Soviet Union | −4.9 | 10.2 | 4.8 |
| North America | −0.7 | 3.9 | 3.2 |
| Oceania | 4.8 | 0.9 | 5.8 |

SOURCE: United Nations (1987). *Global Estimates and Projections of Population by Sex and Age.* Department of International Economic and Social Affairs. ST/ESA/SER.R/70. New York.

**Table 1.4**    Estimated Distribution of Children 5-14 Years of Age, by Regions and Areas of the World, Percentage Distribution 1990, 2000, and 2010, and Percentage Change 1990-2000, 2000-2010, and 1990-2010

| Region of the World | 1990 | 2000 | 2010 |
|---|---|---|---|
| *Numbers in 000s* | | | |
| World | 1,071,250 | 1,197,960 | 1,288,972 |
| More Developed | 173,821 | 177,664 | 177,250 |
| Less Developed | 897,427 | 1,020,294 | 1,111,721 |
| World | 1,071,250 | 1,197,960 | 1,288,972 |
| South Asia | 411,230 | 448,839 | 458,602 |
| East Asia | 221,043 | 228,751 | 234,697 |
| Africa | 174,619 | 237,302 | 307,984 |
| Latin America | 105,216 | 118,873 | 125,517 |
| Europe | 67,270 | 66,157 | 64,641 |
| Soviet Union | 47,874 | 49,794 | 49,517 |
| North America | 39,416 | 43,163 | 42,741 |
| Oceania | 4,582 | 5,080 | 5,274 |
| *Percentage* | | | |
| World | 100.0 | 100.0 | 100.0 |
| More Developed | 16.2 | 14.8 | 15.1 |
| Less Developed | 83.8 | 85.2 | 84.9 |
| World | 100.0 | 100.0 | 100.0 |
| South Asia | 38.4 | 37.5 | 35.6 |
| East Asia | 20.6 | 19.1 | 18.2 |
| Africa | 16.3 | 19.8 | 23.9 |
| Latin America | 9.8 | 9.9 | 9.7 |
| Europe | 6.3 | 5.5 | 5.0 |
| Soviet Union | 4.5 | 4.2 | 3.8 |
| North America | 3.7 | 3.6 | 3.3 |
| Oceania | 0.4 | 0.4 | 0.4 |

| Percentage Change in Number of Persons | 1990 to 2000 | 2000 to 2010 | 1990 to 2010 |
|---|---|---|---|
| World | 11.8 | 7.6 | 20.3 |
| More Developed | 2.2 | −0.2 | 2.0 |
| Less Developed | 13.7 | 9.0 | 23.9 |
| World | 11.8 | 7.6 | 20.3 |
| South Asia | 9.2 | 2.2 | 11.5 |
| East Asia | 3.5 | 2.6 | 6.3 |
| Africa | 35.9 | 29.8 | 76.4 |
| Latin America | 13.0 | 5.6 | 19.3 |
| Europe | −1.7 | −2.2 | −3.9 |
| Soviet Union | 4.0 | −0.6 | 3.4 |
| North America | 9.5 | −1.1 | 8.4 |
| Oceania | 10.9 | 3.8 | 15.1 |

SOURCE: United Nations (1987). *Global Estimates and Projections of Population by Sex and Age.* Department of International Economic and Social Affairs. ST/ESA/SER.R/70. New York.
NOTE: More developed regions include North America, Japan, all regions of Europe, Australia-New Zealand, and the Soviet Union. Less developed regions include all regions of Africa, all regions of Latin America, China, other East Asia, all regions of South Asia, Melanesia, and Micronesia-Polynesia.

**Table 1.5**    Estimated Population of the United States by Age, Race, and Hispanic Origin, 1990-2000, Numeric and Percentage Change by Age (middle series)

| Age (Years) | 1990 Non-Hispanic White | Black | Hispanic[a] | Other Races | 2000 Non-Hispanic White | Black | Hispanic | Other Races |
|---|---|---|---|---|---|---|---|---|
| *Population in 000s* | | | | | | | | |
| Total | 192,040 | 31,412 | 19,887 | 7,456 | 198,919 | 35,753 | 25,225 | 9,548 |
| < 5 | 13,243 | 3,215 | 2,282 | 593 | 11,496 | 3,079 | 2,496 | 704 |
| 5-13 | 22,705 | 5,098 | 3,472 | 1,112 | 23,235 | 5,776 | 4,382 | 1,250 |
| 14-17 | 9,266 | 1,944 | 1,353 | 461 | 10,595 | 2,545 | 1,825 | 525 |
| 18-24 | 18,919 | 3,798 | 2,386 | 826 | 17,200 | 3,773 | 2,766 | 1,022 |
| 25-34 | 32,874 | 5,860 | 3,629 | 1,381 | 26,011 | 5,316 | 3,804 | 1,509 |
| 35-44 | 29,664 | 4,295 | 2,788 | 1,261 | 32,783 | 5,811 | 3,803 | 1,577 |
| 45-64 | 37,836 | 4,624 | 2,851 | 1,298 | 48,097 | 6,479 | 4,430 | 2,142 |
| 65-84 | 24,603 | 2,322 | 1,031 | 484 | 25,216 | 2,563 | 1,551 | 749 |
| 85+ | 2,928 | 257 | 95 | 38 | 4,286 | 412 | 168 | 69 |
| | *Change in Number of Persons in 000s* | | | | *Percentage Change in Number of Persons* | | | |
| Total | 6,878 | 4,341 | 5,338 | 2,092 | 3.58 | 13.82 | 26.84 | 28.06 |
| < 5 | -1,747 | -136 | 214 | 111 | -13.19 | -4.23 | 9.38 | 18.72 |
| 5-13 | 530 | 678 | 910 | 138 | 2.33 | 13.30 | 26.21 | 12.41 |
| 14-17 | 1,329 | 601 | 472 | 64 | 14.34 | 30.92 | 34.89 | 13.88 |
| 18-24 | -1,719 | -25 | 1,387 | 196 | -9.09 | -0.66 | 15.93 | 23.73 |
| 25-34 | -6,863 | -544 | 175 | 128 | -20.88 | -9.28 | 4.82 | 9.27 |
| 35-44 | 3,119 | 1,516 | 1,015 | 316 | 10.51 | 35.30 | 36.41 | 25.06 |
| 45-64 | 10,261 | 1,855 | 1,579 | 844 | 27.12 | 40.12 | 55.38 | 65.02 |
| 65-84 | 613 | 241 | 520 | 265 | 2.49 | 10.38 | 50.44 | 54.79 |
| 85+ | 1,358 | 155 | 73 | 31 | 46.38 | 60.31 | 76.84 | 81.58 |

SOURCE: U.S. Bureau of the Census (1986b).
a. Persons of Hispanic origin may be of any race.

population by 26.8%, and the population of other ethnic groups by 28.0%. The expected changes in the number of persons under 5 years of age range from decreases of 13.2% and 4.2% for white non-Hispanics and blacks, respectively, to increases of 9.4% and 18.7% among Hispanic and other ethnic groups, respectively. Among persons 5-13 years of age, the expected changes are 2.3% for white non-Hispanics, 13.3% for blacks, 26.2% for Hispanics, and 12.4% for other ethnic groups. For persons 14-17 years of age, the expected changes are 14.3% for white non-Hispanics, 30.9 for blacks, 34.9% for Hispanics, and 13.9% for other races. Table 1.5 shows the numerical size of these changes and the resulting age distributions of the respective populations.

**Table 1.6**   Estimated Number of Cases of Mental Disorders Among Children
Under 18 Years of Age, Assuming a Prevalence Rate of 12%,[a] by
Regions and Major Areas of the World, 1990-2000

| Regions and Areas of the World | Number (000s) 1990 | 2000 | Percentage Change | Expected Cases (000s) 1990 | 2000 | Percentage Change |
|---|---|---|---|---|---|---|
| Total | 1,981,348 | 2,179,129 | 10.0 | 237,761 | 261,495 | 10.0 |
| More Developed | 314,874 | 318,976 | 1.3 | 37,784 | 38,277 | 1.3 |
| Less Developed | 1,666,474 | 1,860,153 | 11.6 | 199,976 | 223,218 | 11.6 |
| South Asia | 749,715 | 810,975 | 8.2 | 89,965 | 97,317 | 8.2 |
| East Asia | 418,924 | 414,982 | -0.9 | 50,270 | 49,798 | -0.9 |
| Africa | 332,139 | 444,886 | 33.9 | 39,857 | 53,386 | 33.9 |
| Latin America | 192,502 | 214,388 | 11.4 | 23,100 | 25,726 | 11.4 |
| Europe | 121,701 | 118,894 | -2.3 | 14,604 | 14,267 | -2.3 |
| Soviet Union | 86,059 | 88,957 | 3.4 | 10,327 | 10,674 | 3.4 |
| North America | 71,863 | 76,915 | 7.0 | 8,623 | 9,230 | 7.0 |
| Oceania | 8,445 | 9,132 | 8.1 | 1,013 | 1,096 | 8.1 |

SOURCE: United Nations (1987). *Global Estimates and Projections of Population by Sex and Age.* Department of International Economic and Social Affairs. ST/ESA/SER.R/70. New York.
a. Institute of Medicine (1990, p. 33).

The frequencies of different mental disorders will also vary by country, sex, health, and socioeconomic status of children and their families and other factors (Kramer, 1989a, 1989b). As has been emphasized over and over again, rapid population growth is a barrier to prevention. The size of the problems that exist currently and those that are predicted to occur as a result of such growth will outdistance by far our current capabilities of dealing with them.

### The Effect of Population Growth on Prevalence

I will provide an example to illustrate how the relative increase in population (i.e., the percentage increase in the number of persons in a population) affects prevalence. In the absence of age-specific prevalence rates for mental disorders, I will use the total prevalence rate of these disorders for children under 18 years of age as reported in the recent publication of the Institute of Medicine (IOM), *Research on Children and Adolescents with Mental, Behavioral and Developmental Disorders* (1990).

Let us assume that the IOM's conservative estimate of a prevalence rate of 12% for children under 18 applies uniformly to the children in the various areas of the world listed in Table 1.6. Let us also assume that there will be no change in this prevalence rate between 1990 and 2000. Table 1.6 provides the results of these computations. The total number of cases of mental disorders in children under 18 years of age would increase from 237.8 million in 1990 to 261.5 in the year 2000, an increase of 10%. In the more developed regions the number of cases would increase from 37.8 million to 38.2 million, an increase of 1.3%. In the less developed regions the number of cases would increase from 200.0 million to 223.2 million, an increase of almost 12%. Note that these increases are the same as those for the populations in these regions.

The IOM committee noted that the prevalence rate may exceed 20% in some populations where children are exposed to severe psychosocial adversity. If the 20% rate were used in the above computations, the expected number of total cases in the year 2000 would almost double, to about 436 million cases!

## Urbanization

Another demographic phenomenon that is producing barriers to prevention—and will continue to do so—is the increasing urbanization of the world's population. As stated in the United Nations (1986) *Report on the World Social Situation*:

> Urbanization, largely a result of a long transformation in the structure of economy and technology, brings about changes which are often synonymous with the transition of society from the traditional to the modern, with its accompanying tensions, problems and opportunities. The process of urbanization, or the concentration of a large population in a relatively small area, performing a diverse set of economic and social functions, implies a changing living and working environment, new life styles, aspirations and social institutions. (p. 84)

The percentage of the world's population living in urban areas has increased from about 37% in 1970 to 43% in 1990. It is projected to increase to about 47% in 2000 and to 63% in the year 2025 (United Nations, 1989a).

Between 1990 and the year 2000 the percentage of the population living in urban areas in the more developed regions will have increased from 73% to 75% and that in the less developed regions from 34% to 40% (Table 1.7). This means that by the year 2000 the urban population of the more developed regions will be more than 945 million, and of the less developed regions more than 1,971 million.

Table 1.8 provides data on how much of the world's population will be living in urban areas by regions and areas of the world, 1990-2025. A disturbing feature of this trend is the proliferation of slums and squatter settlements in the developing countries. Between one-fourth and one-half of the urban population in many of these countries live under appalling conditions, lacking the minimum infrastructure and basic amenities of life. The population of such settlements is expected to rise to more than a billion by the year 2000. The World Health Organization (1981a) has commented on the consequences of this unplanned and unchecked urban growth:

**Table 1.7**    Distribution of Population of the World, Its More and Less Developed
Regions, by Urban and Rural Areas (in 000s) and Percentage Change,
1990-2010

| Years | Total | Urban Areas | Rural Areas | Percentage Urban |
|---|---|---|---|---|
| *World* | | | | |
| 1990 | 5,292,178 | 2,260,399 | 3,031,779 | 42.7 |
| 2000 | 6,251,055 | 2,916,501 | 3,334,554 | 46.7 |
| 2010 | 7,190,762 | 3,736,674 | 3,454,088 | 52.0 |
| Percentage Change | | | | |
| 1990-2000 | 18.1 | 29.0 | 10.0 | 9.4 |
| 2000-2010 | 15.0 | 28.1 | 3.6 | 11.3 |
| 1990-2010 | 35.8 | 65.3 | 13.9 | 21.8 |
| *More Developed Region⁻* | | | | |
| 1990 | 1,205,193 | 875,684 | 329,509 | 72.7 |
| 2000 | 1,262,482 | 944,691 | 317,791 | 74.8 |
| 2010 | 1,307,469 | 1,003,753 | 303,716 | 76.8 |
| Percentage Change | | | | |
| 1990-2000 | 4.8 | 7.9 | −3.6 | 2.9 |
| 2000-2010 | 3.6 | 6.3 | −4.4 | 2.7 |
| 1990-2010 | 8.5 | 14.6 | −7.8 | 5.6 |
| *Less Developed Regions* | | | | |
| 1990 | 4,086,985 | 1,384,715 | 2,702,270 | 33.9 |
| 2000 | 4,988,573 | 1,971,809 | 3,016,764 | 39.5 |
| 2010 | 5,883,293 | 2,732,921 | 3,150,372 | 46.5 |
| Percentage Change | | | | |
| 1990-2000 | 22.1 | 42.4 | 11.6 | 16.5 |
| 2000-2010 | 17.9 | 38.1 | 4.4 | 17.7 |
| 1990-2010 | 44.0 | 97.4 | 16.6 | 37.2 |

SOURCE: United Nations (1989a). Reprinted by permission.
NOTE: More developed regions include North America, Japan, all regions of Europe, Australia-New Zealand, and the Soviet Union. Less developed regions include all regions of Africa, all regions of Latin America, China, other East Asia, all regions of South Asia, Melanesia, and Micronesia-Polynesia.

Overcrowded slums are the most glaring result of unplanned and unchecked
urban growth. Tens of millions live in such slums in undeveloped countries
with disastrous effects on the quality of life. Psychological tension, alcohol
abuse and its related problems, traffic accidents, drug dependence, educational
failure, violence and crime are rampant within. (p. 7).

Children living in these slums are at high risk for mental disorders. They are
subjected not only to the problems mentioned above but to other extrinsic factors,

**Table 1.8**    Percentage of the Population of the World That Will Be Living in
Urban Areas, by Regions and Areas of the World, 1990-2025

| Regions and Areas of the World 1990 | | 2000 | 2010 | 2025 |
|---|---|---|---|---|
| World | 42.7 | 46.7 | 52.0 | 60.5 |
| More Developed | 72.7 | 74.8 | 76.8 | 79.0 |
| Less Developed | 33.9 | 39.5 | 46.5 | 56.9 |
| Asia | 29.8 | 35.0 | 41.9 | 53.0 |
| East Asia | 29.4 | 32.6 | 38.6 | 49.0 |
| Southeast Asia | 29.0 | 35.5 | 43.1 | 54.3 |
| South Asia | 27.8 | 33.8 | 41.2 | 52.6 |
| West Asia | 58.2 | 63.9 | 69.4 | 76.3 |
| Africa | 34.5 | 41.3 | 48.1 | 57.8 |
| Latin America | 72.3 | 77.2 | 80.7 | 84.8 |
| North America | 74.3 | 75.0 | 76.1 | 77.9 |
| Europe | 73.1 | 76.0 | 78.8 | 82.3 |
| Soviet Union | 67.5 | 70.7 | 72.7 | 74.1 |
| Oceania | 70.9 | 71.0 | 72.1 | 75.2 |

SOURCE: United Nations (1989a). *Global Estimates and Projections of Population by Sex and Age.* Department of International Economic and Social Affairs. ST/ESA/SER.R/70. New York.
NOTE: More developed regions include North America, Japan, all regions of Europe, Australia-New Zealand, and the Soviet Union. Less developed regions include all regions of Africa, all regions of Latin America, China, other East Asia, all regions of South Asia, Melanesia, and Micronesia-Polynesia.

such as parents having mental disorders, being substance abusers, or both; exposure
to noxious environments; being in families with members who have chronic disabling illnesses and various communicable diseases; being homeless; being subjected to physical and sexual abuse by parents and others; and living in an unstable
family environment.

## Impact of Urbanization on Rural Areas

As a result of the rapid increase in the urbanization of the less developed regions, the percentage of the population living in rural areas is decreasing, but the
number of persons living in these areas is increasing (Table 1.7). Between 1990 and
2000 the rural population of the less developed regions will increase by about 12%,
from 2.7 billion to 3 billion (United Nations, 1989a). In many countries unemployment of the young has swelled the migration from rural to urban areas, where, as indicated above, increasing numbers of young people living in overcrowded
conditions are exposed to unhealthy influences (e.g., drug abuse, alcoholism, smoking, and violence) and the consequent social tensions (WHO, 1986a, 1986c, 1987).

This pattern of migration—from rural to urban areas—leaves a residual population in the rural areas that is weighted heavily with children and adults suffering from physical, mental, social, and economic problems that need attention. As in the urban slums, absolute poverty is rampant in the rural areas, where nearly "1000 million people are trapped in the vicious circle of poverty, malnutrition and disease and despair that saps their energy, reduces their work capacity and limits their ability to plan for the future" (WHO, 1981b, p. 19).

Lack of human, material, and financial resources, along with poor transport and communications in rural areas, are major obstacles to the delivery of health services. As stated by the *World Health Organization Study Group on Mental Health Care in Developing Countries:*

> The vast majority of the population of the developing world does not have access to mental health care. Most of those suffering from epilepsy receive no treatment despite the fact that, for many of them, such treatment is cheap, simple and effective. In some developing countries alcohol abuse is a major public health problem and in others drug dependence has assumed alarming proportions. (WHO, 1984, p. 11)

Thus the conditions in rural areas and in slums of the urban areas of the developing countries exacerbate the "vicious circle of poverty, malnutrition and disease and despair." Such conditions are, indeed, barriers to prevention.

## Changing Household and Family Structure and Living Arrangements

As the World Health Organization (1981a) has stated:

> In contrast to the teeming slums of developing countries, a problem in many developed countries is that up to one third of urban households contain only one person, and small family units that find it difficult to look after a disabled member are much more common than large households which are usually able to buffer stress. (p. 7)

The increase in numbers of persons living alone is only one aspect of a major demographic trend, one that is of considerable importance to mental health and other public health and social programs. This phenomenon is the change in the household and family structure and living arrangements of the populations of the developed world and also of the developing world. International demographic data on these trends are difficult to find, so I will use data from the United States to illustrate barriers that changing U.S. household and family structures are presenting to mental health, physical health, social, and economic problems of children and adults.

Between 1950 and 1990 married-couple families increased by 56%, male householder families without spouse by 115%, female householder families without spouse by 205%, and nonfamily households by 482%. About 90% of the nonfamily households consist of persons living alone (one-person households). The number of one-person households increased by 525% during this period. The trends of the number of households per 1,000 population by type highlight the gradual decline in the number of married-couple families per 1,000 population and accentuate the striking increase occurring in the ratios of the other types of family and nonfamily households (Kramer, Brown, Skinner, Anthony, & German, 1987; U.S. Bureau of the Census, 1985a, 1985b, 1986c).

Two-parent families are also becoming increasingly heterogeneous in the United States. The number of families with only biological children under 18 years of age—the so-called traditional family—decreased between 1950 and 1985. The number of children living with both of their biological parents in married-couple situations dropped from 39.5 million in 1980 to 37.2 million in 1985, a decline of 5.8%. Table 1.9 provides additional data on children living with biological, step, and adoptive married couples by race of mother for the years 1980 and 1985 (Miller & Moorman, 1989).

In 1988, 15.3 million of the 63.2 million children under 18 years (24%) lived with only one parent: 13.5 million with mother alone and 1.8 million with father alone (Table 1.10). This means that one of every four children in the United States now lives in a one-parent family (Rawlings, 1989). These percentages vary markedly by race and Hispanic origin: white, 19%; black, 54%; and Hispanic, 30%. By far the largest percentages are living with mother only: white, 16%; black, 51%; and Hispanic, 27% (Table 1.10) (U.S. Bureau of the Census, 1986a).

Table 1.11 provides data on the changes in living arrangements of children that occurred during the years 1960, 1970, 1980, and 1988 by race and Hispanic origin (U.S. Bureau of the Census, 1989a). Figure 1.4 portrays the dramatic changes that occurred between 1960 and 1985 in the percentages of children under 18 living in one-parent families by marital status and race of parents.

The increases in the number of children in one-parent families mean that there is a striking increase in the proportion of children who will experience part of their lives in single-parent families. Of the children born between 1950 and 1954 who are now adults in their late 30s and early 40s, 19% of whites and 48% of blacks spent some part of their youth in one-parent families. For the generation born in 1980, the corresponding percentages will rise to 70% for whites and 94% for blacks (Morrison, 1986).

Several factors have brought about these changes in household and family structure: the increase in divorce rates; increase in the number of widows and widowers; migration of workers to areas of the country with opportunities for employment; and trends in behavior, life-style, value systems, and aspirations of the various social class strata of our society.

It is well known that persons who are separated, divorced, widowed, never married, living alone, or in nonfamily households and children living with one

**Table 1.9**    Children Living with Biological, Step, and Adoptive Married-Couple
Parents, by Race of Mother: June 1980 and 1985

| | 1980 | | 1985 | |
|---|---|---|---|---|
| Parent Type and Race of Mother | Number (in 000s) | Percentage | Number (in 000s) | Percentage |
| *All races* | | | | |
| Total own children under 18 years | 47,248 | 100.0 | 45,347 | 100.0 |
| Biological mother and father | 39,523 | 83.7 | 37,213 | 82.1 |
| Biological mother-stepfather | 5,355 | 11.3 | 6,049 | 13.3 |
| Stepmother-biological father | 727 | 1.5 | 740 | 1.6 |
| Adoptive mother and father | 1,350 | 2.9 | 866 | 1.9 |
| Unknown mother or father | 293 | 0.6 | 479 | 1.1 |
| *White* | | | | |
| Total own children under 18 years | 42,329 | 100.0 | 39,942 | 100.0 |
| Biological mother and father | 35,852 | 84.7 | 33,202 | 83.1 |
| Biological mother-stepfather | 4,362 | 10.3 | 4,918 | 12.3 |
| Stepmother-biological father | 664 | 1.6 | 676 | 1.7 |
| Adoptive mother and father | 1,209 | 2.9 | 754 | 1.9 |
| Unknown mother or father | 242 | 0.6 | 391 | 1.0 |
| *Black* | | | | |
| Total own children under 18 years | 3,775 | 100.0 | 3,816 | 100.0 |
| Biological mother and father | 2,698 | 71.5 | 2,661 | 69.7 |
| Biological mother-stepfather | 877 | 23.2 | 952 | 24.9 |
| Stepmother-biological father | 46 | 1.2 | 50 | 1.3 |
| Adoptive mother and father | 119 | 3.1 | 76 | 2.0 |
| Unknown mother or father | 35 | 0.9 | 77 | 2.0 |
| *Other races[a]* | | | | |
| Total own children under 18 years | 1,144 | 100.0 | 1,589 | 100.0 |
| Biological mother and father | 973 | 85.1 | 1,350 | 84.9 |
| Biological mother-stepfather | 116 | 10.1 | 179 | 11.3 |
| Stepmother-biological father | 17 | 1.5 | 13 | 0.8 |
| Adoptive mother and father | 22 | 2.0 | 36 | 2.3 |
| Unknown mother or father | 16 | 1.4 | 11 | 0.7 |

SOURCE: Miller and Moorman (1989).
a. "Other races" is a category principally comprising American Indians, Alaskan Natives, Asians, and Pacific Islanders.

parent all suffer relatively high risk for mental disorder. An added risk factor for children living in one-parent families is that a very high proportion of such families are below the poverty level, particularly female householder families with children under 18 (Moynihan, 1986). As of 1987, 46% of all female householder families with children were below the poverty level (U.S. Bureau of the Census, 1989b). Proportions varied dramatically by race: 39% of white families, 60% of

**Table 1.10** Living Arrangements of Children Under 18 Years, by Race and Hispanic
Origin, United States, 1988

| Living Arrangement | All Races | Whites | Blacks | Hispanics[a] |
|---|---|---|---|---|
| | | Numbers in 000s | | |
| Total children under 18 | 63,179 | 51,030 | 9,699 | 6,786 |
| Living with | | | | |
| Two parents | 45,942 | 40,287 | 3,729 | 4,497 |
| One parent | 15,329 | 9,624 | 5,247 | 2,047 |
| mother only | 13,521 | 8,160 | 4,959 | 1,845 |
| father only | 1,808 | 1,464 | 288 | 202 |
| Other relatives | 1,483 | 818 | 620 | 180 |
| Nonrelatives only | 425 | 301 | 94 | 62 |
| *Percentage of Total* | | | | |
| Total children under 18 | 100.0 | 100.0 | 100.0 | 100.0 |
| Living with | | | | |
| Two parents | 72.7 | 78.9 | 38.6 | 66.3 |
| One parent | 24.3 | 18.9 | 54.1 | 30.2 |
| mother only | 21.4 | 16.0 | 51.1 | 27.2 |
| father only | 2.9 | 2.9 | 3.0 | 3.0 |
| Other relatives | 2.3 | 1.6 | 6.4 | 2.7 |
| Nonrelatives only | 0.7 | 0.6 | 1.0 | 0.9 |

SOURCE: Rawlings (1989).
a. Persons of Hispanic origin may be of any race.

black families, and 60% of Hispanic families. As illustrated in Table 1.12, these
percentages have not shown any marked change since 1981, when the proportion of white female householder families with children below the poverty level
was 37%, that of black families was 60%, and that of Hispanic families, 60%.

The changes in family structure occurring in the United States are occurring
in many of the countries in the developed and developing regions of the world
(Hobbs & Lippman, 1990; United Nations, 1989b). To illustrate, in the United
Kingdom 1.6 million children live in 1 million single-parent family units (WHO,
Regional Office for Europe, 1986). Another study reports that in rural Botswana,
43% of the households are headed by women and these households are much
poorer than the others (Kossoudij & Mueller, 1981). The experiences of children in many of the developing regions of the world are incomparably worse
than those of children in the more developed regions: 80 million children in
poor developing countries live without any family, and growing numbers of
children are left to fend for themselves in the cities of developing countries as
economic and social conditions deteriorate (WHO, 1987). The chapter concerned with the changing structure of the family in the 1989 *Report on the*

**Table 1.11** Living Arrangements of Children Under 18 Years, by Race and Hispanic Origin, United States, 1960-1988

| Year | Total Number (000s) | Total | Two Parents | Percentage of Total Living with: Total | One Parent Mother | Father | Other Relatives | Non-related |
|------|------|------|------|------|------|------|------|------|
| *All races* | | | | | | | | |
| 1960 | 63,727 | 100.0 | 87.7 | 9.1 | 8.0 | 1.1 | 2.5 | 0.7 |
| 1970 | 69,162 | 100.0 | 85.2 | 11.9 | 10.8 | 1.1 | 2.2 | 0.7 |
| 1980 | 63,427 | 100.0 | 76.7 | 19.7 | 18.0 | 1.7 | 3.1 | 0.6 |
| 1988 | 63,179 | 100.0 | 72.7 | 24.3 | 21.4 | 2.9 | 2.3 | 0.7 |
| *White* | | | | | | | | |
| 1960 | 55,077 | 100.0 | 90.9 | 7.1 | 6.1 | 1.0 | 1.4 | 0.5 |
| 1970 | 58,790 | 100.0 | 89.5 | 8.7 | 7.8 | 0.9 | 1.2 | 0.6 |
| 1980 | 54,242 | 100.0 | 82.7 | 15.1 | 13.5 | 1.6 | 1.7 | 0.5 |
| 1988 | 51,030 | 100.0 | 78.9 | 18.9 | 16.0 | 2.9 | 1.6 | 0.6 |
| *Black* | | | | | | | | |
| 1960 | 8,650 | 100.0 | 67.0 | 21.9 | 19.9 | 2.0 | 9.6 | 1.5 |
| 1970 | 9,422 | 100.0 | 58.5 | 31.8 | 29.5 | 2.3 | 8.7 | 1.0 |
| 1980 | 9,375 | 100.0 | 42.2 | 45.8 | 43.9 | 1.9 | 10.7 | 1.3 |
| 1988 | 9,699 | 100.0 | 38.6 | 54.1 | 51.1 | 3.0 | 6.4 | 1.0 |
| *Hispanic* | | | | | | | | |
| 1960 | NA | NA | NA | NA | NA | NA | NA | NA |
| 1970 | 4,006 | 100.0 | 77.7 | NA | NA | NA | NA | NA |
| 1980 | 5,459 | 100.0 | 75.4 | 21.1 | 19.6 | 1.5 | 3.4 | 0.1 |
| 1988 | 6,786 | 100.0 | 66.3 | 30.2 | 27.2 | 3.0 | 2.7 | 0.9 |

SOURCE: U.S. Bureau of the Census (1989a).

*World Social Situation* highlights demographic and other factors associated with these changes: declining fertility and mortality rates in the developed regions and, more recently, in developing countries; international migration in response to differential economic conditions between countries; natural disaster, war, and severe economic downturn; increasing number of single-parent families and re-constituted families (United Nations, 1989b).

## Prevalence of Mental Disorder in Families

A study carried out in the Biometrics Branch of the National Institute of Mental Health in 1974 provides an excellent example of the relationship of living arrangements of individuals to the risk of being admitted to a state mental hospital (Redick & Johnson, 1974). Admission rates to these institutions were

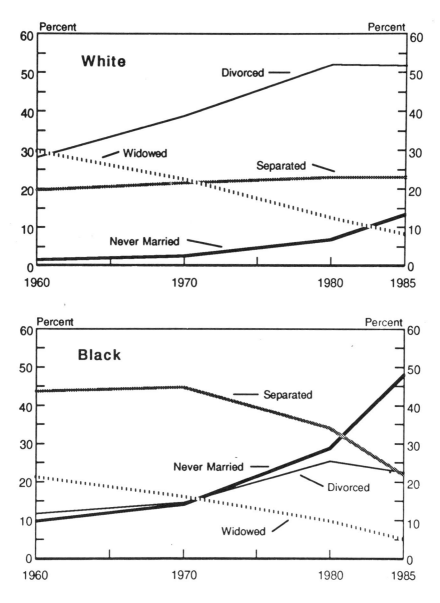

**Figure 1.4.** Children Under 18 Years Living With One Parent, by Marital Status of Parent, 1985, 1980, 1970, and 1960

SOURCE: U.S. Bureau of the Census (1986a).

**Table 1.12** Percentage of Families With Children Below the Poverty Level, United
States, by Race, 1980-1987

| Year | Total | White | Black | Hispanic[a] |
|------|-------|-------|-------|----------|
| *All families* | | | | |
| 1980 | 14.7 | 11.2 | 35.5 | 27.2 |
| 1981 | 15.9 | 12.4 | 37.1 | 28.5 |
| 1982 | 17.5 | 13.7 | 40.7 | 32.6 |
| 1983 | 17.9 | 14.1 | 39.9 | 32.1 |
| 1984 | 17.2 | 13.4 | 39.0 | 31.3 |
| 1985 | 16.7 | 13.3 | 36.0 | 32.1 |
| 1986 | 16.3 | 13.0 | 35.4 | 30.8 |
| 1987 | 16.2 | 12.4 | 37.3 | 32.1 |
| *Married-couple families* | | | | |
| 1980 | 7.7 | 6.8 | 15.5 | NA |
| 1981 | 8.7 | 7.7 | 16.2 | NA |
| 1982 | 9.8 | 9.0 | 17.2 | NA |
| 1983 | 10.1 | 9.2 | 18.0 | NA |
| 1984 | 9.4 | 8.5 | 16.6 | NA |
| 1985 | 8.9 | 8.2 | 12.9 | NA |
| 1986 | 8.0 | 7.5 | 11.5 | NA |
| 1987 | 7.8 | 7.0 | 13.6 | NA |
| *Male householder (without spouse)* | | | | |
| 1980 | 18.0 | 16.0 | 24.0 | NA |
| 1981 | 14.0 | 11.6 | 25.0 | NA |
| 1982 | 20.6 | 17.4 | 32.7 | NA |
| 1983 | 20.2 | 16.8 | 31.1 | NA |
| 1984 | 18.1 | 13.6 | 35.5 | NA |
| 1985 | 17.1 | 14.9 | 29.0 | NA |
| 1986 | 17.8 | 14.5 | 31.5 | NA |
| 1987 | 17.6 | 15.1 | 29.6 | NA |
| *Female householder (without spouse)* | | | | |
| 1980 | 42.9 | 35.9 | 56.0 | NA |
| 1981 | 44.3 | 36.9 | 59.5 | 60.0 |
| 1982 | 47.8 | 39.3 | 63.7 | 63.8 |
| 1983 | 47.1 | 39.8 | 60.7 | 63.4 |
| 1984 | 45.7 | 38.8 | 58.4 | 62.8 |
| 1985 | 45.4 | 38.7 | 58.9 | 64.0 |
| 1986 | 46.0 | 39.8 | 58.0 | 59.5 |
| 1987 | 46.1 | 38.7 | 59.5 | 60.7 |

SOURCE: U.S. Bureau of the Census (1989b).
NOTE: Persons of Hispanic origin may be of any race.

calculated specifically for type of family in which persons live. The rates were excessively high for sons 18-24 years of age living in female householder families compared with sons of this age living in married-couple families (1,500 per 100,000 versus 441 per 100,000). The rates were also much higher for daughters in this age group living in female householder families than for daughters living in married-couple families (539 per 100,000 versus 254 per 100,000). Data such as these are needed currently to provide information on the relationship of living arrangements of children to their risks of being admitted to inpatient and outpatient mental health services and other types of health and human services.

More recently, the Eastern Baltimore Mental Health Survey provided a unique opportunity to collect data in a way that made it possible to allocate persons with a DIS mental disorder to type of household in which they lived and to determine prevalence rates of specific DIS/DSM-III disorders among persons living in different types of families and households (Kramer et al., 1987). These data underscore the significantly higher prevalence of mental disorders in members of male-only and female-only householder families and nonfamily households, compared with that found in members of married-couple families (Figure 1.5).

As a result of changes in the household composition of the United States during the last 30 years, results similar to those reported for Eastern Baltimore are likely to be quite general throughout the United States and probably in other developed countries. This follows from the fact that female and male householder families and nonfamily households are heavily weighted with persons at high risk for mental disorder. As a result of the expected increase in the number of such households between 1990 and 2000, shown in Table 1.13, and the high prevalence of mental disorders in these households, a marked increase can be expected in the number of U.S. households in which one or more members will have a mental disorder.

As a result of the continuing emphasis on community care in the United States, it is important to learn more about the living arrangements of persons in these high-risk groups—who among them has a mental disorder, the role of this person in the household (i.e., head of household, spouse of head, child, or other relative), the impact of the person with a disorder on the other persons in the household, and vice versa—and to gather additional information about the familial aggregation of mental disorders (Downes & Simon, 1954; Kellam, Adams, Brown, & Ensminger, 1982; Kellam & Ensminger, 1980; Quinton, Rutter, & Gulliver, 1989; Rutter & Quinton, 1984; WHO, Regional Office for Europe, 1986). Indeed, more knowledge is needed about the family-household aggregation of mental and physical disorders in an era when the importance of primary health care and family-based preventive care is being increasingly emphasized.

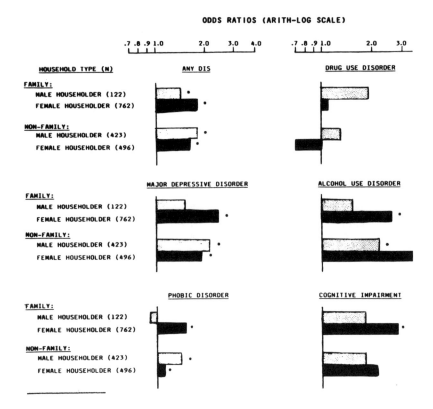

**Figure 1.5.** Odds Ratios for Prevalence Rates by Type of Household[a] (relative to rates for married-couple families): Any DIS/DSM-III Disorder and Selected Disorders

SOURCE: Kramer et al. (1987).
a. Adjusted for age, race, and sex.
*Rates are significantly higher than those for persons living in married-couple families.

### Refugees and the Homeless

Another group of persons at high risk for MNP disorders and many other health problems are refugees. It is estimated that there are between 10 and 15 million refugees in the world, that their number is increasing at a rate of about 3,000 per day and that half of them are children (WHO, 1987b). To quote this World Health Organization report:

Events have once again demonstrated the magnitude and complexity of the refugee problem, which in the final analysis is a reflection of the troubled

**Table 1.13** Types of Households and Family Units, United States, 1990-2000

| Type of Household and Family | 1990 | 2000 | Percentage Change |
|---|---|---|---|
| | | Number (000s) | |
| Total | 94,227 | 105,933 | 12.4 |
| Family households | 66,758 | 72,277 | 8.3 |
| married couple | 53,012 | 56,294 | 6.2 |
| male householder | 2,581 | 3,282 | 27.2 |
| female householder | 11,165 | 12,701 | 13.8 |
| Nonfamily households | 27,469 | 33,656 | 22.5 |
| male householder | 11,946 | 15,452 | 29.3 |
| female householder | 15,523 | 18,204 | 17.3 |
| living alone | 23,623 | 28,944 | 22.5 |
| two or more persons | 3,849 | 4,712 | 22.4 |
| *Percentage of Total* | | | |
| Total | 100.0 | 100.0 | 100.0 |
| Family households | 70.8 | 68.2 | -3.7 |
| married couple | 56.3 | 53.1 | -5.7 |
| male householder | 2.7 | 3.1 | 14.8 |
| female householder | 11.8 | 12.0 | 1.7 |
| Nonfamily households | 29.2 | 31.8 | 8.9 |
| male householder | 12.7 | 14.6 | 15.0 |
| female householder | 16.5 | 17.2 | 4.2 |
| living alone | 26.2 | 27.3 | 4.2 |
| two or more persons | 4.1 | 4.5 | 9.8 |
| *Number of Households per 1,000 Population* | | | |
| Total | 376.3 | 395.3 | 5.0 |
| Family households | 265.6 | 269.7 | 1.5 |
| married couple | 211.7 | 210.1 | -0.8 |
| male householder | 10.3 | 12.2 | 18.4 |
| female householder | 44.6 | 47.4 | 6.3 |
| Nonfamily households | 109.7 | 125.6 | 14.5 |
| male householder | 47.7 | 57.7 | 21.0 |
| female householder | 62.0 | 67.9 | 9.5 |
| living alone | 98.7 | 108.0 | 9.4 |
| two or more persons | 15.3 | 17.6 | 15.0 |
| Total Population (000s) | 250,410 | 268,266 | 7.1 |

SOURCE: U.S. Bureau of the Census (1986c).

conditions of today's world. Concentrations and movement of refugees, often sizeable, have been reported in almost all geographical areas. It is estimated that there are between 10 and 15 million refugees in the world, their number increasing at a rate of about 3,000 per day, and half of them children. (p. 11)

A problem that bears some resemblance to that of refugees and other homeless persons in the developing areas of the world is that of the homeless in the developed areas of the world. The refugee problems in the developing areas of the world have been created by international sociopolitical and economic policies of nations that have deprived persons and their families of a permanent residence. Almost all arise for socioeconomic reasons, particularly the migration of large numbers of persons from rural to urban areas to find better economic opportunity. In the United States, some persons have become homeless for these same reasons, but some for other reasons, including loss of employment resulting from major changes in industry, agriculture, and other segments of the economy; migration to other sections of the country to seek employment opportunities; government policy that has promoted deinstitutionalization of large number of patients from state mental institutions into communities, without adequate housing or services; severe alcohol and drug abuse problems that have caused family breakdown; loss of friends, loss of finances, loss of job and affiliative relationships; and desire on the part of some individuals to escape from a society that is too complicated and stressful for them (Breakey, 1987; Fischer & Breakey, 1987). Whatever the reasons, there are in the United States an estimated 250,000 homeless on any given night and as many as 3 million who experience some type of homelessness during a year (Ropers & Boyer, 1987). A very high proportion of the homeless are known to have both mental and physical health problems (Breakey et al., 1989).

The homeless problem is exacerbated by the fact that there is a marked increase in the number of families who have become homeless because of their inability to find or maintain stable housing. The number of children who are homeless is difficult to establish. It is estimated in Baltimore that 20% of shelter users are children and adolescents (Breakey & Fischer, 1990; Health and Welfare Council of Central Maryland, 1986). Estimates for New York have been as high as 12,000 children in the shelter system and 10,000 adolescents on the streets (Alperstein & Arnstein, 1988). As stated by Breakey and Fischer (1990):

That the homeless way of life is harmful for children and adolescents seems self-evident. The younger children of homeless families are placed at risk at crucial stages of their development. Basic aspects of child-care become very difficult, immunization schedules are neglected and the children's health status is impaired (Alperstein & Arnstein, 1988; Miller & Linn, 1988). Children in homeless families too often move from shelter to shelter, they live in cramped and dangerous accommodations, their schooling is interrupted and opportunities for social development are minimal. In most cases they are in single-parent families, and even when both parents are with the family, the father may be banished at night time because the shelter where they are staying can not accommodate men. Young children of families in shelters in Massachusetts were found, after systematic and careful evaluation, to manifest greatly increased levels of anxiety and depression and to be markedly delayed in their general development, specifically in their language development (Bassuk et al., 1986; Bassuk & Rosenberg, 1988). (pp. 37-38)

## Implications of the Rising Pandemic of AIDS for MNP Prevention Programs

One other major barrier to prevention of mental disorders of both adults and children that must be mentioned is the rising epidemic of human immunodeficiency virus (HIV) syndrome. The HIV epidemic presents an unprecedented challenge to biomedical research and to public health and mental health: to biomedical research, the development of vaccines to protect persons against HIV infection and therapies to treat persons with AIDS and AIDS-related illnesses; to public health, the development of effective prevention and control programs to reduce morbidity and mortality from these illnesses and to ease the socioeconomic burdens and stress they cause the community; to mental health, to provide counseling, support systems, and preventive education (see Mays, Albee, & Schneider, 1989).

The former Director for the World Health Organization Special Program on AIDS stresses the considerable social and economic costs of the HIV epidemic to both the developed and developing countries of the world:

The personal, social and economic costs of the HIV epidemic are very high. Uncertainties regarding prognosis, along with fears and realities of exposure and ostracism, lead HIV-infected but asymptomatic persons to experience higher levels of stress than AIDS patients themselves. The family structure and function is threatened by infection and the loss of mothers and fathers. The social and economic fabric is seriously affected by the epidemic of illness and death among productive 20-40 year olds, which is typical of AIDS epidemiology in industrialized and developing countries. In Africa, social and economic development may be threatened by the loss of a substantial proportion of 20-40 year-old persons, particularly among the urban elites. The direct economic costs of AIDS are also enormous. For example, in the United States, it is estimated that the total cost of direct medical care for AIDS patients in 1991 will reach U.S. $16 billion. In some central African hospitals, 20-50% of adult patients on medical wards have AIDS or other HIV-related conditions, placing an additional burden upon already limited health care systems. The combined impact of the HIV pandemic, of AIDS, AIDS-related disease and neurological disease upon health care, insurance and legal systems, economic and social development, and indeed entire cultures and populations is already extraordinary and will become increasingly profound. (Mann, 1987, p. 190)

A recent front-page *New York Times* article provides a poignant example of the impact of the AIDS epidemic on an area of Africa:

> In Rakai, a county of about 300,000, AIDS kills the breadwinners and leaves behind the most helpless: children. From all the thousands of AIDS deaths of mothers and fathers, up to 40,000 children in the county have been orphaned by a disease they understand to mean daily funerals and impoverishment. In many villages of Rakai, rows of houses stand silent, shuttered and abandoned, the parents dead and the children taken to usually less prosperous and aging grandparents. (Perlez, 1990, p. A1)

This quote emphasizes the extraordinary barrier that the HIV epidemic presents to the development of activities to improve the lives of children and adults in Africa and other countries in the developing regions of the world.

The HIV epidemic is also taking its toll in countries of the more developed regions, but, as yet, in not as devastating a way as has occurred in Uganda and other countries of Africa. To illustrate, in the United States, between January 1, 1981, and September 1989 a total of 106,270 cases of AIDS were reported to the AIDS Program of the Centers for Disease Control. Of these cases, 1,773 have been among children under 13 years of age and 22,051 among adolescents and young adults 13-29 years of age. During the same period there were also 63,159 AIDS-related deaths reported, of which 980 were children and 12,480 adolescents and young adults. As of 1987, the HIV death rate of 1.3 per 100,000 population for adolescents and young adults 15-24 years of age ranked seventh among the causes of death for that age group (National Center for Health Statistics, 1989).

In addition to the considerable toll the HIV epidemic has been taking in the lives of affected individuals and the problems it has created for the families and friends of these individuals and the communities in which they live, it also has its economic consequences. In 1988 alone the total cost for AIDS-related expenditures was estimated to be $4.1 billion. This total includes federal government outlays of $626 million for research and $354 million for education and prevention as well as expenditures covered by private health insurance, out-of-pocket costs to patients, and the states' share of Medicaid, public hospital, and other local expenditures (Winkenwerder, Kessler, & Stolek, 1989).

## Poverty

In the preceding sections mention has been made of the extensive poverty that exists in the world. The World Health Organization (1987) has underscored the dramatic increase in poverty in the developing countries: "Absolute poverty traps almost one thousand million people, 90% of whom live in rural areas; more than 50% are small farmers and almost 25% are laborers without land" (p. 20).

There is also evidence that growing numbers of elderly persons in the developed countries live in poverty, particularly among the elderly who live alone, and, as already indicated, the same is true among the increasing number of one-parent families (Commonwealth Fund Commission on Elderly People Living Alone, 1987; U.S. Bureau of the Census, 1989b; U.S. House of Representatives Select Commission on Aging, 1987; U.S. Senate Special Commission on Aging, 1986).

Many epidemiologic surveys of mental disorders have demonstrated the inverse relationship between socioeconomic status and the prevalence of specific MNP disorders (Eaton, 1986; Roman & Harrison, 1967). The effect of poverty on disease is well summarized in this World Health Organization (1987) statement: "The risk of disease and disablement is much greater for the poverty-stricken, threatening families with further demands on their limited resources and thus even deeper poverty" (p. 21).

## Other Barriers to Prevention

The preceding sections have provided a review of demographic and related factors that are barriers to prevention of MNP disorders in children and to improving their lives. There are many other health, social, cultural, and economic factors that place major obstacles in the way of preventing these disorders and their disabling consequences, that can only be touched on here. Among these are hunger, malnutrition, and nutritional deficiencies; inadequate prenatal and perinatal care; acquired lesions of the central nervous system; lack of shelter and ancillary services; illiteracy; lack of programs and trained personnel, particularly in developing countries; suicide among adolescents and young adults; natural disasters; discrimination against girls and women; racism and apartheid; torture; ongoing military actions and conflicts; deterioration and pollution of the environment; and, last but not least, the collapse of the communist regimes in Eastern Europe and the Soviet Union and the resultant turmoil among the citizens of these countries and their ruling parties during the periods of transition to democratic forms of government. A detailed exposition is given in the *Seventh Report on the World Health Situation* (WHO, 1987), and possible preventive strategies are summarized in the report of WHO's Director General (WHO, 1986a).

## Inadequate Information Support for
## Planning Programs for Prevention of MNP Disorders

There is still another barrier to the prevention of MNP disorders both in children and adults: the lack of epidemiological, demographic, and health services information needed for sound planning of programs to accomplish this. In its evaluation of progress being made by member states in their formulation of national strategies for achieving the goals of "health for all by the year 2000," the World Health Organization (1987) found that practically all reported that inadequate information support was the main constraint to the development of these strategies.

With respect to MNP disorders the lack of essential information is particularly critical. Only a few countries have the trained personnel and resources needed to collect systematic data about the prevalence of these disorders in the various demographic and geographic subgroups of their populations and to monitor trends of these rates. There is an associated problem with respect to the collection and analyses of data on the utilization of health, mental health, and related human services by persons with MNP disorders and of the additional data needed to evaluate the effectiveness of these services (Freeman, Fryers, & Henderson, 1985).

The lack of such data is particularly critical with respect to need for reliable data on the disorders of children and on the use of health and mental health services by children with these disorders. Such data are needed for planning services and determining personnel needs and other resources required to meet the needs of children with these disorders, as well as to provide clues to causes of these disorders. Follow-up data are needed to provide knowledge of the clinical course of these disorders and their effect on the development and future lives of the children so affected (Morris, 1975). The Institute of Medicine (1990) has recognized this problem and has made a strong recommendation to the National Institute of Mental Health to stimulate and support epidemiologic, health services, and longitudinal research so as to fill in these gaps in our knowledge.

**Conclusion**

This review has dealt with what I perceive to be major barriers to prevention of MNP disorders and associated disabling conditions among children and adolescents in the developed and developing countries of the world. Many of these problems are caused by the behavior of people living in these areas. Others are the result of actions of governments, some of which have enacted policies and laws intended to improve the mental, physical, and social well-being of the men, women, and children under their jurisdictions, while others have conducted policies that maintain the status quo of conditions known to result in MNP problems and still others have actively increased world tensions that are a threat to the physical and mental health of their populations and their state of well-being.

It is quite clear that much more research will be needed on the biopsychosocial factors that determine the differential incidence and prevalence of MNP disorders in both children and adults and their outcome and the organizational, human, and financial resources needed to apply the results of these research ef-forts. However, it must be emphasized that progress in achieving the goals of prevention is very much dependent on social and economic progress, and much remains to be done to remove the obstacles that are preventing this progress (United Nations, 1986). To quote from the World Health Organization's *Seventh Report on the World Health Situation* (1987):

> The Global Strategy for Health for All by the Year 2000 stresses the close and complex links that exist between health and socioeconomic development. Health not only results from genuine socioeconomic development as distinct from mere growth, it is also an essential investment in such development. The economic development of a country is clearly limited when one out of five children dies before completing one year of life, when a high proportion of children suffer from stunted growth due to malnutrition, when a lifetime can be shortened by as much as a tenth by disease, or when a person is beset by disability and disease at what is potentially the most productive age.
>
> Achievement of health goals is determined to a large extent by policies that lie outside the health sector and in particular by policies, whatever their na-ture, aimed at assuring universal access to the means to earn an acceptable in-come. But a mere increase in income is no guarantee of health. Health authorities will have to be vigilant in identifying those aspects of development that can threaten health and in introducing the elements that are essential to healthy development in national, regional and global socioeconomic develop-ment plans. (p. 8)

It is my hope that the participants in this Vermont Conference, members of the professional and nongovernment organizations in attendance, and the people themselves will continue to put pressure on governments and institutions to re-move the social, economic, psychological, and political barriers that continue to thwart our efforts to prevent mental, neurological, and psychosocial disorders and their disabling effects and other health, social, and economic problems that currently affect such a large portion of the world's children, adolescents and adults.

## References

Alperstein, G., & Arnstein, E. (1988). Homeless children: A challenge for pediatricians. *Pedi-atrics Clinics of North America, 35*, 1413-1425.

Bassuk, E. L., & Rosenberg, L. (1988). Why does family homelessness occur? A case control study. *American Journal of Public Health, 78*, 783-788.

Bassuk, E. L., Rubin, L., & Lauriat, A. S. (1986). Characteristics of sheltered homeless fami-lies. *American Journal of Public Health, 76*, 1097-1101.

Breakey, W. R. (1987). Treating the homeless. *Alcohol, Health and Research World, 11*, 42-46.

Breakey, W. R., & Fischer, P. J. (1990). Homelessness: The extent of the problem. *Journal of Social Issues, 46,* 31-47.

Breakey, W. R., Fischer, P. J., Kramer, M., Nestadt, G., Romanoski, A. J., Ross, A. Royall, R. M., & Stine, O. C. (1989). Health and mental health problems of homeless men and women in Baltimore. *Journal of the American Medical Association, 262,* 1352-1357.

Commonwealth Fund Commission on Elderly People Living Alone. (1987). *Old, alone and poor, A plan for reducing poverty among elderly people living alone.* Baltimore: Author.

Downes, J., & Simon, K. (1954). Characteristics of psychoneurotic patients and their families as revealed in a general morbidity study. *Milbank Memorial Fund Quarterly, 32,* 1-23.

Eaton, W. W. (1986). *The sociology of mental disorders* (2nd ed.). New York: Praeger.

Fischer, P. J., & Breakey, W. R. (1987). Profile of the Baltimore homeless with alcohol problems. *Alcohol, Health and Research World, 11,* 36-37, 61.

Freeman, H. L., Fryers, T., & Henderson, J. H. (1985). *Mental health services in Europe: 10 years on* (Public Health in Europe 25). Copenhagen: World Health Organization, Regional Office for Europe.

Health and Welfare Council of Central Maryland. (1986). *Where do you go from nowhere? Homelessness in Maryland.* Baltimore: State of Maryland, Department of Human Resources.

Hobbs, F., & Lippman, L. (1990). Children's wellbeing: An international compassion. In *Report of the Select Committee on Children, Youth and Families* (101st Congress, 2nd session, Report No. 101-628). Washington, DC: Government Printing Office.

Institute of Medicine. (1990). *Research on children and adolescents with mental, behavioral and developmental disorders.* Washington, DC: National Academy Press.

Kellam, S. G., Adams, R. G., Brown, C. H., & Ensminger, M. E. (1982). Longterm evolution of the family structure of teenage and older mothers. *Journal of Marriage and the Family, 44*(3), 539-554.

Kellam, S. G., & Ensminger, M. E. (1980). Theory and method in child epidemiology in studies of children. In F. Earls (Ed.), *Monographs in psychological epidemiology* (pp. 145-179). New York: Prodist.

Kossoudij, S., & Mueller, E. (1981). *The economic and demographic status of female headed households in rural Botswana* (Research Report No. 81-10). Ann Arbor: University of Michigan, Population Studies Center.

Kramer, M. (1989a). Barriers to prevention. In B. Cooper & T. Helgason (Eds.), *Epidemiology and the prevention of mental disorders* (pp. 30-55). London: Routledge.

Kramer, M. (1989b). The biostatistical approach. In P. Wilson, G. Wilkinson, & K. Rawnsley (Eds.), *The scope of epidemiological psychiatry* (pp. 86-107). London: Routledge.

Kramer, M., Brown, H., Skinner, A., Anthony, J., & German, P. (1987). Changing living arrangements in the population and their potential effect on the prevalence of mental disorder: Findings of the Eastern Baltimore Mental Health Survey. In B. Cooper (Ed.), *Psychiatric epidemiology: Progress and prospects* (pp. 3-26). London: Croom Helm.

Mann, J. M. (1987). The global AIDS situation. *World Health Statistics Quarterly, 40,* 185-192.

Mays, V., Albee, G., & Schneider, S. (Eds.). (1989). *Primary prevention of AIDS: Psychological approaches.* Newbury Park, CA: Sage.

Miller, D. S., & Linn, E. H. B. (1988). Children in sheltered homeless families: Reported health status and use of health services. *Pediatrics, 81*(5), 668-673.

Miller, L. F., & Moorman, J. E. (1989). Married couple families with children. In U.S. Bureau of the Census, *Studies in marriage and the family* (Current Population Reports, Special Studies, Series P-23, No. 162) (pp. 27-36). Washington, DC: Government Printing Office.

Morris, J. N. (1975). *Uses of epidemiology.* Edinburgh: Churchill Livingstone.

Morrison, P. A. (1986). *Changing family structure: Who cares for America's dependents?* Santa Monica, CA: RAND Corporation.

Moynihan, D. P. (1986). *Family and nation: The Godkin Lectures, Harvard University, 8-9 April 1985.* New York: Harcourt Brace Jovanovich.

National Center for Health Statistics. (1989). *Health, United States, 1989 and prevention profile.* Washington, DC: Government Printing Office.

Perlez, J. (1990, June 10). In AIDS-stricken Uganda area, the orphans struggle to survive. *New York Times*, p. A1.

Quinton, D., Rutter, M., & Gulliver, L. (1989). Continuities in psychiatric disorder from childhood to adulthood in the children of psychiatric patients. In L. N. Robins & M. Rutter (Eds.), *Straight and devious pathways from childhood to adulthood* (pp. 259-278). New York: Cambridge University Press.

Rawlings, S. W. (1989). Single parents and their children. In U.S. Bureau of the Census, *Studies in marriage and the family* (Current Population Reports, Special Studies, Series P-23, No. 162) (pp. 13-26). Washington, DC: Government Printing Office.

Redick, R. C., & Johnson, C. (1974). *Marital status, living arrangements and family characteristics of admissions to state and county mental hospitals and outpatient psychiatric clinics, United States 1970* (Statistical Note 100). Rockville, MD: National Institute of Mental Health, Division of Biometry.

Roman, P., & Harrison, M. T. (1967). *Schizophrenia and the poor.* Ithaca: New York State School of Industrial and Labor Relations.

Ropers, H. R., & Boyer, R. (1987). Homelessness as a health risk. *Alcohol, Health and Research World, 48*, 38-41.

Rutter, M., & Quinton, D. (1984). Parental psychiatric disorder: Effects on children. *Psychological Medicine, 41*, 853-880.

United Nations. (1985). *World population prospects: Estimates and projections as assessed in 1982* (Department of International Economic and Social Affairs, Population Studies No. 86, ST/ESA/SER.A/86; United Nations 1985 Sales No. E.83 xiii.5.). New York: Author.

United Nations. (1986). *Report on the world social situation* (Department of International Economic and Social Affairs, ST/ESA/165.ECN-5 1985 Revision 1). New York: Author.

United Nations. (1987). *Global estimates and projections of population by sex and age: The 1984 assessment* (Department of International Economic and Social Affairs, T/ESA/SER.R/70). New York: Author.

United Nations. (1989a). *World population prospects, 1988* (Department of International Economic and Social Affairs, ST/ESA/SER.A/106; United Nations 1989a Sales No. E.88.xiii.7.). New York: Author.

United Nations. (1989b). *World social situation, including the elimination of all major social obstacles: 1989 report on the world social situation* (Economic and Social Council, E/CN-5/1989/2, 15 February 1989). New York: Author.

U.S. Bureau of the Census. (1985a). *Households, families, marital status and living arrangements, March 1985 (advance report)* (Current Population Reports, Series P-20, No. 402). Washington, DC: Government Printing Office.

U.S. Bureau of the Census. (1985b). *Marital status and living arrangements, March 1984* (Current Population Reports, Series P-20, No. 399). Washington, DC: Government Printing Office.

U.S. Bureau of the Census. (1986a). *Marital status and living arrangements, March 1985* (Current Population Reports, Series P-20, No. 410). Washington, DC: Government Printing Office.

U.S. Bureau of the Census. (1986b). *Projections of the Hispanic population 1983 to 2080* (Current Population Reports, Series P-25, No. 995). Washington, DC: Government Printing Office.

U.S. Bureau of the Census. (1986c). *Projections of the number of households and families, 1986-2000* (Current Population Reports, Series P-25, No. 986). Washington, DC: Government Printing Office.

U.S. Bureau of the Census. (1989a). *Marital status and living arrangements* (Current Population Reports, Series P-20, No. 433). Washington, DC: Government Printing Office.

U.S. Bureau of the Census. (1989b). *Poverty in the United States, 1987* (Current Population Reports, Series P-60, No. 163). Washington, DC: Government Printing Office.

U.S. House of Representatives Select Commission on Aging. (1987). *Long term care and personal impoverishment: Seven in ten elderly living alone at risk* (Commission Publication No. 100-631). Washington, DC: Government Printing Office.

U.S. Senate Special Commission on Aging. (1986). *The graying of nations II* (July 12, 1985; Serial No. 99-7). Washington, DC: Government Printing Office.

Winkenwerder, W., Kessler, A. R., & Stolek, R. M. (1989). Federal spending for illness caused by human immunodeficiency virus. *New England Journal of Medicine, 320*(24), 1598-1603.

World Health Organization. (1981a). *The social dimensions of mental health.* Geneva: Author.

World Health Organization. (1981b). *Global strategy for health for all by the year 2000* (Health for All Series, No. 3). Geneva: Author.

World Health Organization. (1984). *Report of the WHO Study Group on Mental Health Care in Developing Countries: A critical appraisal of research findings* (Technical Report Series, No. 698). Geneva: Author.

World Health Organization. (1986a). *Prevention of mental, neurological and psychosocial disorders* (Report by the Director General, A39/9, February 25, 1986). Geneva: Author.

World Health Organization. (1986b, June). Smoking, alcohol and drugs. *World Health*, pp. 1-31.

World Health Organization. (1986c). *World health statistics annual.* Geneva: Author.

World Health Organization. (1987). *Evaluation of the strategy for Health for All by Year 2000: Seventh report on the world health situation—global review.* Geneva: Author.

World Health Organization, Regional office for Europe. (1986). *Children and family breakdown* (Report on a WHO meeting, Kiel, December 4-7, 1984; EURO Reports and Studies, No. 101). Copenhagen: Author.

# 2
# Life on the Brink

## Alan Durning

Historians of the world's fortunate class—those billion-odd people who inhabit industrial lands—have already labeled the twentieth century an era of economic miracles. The poor tell a different tale. The disparities in living standards that separate them from the rich have never been greater. Indeed, they verge on the surreal.

The world has 157 billionaires and perhaps 2 million millionaires, but 100 million people around the globe are homeless, living on sidewalks, in garbage dumps, and under bridges. The concerns of the rich contrast violently with those of the poor. Americans spend $5 billion each year on special diets to lower their calorie consumption, while the world's poorest 400 million people are so undernourished they are likely to suffer stunted growth, mental retardation, or death.

As water from a single spring in France is bottled and shipped to the prosperous around the world, 1.9 billion people drink and bathe in water contaminated with deadly parasites and pathogens. More than half of humanity lacks sanitary toilets. In 1988 the world's nations devoted $1 trillion—$200 for each person on the planet—to the means of warfare, but failed to scrape together the $5 per child it would have cost to eradicate the diseases that killed 14 million that year.

In the 1980s the histories of rich and poor diverged sharply. For industrial nations, the decade was a time of resurgence and recovery after the economic turmoil of the 1970s. For the poor, particularly in Africa and Latin America, the 1980s were an unmitigated disaster, a time of falling earnings and rising debt, of contracting food supplies and escalating death rates.

Once entered, destitution in the modern era is perpetuated by a set of mutually reinforcing factors that form a poverty trap. Locally, poor people's lack of productive assets, their physical weakness, susceptibility to illness, and powerlessness combine with rapid population growth to keep them in straitened circumstances. Nationally, government policies in many sectors favor the urban fortunate over the rural masses. And, at the international level, interlocking patterns of debt, trade, and capital flight during the 1980s made the rich richer and the poor poorer.

AUTHOR'S NOTE: This chapter was published originally in *World Watch*, Vol. 3, No. 2 (March 1990), pp. 22-30. Copyright 1900 by the Worldwatch Institute, 1776 Massachusetts Avenue, N.W., Washington, DC 20036, USA. Reprinted by permission of the publisher.

Still, there is hope for prying open the poverty trap. Poor people have formed hundreds of thousands of grass-roots organizations to help themselves gain what official development programs have failed to provide. In some cases, enlightened governments and international agencies have sponsored these groups. Ultimate success, however, depends on turning these hopeful beginnings into full-fledged mobilization to end poverty.

### Poverty in the Extreme

In 1978, Robert McNamara, then president of the World Bank, gave what stands as the classic description of absolute poverty: "A condition of life so limited by malnutrition, illiteracy, disease, squalid surroundings, high infant mortality, and low life expectancy as to be beneath any reasonable definition of human decency." As McNamara's words suggest, poverty is far more than an economic condition.

Although usually measured in terms of income, poverty's true horror extends into all aspects of an individual's life. Susceptibility to disease, limited access to most types of services and information, lack of control over resources, subordination to higher social and economic classes, and utter insecurity in the face of changing circumstances are the norm for a poor person. Flowing from these physical dimensions, poverty's psychological toll is equally severe: the erosion of human dignity and self-respect.

Unfortunately, even the most basic poverty indicator—income—is hardly monitored. It is possible to know precisely how much money is in circulation in Haiti, how much steel is produced in Malaysia, and how many automobiles there are in the Congo. But the number of people living in the wretched misery of poverty is a matter largely left to conjecture, since little information is gathered. What information does exist is often inconsistent, outdated, or unreliable.

In this chapter, *absolute poverty* is defined as the lack of sufficient income in cash or kind to meet the most basic biological needs for food, clothing, and shelter. From country to country, the income threshold for absolute poverty varies between $50 and $500 per year, depending on such factors as prices, access to subsistence resources, and availability of public services.

In the early 1980s, World Bank and U.S. Food and Agriculture Organization (FAO) estimates of the number of people living in absolute poverty ranged between 700 million and 1 billion. Since then, most indicators suggest that poverty has increased dramatically in sub-Saharan Africa, Latin America, and parts of Asia, swamping reductions in China and India. The result is that approximately 1.2 billion people live in absolute poverty, at least 200 million more than in 1980 (see Table 2.1). World Bank figures suggest that the global poverty rate stood at 22.3% in 1980, after declining gradually but steadily since mid-century. The new poverty

**Table 2.1** People Estimated to Be Living in Absolute Poverty, 1989

| Region | Number of People (millions)[a] | Share of Total Population (percentage) |
|---|---|---|
| Asia | 675 | 25 |
| Sub-Saharan Africa | 325 | 62 |
| Latin America | 150 | 35 |
| North Africa and Middle East | 75 | 28 |
| World | 1,225 | 23 |

SOURCE: Worldwatch Institute.
a. Estimates are best thought of as midpoints of ranges that extend 10% above and below the listed figures.

estimate of 1.2 billion people translates to a poverty rate of 23.4%. During the 1980s, then, the global poverty rate not only stopped falling, it rose.

**The Rich Get Richer**

Perhaps the best way to analyze income per person, or average income, was developed by Robert Summers and Alan Heston, economics professors at the University of Pennsylvania. Their data base incorporates per capita gross domestic product figures on 130 nations compiled from two decades of reports by the United Nations, World Bank, and Organization for Economic Cooperation and Development. Their key innovation was to make systematic adjustments that reflect the widely varying purchasing power for goods and services from country to country. The result is a much more realistic picture of income levels.

Based on Summers and Heston's data, average income per person worldwide in constant 1980 U.S. dollars has doubled to $3,300 since 1950. The fruits of global economic growth, however, have almost all gone to the fortunate. Grouping the world's nations into four classes based on their 1985 per capita income brings the disparities into sharp focus. Wealthy nations, including those in Europe and North America, almost tripled their per capita incomes over the last 40 years. Middle-income countries, such as Brazil, Mexico, and Turkey, more than doubled theirs before entering a period of stagnation around 1980. Poor nations, including China, Egypt, and the Philippines, experienced some rise, but the per person income of the poorest countries, including much of the Indian subcontinent and Africa, has remained effectively level since mid-century.

Wide as the gap between the world's rich and poor appears when measured in average income, the real situation is worse. Averages disguise the gross disparities in income distribution that characterize the majority of countries. Between 60% and 70% of the people in most countries earn less than their nation's

Table 2.2   Approximate Income Distribution, Selected Nations, Most Recent
Available Year

| Country | Equity Ratio[a] |
|---|---|
| China (cities) | 3 |
| Soviet Union | 4 |
| Japan | 4 |
| Bangladesh | 7 |
| Indonesia | 8 |
| India | 10 |
| United States | 12 |
| Mexico | 18 |
| Brazil | 28 |
| World[b] | 15 |

SOURCE: Worldwatch Institute.
a. Ratio of share of national income of richest 20% of households to share of national income of poorest 20% of households.
b. Estimated from average national incomes; true world income distribution is less equitable.

average income. Almost nowhere does the poorest fifth of households collect even 10% of national income, while the richest fifth commonly receives half.

Among the world's most populous nations, China, the Soviet Union, and Japan have relatively equitable income distributions, with the richest fifth of households in the nation receiving between three and four times as much per year as the poorest fifth. Indonesia and India fall in the middle of the range, with the rich earning 8 to 10 times as much as the poor. Mexico is worse, with a factor of 18 separating top and bottom, while in Brazil members of the richest fifth earn 28 times as much as members of the poorest fifth (see Table 2.2).

Data on income distribution and average income can be combined to help reveal the extent of poverty. The poor may be fairly well off even when average income is low, or suffer greatly where average income is high. In 1985, for example, Egypt's per capita income was about half of Peru's, but because Egypt is more equitable, poor Egyptians earned one-third more than poor Peruvians. Likewise, Brazil's average income was twice Sri Lanka's, but the Sri Lankan poor earned more than the Brazilian poor.

In terms of economic security, what different classes own is as important as what they earn. Although reliable information is scarce, the disparity in distribution of wealth appears to be wider than the disparity in distribution of income. The situation in India is probably representative of developing countries generally. There, the richest tenth of households receive income worth 25 times as much as the poorest tenth of households, but own assets worth 250 times as much.

**A Cruel Decade**

For the poor of Africa, Latin America, and parts of Asia, the 1980s were a time of cruel reversals, a period when the global economy seemed to conspire against them. On top of the runaway population growth and accelerating environmental decline that were already dragging down living standards across the Third World, prices for poor nations' exports plummeted, and international debt siphoned a growing share of their income into the hands of foreign financiers. The poor, in short, earned less and paid more. Consequently, they ate less.

Developing nations' debt of $1.2 trillion caused a reversal of the flow of international capital. Today, poor nations are paying rich ones $50 billion each year in debt and interest payments beyond what they receive in new loans. Capital flight from wealthy people in poor lands may bring the exodus up to $100 billion each year. Trade protectionism in industrial countries results in annual losses on a similar scale, as Third World export prices fall and markets shrink.

This massive hemorrhage of financial resources from poor regions only augments their destruction of natural resources. Poor countries are forced to exploit mineral deposits, forests, and fisheries to meet debt obligations. And they are left with few resources to alleviate poverty. The poor turn to the only means of survival available to them: marginal lands. They plow mountain slopes, burn plots in tropical forests, and overgraze grasslands, often knowing full well that their actions are destructive to the environment and therefore cannot last.

Close to half of the absolute poor now live in regions of marginal agriculture productivity, where they are falling into a downward spiral of ecological and economic impoverishment. The stark choice for the dispossessed, trapped as they are in stagnant economies that are exporting precious resources to pay bank debts, is between sacrificing their environment and sacrificing their children.

**One Step Forward, Two Steps Back**

From 1950 to 1980, the gap between rich and poor nations has grown, mostly because the rich got richer. Since 1980, the poor in many developing countries have been getting poorer, too. More than 40 Third World nations probably finished the decade poorer, in per capita terms, than they started it. The 14 most devastated countries—including Zambia, Bolivia, and Nigeria—saw per capita income plummet as drastically as did the United States during the Great Depression. In fact, the term *developing nation* has become a cruel misnomer; many countries are no longer so much developing as disintegrating.

The human impact of the decade's economic backslide in Africa, Latin America, and parts of Asia has been ruinous. Malnutrition is documented to have risen in Burma, Burundi, the Gambia, Guinea-Bissau, Jamaica, Niger,

Nigeria, Paraguay, the Philippines, Nicaragua, El Salvador, Peru, and undoubtedly elsewhere. The World Bank reports that from 1979 to 1983, life expectancy fell in nine African countries, and more than 100 million Africans are thought to lack sufficient food to sustain themselves in good health.

The economic turmoil of the 1980s truly wreaked havoc south of the Sahara. Income per capita peaked in 1974, stumbled along until 1980, and then plunged, dropping 25% by 1988. Nigeria, Zaire, and Zambia, dependent on exports of mineral resources, and war-torn Angola, Ethiopia, Mozambique, and Sudan saw their economies unravel more rapidly still. North African and Middle Eastern nations suffered less than most in the early 1980s, but with the drop of oil prices in mid-decade, unemployment spread and poverty rose again.

In Latin America, per capita income stood at almost $3,400 in 1980. Sadly, skewed income distribution meant that destitution continued to be the lot of a large share of the population. The 1980s darkened the outlook across the region, but were especially gloomy for the poor. As Inter-American Development Bank President Enrique Iglesias said in September 1988, "The per-capita income of the average Latin American is 9 percent lower today than it was in 1980. This is average. In some countries the standard of living has slipped back to what it was 20 years ago. It does not take much imagination to realize that behind this statistic are plummeting real wage levels, soaring unemployment . . . increased levels of marginality, and acute poverty—in short, an erosion of every measure of social well-being."

El Salvador, Nicaragua, and Peru, all torn by war, went into economic tailspins. Peruvian children are malnourished to the point that one in three has stunted growth, according to the government's National Investigation of Nutrition and Health. In El Salvador, staples such as beans are now called "rich people's food" and health workers report that infant mortality is surging.

Asian economies were sharply divided during the turbulence of the last decade. In China, average income rose by more than 60% since 1980. India, Indonesia, Pakistan, and Thailand also raised per capita income appreciably during the 1980s, in some cases at a faster rate than in earlier decades. Bangladesh, Burma, and Vietnam, by contrast, stagnated, and the Philippines experienced a sharp decline.

Asian countries that did well during the 1980s—coincidentally, among the few countries for which fairly reliable poverty estimates exist—also made strides in alleviating poverty. The extent of absolute poverty in China was cut dramatically during a period of rapid economic growth. In 1980, according to a World Bank estimate, 150 million Chinese lived in poverty; by 1988, best estimates put the number at 70 million, even though the country's population has grown by 69 million over this period.

Indonesia, meanwhile, reduced the portion of its population in poverty by between one-fourth and one-half since 1970, according to different estimates. Thailand reportedly made a 50% reduction since 1960. Although still controversial, indications are that the poverty rates in India and Pakistan declined by several percentage points in the 1980s.

## Who Are the Poor?

Poor people are not a homogeneous group. Nonetheless, a few generalizations help answer the question, Who are the poor? Despite rapid urbanization and growing urban poverty in much of the world, four-fifths of those in absolute poverty still live in rural areas. Only in Latin America do a large share of the poor—nearly one-half—live in cities. Almost all of the poor live in, and are culturally shaped by, the world's 2 million villages—the tightly knit social and economic institutions that have been at the center of human life since the dawn of agriculture.

Even among the absolute poor, degrees of poverty can be distinguished. Michael Lipton, director of the Food Consumption and Nutrition Program at the International Food Policy Research Institute in Washington, DC, has demonstrated that those at the very bottom of the economic ladder form a distinct subclass. Defined as those who spend 80% of their income on food but still lack sufficient calories to meet their metabolic needs, this undernourished class accounts for perhaps one-third of the absolute poor, or 400 million people. All of the poor eat boring, monotonous, and unappetizing diets of cereals, roots, and legumes day after day. All may be hungry periodically.

The world's poor are overwhelmingly illiterate and therefore lack access to information and ideas that could help them escape poverty. Indeed, social scientists studying poverty through statistical analysis commonly find educational level to be the variable that correlates most closely to standard of living. Even among landless laborers, where literacy would seem to matter little, those who can read tend to earn more than those who cannot.

The poor are often distinct from dominant wealthy groups in race, tribe, or religion. In Africa, with its hundreds of different cultural groups, economic strata are often drawn along tribal lines. Indian poverty is concentrated among tribal peoples and lower castes. The hill tribes of Southeast Asia and the Philippines fall at the bottom of the economic ladder, while Latin American Indians are the poorest of that region, particularly in Guatemala, Peru, and Bolivia, where they form a majority of the population.

The poor are slightly more likely to be female than male, particularly in urban areas, leading some analysts to speak of a global "feminization of poverty." Although the true extent of female poverty remains uncertain, there is no question that life is harsher for poor women than for poor men. Women's burdens multiply endlessly. They are paid less than men (in Egypt, half as much for farm labor), but they work more—up to three additional hours each day, according to studies of villages in four countries. They are less educated—female literacy trails male literacy by 38 percentage points on average in the world's worst-off countries—but bear greater responsibility for the health of children.

Women are expected to give birth to, raise, and feed numerous (preferably male) offspring, and consequently grow weak and ailing as their bodies are exhausted by the cycle of repeated pregnancy and childbirth. They are often abused and beaten at home, but have few legal rights and fewer property rights. They cannot leave their husbands unless they are willing to lose their social standing, their economic security, and their children. For poor women, as a peasant woman from the Brazilian state of Minas Gerais says, "the only holiday . . . is when you are asleep."

The work of the poor is concentrated at the fringes of the global economy. Most are landless agricultural laborers, sharecroppers, marginal farmers, or, if they live in cities, unskilled laborers in the underground economy. Landlessness has been on the rise as small farms are divided into plots too tiny for subsistence and as agricultural commercialization pushes tenants and sharecroppers out of fertile zones. Landless and near landless rural households probably number near 200 million in developing countries.

What work the landless can find is usually piecemeal, unstable, and insecure, not to mention backbreaking and tedious, yet they work hard day in and day out. As Professor Robert Chambers of the Institute for Development Studies in Brighton, England, puts it, "People so close to the edge cannot afford laziness or stupidity. They have to work, and work hard, whenever and however they can. Many of the lazy and stupid poor are dead."

**A Painful Inheritance**

Poverty's most savage toll is measured in the lives of children. As income declines, family size increases. Lipton reports that whereas 15-30% of families in developing countries have eight or more members, 55-80% of poor families are that large. Consequently, perhaps two thirds of the world's absolute poor are under the age of 15. The prospects for these young people are even worse than for their parents.

Not surprisingly, at lower incomes infant death rates turn sharply upward. Wracked by disease, lacking sufficient nourishment and clean water, perhaps one third of these youngsters die before their fifth birthdays. Many of those who survive are physically stunted and mentally impaired as a result of chronic hunger during the critical age of 6 months to 2 years, foreclosing their already slim chances of escaping poverty.

In Zambia, twice as many children died from malnutrition in 1984 as in 1980. The infant mortality rate in Brazil rose in 1983 and 1984 for the first time in decades—rising more steeply in the poorest regions. Similar trends are afoot in much of the Third World, leading UNICEF to conclude in its 1989 annual report that "hundreds of thousands of the developing world's children have given their lives to pay their countries' debts, and many millions more are still paying the interest with their malnourished minds and bodies."

### Hunger in the Lap of Luxury

Absolute poverty is rare in affluent lands, yet it is worth noting that in industrial countries less severe forms of poverty also rose during the 1980s, particularly in the United States, the United Kingdom, and Eastern Europe. With glasnost, the Soviet Union and Eastern European countries have begun to reveal the extent of deprivation within their borders. One fifth of Soviet citizens reportedly live below the official poverty line of 75 rubles ($116) a month, and many Poles have seen their livelihoods wither as their economy unravels.

In the United States, the last decade saw more people living below the poverty line—which stood at just over $12,000 per year for a family of four in 1988—than at any time since the War on Poverty was initiated in the mid-1960s. In 1979 the equity of income distribution began to deteriorate rapidly; by 1986, disparities in earnings were the worst on record. Meanwhile, the median  family income was lower in 1988 than in 1973, measured in constant dollars, and average weekly earnings were lower than in 1962.

Falling real wages and greater inequality led inevitably to rising poverty: In 1988, some 32 million Americans lived below the official poverty line. Most severely affected are minorities, female-headed households, and the young. One-fifth of American children are growing up in poverty. With widening income disparities around the globe, it will not be long before there is a Third World within the First World, and a First within the Third.

### Ending Poverty

Alleviating poverty worldwide will require national governments and international agencies to redefine development away from generalized aid for entire regions. True development is the struggle to help the poorest break out of the poverty trap. The touchstone of true development was best expressed decades ago by Mahatma Gandhi: "Whenever you are in doubt . . . apply the following test. Recall the face of the poorest and the weakest man whom you may have seen, and ask yourself if the step you contemplate is going to be of any use to him. Will he gain anything by it? Will it restore him to a control over his own life and destiny?" Given the changing profile of poverty, the only updating Gandhi's principle needs is to substitute "poorest child" for "poorest man."

A variety of innovative grass-roots strategies from around the world have now proven that effective assaults on poverty begin by putting the poor in control. As nutrition analyst Paulus Santosa put it, "It would be very hard to find professional nutrition workers in Indonesia today who can raise a family of five with U.S. $0.50 per day and stay healthy." The only true experts on poverty are the poor.

Critical components of grass-roots mobilization against poverty are female education, redistribution of farmland, empowerment of communities to control local natural resources, extension of credit, and provision of clean water, primary health care, and family planning services.

In West Bengal, India, "untouchables"—those at the bottom of the country's caste system—who received tiny allotments of scrub land from the state started tree farms that enabled them to buy fertile plots from absentee landlords. They helped themselves and the environment. In the highlands of Bolivia, home of the Quechua Indians, local efforts to start a community newspaper unleashed local knowledge and energy that has since flowed into dozens of activities, including soil and forest conservation.

The state of Kerala, India, provides a model of fighting poverty with grass-roots participation. The state's success speaks for itself. Despite per capita income one-third below the Indian average, the state's literacy rate is almost twice the national mark; the state's people typically live 11 years longer, the birthrate is one-third lower, and the infant death rate is two-thirds lower than the national average.

Yet local and national efforts will amount to little in the absence of fundamental changes at the international level. Without accords to reduce debt dramatically, lower protectionist barriers to Third World exports, and slow the astronomical rate of capital flight, poverty will continue to rise during the 1990s.

### Voices of the Powerless

Described in numbers, poverty seems horrible enough; in the words of the poor, however, its full cruelty is revealed. A young woman from the highlands of Guatemala describes the misery and powerlessness of life, and death, on the coffee plantations where her family and thousands of other Indians worked as migrants:

> Two of my brothers died in the plantation. The first, he was the eldest, was called Felipe. . . . They'd sprayed the coffee with pesticide by plane while we were working, as they usually did, and my brother couldn't stand the fumes and died. . . . The second one . . . his name was Nicolas . . . died when I was eight. . . . He was two then. When my little brother started crying, crying, crying, my mother didn't know what to do. . . . He lasted fifteen days. . . .
>
> The little boy died early in the morning. We didn't know what to do. Our two neighbors were anxious to help my mother but they didn't know what to

do either—not how to bury him or anything. Then the overseer told my mother she could bury my brother in the plantation but she had to pay a tax to keep him buried there. My mother said, "I have no money at all." He told her: "Yes, and you already owe a lot of money for medicine and other things, so take his body and leave." . . . It was impossible to take his body back to the highlands. . . . So my mother decided that, even if she had to work for a month without earning, she would pay the tax to the landowner, or the overseer, to bury my brother in the plantation. . . .

One of the men brought a little box, a bit like a suitcase. We put my brother in it and took him to be buried. . . . That night the overseer told us: "Leave here tomorrow."

They were fired for missing work to bury Nicolas. For the Indians of Guatemala, like the rest of the poor, life is a grueling ordeal. Days before his own death, a farm laborer in Bangladesh named Hari reflected on his years: "Between the mortar and the pestle, the chili cannot last. We poor are like chilies— each year we are ground down, and soon there will be nothing left."

The poor, more than ever, are rallying to their own defense, but the global poverty trap only tightens around them. The challenge of forestalling Hari's prophecy falls largely to the rich.

**A Few Entry Points for Fighting Poverty**

Support poor people's grass-roots organizations through

Oxfam-America
115 Broadway
Boston, MA 02216
(617) 482-1211

Promote reform of international development agencies through

Bread for the World
802 Rhode Island Avenue, N.E.
Washington, DC 20018
(202) 269-0200

and through

The Global Tomorrow Coalition
1325 G Street, N.W.
Washington, DC 20005
(202) 628-4016

Educate yourself on a Third World study tour with

Global Exchange
2141 Mission Street, Suite 202
San Francisco, CA 94110
(415) 255-7269

# 3

# An Epidemiological Study of Mental Disorders During Early Childhood in the Soviet Union

Olga V. Bazhenova
Anna V. Gorunova
Galina V. Kozlovskaya
Galina V. Skoblo

The first and most sensitive period of mental development is in infancy and early childhood, embracing the time from birth to 3-4 years old. The sensitivity of this period results from high rates of psychic and physical development (comparable to the rates of changes that take place during puberty) with imperfect adaptation mechanisms. These imperfect mechanisms provoke the appearance of different mental disorders if the child has biological or social risk factors. The qualification of these factors, finding out the mechanisms of their interaction, and the direct study of the specific features of psychopathology and of the psychology of early childhood are all essential conditions for the development of primary preventive measures.

Until recently little attention has been given to these research directions in the Soviet Union, or to their introduction into practice. A number of Soviet works on the psychopathology of early childhood, written from the 1920s through the 1960s, did not constitute a sufficient theoretical base. The problems of prevention of mental disorders were not practically covered in those early studies. Work in the field of Soviet psychology and in the psychopathology of early childhood is at an initial stage of development. Practical psychiatric intervention with young children is not widely accessible in the Soviet Union. According to the existing official provisions, psychiatrists start observing children from the age of 3 years. Before that, assessments of the mental health of children are made by pediatricians and neuropathologists. However, these specialists (including child psychiatrists) are not, as a rule, competent in the problems of the psychiatry and psychology of early childhood, as these subjects are not included in their professional training. Until now the practice of psychological aid in early childhood (and particularly in mother-child interactions) has not been established because of the lack of specialists in this field.

Recently, however, attempts have been made to provide special medical and preventive assistance to children in the early years, to those who already have mental disorders, or to those who belong to high-risk groups; a new wave of scientific work in this field has begun to appear.

Attention to the primary prevention of early childhood mental disorders has arisen first of all because of practical needs. In the mid-1980s, a network of state nursery schools was developed on a large scale. These are special institutions for the organized care of young children. Every institution of this kind can accommodate 100-120 children between the ages of 1 and 3 years. Children can stay during the day, and in the evening return to their families. Children might also stay at such institutions for as much as a week at a time. In these nursery schools, the children are observed by medical workers of the local children's outpatient hospital and by people with special pedagogical education. One person with this special training usually observes 20-25 children.

Sending a 1-year-old child for observation to the state institution, often for a stay of five or six days, has not been a widespread phenomenon, especially among young families, due to insufficient state material support and to the long tradition in the Soviet Union of the collective upbringing of children. This latter tradition has led to a noticeable deterioration of the mental and somatic health of children. It was one of the reasons a law was adopted that provides mothers with three-year partly paid job leaves so that they can stay home and take care of their children. On the other hand, the appearance of a large number of children with emotional disorders has made it necessary to establish special psychoneurological nursery schools (in Moscow there are 13 of them), as a result of which new groups of child psychiatrists, neuropathologists, and psychologists have begun their research work. The largest team of such specialists was established in 1987 in the Department for Child Preventive Psychiatry at the All-Union Mental Health Research Center of the USSR Academy of Medical Sciences, a department we helped to establish. The practical base of our department, besides nursery schools, is the state children's outpatient hospitals of Moscow.

In the years 1987-1990, our department carried out an epidemiological study of the mental health of children during the first three years of life. Child psychiatrists, psychologists, and neuropathologists took part in this research, the goals of which are to determine the distribution and structure of mental disorders in the urban child population, to study the dynamics of these disorders in the preschool years, and to find risk factors for the development of psychopathological disorders.

The children studied were 370 individuals from state nursery schools who were selected at random from a typical state pediatric outpatient hospital. To carry out this research we designed a special scheme for psychoneurological examination of the young child. To classify disorders, we adapted classifications in the *Manual of the International Statistical Classifications of Diseases, Injuries, and Causes of Death* (9th ed.; World Health Organization, 1977). (The tenth edition of this volume is only now being adapted for use in the Soviet Union.)

The psychoneurological examination was aimed at obtaining data on peculiarities of development and disorders of different mental functions, as well as the dynamic assessment of the neurological status of the child. The main parameters of development and deviations, of vegetative-instinctive, sensory, emotional, motor, and cognitive spheres, as well as attention, speech, communication, and peculiarities of social behavior, were reported on a clinical level.

Among the risk factors, genetic, exogenous-organic, and social factors were studied. These involved the presence in the families of mental diseases or apparent mental anomalies. Psychiatrists treating adults were involved in this research. Exogenous organic influences, data on the progress of pregnancy and childbirth, the presence of cranial/brain damage, infection with brain process, and somatic diseases were studied. Among social parameters were the composition of the family, its material well-being, the professional level of the parents, peculiarities of parental care, and the family situation as a whole. Separation of parents was taken into consideration.

As a result of the epidemiological research on the mental health of this sample of children, three groups were identified: the pathological group (14%), the group at risk (30.5%), and the normal group (55.5%). In the pathological group the following disorders were obvious: mental retardation (4.5%), serious behavior deviance (3.7%), apparent neurotic and neurosis-like disorders (3.5%), psycho-organic syndrome (.8%), psychosis of early childhood (.6%), episyndromes (.6%), and hyperkinetic syndrome with attention disorders (.5%). These indications of pathology were found in observations as the children were reaching 3 to 4 years. In earlier ages the total indication of apparent mental disorders was less, amounting to about 8%. We concluded that there is a tendency toward increased "crystallization" of mental disorders with the time of "growing up" of the children's sample studied. Generally, the fact of widespread mental disorders in early childhood has been established.

In our opinion, two observations can be made based on these data that are of particular interest. First, the manifest psychoses in nonselected epidemiological examination of the young group (.6%) proved to be numerically close to the spreading psychoses (schizophrenia) among the adult population in the city of Moscow in 1988. The discovered cases of psychosis (one in a girl and one in a boy) were diagnosed at the age of 1 to 1.5 years. Before that, both children had been described as "behavior deviant with considerably disturbed adaptability." Moreover, the state of these children before the time of the manifestation of psychosis could be described within the framework of "neurointegrative defect" (a term introduced by American scientist B. Fich, 1978). In Soviet terminology this would be called "schizotypical diathesis." These states are determined by specific apparent features of the clinical picture that incorporate a characteristic dissociation of development along with elements of deficiency in a number of mental spheres. The greatest changes on the clinical level are found in the vegetative-instinctive, motor developmental, emotional, and communicative spheres.

The second interesting observation is that the state of schizotypical diathesis was diagnosed in six more children in the sample. These children, characterized by behavior disorders that considerably disturbed their adaptability, were classified under the relative general section. During the whole period of examination no psychotic symptoms had been discovered in them. However, there are grounds to believe that it is this group of children who present the greatest risk for manifestation of psychoses. Besides the specific picture of schizotypical diathesis, the genealogical study of families convinced us of this conclusion. In the families of all these children (usually the first degree of relationship) we found members suffering from schizophrenia or disorders of the schizophrenia spectrum.

The second big group (those "at risk") of the observed contingent (30.5%) consisted of children having less apparent mental disorders than in the pathological group. These children were observed to have disturbances of sleep at times, transitory indigestion, psychogenically conditioned disturbances of temperature regulation and other somatovegetative dysfunctions, hyperkinetic reactions (not reaching the degree of the definite hyperkinetic syndrome), nonpersistent tics, stammering, phobias, pathological habits, momentary febrile convulsions, and isolated mental retardation (of speech development). Usually such symptoms were found in children under the age of 3 as a complex of the described dysfunctions. These children were in the at-risk group for the development of nondifferential mental deviations. The prospective observation of this group until the age of 5 showed that only 10% of these children could be considered healthy, and 25% had some deterioration of their health as they grew up; there were no essential changes in the state of the other children.

The neurological examination of the population showed the presence of some pathological changes, the frequency and appearance of which were separate from the distribution of children in healthy groups. So in the pathological group neurological disturbances were found in all the children. In cases of schizotypical diathesis they had the specific character described elsewhere in our research. In other cases, dispersed neurological inclinations were observed as a consequence of pre- and antenatal brain damage usually moderately expressed. By the age of 3 the neurological symptoms were considerably regressed to the level of the syndrome of minimal brain dysfunction. In the risk group neurological deviations occurred less often and were, as a rule, less prominent. We suppose that the neurological disorders found in infancy and early childhood form the biological background for the development of mental disorders in the presence of negative social factors.

In this epidemiological research systematic analysis was made of the risk factors for mental pathology of children in the first years of life. The main biological and social risk factors are as follows: (a) early infantile encephalopathy both of hypoksical and traumatic origin; (b) the specific liability to genetically determined conditions that include diseases such as schizophrenia and diseases of the schizophrenia spectrum, affective psychoses, constitutional psychopathy, epilepsy, and mental retardation; (c) neuropathetic constitution, conditioned by genetically determined dysfunction of the higher centers of vegetative regulation or their morphofunctional immaturity at birth; (d) frequent somatic diseases; and (e) postnatal diseases and injuries of the nervous system.

Among the main social risk factors for the appearance of psychopathology the following can be pointed out: (a) the upsetting of "mother-child" interaction, (b) unfavorable family situations, (c) low material well-being of the family, (d) separation influences (hospitalization without mother, early attendance at preschool institutions and others), and (e) depriving influences of preschool institution.

The data from the epidemiological screening of the population of children indicated a high frequency of social risk factors amounting to 100% in the pathology group. The main conclusion of the research is as follows: It is imperative that prevention measures be worked out early by mental health professionals and put into practice early.

A new program of research has been started, the aim of which is to work out the problems of the prevention of mental pathology in early childhood. The program covers several aspects and is carried out by four groups of specialists: child psychiatrists, neuropathologists, psychologists, and the genealogical group (psychiatrists treating adults). The ideological foundations of the research are as follows:

(1) The prevention of psychopathological disorders in early childhood is a complex problem.

(2) The formation of psychopathological deviations is conditioned by the presence of predisposing risk factors of biological and social origins.

(3) The prevention of psychopathological deviations depends on reducing or eliminating the risk factors. This can be achieved by both social psychological and biological influence.

(4) The identification of clinical presymptoms ("markers of disease") in early childhood can be carried out on psychiatric, neurological, and psychological levels.

(5) The primary prevention of psychopathology can be carried out from the pre- and perinatal periods of child development.

(6) Adequate prevention of psychopathological deviations in the child can be effected only in the process of intensive work with the family.

The organizational and methodological aspects of the work are as follows. The intervention will be carried out in a typical district of Moscow. We plan to observe many groups of pregnant married women giving birth to their first child, and then, within three years, to observe the state of their children's mental health. The observations of expectant mothers and their husbands will be made by psychologists and psychiatrists.

Psychological assessment of the peculiarities of the parents' personalities, emotional and cognitive components of the readiness for maternity, and family relations will be made. Widely known tests (MMPI, Rorschach, Luscher, and others) as well as tests created in the Soviet Union (Color Test of Relations, Joint Rorschach, and others) and methods specially designed in the interests of the research (structured interviews, projective tests for the evaluation of family relations and the feeling of support experienced by women, methods of the observation of family communications, and others) will be used.

Steps in the study are as follows. The psychiatrist makes the clinical evaluation of the mental state of the expectant mother and of the future child's father, and also the assessment of the state of mentally sick relatives. The diagnosis of mental illness is made within the framework of the criteria based on our adaptation of classifications found in the *Manual of the International Classification of Diseases.*

The children's psychologist starts the observation of children at the age of 1 month. To assess the development of infants the Soviet method of differentiated quality-quantity diagnosis of the development of 1-year-old children (Bazhenova, 1986) is utilized. Later, the traditional USSR psychopathological diagnosis of development is made.

Both neuropathologist and psychiatrist also observe children jointly from the age of 1 month, applying specially designed schemes. The qualification of the neurological state is based on the criteria adapted in Soviet childhood neurology. The qualification of the mental disorders of infants and toddlers in the first year of life is carried out on both syndrome and symptomatic levels. In the first case the variant of the *International Classification of Diseases* we adapted for young children, applying established diagnoses from worldwide psychoneurological practice (hospitalization, anaclitic depression, affect-respiratory attacks, and others), as well as our own diagnostic procedures (schizotypical diathesis and others) are utilized.

As soon as family or infant risk factors are found, intervention for the secondary prevention of mental disorders and minimizing of unfavorable influences begin. First, psychological consultation is undertaken with the parents, taking into consideration their personal peculiarities, the situation in the family, and their attitude toward the child. In the case of a mother having psychopathological disorders, the psychiatric treatment (including medical treatment) is started (with the mother's consent). Mothers more often accept such help than do fathers. When diagnosing psychological causes for parent's lack of adaptability, the psychotherapeutic work is carried out with the parents. The parents are informed of presymptoms of psychopathological disorders in the child and are given the general prognosis for the child's development. They are offered free medical and psychotherapeutic aid. If the family agrees to accept all this, there are two possibilities. In the first case the child receives psychological help aimed at the elimination of socially determined deviations and compensation of emotional and interactive defects. In the second case a similar type of intervention is combined with medical treatment if necessary.

## A Clinical Case

A child, M.A., a boy, was born after 37 weeks of pregnancy; he weighed 3 kilograms. The diagnosis made at the maternity home was morphofunctional immaturity.

The boy's mother is 24 years old and a teacher of history; she suffered several attacks of depression before and during pregnancy. Psychological observation during the pregnancy revealed that, according to the self-attitude questionnaire, she has a low level of self-acceptance; her MMPI scores show incomplete acceptance of the feminine social role, suppressed self-fulfillment, concentration on her own somatic health, and unreasonable demands on herself, as well as adherence to conventional norms of behavior (an elevation on 5, 1, and 8 scales).

The father is 28 years old and a history teacher—one of his school's best. In his childhood he was in a lengthy deprivation situation (from the age of 3 months he was brought up in state institutions). The psychological examination and observation revealed that, according to his scores on the MMPI, he is open to communication, likes to be the center of attention, is persistent in achieving this goal, is capable of involving people, has an apparent feeling of competition, and is highly impulsive and emotionally unstable (an elevation on 9, 3, 4, and 6 scales).

Family interaction (according to joint settlement of family tasks) observation revealed an apparent dominating position of the father and his ability to organize family interaction, with the wife's position being one of passively following the husband's recommendations.

Until the age of 2 months, the child experienced a prolonged period of maladaptation explained by morphofunctional immaturity: He slept almost without the normal intervals of actively remaining awake, apparently did not have the feeling of being sated (that is, he overate), gave negative reactions to swaddling and bathing, and did not smile. He gained weight well. It was recommended that he be cared for following a special protective regime from the age of 2 months—the period of intensive mental development and improvement of the general state. The examination at the age of 3.5 months indicated retardation of development in all spheres of psychic (especially sensory) reactions and concrete activities. In addition, the child began waking up at night very frequently, refused to be breast-fed, and, apparently because of loss of appetite, did not gain weight normally. He was prone to crying and caprice, and often sucked his fist. By the age of 4 months he began to balance on all fours, and an irregular phenomenon of pseudodeafness was observed. The psychiatric observation of the mother revealed her depressive state of mind (average degree), which started when the child was 3 months old. The disturbance of the mother-child interaction became apparent: The mother, according to her own words, felt alienated from the child ("as if it were not mine"—a symptom of depression), could not develop sufficient child-care skills, adhered in his upbringing to a strictly regulated system approved by the father, did not approach the child for long periods when he was crying, and tried "not to train the child to be carried," not to pamper him, to bring him up to be "courageous." The described case indicates a depressive state in infancy as a result of deprivation (mother's depression, the disturbance of the mother-child interaction).

The family was offered psychotherapeutic help and the mother was recommended for drug treatment. The parents' personal peculiarities were corrected, as well as their interaction; explanations were given to adjust the mother-child interaction. Infusion of sedative herbs for the child was recommended to reduce his excitement and to improve his sleep and appetite. During three months the mother's and child's states were gradually improved. The psychological observation at the age of 6 months indicated positive improvement in mental development. The child's sleep patterns had improved considerably, as well as his appetite and mood; his swaying stopped. However, the child remains emotionally unstable. Supportive guidance for the family is continuing.

This described approach to the secondary prevention of mental disorders is not fully adopted in the Soviet Union, and is used only within the framework of the All-Union Mental Health Research Center. Experience in carrying out this work indicates that, at the present time in the Soviet Union, under conditions of intense psychological stress, the support and aid of psychologists and psychiatrists are needed for young families and disturbed children.

The social changes taking place in the Soviet Union currently are enormous, although at times unpredictable. So far, these changes have not always made people's lives optimal. The future, which is difficult to predict, and the crises of the present are two acute social factors that are exercising influence nowadays, especially on families. All of this experience indicates, once more, that it is impossible to solve the problems of the primary prevention of mental disorders, even at an early age, apart from social reality.

## References

Bazhenova, O. V. (1986). *Djagnostika psixicheskogo raswitija detei perwogo goda zisni* [The diagnostics of psychophysical development during a child's first years]. Moscow: Uniwersit.

Fich, B. (1978). Neurobiologic antecedents of schizophrenia in children. In S. Chess & A. Thomas (Eds.), *Annual progress in child psychiatry and child development* (pp. 442-485). New York: Brunner/Mazel.

World Health Organization. (1977). *Manual of the international statistical classifications of diseases, injuries, and causes of death* (9th ed.). Geneva: Author.

# 4

# One Little Girl

On January 31, 1990, National Public Radio (NPR) featured an interview broadcast by correspondent Daniel Swerdling-Rothschild, who had been allowed inside a prison in Pakistan. He discovered that many of the inmates were girls, women, and even babies and very small children. In interviews with them he learned that many of the women and girls had been transported from Bangladesh by human traffickers. Many of them were brought into Pakistan (and other countries as well) to be sold as permanent household "maids" or to meet the demand for girls and young women as prostitutes.

Many of these girls and young women had attempted to leave Bangladesh and their poverty-stricken lives in the hope of finding jobs in Pakistan. They were often picked up by agents, or they voluntarily paid agents, who promised job placements. Some came alone, some with relatives, often walking from Bangladesh across northern India to Pakistan, crossing international boundaries at night in an effort to avoid detection. Those who were captured by the authorities were incarcerated in Pakistan, usually without a trial and, often, without hope. Many of those interviewed by the NPR correspondent had been in prison for months or years without hope of release. Many of them had borne children while in the prison.

Mr. Swerdling-Rothschild interviewed, via an interpreter, a tearful little girl of 8 or 9 years old who said her name was Fatma (or Fatima). She said she was from Bangladesh, that she had had an argument with her mother and decided to run to her sister's house. But she was caught and kidnapped en route and brought by her captors to Pakistan. In January 1990, during a raid on the house where she was being kept, she was found, arrested by the police, and jailed as an illegal immigrant. During the interview the child wept, stating that she knew her parents had no idea where she was. She begged to be allowed to return home.

Fatima had been brought to Pakistan by a slaver and sold to a family who mistreated her and forced her to do all the household work. "They always used to beat me," she said. For some reason the house was raided by the police. The agent who sold her to the family was also arrested, but was released from jail

EDITOR'S NOTE: This account is a brief summary of materials provided by attorney Debra Weecks and Barry Jay, Ph.D. We deeply appreciate their efforts and concern about this case and the issues it raises. Detailed accounts of human trafficking problems may also be obtained from the International League for Human Rights (432 Park Avenue, New York, NY 10016, USA) and the Anti-Slavery Society (180 Brixton Road, London SW9 6AT, England).

after just a few days. In the prison she pointed out that her "bed" was the floor in a room with at least 75 other women and children, and only approximately 25 beds. She slept without bed clothes or covers. Many of the women in the room seemed protective of this little girl, but they were all housed in the same desperate, overcrowded way and all were underfed. Of these women, those who are eventually released are frequently recaptured in the streets outside the prison and enslaved all over again.

There is no word about the current whereabouts of Fatima. The Anti-Slavery Society, which has inquired into her fate, is concerned that she might have been released into the custody of known human traffickers. The Anti-Slavery Society has sent a series of questions to the representative of Pakistan, but as a consequence of the recent abrupt change in the Pakistani government, no information has been released. Fatima is now missing. She cannot be found.

An American attorney, Debra Weecks, heard the NPR broadcast and spearheaded an attempt by a number of Americans, including U.S. government agencies and members of Congress, to win Fatima's release and return her to Bangladesh, with the intent of reuniting her with her family. Weecks was instrumental in persuading the Pakistani government to release the child to a responsible third party until the child's parents could be found. A third party was secured, the Rainbow House International, a foster home in Bangladesh. Airline transportation for Fatima from Pakistan to Bangladesh was arranged. Indeed, the Pakistani government further agreed to release all of the women and children incarcerated in the Karachi prison. The only obstacle at the time was authorization by the Bangladeshi government for the child to be returned to her country, as she had no papers indicating that she was a Bangladeshi citizen.

Several U.S. senators, including Claiborn Pell, Joseph Lieberman, and Carl Levin, intervened with the Bangladesh government on Fatima's behalf, and in a letter dated April 11, 1990, Bangladesh Foreign Secretary Abul Ahsan indicated that his government would work toward Fatima's reparation "on a priority basis."

Time passed and no word was received about the status of Fatima's reparation or of the child's health and welfare. On May 16, 1990, the Bangladesh minister of foreign affairs, director general for South Asia, Ambassador Mostafa Faruque Mohammed sent a telex to the U.S. State Department with the information that shortly after the interview with Mr. Swerdling-Rothschild, Fatima had been released from prison and apparently returned to her abductors, and that no further information was available about her whereabouts or her well-being. Additionally, there were no reports of the other women and children being released from the prison.

Dr. Arshad Husain, cochair of a World Federation for Mental Health Committee, on a visit to Pakistan in December 1990, reported that it was believed Fatima was smuggled to India after her prison release.

The case of Fatima is only one of thousands or hundreds of thousands. During the 1990 Vermont Conference on the Primary Prevention of Psychopathology, we heard of the common practice of children being employed in the manufacture of "Oriental carpets," where they are required to sit and tie knots 12 hours a day, 7 days a week, for pitifully small wages and meager food rations—small hands tie tighter knots. Many of these children become crippled from sitting in the same position all day, every day, but there is no escape. Other children are indentured by their parents to pay off debts incurred with unscrupulous lenders who charge high interest. Sometimes these children are bonded to a creditor for a year, but after a year the creditor has accumulated charges against the child for food and housing, requiring continued bonded servitude. We heard of thousands of girls, throughout a number of countries, who were sold by their parents or otherwise turned over to human traffickers with the promise that the girls would be taken to the cities for gainful employment. A very large proportion of them wound up in houses of prostitution from which there was no escape. Conference attendees agreed that it is imperative that the world focus on the tragedy of human trafficking.

The international news media have publicized the truth, especially the media in Pakistan and Bangladesh. The United Nations has appointed a special rapporteur who gave his first report to the U.N. Commission on Human Rights in January 1991. Two prominent groups, the International League for Human Rights and the Anti-Slavery Society, issued statements in Geneva in July 1990, at the meeting of the U.N. Working Group on Slavery.

According to the U.S. State Department, the problem is compounded when women try to migrate illegally from Bangladesh to Pakistan by way of India in search of employment and an escape from the extensive poverty in Bangladesh. People without documentation are accorded no rights and become objects of exploitation. Many of them may end up in detention. Human rights groups, government-sponsored commissions, the press in Pakistan, and other voluntary citizens' groups around the world have all expressed concern about this exploitation of illegal immigrants. Unfortunately, the human traffickers and smugglers are well organized, enjoy enormous profits, and sometimes even have the cooperation of their victims.

Barry Jay, Ph.D., having also heard the report about Fatma (Fatima) on National Public Radio, brought the child's problem to the attention of persons attending the June 1990 Vermont Conference on the Primary Prevention of Psychopathology. Dr. Jay met with Max Abbott, president-elect of the World Federation for Mental Health (WFMH), and also had extensive discussions with Arshad Husain, M.D., and others who were present as invited speakers at the conference. During the course of the conference everyone was struck by the frequency of reports of human trafficking in women and children. Several ad hoc meetings were held with Dr. Abbott and Dr. Arshad Husain. These meetings included Chok Hiew, Ph.D., and Mawaheb El-Mouelhy, M.D.

Everyone agreed that the case of little Fatima typified a widespread problem in the trafficking of women and children. Subsequently, Dr. Abbott, as president-elect of the WFMH, advised interested groups that the WFMH had established a

Committee on Commercial Sexual Exploitation of Children. Dr. Arshad and Dr. El-Mouelhy have agreed to cochair the committee, the mandates of which are as follows:

(1) to provide information concerning the commercial sexual exploitation of children, including an assessment of the magnitude of these practices in various countries

(2) to describe the social, cultural, and economic factors that have contributed to the evolution of this phenomenon

(3) to make recommendations to the governments involved about the sequence of legal, cultural, and economic measures that could be expected to ameliorate or prevent the commercial sexual exploitation of children within their borders

Dr. Abbott's proposal for the establishment of this committee stated, "This practice has such detrimental effects for the individuals, families, and societies within which it occurs that it warrants specific investigation. The findings of such investigation require wide dissemination including presentation to appropriate United Nations agencies."

The WFMH committee is scheduled to present an informational session at the World Federation for Mental Health Congress in Mexico City in August 1991, where it will report on the responses of the Pakistani government about the fate of Fatima, the women and children in the Karachi prison, and the amelioration of human trafficking within its borders. The committee will also present its preliminary findings on the verifiable evidence of commercial sexual exploitation of children in other regions of the world.

Meanwhile, there is no word as to the whereabouts or the fate of Fatima.

Individuals or organizations interested in collaborating in the efforts of the committee are encouraged to phone Attorney Debra Weecks at (203) 787-4191 or Barry Jay at (313) 349-8000, or to contact the World Federation for Mental Health Committee, c/o Max Abbott, Director, Mental Health Foundation of New Zealand, Auckland, New Zealand.

# PART II

# Sources of Stress:

## PARENTING, POVERTY, SEXISM, WAR

Around the world multiple sources of stress affect families and children. All too often they appear chronic in nature. While certain of the stressors are unique to given regions and populations, others are shared across many nations, calling us to consider and communicate carefully strategies for improving the lives of our people. In this section of the book authors examine significant sources of stress affecting families and children in Ghana, Pakistan, Egypt, Czechoslovakia, Thailand, and other nations, and the implications of these stressors for effective prevention efforts.

The first chapter in this section is by Araba Sefa-Dedeh, Ph.D., one of a very small number of clinical psychologists practicing and teaching in Ghana. With great interest in primary prevention, she gives a broad overview of some of the problems affecting children in a country on the west coast of Africa that was once a part of the powerful and extended Ashanti Empire. European colonial powers carved up the Ashanti lands and arbitrarily divided the empire into British, French, and other European pieces that were exploited for many years in the traditional colonial pattern. Dr. Sefa-Dedeh describes problems that affect infants and young children as a consequence of poverty, nutritional deficiencies, and common childhood diseases that are completely preventable, and other endemic conditions such as malaria and kwashiorkor. The problems of poverty, urbanization, and family stresses are also addressed. Clearly, her chapter identifies issues common in a great many emerging and developing nations around the world.

Syad Arshad Husain, M.D., is a distinguished child and adolescent psychiatrist and head of the Child and Adolescent Psychiatry Program at the University of Missouri Medical School. He also is a frequent visitor to Pakistan, where he maintains close ties with Pakistani psychiatry. As someone who is bilingual and bicultural, Dr. Arshad Husain is in a unique position to compare and understand Third World psychiatric problems and their origins. In his chapter he describes characteristics of Pakistani family life affected by problems such as poverty, massive migration, and absentee fathers who for many years have worked in the (Persian) Gulf states. He also describes a simple but effective prevention program being applied in schools in a large area of Pakistan.

Mawaheb El-Mouelhy, M.D., an Egyptian physician trained in obstetrics and gynecology, is an active worker and spokesperson for the empowerment of

61

women in the Arab world. She has worked in Saudi Arabia and the United Arab Emirates and has long been concerned with family planning and women's health. Her chapter documents the effects of women's health and status on the lives of children. She considers major sources of stress, especially those affecting women and children in less developed countries, where rapid population growth, malnutrition, and poverty are major influences. It becomes clear that a host of preventable problems are rampant as a function of these stressors coupled with cultural practices that discriminate against females.

Zdenek Dytrych, M.D., is head of the Department of Social Psychiatry at Prague's Psychiatric Research Institute. He provides compelling empirical data about the long-term consequences of being born of an unwanted pregnancy. By following a cohort of individuals whose mothers had twice sought and twice been refused abortion, he and his colleagues (including especially Henry David, Ph.D., in the United States) have been able to document the long-term negative consequences for children with this history. Integrating his own research and that of others, Dr. Dytrych provides us with compelling arguments to support the view that children's emotional growth and development are influenced by parental attitudes toward their conception and birth.

Milton Schwebel, Ph.D., has had a long and distinguished career in clinical psychology. Professor emeritus at Rutgers University, he is also senior research scholar at the Center for Psychological Studies in the Nuclear Age at Harvard Medical School. His explorations into the meaning of the threat of nuclear war for children and adolescents and his work on child cognitive development have resulted in a large number of books and articles. Clearly, we live in a world where children experience directly and indirectly the nearly chronic stresses associated with both the threat and the reality of war and mass destruction. Dr. Schwebel presents evidence for the compelling necessity of developing effective strategies for helping young people to cope with this major source of stress—strategies that are sensitive to the developmental needs and capabilities of our youth.

Finally, Professor Chok C. Hiew of the University of New Brunswick reports on his findings in Thailand of the consequences associated with rural-urban migration, the effects of poverty, and overpopulation. His central theme is that rapid economic developments in Asia have altered the family unit and have resulted in an increase of fragmented nuclear families and changes in traditional Asian family structure. He describes the endangered children of Thailand and gives some dramatic specific examples that provide powerful evidence of the consequences of massive social change. Again we encounter the problems in families with absentee fathers, with a major escalation of child labor, and with widespread child prostitution catering to a major sex-oriented tourist industry. This last development has resulted in a sharp increase in the incidence of AIDS. Dr. Hiew makes a number of suggestions for prevention programs in Thailand that have applicability to other countries as well.

# 5

# Improving Children's Lives: The Case for Primary Prevention in Ghana

## Araba Sefa-Dedeh

Ghana lies almost in the center of the countries along the Gulf of Guinea on the west coast of Africa. The country is about 420 miles from north to south and about 350 miles from east to west. It has an area of about 92,100 square miles. To the east of Ghana is Togo, to the west is the Ivory Coast, and to the north is Bukina Faso.

Ghana is not far from the equator, so the climate is tropical. Temperatures are high, with little variation from season to season. In the south they range between 70° and 90° and in the north between 60° and 110°.

Rainfall is seasonal, resulting in a dry season and a wet season. November through April is generally dry, with major rains from May until July and minor rains from September to October. The Harmattan, which is the name given to the northeasterly winds blowing from the Sahara to Ghana, brings with it cool nights and hot days and low relative humidity during the dry season. Its effects are more evident in the north than in the south.

Ghana became a colony of Britain in 1874 in the teeth of much resistance. It was not until 1901 that the extended Ashanti Empire was finally conquered by British forces. Ghana remained a colony until 1957, when it became the first country south of the Sahara to win independence from British rule. Many of Ghana's current social problems typify countries in the Third World that were once part of a colonial empire.

For historical reasons, Ghana's economy is largely dependent on a single main agricultural commodity, cocoa. The economy rises and falls with the demand for cocoa. Ghana also exports timber, gold, bauxite, and diamonds, and the market for these is also determined by external forces.

Since independence in 1957, Ghana has had six different governments. Three of these were elected governments, and three were military regimes that seized power. The present government came to power in a coup d'état on December 31, 1981. Between 1980 and 1984 Ghana went through severe drought conditions and general economic recession. The economy is now gradually recovering under a structural adjustment program.

Ghana's present population is about 14 million, divided among several ethnic and language groups that cross national boundaries. The population is growing at an annual estimated rate of 2.6%. Most of Ghana's people are rural dwellers. In the south about 68% and in the north 85% live in rural areas. Nearly half of Ghana's population is under age 15, resulting in a high age-dependency burden on the working population.

## Child Health Risks

Children under the age of 5 years form about 20% of Ghana's population, but they contribute 50% of all registered deaths. The death of children is a major source of stress in a culture where family is important.

### Children's Killer Diseases

Infant diarrhea is a major preventable cause of early death. The condition, which is easily treatable if resources are available, could be prevented with universal access to pure water. Recently, oral rehydration therapy has done a great deal to cut down on deaths due to infant diarrhea. Other diseases that contribute to the high percentage of early death could be prevented with adequate immunization. They include the following:

- *Tuberculosis:* About 0.5-1% of the general population is affected. By age 14, 1 out of 10 children will be exposed to the disease and may develop it.
- *Whooping cough:* This causes a lot of illness and death among children less than 1 year old, especially during the dry season.
- *Neonatal tetanus:* Nearly 1 in 10 children dies of this disease every year.
- *Poliomyelitis:* Polio affects mainly children younger than 5 years. Paralysis due to the disease is found in 7 out of every 1,000 in the population.
- *Measles:* About 75% of all children who are not immunized will be affected by age 2 and nearly 1 out of every 12 affected children will die (Adjei, 1986).
- *Malaria:* Endemic malaria causes many deaths in those less than 5 years old.

Recently, HIV infection has added to the toll of deaths in children. In Ghana as of February 1989, 452 females and 68 males were known to be HIV positive. Though exact statistics are not available, some of the women have had babies who are also HIV positive and have died. The few who have survived face rejection from the extended family out of fear of AIDS, and consequent malnutrition.

Moreover, mothers dying from AIDS and other preventable diseases leave orphaned children who are at greater risk for malnutrition.

### Malnutrition and Poverty

It is not only these killer childhood diseases that contribute to the registered deaths; malnutrition takes its toll as well. A trend away from breast-feeding in the cities has contributed to the problems of infant malnutrition and diarrheal diseases. There are no statistics available concerning the number of children who are sick or hospitalized every year with kwashiorkor—protein deficiency malnutrition—or marasmus, but the fact that the word *kwashiorkor* was coined from a Ghanaian language indicates the endemic nature of this problem in Ghana. Infant malnutrition in Ghana cannot be discussed in isolation because associated with it are poverty, unsanitary living conditions, exposure to infectious diseases, inadequate food supplies, and minimal education.

Not only do all these contribute to loss of life, but even more sobering is the fact that for every child who dies, there are others who survive as mere shadows of their actual physical, emotional, and intellectual potential. In Ghana, mental retardation is one of the major tragic consequences of the endemic health problems of children.

### Mental Handicap

It is impossible to estimate the number of children with mental handicaps in the country because many such children are not taken to government health institutions for evaluation. However, in 1986 a total of 998 children (494 males and 504 females) between the ages of 1 and 14 were seen at the Accra Psychiatric Hospital. In 1987 the total was 1,075 children (638 males and 437 females). The majority of these were diagnosed as epileptic, mentally retarded, or both.

The most common symptom in the etiology of these diagnoses was convulsions that resulted from viral and bacterial infections or sometimes from prenatal and congenital factors that led to poor brain development and brain injury. Nearly all the children who were retarded were classified as moderately, severely, or profoundly retarded. Most of these cases could have been prevented through immunizations and good maternal and child health care.

### Reduced Intellectual and Physical Functioning

In addition to those obviously retarded, there are many who are not classified as retarded but who have reduced mental and physical functioning. Several studies illustrate this. Some research findings, beginning with Gerber and Dean (1957), indicate that full-term African babies are often more precocious in their development for the first year of life when compared with European babies

(Goldberg, 1970; Kilbride, Robbins, & Kilbride, 1970). A few studies have not found these systematic differences (Falmagne, cited in Wober, 1985; Warren, 1972), but no study has found normal African babies to be developmentally slower. A disturbing finding that emerges from these studies is that precocious developmental quotients of African babies start falling at as early as 6 months of age; by 2 years, when most of the children have been weaned, their developmental quotients lag behind Western norms. This may demonstrate the effect of an environment that becomes increasingly more hostile and impoverished as the child grows, in terms of lack of nutritionally adequate food, exposure to infectious diseases, and lack of adequate stimulation for intellectual growth. A study by Lakhani, Jansen, and Gemert (1987) clearly illustrates this. These researchers compared middle-income Kenyan children with rural Kenyan children and U.S. reference norms, and found that the urban group gained weight in a way similar to that of the U.S. reference norms. Their height gains were higher than those of the reference norms. However, the rural group gained weight in a similar manner to the urban group only in the first six months. After that they lagged behind. Height gains were particularly retarded.

**Poor Education**

For children who survive physically but are caught in the poverty trap, education that is available in the rural areas may only serve to aggravate conditions. In Ghana, primary school education is free. However, despite this and the fact that the government spends 24% of its budget on education, many schools in the rural areas of Ghana are hardly functional. Inadequate buildings, furniture, equipment, books, and teaching methods often result in pupils who are still illiterate both in English and in their native language by the time they graduate. Moreover, having spent an inordinate amount of time in unproductive schools, these individuals have had little time to learn adequate survival skills in or out of school. This is part of the impoverishment process: Individuals' inability to compete or functionally survive relegates them to a lifetime of continuing poverty—that is, working hard all their lives for less than subsistence.

**Traditional Practices and Status of Women**

It is difficult to separate children's and women's problems in Ghana; the two clearly influence each other. As in other countries, children of poor, uneducated mothers are at more risk for malnutrition and childhood diseases. Adolescent pregnancies are also common in Ghana. In Korle Bu Hospital in Accra, 21.2% of total deliveries in 1983 were by teenagers; this figure rose to 21.8% in 1985 (Ampofo & Gyepi-Garbrah, 1986). The rates are likely to be higher in rural areas, especially in the north, where early marriages are common. Girls who are illiterate or who drop out of school are more likely to get pregnant. Those in school who get pregnant drop out of school. Associated with these pregnancies are higher risks for antenatal complications, maternal and infant mortality, and low birth weights (Adjei & Ampofo, 1986).

Traditional practices often result in problems for both women and children. In many households in rural Ghana, men eat first and get the best part of the food; children are fed next, and are often given few protein foods; women eat last and end up undernourished, with little strength for childbearing and their many labors—a vicious cycle. In some areas in Ghana food taboos exacerbate malnutrition. For example, it is said that children should not be given meat or they will become thieves; eggs will make an infant have smelly stools and become ill. In the cities, malnutrition may result from a replacement of traditionally nutritious foods and snacks made from legumes—such as koose, nuts, and whole grains—with foods made from commodities imported from developed countries, such as white bread, tea, carbonated drinks (Coca-Cola, Sprite, and so on), and cakes and cookies made with little but white flour, sugar, and oil.

In the rural areas of the Upper Region of Ghana, female circumcision is still practiced, contributing to an increase in neonatal and maternal deaths. Polygamy is still practiced in Ghana and has implications for increased fertility and malnutrition, since polygamous men sometimes have trouble supporting their many children. Many women in such relationships often have sole responsibility for the financial upkeep of their children.

A pressing need of urban women is day-care services for their children. In the absence of adequate day care many women leave their children with "house help," who are often young girls in need of mothering themselves. This sometimes results in poor care and even abuse of children left in their care. The practice of sending young girls from the rural areas to the cities to be employed as house help in itself contributes to child abuse in some cases and to teenage pregnancies in others. Such children and adolescents are at increased risk for emotional and physical problems. Such practices are perpetuated by rural poverty that results in families sending their young children to be employed in the cities to boost family income and to decrease the number of children they have to feed. Davison and Neale (1974) summarize the poverty problem most succinctly:

> The child reared in poverty is affected by innumerable intellectually (and emotionally) stunting factors both organic and environmental—ranging from the poor nutrition and lack of prenatal care of his mother to his own malnutrition, his emotionally and intellectually depriving home and neighborhood and the failure of his school system. (p. 451)

No country, especially one that is dependent on trained human resources to supervise its many development projects, can afford such a waste of human potential. What should be done about this? The only viable answer is prevention.

In a country with scarce mental health resources (12 psychiatrists and 2 clinical psychologists in the entire country, with 8 of these in Accra) there is little that can be done for those who have already fallen victim.

## Prevention

Prevention strategies that could deal (positively) with the problems enumerated above include immunization, family planning, health education, improved nutrition, parenting skills training, raising women's status in society, family support (especially economic), and improved educational programs for rural children.

The idea of prevention is not new to Ghana. The thrust of health policy in Ghana now is primary health care that stresses prevention and community intervention for physical health. The problem is acquiring resources for implementation.

### Immunization

Since 1976, national immunization programs have been organized with varying success. The last five years have been more successful than previous years. Statistics from 1987 indicate that immunization coverage has increased substantially, with average coverage levels of 30-40% for total vaccination, compared with 5% in 1984. In some regions as many as 70% of all children have been immunized, resulting in a drop in hospitalizations for childhood diseases. For example, when immunization for measles was about 60-70% coverage there was a 75% drop in cases sent to clinics in the country (Adjei, 1986). There is definitely a need to continue the immunization programs and increase their efficiency.

### Family Planning

Ghana has had a comprehensive policy on population since 1969. It was the second African country (after Kenya) to adopt such a policy. The policy recognizes the negative effects of unregulated population growth on national development and on individual and family welfare. A year later, in 1970, the Ghana National Family Planning Programme Secretariat was established. However, despite all efforts, the practice of family planning in rural areas remains low. In 1986, the Ghana National Conference on Population and National Reconstruction was held at the University of Ghana to provide a forum for a critical look at Ghana's population policy, especially its family planning program, and to make recommendations to the government on a plan of action. Recommendations spanned the broad areas of maternal and child health and family planning as well as education, agriculture and nutrition, women and development, migration and urbanization, and economic development. Some relevant specific recommendations included social marketing of contraceptives; integration of sex and family life education into teacher training and school curricula; more intensive efforts, using mass communication methods and community involvement, to reach rural communities with family planning programs; intensifying efforts to ensure the rights of women in education, employment, and decision making; increasing efforts to make education more relevant to human resources needs; and implementing integrated rural development so that the rural sector can take advantage of those factors that otherwise draw people to the urban centers (Population Prevention, 1987).

The importance of family planning for child health can be illustrated by startling statistics from Ghana's 1980 Fertility Study. The infant mortality rate for children born less than two years after a preceding birth was about 115 per 1,000 births. This dropped to about 58 per 1,000 for children born after an interval of two years after a preceding birth and dropped to 40 per 1,000 for those born three years after a preceding birth. Infant mortality would thus decline about 17% if all children are born at least two years after preceding births (Population Prevention, 1987). These recommendations are still pertinent and have implications for the mental health of the population also. In addition to immunization and family planning, other prevention efforts have also centered on physical health.

### Nutrition and Health Education

The Primary Health Care Program of Ghana ensures that health and nutrition information is disseminated particularly to mothers, through well-baby clinics as well as in communities, especially rural communities. Health education in urban areas is usually given by public and community health nurses. Since 1975, a few community psychiatric nurses have been trained each year to follow up psychiatric patients who are discharged into communities. They are not part of the primary health care team, but they give mental health information to outpatients who come to the hospitals from which they work. In rural areas, health education is usually given by traditional birth attendants. These are generally older women who act as midwives for their communities. The Primary Health Care Program has made training in general hygiene, obstetrics, and gynecology available for such women. After training, they graduate in a public ceremony and are given certificates that enhance their status not only as traditional caregivers but as modern caregivers in their communities. They thus become effective agents for change.

Village health workers who are members of the community they work in are also trained for three months to give basic health care and health education. So far, only physical health issues have been dealt with. There is a need for mental health information and programs to be integrated into primary health care. The structures for primary health care are already in place. It should not be difficult to train village health workers and birth attendants to understand and add information on mental health to what they already disseminate or to bring up mental health issues in village meetings and discussions. Issues of importance are the link between physical and mental health, the effect of various socialization styles and lack of nurturing on emotional health, the possibility of community and school nurturing of children's self-esteem and intellectual and social skills, the impact of traditional practices on physical and emotional health, and the early learning of coping skills to deal with the many problems children face.

### Women's Issues

In Ghana many organizations are working to raise the consciousness of women, to help them know what they can do to improve life socially and economically for themselves and their children. They are working to help eradicate traditional practices that are inimical to women and children as well as to enact and enforce laws that support children and women. Ghana has ratified the U.N. Convention on the Rights of the Child. The Ghana National Commission on Children has the job of ensuring children's rights in the country, and has been instrumental in the building of parks and libraries for children in both rural and urban communities. In the last year it has been very vocal about child labor issues. The National Council on Women and Development, created in 1975, coordinates women's work in Ghana and organizes seminars and workshops for leaders of rural and urban women as well as staff of organizations that work with women. The 31st of December Women's Movement was started by the wife of the head of state and has been instrumental in the building of day-care centers in many markets in both rural and urban Ghana and has also organized cottage industries in many rural communities. Women lawyers have formed an association that gives free legal services to poor women, especially when their cases involve child support or inheritance disputes. This association has been especially instrumental in passage of the Intestate Succession Law, which ensures that wives and children of men who die intestate in matrilineal communities have inheritance rights. Women lecturers at the University of Ghana have formed the Women's Research Group, which encourages research on women's issues. Women's clubs such as Zonta, Inner Wheel, and the Ghanaian Association for Women's Welfare and many religious organizations sponsor programs for women and children. Rural women especially in northern Ghana are banding together to form cooperatives to help them obtain bank credit to expand their farms or cottage industries or to market their produce more profitably. Traders and market women have always had associations that give them economic and social benefits. Generally, the last decade has been an exciting one for Ghanaian women, as women and children's issues have received much publicity and work.

However, there is much prevention work yet to be done in changing attitudes that diminish the emotional and physical health of women and children, especially in rural Ghana. What is needed is a united focus for the many organizations that seek to help women and children, a focus that needs to include not only physical health but mental health also and a unity that would increase the impact and effectiveness of change programs in communities.

### Family Support

One obvious major strength of most Ghanaian communities is the social and family support that exists. Extended families provide needed support for all members, thus children who are orphaned or who need care are adopted or helped through informal extended family or community arrangements. There is a tremendous need for a deliberate nurturing of this strength, because the exigencies of urban living are gradually eroding families' willingness to provide support. Without this informal support system, no government program could cope with all the problems faced by Ghana's citizens. There should be government support for these family and community systems, so they can continue to be effective in the face of endemic economic hardship.

### School Systems

Schools should function not only to develop academic competence but to prepare individuals to function productively in their communities. The effectiveness of school as a primary prevention agent is attested to by many reports in the literature (Bond & Compas, 1988; Goodlad, 1983). In rural Ghana, schools fall short of both of these functions. The tendency is to produce graduates who are unprepared for effective living in either rural or urban Ghana. The resulting frustration and bitterness bode ill for individuals, their families, and the nation. There is a need to rethink educational policy, curricula, and methods of teaching if this problem is to be addressed.

### Poverty

Of even more importance than any of the issues addressed above is the need to ameliorate the extreme poverty that is the lot of most rural and some urban Ghanaians. The 1989 statistics indicate that the Ghanaian government spends 24% of its total budget on education and 8% on health, which translates to about $7.50 per person for education and $2.60 per person for health. Thus it is obvious that economics is an important aspect of any prevention program in Ghana. Communities need help in identifying and exploiting possible sources of wealth. Clearly, if we really want to improve children's lives throughout the world, we must face the glaring inequalities that exist and work toward assuring an equitable world for all.

### Summary

Ghanaian children, like children in other Third World countries, die or are diminished because of problems that are preventable. Poverty, ignorance, and the low status of women, with its resultant inadequate health care and malnutrition, often lead to both physical and emotional debilitation for which few services exist. Prevention is the only viable alternative in such a situation. Through better maternal and child health care, health education that encompasses emotional and physical health, improved school systems, and improvement of the economic and social status of women, much of the waste in human lives can be prevented.

Prevention as a health strategy is accepted by the government of Ghana, and already much prevention work is being done, especially through the Primary Health Care Program. The problem is that resources are lacking to expand such prevention programs and to include areas other than physical health. However, for a Third World country, burdened with debt and with an economy at the mercy of market forces it cannot control, finding enough resources for more prevention efforts may be a dream unless together we work for a more just and equitable world.

## References

Adjei, S. (1986). *Report on immunization in Ghana*. Accra: Ghana Ministry of Health, Epidemiology Division.

Adjei, S., & Ampofo, D. A. (1986, April). *Adolescent fertility: Social and medical problems in Ghana*. Paper presented at the National Conference on Population and National Reconstruction, University of Ghana.

Ampofo, D. A., & Gyepi-Garbrah, B. (1986, April). *Dimensions of adolescent pregnancy in Korle-Bu Teaching Hospital, 1983-1985*. Paper presented at the National Conference on Population and National Reconstruction, University of Ghana.

Bond, L. A., & Compas, B. E. (Eds.). (1988). *Primary prevention and promotion in the schools*. Newbury Park, CA: Sage.

Davison, G. C., & Neale, J. M. (1974). *Abnormal psychology: An experimental clinical approach*. New York: John Wiley.

Gerber, M., & Dean, R. F. A. (1957). Gesell tests on African children. *Pediatrics, 20*, 1055-1065.

Goldberg, S. (1970). *Infant care, stimulation and sensori-motor development in a high density urban area of Zambia* (Human Development Research Unit Report No. 15). Lusaka: University of Zambia.

Goodlad, J. (1983). *A place called school: Prospects for the future*. New York: McGraw-Hill.

Kilbride, J. E., Robbins, M. C., & Kilbride, P. L. (1970). The comparative motor development of Baganda, American white and American black infants. *American Anthropologist, 72*, 1422-1428.

Lakhani, S., Jansen, A. A. J., & Gemert, W. (1987). Growth of middle-income urban African infants. *East African Medical Journal, 64*, 388-395.

Population Prevention. (1987). *Population impact project*. Accra: University of Ghana.

Warren, N. (1972). African infant precocity. *Psychological Bulletin, 78*, 353-367.

Wober, M. (1985). *Psychology in Africa*. London: International African Institute.

# 6

# Prevention of Mental Illness in Children in Third World Countries: A Pakistani Perspective

## Syed Arshad Husain

George Albee, a leader in the field of the prevention of psychopathology for many decades, has developed a formula relating the incidence of psychopathology to difficult life circumstances on one hand and to available strengths and resources on the other (Albee & Joffe, 1977). He considers organic factors, stress, and exploitation as deficits, and balances these with resources such as coping skills, self-esteem, and social supports. He asserts that a change in one or more of the components in the equation may result in changes in the emotional stability or disability of an individual.

Utilizing this approach, four major areas of resources are recognized for good mental health: biological integrity, psychosocial competence, social support, and societal policies and attitudes. These are discussed in turn in the sections that follow.

### Biological Integrity

Some mental-emotional illnesses can be prevented through the achievement of optimum physical fitness. Until recently, physical and mental health were viewed as separate concepts by most people, but now the influence of physical fitness on emotional health is being recognized more and more. The role of adequate nutrition on brain development and the effect of exercise on emotional well-being are examples of such influence.

By taking specific steps to prevent injury to the brain and the nervous system, it is possible to prevent mental and emotional disability. For example, low birth weight, a factor strongly associated with neurological problems, can be prevented through adequate maternal nutrition and sound perinatal care. There is a well-documented link between early nutrition and development of the brain.

73

This applies to the nutrition of both the pregnant mother and the child, especially before the age of 3.

Accidents, physical abuse, and exposure to drugs or to environmental hazards such as lead, other heavy metals, and environmental pollutants may cause brain damage (Husain & Fahim, 1975; Husain & Kashani, 1978) and preventive measures against these factors can also prevent brain damage.

### Psychosocial Competence

The second ingredient proposed by Albee is psychosocial competence, which involves the ability of an individual to relate to others, to use various coping skills, and to get along in the world. Mental and emotional disability can be prevented by ensuring that individuals have skills for relating to others and capabilities to handle crises.

The capacity to initiate and maintain meaningful and mutually satisfying relationships is central to good mental health. This skill is achieved mostly through early experiences with parents and other caregivers.

Self-esteem is another important component of psychosocial competence. Self-esteem is enhanced by factors that promote an individual's sense of personal control and self-determination. Success experiences in early life inculcate feelings of self-confidence and self-worth in adults.

Child-rearing practices may foster or hinder the development of psychosocial competence. In a study of child-rearing practices of six cultures, American children were found to be repressed in aggressive acts toward peers only 8% of the time; Mexican children were repressed 91% of the time; Okinawan children, Indian children, and Kenyan children each about two-thirds of the time; and Filipino children, 57% of the time (Minturn & Lambert, 1964). It was concluded that the American children, although allowed to express aggression and to be assertive, also learned to accept differences of opinion, whereas Mexican, Okinawan, Indian, and Kenyan children learned to be subservient to authorities—namely, their parents and other elders—but did not learn to accept differences of opinion, particularly from younger persons or from persons inferior in rank.

### Social Support

The third ingredient in good mental health is social support, or the availability of others to provide nurturance and security. Infants and children need a stable and nurturing relationship with those who care for them. If such a relationship does not develop or is disrupted, the child has an increased risk for deficit in physical, cognitive, social, and emotional development. Research on primates has shown that offspring deprived of their mothers' care (either by absenting the mothers or by impairing the quality of the mothering) grew up to be inadequate as adults (Harlow, 1970). Females could not parent their own offspring and even at times mutilated or killed them. They also could not mate properly and became disruptive as members of their community.

Similar observations have been made concerning human infants who were brought up in orphanages. In a study conducted by Spitz (1946), the orphan infants observed failed to gain weight, looked depressed and listless, and were more prone to infectious diseases than other children. The mortality rate among these infants was two or three times higher than that found for infants brought up with their mothers. Also, the quality of mothering can be compromised by bereavement, multiple pregnancies, or physical and sexual abuse of the mother. Multiple siblings, poor supervision, and physical abuse are often found in the histories of juvenile delinquents (Robins, 1978).

It is now well accepted that people who belong to a network of social support fare much better in coping with stress and crises than those who are isolated and alienated. This observation has led to the development of a variety of social support groups in many communities that target high-risk populations such as the bereaved, the chronically ill, and the unemployed.

## Social Policies and Attitudes

By defining and working toward a society that encourages mentally healthy behavior, we may be able to prevent some mental-emotional disabilities. Organizations such as hospitals, schools, workplaces, health care systems, and legal and government systems play crucial roles in all our lives. The practices and policies of these institutions can determine how effective they will be in promoting mental health or emotional disability. Societies that choose to limit the options of people through insensitive policies may adversely affect families' education and employment as well as the rights of welfare recipients and various other groups.

People who live in poverty, and this includes a majority of Third World children, have more mental and emotional illnesses than people with greater resources. Social policies need to address widespread poverty.

## The Third World

With the above background in mind, let us review the situation in the Third World. There are about 1.3 billion children under the age of 15 years in the world, and approximately 83% of them live in the developing countries. Children constitute about 40% of the Third World population (World Health Organization, 1977); by contrast, children constitute only 25% of the population of the developed countries.

There is a sixfold difference in infant mortality rates between the developed and the developing countries. In all countries, socioeconomic level is the most important variable affecting infant mortality. The main killers of these children are infectious diseases and malnutrition, and these are also the principal direct and indirect causes of morbidity. According to some estimates, 25% of children living in developing countries receive nutrition that is below an acceptable lower limit; in the developed countries, this figure is 3%.

Urbanization, a phenomenon that is proceeding rapidly in the Third World, is another cause of severe stress on children and their families. As economic problems increase, many fathers of rural families move toward the urban centers in pursuit of employment and better income. These internal migrants often live under very unsatisfactory conditions in shantytowns on the edges of urban centers, with no access to health and welfare services.

Urbanization is also taking its toll on family life. There have been many reports indicating family breakdown in urban areas in the developing countries. This breakdown is following the pattern of the increased divorce rate that is usually reported in the developed countries. Thus the result is an increasing number of children who are growing up in broken homes. Again, mostly due to the economic constraints, more and more women are entering the labor force in the developing countries, resulting in a large number of children being forced to receive alternative and low-quality care in privately run or informal day-care centers.

In summary, because of the changing world, a number of new factors have emerged that are negatively influencing the lives of children in the world at large, but especially of the children of developing countries. In the discussion that follows, I will focus mainly on the children of Pakistan. I will make an effort to identify some of these factors as they relate to Pakistan and how they are influencing the lives and mental health of the children in that country. I will also discuss some of the prevention efforts that have been made to attenuate the effects of the factors.

Pakistan is a country of 100 million people, approximately 40% of whom are less than 15 years old. However, the stage of "childhood" as it is perceived and defined in the developed countries is very short in Pakistan; for most of the population it does not last past the age of 6 or 7. A majority of children in Pakistan are in jeopardy from the time of conception. Their mothers are generally multiparous and malnourished, and have no access to health care facilities. Consequently, the rate of premature births is very high and perinatal complications are extremely common. The infants who survive these ordeals are faced with poor nutrition, environmental pollutants, accidents, and numerous psychosocial stresses. The Western concept of childhood, according to which children are meant to be nurtured, educated, and allowed to grow in a safe and protected environment, does not exist.

In a typical urban center the people living in huts along the roadsides inhale from dawn to dusk the lead-filled fumes emitted by automobiles and motor scooters; such hazards cause further insult and injury to the developing nervous systems of infants and young children.

In Pakistan, children are forced to work because of family poverty. Most come from large families with limited resources and thus are required to work to supplement their families' incomes. It is not unusual to see children under 9 years of age working at demanding and sometimes dangerous jobs, such as lathe operating, automobile repair and service station work, welding, housekeeping in roadside hotels, tailoring, or tin packaging.

According to a 1985 survey, a Pakistani child under 9 years of age works on the average of nine hours per day. The majority of these children are exploited; the remuneration they get for their work is grossly inadequate. For example, in the well-known carpet industry of Pakistan, children under 9 are frequently employed. This job involves sitting in one position before a loom for about eight hours a day. The children doing this work receive 110 rupees a month, which is equivalent to U.S. $6.00. They frequently develop rickets and deformed bones. Industrial injuries are also quite common. Although the Constitution of Pakistan prohibits child labor below 14 years in factories, mines, and other hazardous employment, children are still forced to work in these jobs, according to the Defense of Children International of Pakistan. Sometimes they are kidnapped and bonded to labor camps and forcibly employed by contractors during the day and are chained at night to prevent them from escaping.

Another source of stress among children is the family disintegration that is brought about by the economic demands that force the heads of families to leave their homes for big cities or for other countries, in search of better-paying jobs. According to surveys, more than 2.5 million adult workers have migrated in the last two decades from Pakistan to oil-rich Middle Eastern countries. The peculiar immigration policies of those countries do not allow these migrants to bring their families to live with them, thus creating a situation whereby more than 7.5 million dependents of these adults are left behind in Pakistan. This dependent group mainly comprises wives, children, and elderly people who are already vulnerable and predisposed to a variety of stresses and turmoil. Clinical studies done in Pakistan have described a syndrome among females called the "Dubai syndrome" (after the Persian Gulf state, Dubai). Women whose husbands have gone overseas to work often suffer from chronic depressive illness, and their children manifest a variety of behavior disorders and are likely also to be depressed.

Children in Pakistan are also jeopardized by child-rearing practices that have been in place for centuries and that discourage the overt expression of feelings and emotions. In a study using diagnostic interview schedules for children and parents, it was found that the parents reported that 12% of their children had worries, phobias, and other anxiety disorders, but two-thirds of the children admitted having a variety of fears, phobias, and anxiety disorders (Husain & Haroon, 1988). These disparate findings suggest that a lack of communication exists between children and their parents in Pakistan. Children, according to Pakistani child-rearing practices, should be seen and not heard. They are generally hushed when they make an effort to communicate with their parents and express their feelings and emotions. At a recent workshop in which parents were invited to discuss their child-rearing practices, the fathers were asked why they do not interact with their children in any type of play activities. The men argued that such practices would undermine their control over their children.

In summary, a number of stressors are encountered by the children of Pakistan that affect their emotional and psychosocial development. Although very few epidemiological studies have been conducted of mental illness in the children of Pakistan, it is agreed that 5-15% of Pakistani children have mental health problems requiring psychiatric intervention. Mental retardation and epilepsy are considered to be more prevalent in the developing countries, including Pakistan, than in the developed countries. In Pakistan, there are regions where mental retardation is common, caused by the simple absence of iodine in the soil and water. High rates of epilepsy in children are found to be due to poor perinatal care and malnutrition before and after birth.

It may be worthwhile to mention here a few facts about the health care resources available in Pakistan. There is a serious shortage of both trained personnel and treatment facilities in the health care field. For example, there is 1 doctor per 2,100 persons. There is a single psychiatrist per million individuals, 1 paramedic for 13,000, and 1 nurse per 4 hospital beds (reflecting the small number of beds). There is 1 hospital bed per 10,692 citizens and 1 primary health care center per 15,000 population. There are 349 rural health care centers, 3,441 dispensaries, and 632 subcenters (see Ahmed, 1988).

The professionals and mental health facilities serving children are even sparser. There are only three practicing child psychiatrists in all Pakistan—two in Karachi and one in Lahore. There are only two child guidance clinics, one in Lahore and the other in Karachi, and only one residential facility for emotionally disturbed children, located in Lahore. There are many small private facilities for mentally retarded children, mainly established by the rich and influential parents of these children.

Child and adolescent psychiatry in Pakistan is still in its infancy and is mostly limited to diagnosis and management of mental retardation. Until 1985, only one child and family psychiatry department existed in the country (in Lahore). The complement of multidisciplinary staff in this clinic comprised a self-trained child psychiatrist, a psychologist, a social worker, and a speech therapist. In the 12 years of its existence this department has provided psychiatric services to 5,760 children covering the whole spectrum of psychiatric diagnoses. The clinic is also involved in some epidemiological research activities.

There is no national policy for children's mental health in Pakistan. The federal government has developed a comprehensive national policy on disability with the inclusion of children, and under this policy funds are appropriated to develop programs and facilities for early detection of mental illness, training, and rehabilitation.

There is no compulsory schooling requirement in Pakistan, and only 20% of children go to school. Most of these are from more advantaged families. There is no policy or provision for school health or mental health programs. Discussions held with teachers and parents have revealed that children who go to school are under severe pressure from their middle-class and upper-middle-class parents to achieve academic excellence. School curricula usually have no provision for organized sports or for any other recreational and physical activities.

However, Pakistan is a signatory to the Alma Ata Declaration (Health for All by the Year 2000), and is the first country in the eastern Mediterranean region to develop its own national mental health program. This program outlines the background of the mental health situation in Pakistan, identifies objectives and strategies, and specifies necessary actions. This plan seeks to integrate mental health services with the general health care plan as recommended by the World Health Organization. One of the major objectives of Pakistan's national mental health program is to develop an alternate mental health delivery system utilizing the existing health infrastructure without exerting an additional load on resources. This has been achieved in some areas; in the following section I describe one project that is in operation in the northwestern region of Pakistan.

## A Community-Based
## Rural Mental Health Care Program

This four-phase project was started in 1985 in an area northeast of Islamabad (the capital of Pakistan) that includes 380 villages with total population of 417,000, including a rural population of 378,000 (density of population is 742 per square mile) (Mubbahar, Malik, Zar, & Wig, 1986). The first phase involved collection of background information on the social and demographic characteristics of the project area, the existing health facilities, and the current health problems. In addition, interviews with health personnel were arranged in order to assess their current mental health knowledge, the extent of mental health care provided, and their willingness to take on mental health work. The community's general perception of mental disorders was also elicited. During this phase a weekly psychiatric clinic was set up in the area.

The second phase of the project involved the training of primary health care personnel in a task-oriented manner. This training was carried out at the district hospital and at the Department of Psychiatry at Rawalpindi Medical College. The third phase involved monitoring of the mental health care personnel. Data were maintained regarding case identification, treatment provided, referral, and outcome. The fourth phase dealt primarily with an analysis of the results and an in-depth study of the attitudes of the health staff and of the community toward mental health.

The project was planned in close collaboration with the deputy director of health services, the staff at the rural health center, and the basic health units. Cooperation was also obtained from the Union Council, the District Council, and local community leaders. The project coordinator visited the area extensively for a number of weeks and addressed many meetings of community members.

A team from the Department of Psychiatry, Rawalpindi Medical College, visited the rural health center, the basic health center, the Union Council, and the District Council in order to create a climate of better understanding and cooperation. A training program was developed for health staff, primary health care physicians, and multipurpose health workers. The objectives of the training program included (a) to provide basic knowledge about the importance of human behavior in health and disease; (b) to make health personnel familiar with the wide prevalence of mental, neurological, and psychosocial disorders in primary health care; and (c) to enable recognition in management of the priority disorders of severe depression, neurosis, psychosis, epilepsy, mental retardation, and drug dependency.

A massive community orientation program was also launched, aimed at reaching as many of the general public as possible. To this end, teams from the Department of Psychiatry addressed congregations of people during their religious gatherings. The community was also reached through the school system, the local health facility, and the village headman. Health committees were also formed in each basic health unit; these committees included religious leaders, teachers, counselors, and other influential people in the community.

One component of the project needs special mention for its novelty and effectiveness in the promotion of mental health through school systems. After imparting basic mental health education to teachers in a weekly series of lectures, project personnel persuaded the school authorities to permit teachers to spend five minutes daily with their classes teaching principles of mental health, concentrating on only three messages:

(1) Smoking is injurious to health (and is also the starting point for future drug abuse).

(2) Mental illnesses are, like physical illnesses, due to natural causes and are treatable. Mental illnesses are not due to curses of God or evil spirits.

(3) If you see a child with a physical or mental handicap, you should not laugh at him or her; rather, you should try to help.

Schoolchildren recite these principles daily. The program has become very popular and is being introduced increasingly in other schools. The principal of one school has had these slogans written on classroom walls and printed on the backs of all school report cards for the parents to see. Recent reports indicate that the program has already had very positive results. Children have identified mentally ill relatives and have brought them to rural clinics for treatment, thus reducing family stress and increasing the efficiency of primary health care units. Smoking among teachers has been reduced, and handicapped children seem to be better accepted by their classmates and better looked after by their teachers.

As part of the project, essential drugs have been provided at different levels of the health care delivery system. The multipurpose health workers have been provided with phenobarbital, Thorazine, and imipramine, and the medical officers at basic health units with phenobarbital, Thorazine, imipramine, and injection fluphenazine. The medical officers at the rural health centers have diazepam in addition to the other listed drugs.

The trained mental health care personnel are expected to identify the mentally ill during visits to the villages and to work in close collaboration with the health care delivery system. Special referral cards were introduced to enable quick referral from the periphery to the center and back. A community mental health center was established in the Department of Psychiatry at Rawalpindi Medical College to coordinate these activities.

After one year it was seen that several significant changes had occurred as a result of this project. The evaluation indicated that there was widespread community acceptance of delivery of mental health services at the primary health care level. In the past, mentally ill patients from rural areas had to be taken to the big city, a long journey that was prohibitively expensive. As a result of the new service, many mental patients who had been distressed for a number of years received adequate psychiatric treatment for the first time, reducing their families' stress significantly.

Another significant change noticed by health staff was that as a result of the introduction of mental health training they started spending more time talking with patients and their families. This led to an increase in the total attendance at the rural clinic and consequently to better overall utilization of services. The cooperation of the health staff at the primary health center was generally very good, and staff members seemed to like their new role as providers of mental health services. However, for the success of the project adequate supervision, quick referral facilities, and the continuous supply of essential drugs were considered essential.

In summary, Third World children are facing severe biological, psychosocial, and emotional stresses. The treatment and prevention resources of their countries are seriously limited. Western strategies of intervention are neither possible nor practical. Innovative methods are being developed, however, and are showing some results. The path to mental health in these countries is tortuous, and they have a long way to go. Will they reach their destination? Only time will tell.

## References

Ahmed, S. H. (1988). Economics of health. In S. A. Ahmed (Ed.), *Health policy and planning perspective* (pp. 6-14). Karachi: Pakistan Medical Association.

Albee, G. W., & Joffe, J. M. (Eds.). (1977). *The primary prevention of psychopathology. The issues.* Hanover, NH: University Press of New England.

Harlow, H. F. (1970). The nature of love. *American Psychologist, 25,* 161-168.

Husain, S. A., & Fahim, M. (1975). Chemical environment and child behavior. *Journal of the Pakistan Medical Association, 25,* 248-252.

Husain, S. A., & Haroon, A. (1988). Prevalence of anxiety symptoms and worrisomeness in a sample of high school boys in Karachi, Pakistan. In *Proceedings of the 7th International Conference.* Karachi, Pakistan.

Husain, S. A., & Kashani, J. (1978). Maternal medication and MBD: A possible relationship. *Missouri Medicine, 76,* 508-511.

Minturn, L., & Lambert, W. (1964). *Mothers of six cultures: Antecedents of child rearing.* New York: John Wiley.

Mubbahar, M. H., Malik, S. J., Zar, J. R., & Wig, N. N. (1986). Community based rural mental health care programs: Report of an experiment in Pakistan. *Eastern Mediterranean Region Health Services Journal, 1,* 14-20.

Robins, L. (1978). Sturdy childhood predictors of adult antisocial behavior: Replication from longitudinal studies. *Psychological Medicine, 8,* 611-622.

Spitz, R. A. (1946). Anaclitic depression: An inquiry into the genesis of psychiatric conditions in early childhood. *Psychoanalytic Study of the Child, 2,* 313-342.

World Health Organization. (1977). *Expert committee report on child mental health and psychosocial development* (Technical Report Series, No. 613). Geneva: Author.

# 7

# The Impact of Women's Health and Status on Children's Health and Lives in the Developing World

## Mawaheb El-Mouelhy

Healthy children are the greatest investment a nation can make; children's health is tomorrow's wealth. Protecting the health of infants and young children will protect the health of the next generation. Moreover, children's health and women's health are intimately linked. In their capacities as mothers, teachers, and governesses, women play unique and important roles in contributing to the emotional and physical makeup of children; improving the health of young girls who will have these roles in the future will have a great impact on the health of future families.

Ill health of women itself reflects on the well-being of children. Women cannot effectively produce and rear healthy babies if they themselves are ill, malnourished, overworked, insecure within their families, and treated by the society as a disadvantaged group. Figure 7.1 summarizes the relationship between the health of children and the health and status of women and the factors that contribute to the latter.

Third World women are largely responsible for food production and for most of the basic work in the household; it is through them that children are born and reared. But Third World women suffer the consequences of the deteriorating economy in their countries; they suffer from lack of support and reproductive ill health from increasing birthrates, child marriage, wife abuse, illegal abortions, and venereal diseases; they suffer from their inability to make decisions concerning their health and to take proper care of their children because of poverty and powerlessness.

## The Child

There are tremendous variations in infant and early childhood mortality from country to country (see Table 7.1), and factors affecting the basic physical

AUTHOR'S NOTE: I would like to thank the VCPPP, Dr. L. Bond, and her team for their great help and assistance in producing this chapter.

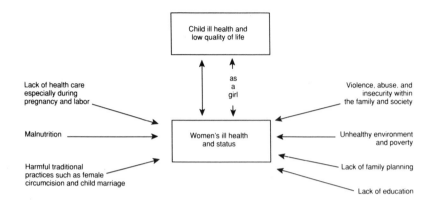

**Figure 7.1.** The Relationship Between Health of Children and the Health and Status of Women

survival of children are poorly controlled in many nations. Health, as defined by the World Health Organization (WHO) constitution, is a state of complete physical, mental, and social well-being, and not merely the absence of disease or infirmity ("Mothers' Lives Matter," 1988; WHO, 1980). Achievement of this state of health for the infant or the child requires certain conditions: good nutrition and health care (both physical and mental), healthy environmental conditions, education, healthy mothers, small families, and a secure and peaceful family atmosphere.

Children in the developing world suffer from low standards of care at levels of both family and society, which may result in serious social, physical, psychological, economic, demographic, and political consequences. The neglected child is a serious problem at the individual level as well as the national level.

In a large, poor family, surrounded by unhealthy environmental conditions, with family problems such as divorce or polygamy and with an ill, illiterate, and overworked mother, children are not going to have the proper attention and care necessary to their development. The natural escape for such children is usually the street, where they gather with friends who live in similar circumstances to play with mud and stones instead of toys that can help to develop their mental capabilities. The street also exposes children to poor environmental conditions that can contribute to further health hazards. Street children can be picked up easily, and recruited and trained to participate in illegal activities such as distributing drugs or stealing, a disaster for both family and society. The alternative for these children is to work to feed themselves and possibly their families, too. At an early age, these children become responsible for others, when others should be responsible for them. The result is total deprivation from natural childhood.

**Table 7.1**  Aspects of Women's and Children's Health in Selected Countries, 1980-1985

| Country | Infant Mortality Rate[a,b] | Under 5 Mortality Rate[a,c] | Percentage of Literate Adults (Male/Female)[d] | Percentage of Age Group Enrolled in Primary School (Male/Female)[d] |
|---|---|---|---|---|
| Bolivia | 124 | 197 | 76/51 | 94/81 |
| Bangladesh | 128 | 204 | 40/18 | 74/46 |
| India | 110 | 167 | 55/26 | 100/68 |
| Yemen | 135 | 223 | 18/2 | 99/17 |
| Poland | 20 | 22 | 99/98 | 100/100 |
| Finland | 6 | 8 | — | 100/100 |
| Egypt | 100 | 148 | 54/22 | 100/76 |
| Senegal | 142 | 240 | 31/14 | 61/41 |
| Morocco | 97 | 142 | 41/18 | 100/62 |
| Guatemala | 70 | 118 | 54/39 | 78/67 |

SOURCE: Belsey and Royston (1987).
a. Per 1,000 live births.
b. Figures are from the United Nations.
c. Figures are from UNICEF.
d. Figures are from UNESCO.

*Children's work.* Millions of children under age 15 are believed to be working in the developing world to support themselves and their families, despite the laws forbidding young child labor in many of these countries. In Egypt, as an example of a developing country where more than 40% of the population is under 15, the 1976 census showed that 17.2% of children between ages 6 and 14 are working or looking for jobs (Koraim, 1988). In the majority of these cases, the children are forced to accept exhausting, difficult, and unrewarding jobs.

*Education.* Children who are forced to work early in childhood, or female children who are kept at home in preparation for early marriage, will not attend or continue in school. Primary school enrollment in most developing countries is well below 100%, and secondary school enrollment is even lower (WHO, 1985). Enrollment for females in these countries is usually lower than for males.

*Low birth weight.* Low birth weight seems to constitute a serious problem in less developed countries. WHO has estimated that 16% of all infants born in the world have low birth weight; 95% of these infants are born in developing countries. The highest percentages are found in southern Asia (31%), Africa (10-20%), and Latin America (11%), compared with 6-7% in developed countries (WHO, 1985) (see Table 7.2).

Table 7.2    Aspects of Women's and Infants' Health in Selected Countries

| Country | Total Fertility Rate, 1985-1990[a] | Percentage of Women Aged 15-19 Married, 1980[b] | Percentage of Contraceptive Prevalence, 1970-1984[a] | Percentage of Anemic Pregnant Women[c] | Percentage of Low Birth Weight Infants, 1982[c] |
|---|---|---|---|---|---|
| Kenya | 8 | 34 | 17 | 40 | 13 |
| Zambia | 7 | 37 | 1 | 50 | 14 |
| Egypt | 5 | 30 | 30 | 75 | 7 |
| Jordan | 7 | 28 | 26 | 50 | 7 |
| Mexico | 5 | 20 | 41 | 38 | 12 |
| Peru | 5 | 16 | 43 | 35 | 9 |
| Indonesia | 4 | 32 | 40 | 44 | 14 |
| Pakistan | 6 | 31 | 3 | 65 | 27 |
| Denmark | 2 | 2 | 63 | — | 6 |
| United States | 2 | 11 | 68 | — | 7 |

SOURCE: Belsey and Royston (1987).
a. Figures are from UNFPA.
b. Figures are from UNICEF.
c. Figures are from WHO.

Factors such as the mother's prepregnancy weight, weight gain during pregnancy, height, and nutritional status, as well as the presence of sexually transmitted diseases and the mother's use of alcohol and tobacco, can all influence the outcome of pregnancy and the birth weight of the infant (Belsey & Royston, 1987). An underweight infant is more likely to die or to suffer short- and long-term disabilities than its fellows born with normal weight (Donald, 1979).

*Malnutrition, physical growth, and development.* Malnutrition is still widespread among infants and children in the developing world. Nutritional deprivation in childhood is closely correlated with subsequent adult weight and height, which, in turn, can have a great impact on the productivity and working capacity of the individual.

Anemia among children up to 4 years old affects 51% in developing countries, compared with 12% in developed countries (DeMayer & Adiels-Tegman, 1985; cited in Winikoff, 1988) (see Table 7.2), while iodine deficiency among neonates affects 4% in Zaire and 10% in India, compared with 0.02% in developed countries (Hetzel, 1986; cited in Winikoff, 1988).

Inadequate caloric intake and protein deficiency in diet can seriously affect the physical growth of children. Studies in 25 developing countries have shown that up to one-fourth of 1-year-olds were malnourished judging by the weight for height standard (wasting), while up to three-fourths were malnourished judging by the height for age standard (stunting) (Keller & Filmore, 1983; cited in

"Healthier Mothers," 1984). Slow physical growth and development of children also seems to be related to maternal age, large family size, and short birth intervals (Christiansen, Mora, & Herrera, 1975; cited in "Healthier Mothers," 1984).

*Birth defects and congenital abnormalities.* Birth defects and congenital abnormalities arise from a multitude of causes, genetic and environmental, including mother's ill health and malnutrition. While there are many possible links between high-risk pregnancies and various birth defects, the evidence is clearest for the association between Down's syndrome and maternal age. Among young mothers, the incidence of this syndrome is approximately 1 per 1,000 births; the incidence rises sharply to reach 1 per 40 births at age 45 (Smithells, 1978).

Birth defects resulting from exposure of the mother to viruses or drugs during pregnancy are well documented. The rubella virus and the case of Thalidomide are outstanding examples. Teratogenesis may also result when the mother takes certain drugs, such as antibiotics, while pregnant. Exposure of the pregnant woman to large doses of radiation may result in central nervous system defects in the infant, or may lead to early childhood leukemia (Smithells, 1978). Consanguinity in marriage is also believed to increase the risk of certain congenital abnormalities.

Childbirth patterns can affect infants as well. Short- and long-term effects of birth trauma can be seen after instrumental or difficult labor. Nerve injuries, brain damage, fractures, and rupture of abdominal viscera at the time of birth may leave a child handicapped for life.

*Infections and immunization.* Diarrheal diseases, respiratory tract infections, and other infectious diseases still kill or cause ill health among many children in developing countries. Children in large families may suffer from infectious diseases more often because their siblings are a major source of infection. In a study in rural Egypt among children under 5 years old, intestinal parasites were found in 57% of those in the smallest families, 64% of those in families with three or four children, and 77% of those in families with more than four children (Sherbini, Hammam, Omran, Torky, & Fahmy, 1981). Similar findings have come from Pakistan (Saeed Qureshi & Omran, 1981; cited in "Healthier Mothers," 1984) and South Korea (Kwon, Kim, Hong, Ahn, & Kim, 1975; cited in "Healthier Mothers," 1984).

One of the primary mechanisms for improving child survival and health is to increase the proportion of children protected from the main preventable childhood infectious conditions through immunization. Table 7.3 presents the rates of infant immunization in a selected representation of countries. In the late 1980s, WHO researchers showed that 45% of infants in the developing world received the third dose of DPT (diphtheria, pertussis, and tetanus) and polio vaccines, while 35% received measles immunization (Belsey & Royston, 1987). Although these figures seem to be modest, approximately 30% of expected deaths from pertussis have been prevented through this immunization, as have nearly 40% of the expected cases of polio.

**Table 7.3**    Percentage of Children Under 1 Year Old Fully Immunized in Selected Countries

| Country | BCG[a] | DPT[b] | Polio 3 | Measles |
|---|---|---|---|---|
| Zaire | 57 | 37 | 34 | 40 |
| Ghana | 31 | 19 | 17 | 1 |
| Chile | 90 | 89 | 89 | 91 |
| Egypt | 84 | 95 | 95 | 74 |
| Algeria | 88 | 54 | 55 | 51 |
| El Salvador | 50 | 54 | 54 | 71 |
| Philippines | 76 | 59 | 61 | 55 |
| Afghanistan | 17 | 15 | 15 | 14 |
| Hungary | 99 | 99 | 99 | 99 |
| United Kingdom | 5 | 60 | 78 | 62 |

SOURCE: Belsey and Royston (1987). All figures are from the WHO Expanded Program on Immunization.
a. Vaccination against tuberculosis.
b. Vaccination against diphtheria, pertussis, and tetanus.

### The Girl Child

The girl child in the developing world has additional problems of her own. In these societies, the girl is considered a burden and a less useful member of the family; she will not contribute to family income or be the source of security for her parents when they grow older, nor will she serve as a defender of family rights and interests.

There are reasons to believe that girls in these societies are unfairly treated and are more neglected compared with boys within the family. The inadequate care that girls receive and the emotional starvation to which they are exposed can affect their psychological, social, and physical well-being throughout their lives.

*Son preference.* Son preference is common throughout the world, but seems especially widespread in certain societies. Economic, religious, cultural, and traditional reasons are behind this kind of discrimination. The index of son preference (ratio of the number of mothers who prefer their next child to be male to the number who prefer their next child to be female) is high in countries such as Pakistan and Bangladesh (4.9 and 3.3, respectively) and moderate in such countries as Egypt and Mexico (1.5 and 1.2, respectively) (World Fertility Survey, 1983; cited in WHO, 1986). Wherever son preference is strong, it is invariably accompanied by discriminatory practices against daughters, many of which could lead to serious short- and long-term consequences for girls' well-being.

*Malnutrition.* During childhood, both boys and girls require equal amounts of nutrients, yet in many areas in developing countries, little girls receive less from the family pot than do their brothers. Undernourishment in the early years of childhood can lead to stunted growth and deformity in girls' pelvic structure, which may result in complications for them later during pregnancy and labor.

Studies from different parts of the world affirm that malnutrition among girls is higher than it is among boys. A study carried out in Bangladesh in 1981 found that 26% of female children up to 5 years old were severely stunted, compared with 18% of boys of the same age (Chen, Huq, & D'Souza, 1981; cited in WHO, 1986). Another study in a low-income district in Cairo found that female infants suffer malnutrition 1.25 times more than male infants at age 3 months and 1.8 times at age 9 months (Ahmed, Beheiri, Drini, Manala, & Bulbul, 1981).

The same kind of discrimination is found with regard to medical care given to children. One study in India found that boys admitted to a hospital suffering from protein energy malnutrition outnumbered girls by between 47 and 53 to 1, although the condition was 4 to 5 times more common among girls in the research area (Goplan & Naidu, 1972; cited in WHO, 1986). Similar evidence on unequal care for girls has come from Egypt (Makinson, 1985; cited in WHO, 1986), Nigeria (Akesode, 1982; cited in WHO, 1986), and Bangladesh (Greenhalg, 1985; cited in WHO, 1986).

*Education.* Traditionally, boys have better chances than girls for education, particularly in less developed areas (see Table 7.1). Enrollment in schools is almost always higher for boys than for girls. In the early 1980s the percentage of boys enrolled in primary schools was 1.4 times higher than for girls in Africa and 1.35 in Asia, compared with 1.0 in North America and Europe. Furthermore, of the girls enrolled in primary schools, just over half reach secondary schools, and less than one-sixth of them continue to higher education (WHO, 1985). It appears that where customs and tradition have deep roots there is resistance to education for girls. In these societies, poor educational levels and child marriage go hand in hand.

*Female circumcision.* Female genital mutilation is a traditional practice that is widespread in many countries in Africa and some countries in Asia. The procedure varies in severity from removing parts of the outer genitals to infibulation that almost closes the vaginal opening. This severe degree of mutilation is reported mainly in the Sudan, Somalia, southern Egypt, and Ethiopia. It is estimated that in Africa more than 50 million women are circumcised (Rushwan, 1984; cited in "Mothers' Lives Matter," 1988).

The procedure is usually carried out on girls before puberty and is done mainly by traditional birth attendants and healers who do not usually possess the means to perform clean surgical procedures. Immediate effects include shock, severe pain, infection, bleeding, urine retention, and accidental damage to surrounding organs; long-term complications, especially from infibulation, include scarring, painful intercourse, obstetric complications, and psychological effects. Research and reports on the subject have revealed that ambiguous motives lie behind the practice: tradition, religion, hygiene, and attenuation of sexual desire (Assaad, 1980).

*Child marriage.* Early marriage is the norm in many cultures, based upon not only tradition but also economic factors. Most common in Africa and the Indian subcontinent, girls in some of these areas may get married when they are as young as 10-11 years old. In the 1980s, it was estimated that the percentage of women aged 15-19 currently married was 44% in Africa, 42% in Asia, 16% in Latin America, 11% in North America, and 7% in Europe (WHO, 1985) (see Table 7.2).

Girls who get married at such early ages can face tremendous psychological and physical risks. They may suffer mental health problems serious enough to threaten their lives and the safety and health of their children. An inquiry into high suicide rates among 15- to 30-year-old women in India blamed childhood marriage and the stress caused when girls leave their family homes to live in their husbands' houses (Devi, 1980; cited in World Federation of Public Health Associations, 1986). Stress weakens girls' and women's resistance to physical disease and may reduce their capacity for essential family activities.

Girls who get pregnant at such early ages are exposed to many further risks. Among other complications, their small and immature pelvises can result in obstructed labor; eclampsia and increased rate of pregnancy wastage are also well documented. The risks of pregnancy in the very young extend to their infants as well. Low birth weights and infant mortality rates are high among these young girls.

## The Woman

The quality of life, health, and survival of children are determined by the mother's health and status. It is estimated that 18-30% of the world's families are supported solely by women (World Federation of Public Health Associations, 1986). Women's health and status are closely related to the types of lives they lead, the roles they play within the family and in the society, and the environmental conditions that surround them.

*Mental health.* Women are more prone to mental illness than are men, because of severely conflicting family and cultural expectations, the trauma of overwork, repeated childbearing, and feelings of insecurity within the family. Polygamy and men's right to divorce at will in certain areas add greatly to women's insecurity. In Bangladesh, for example, women outnumber men among the mentally ill by two to one (World Federation of Public Health Associations, 1986).

Violence against women within the family is common in all countries and societies, including developed countries. Forms of abuse range from humiliation and economic blackmail to physical brutality. The consequences can affect the mental and physical health of many women for life. Such violence leaves its marks on society as a whole and on the children in particular.

*Education and employment.* Education is the master key to the status of women. It is an important determinant of health. Studies have shown strong correlations between children's health and survival and mothers' education. Illiteracy rates among women, particularly in the developing world, are still very high, the highest being in Africa, with 85%, Asia with 66%, and Latin America with 30%, compared with 7% in Europe and 1% in North America (WHO, 1985). Table 7.1 shows the variation in literacy rates of women and men across a selected group of countries.

Educated women are more ready to reject harmful traditional practices. They are more likely to marry later, delay the onset of childbearing, and have fewer and more optimally spaced children. Generally, women with no schooling have almost twice as many children on average as those with seven or more years schooling (Belsey & Royston, 1987).

Educated women are more likely to use available health services and to have their children immunized. A demographic health survey in the 1980s in Egypt revealed that the mother's educational attainment was inversely related to children's immunization coverage rates. The proportion of fully immunized among children 12-23 months with birth records ranged from almost 25% of those whose mothers had never attended school to 54% among children whose mothers had a secondary education. Children of mothers working for cash were also more likely to have been immunized than children of other mothers (Sayed, Osman, Zanaty, & Way, 1988).

*Malnutrition.* Women need to eat well throughout their lives, and if they are to produce healthy babies and reduce the risks they may face during their reproductive years, they must give particular attention to the quality and quantity of food they eat during pregnancy. During pregnancy and breast-feeding, a woman's body has extra nutritional demands for protein, calories, various vitamins and minerals, and particularly iron. A pregnant woman in her last six months of pregnancy needs an additional 350 calories per day; a breast-feeding mother needs an additional 550 calories per day (WHO/FAO, 1973, pp. 34-35; cited in "Healthier Mothers," 1984).

In many areas, the type and amount of food, endemic diseases, hard physical work, and intestinal parasites leave women anemic and malnourished. The extra demands of pregnancy and lactation worsen their nutritional status; WHO has estimated that almost half of nonpregnant and nearly two-thirds of pregnant women in developing countries suffer from iron deficiency anemia (Belsey & Royston, 1987); the highest rates are found in South Asia and Africa. A survey of diets in more than 80 developing countries found that 20-45% of women aged 15-44 have inadequate daily caloric intake (Hamilton, Popkin, & Spicer, 1984; cited in "Mothers' Lives Matter," 1988).

Discrimination in distributing high-value food in some areas is obvious. The nutritional needs of men are met first, followed by children and finally women.

*Sexually transmitted diseases.* Women often carry the blame for passing sexually transmitted diseases (STDs) to their infants, when in fact they are victims who contracted these diseases from their male partners. STDs affecting women can have grave consequences for children. Syphilis, gonorrhea, chlamydia infections, and other STDs affecting the mother during pregnancy may result in harmful effects for the infant, including low birth weight and neonatal morbidity, conjunctivitis, corneal ulceration, congenital syphilis (Ross, 1982), and now the deadly AIDS. A rough estimate of 35-50% of stillbirths in Ethiopia can be attributed to syphilis, and one-third of low birth weight infants born each year in Kenya can be attributed to STDs (Belsey & Royston, 1987).

*Antenatal and intrapartum care.* Antenatal care helps women have safer pregnancies and healthier babies. It prevents or reduces both maternal and fetal mortality and morbidity rates. Wide variations in the proportion of women receiving antenatal care exist within geographic areas, but coverage rates are still lowest in Africa and Asia (Belsey & Royston, 1987).

An Egyptian study has found that the rate of low birth weight infants among mothers who received late antenatal care (after the seventh month) was 6.3 times higher than among mothers who had early antenatal care (Wakeil, Abdallah, El-Rafei, & Naeim, 1983).

What applies to antenatal care applies to intrapartum care. Although almost 100% of deliveries in developed countries are attended by trained personnel, less than half of deliveries in developing countries (where 85% of world deliveries take place) receive the same kind of care (Belsey & Royston, 1987).

*Family planning and unwanted pregnancy.* The United Nations Children's Fund (UNICEF) has endorsed family planning as one of the high-priority techniques for improving child health ("Healthier Mothers," 1984). Family planning lowers child mortality and morbidity rates by preventing high-risk pregnancies, giving women more control over the number of children they have, spacing pregnancies, and avoiding the births of unwanted children.

Women who do not want their pregnancies will most probably resort to abortion, which could have grave consequences for the women's health and lives. When abortion cannot be obtained for one reason or another, these women are forced to continue with their unwanted pregnancies. In many instances the outcome is undesirable, especially when the infant is a girl. The "unwantedness" often may eventually be translated into less care, less love, and more neglect, which could greatly affect the mental and physical health of the child.

Several studies in different parts of the world have found a relationship between high birth order, large family size, and short birth intervals on the one hand and low birth weight, high infant mortality and morbidity rates, and low standard of intelligence and academic achievement on the other ("Healthier Mothers," 1984).

Despite its apparent increase, contraceptive prevalence (as a measure of family planning program effectiveness) is still below the desirable standard in many developing countries (see Table 7.2). Moreover, failure and discontinuation rates are still high in these countries. The World Fertility Survey (1983; cited in WHO, 1986) has shown a marked discrepancy in many countries between current

**Table 7.4**    Percentage of Currently Married Fertile Women Not Wanting More Children and Percentage of This Group Using Effective Contraception in Selected Countries

| Country | Percentage of Married Fertile Women Not Wanting More Children | Percentage of Married Fertile Women Not Wanting More Children Who Use Effective Contraception |
|---|---|---|
| Egypt | 53 | 46 |
| Ghana | 12 | 17 |
| Tunisia | 47 | 48 |
| Kenya | 17 | 17 |
| Sudan | 17 | 16 |
| Bangladesh | 61 | 14 |
| Pakistan | 49 | 17 |
| Philippines | 54 | 29 |
| Thailand | 57 | 66 |
| Colombia | 80 | 40 |
| Mexico | 57 | 48 |

SOURCE: Herz and Measham (1987).

fertility figures, numbers of unwanted births per woman, and contraceptive prevalence. In Africa, for example, only 23% of women not wanting any more children are practicing contraception; the corresponding figure in Asia is 43%, and in Latin America it is 57% (Belsey & Royston, 1987). Table 7.4 presents related data for a selected group of individual countries.

## Intervention

The above sections have described the link between women's health and status and children's health, emphasizing the important role played by women in improving the health and the quality of life of their children, and concluding that women's health and status should be a major concern, in part because of their influence on children's health and survival and on the mother's ability to provide child care. Women and children's health care should be integrated. Maternal and child health care (MCH) must be considered a priority. With a little more attention to the M component, the C component will improve automatically. As women's contributions and standing improve, society will be more willing to do what is necessary to improve women's health, which, in turn, will improve children's health.

What is urgently needed is a firm political commitment. Women's health and status constitute a political issue. Policymakers and opinion leaders such as ministers, members of Parliament, religious and community leaders, broadcasters, and news editors have to unite their efforts and give the matter high priority. Although developing countries have common problems, sociocultural differences exist; therefore, the strategy should be adapted to the social, cultural, economic, and environmental needs and resources of each region. This commitment should also give more attention to improving environmental conditions by providing safe water and adequate sanitation. It should also work to enhance the status of women by supporting women's groups and nongovernment organizations (NGOs), and by modifying the laws and regulations that affect women's status.

As education is a key factor in improving both women's and children's health, every effort must be made to promote both formal and informal education. Governments should modify their regulations to improve children's (especially girls') and women's education, while NGOs can participate by disseminating necessary information on health, nutrition, and personal hygiene.

Because they provide opportunities to improve earning capacity, income-generating activities and projects for women must be encouraged by governments as well as donor agents. A little more cash in women's hands will help them to purchase food and health care for their children and themselves.

Creating strong community-based health care for women and children is an excellent idea. The system can work through using trained local community health workers, such as traditional birth attendants, to promote better nutrition, immunization, and family planning; to provide sound antenatal care; and, in time, to recognize and refer high-risk cases to experts for further management. The infrastructure can help by providing necessary backup, making referral facilities and transport available. A good example of this system is the strong family planning program in Indonesia.

The role that NGOs can play is crucial. These organizations, especially those concerned with health, as well as women's groups, with their flexibility and determination, can provide women with needed information and, if strong enough, can create pressure on governments. Feminist health advocates in Brazil have succeeded in persuading the government to adopt a comprehensive women's health policy that includes family planning as a basic component (Germain, 1987). Campaigns against female circumcision in Egypt are undertaken solely by NGOs.

The media, especially television and radio, have a powerful role to play in bringing vital health matters to people's attention, disclosing facts and figures about health matters concerning women and children. With such facts more widely known, national and local leaders will be more likely to respond to the pressure, reinforce statements, modify laws and regulations, and take action. A good example is the oral rehydration therapy program presented on Egyptian television that helped a great deal in lowering the rates of infant mortality from diarrheal diseases (Hirschhorn, 1985; cited in "Radio Spreading the Word," 1986).

Developing countries face many economic difficulties. The deteriorating economic conditions in these countries hit women and children first. Projects concerned with the health of women, in particular, are not usually given priority by governments. Donors from international organizations should support these projects by providing both technical and financial assistance when required. They must be ready to cooperate with both governments and NGOs.

Several organizations, such as WHO, UNICEF, and UNESCO, are already involved in some projects concerned with health, informal education, income-generating activities, and nutrition. It must be emphasized that the role of these donors has a significant impact on women's and children's health. The existing projects may not survive and new ones may not see the light of day if the international community loses interest in supporting the less developed, poor, and disadvantaged parts of the world. Donors should help poor countries to bring the goal of "health for all by the year 2000" closer.

## References

Ahmed, W., Beheiri, F., Drini, H., Manala, D., & Bulbul, A. (1981). Female infants in Egypt: Mortality and child care. *Population Sciences, 2,* 25-39.

Akesode, F. (1982). Factors affecting the use of primary health care clinics for children. *Journal of Epidemiology and Community Health, 36,* 310-314.

Assaad, M. B. (1980). Female circumcision in Egypt: Current research and social implications. *Studies in Family Planning, 11*(1), 3-16.

Belsey, M., & Royston, E. (1987). *Overview of the health of women and children* (World Health Organization Report). Paper presented at the International Conference on Better Health for Women and Children Through Family Planning, Nairobi, Kenya.

Chen, L. C., Huq, E., & D'Souza, S. (1981). Sex bias in the family allocation of food and health care in rural Bangladesh. *Population and Development Review, 7*(1), 55-70.

Christiansen, N., Mora, J. O., & Herrera, M. G. (1975). Family social characteristics related to physical growth of young children. *British Journal of Preventive and Social Medicine, 29*(1), 121-130.

DeMayer, E., & Adiels-Tegman, M. (1985). The prevalence of anaemia in the world. *World Health Statistics Quarterly, 38,* 302-316.

Devi, P. K. (1980, June). Traditional patterns. *World Health,* pp. 6-9.

Donald I. (1979). Prematurity. In I. Donald (Ed.), *Practical obstetric problems* (5th ed., pp. 939-977). London: Lloyd-Luke.

Germain, A. (1987). *Reproductive health and dignity: Choices by Third World women.* Paper presented at the International Conference on Better Health for Women and Children through Family Planning, Nairobi, Kenya.

Goplan, C., & Naidu, A. (1972). Nutrition and fertility. *Lancet,* 1077-1079.

Greenhalg, S. (1985). Sexual stratification: The other side of "Growth with equity" in East Asia. *Population and Development Review, 11*(2), 265-314.

Hamilton, S., Popkin, B., & Spicer, D. (1984). *Women and nutrition in Third World countries.* New York: Praeger.

Healthier mothers and children through family planning. (1984). *Population Reports* (Series J, No. 27).

Herz, B., & Measham, A. (1987, February). *The safe motherhood initiative: Proposals for action* (World Bank Report). Paper presented at the International Conference on Safe Motherhood, Nairobi, Kenya.

Hetzel, B. (1986). Iodine deficiency disorders: A maternal and child health issue. In D. B. Jellife & E. F. Jellife (Eds.), *Advances in international maternal and child health* (Vol. 6, pp. 79-107). Oxford: Clarendon.

Hirschhorn, N. (1985). *Oral rehydration therapy program in Egypt.* Arlington, VA: John Snow Public Health Group.

Keller, W., & Filmore, C. M. (1983). Prevalence of protein energy malnutrition. *World Health Statistics Quarterly, 36*(2), 129-168.

Koraim, K. (1988). *The impact of economic adjustment policies on the vulnerable families and children in Egypt.* Report prepared for Third World Forum and UNICEF.

Kwon, E., Kim, T., Hong, J., Ahn, Y., & Kim, E. (1975). The interrelationship between family planning and child health. *Seoul Journal of Medicine, 16*(4), 217-227.

Makinson, C. (1985). *Age and sex differences in treatment of childhood diarrheal episodes in rural Menoufia.* Unpublished manuscript, American University, Social Research Center, Cairo.

Mothers' lives matter: Maternal health in the community. (1988). *Population Reports* (Series L, No. 7).

Radio-spreading the world on family planning. (1986). *Population Reports* (Series J, No. 32).

Ross, S. M. (1982). Sexually transmitted diseases in pregnancy: Obstetric problems in the developing world. *Clinics in Obstetrics and Gynaecology, 9*(3), 565-589.

Rushwan, H. (1984). Female circumcision: A reproductive health problem. In J. K. G. Mati, O. A. Ladipo, R. T. Burkman, R. H. Magarick, & D. Huber (Eds.), *Reproductive health in Africa* (pp. 178-180). Baltimore: Johns Hopkins Program for International Education in Gynecology and Obstetrics.

Saeed Qureshi, M., & Omran, A. (1981). Pakistan. In A. R. Omran, C. C. Standley, G. Ochoa, A. Gil, H. Hammam, F. Sherbini, B. Raza, T. Khan, & F. Boustani (Eds.), *Family formation patterns and health: Further studies* (pp. 164-172). Geneva: World Health Organization.

Sayed, H., Osman, M., Zanaty, F., & Way, A. (1988). Maternal and child health. In *Egypt's demographic and health survey* (p. 170). Cairo: National Population Council.

Sherbini, F., Hammam, H., Omran, A., Torky, M., & Fahmy, S. (1981). Egypt. In A. R. Omran, C. C. Standley, G. Ochoa, A. Gil, H. Hammam, F. Sherbini, B. Raza, T. Khan, & F. Boustani (Eds.), *Family formation patterns and health: Further studies* (pp. 154-164). Geneva: World Health Organization.

Smithells, R. W. (1978). Prevention and prediction of congenital malformation. In R. MacDonald (Ed.), *Scientific basis of obstetrics and gynaecology* (2nd ed., pp. 275-299). London: Churchill Livingstone.

Wakeil, F., Abdallah, N., El-Rafei, M., & Naeim, H. (1983). Effect of maternal and socioeconomic factors on the outcome of pregnancy. *Bulletin of Faculty of Agriculture, Cairo University, 34,* 19-37.

Winikoff, B. (1988). Women's health: An alternative perspective for choosing health intervention. *Studies in Family Planning, 19*(4), 197-214.

World Federation of Public Health Associations. (1986, March). *Women and health: Information for action* (issue paper for the Aga Khan Foundation and UNICEF). New York: Author.

World Fertility Survey. (1983). *Cross-national summaries, 27.*

World Health Organization. (1980). World Health Organization constitution. In World Health Organization, *Basic documents* (30th ed., pp. 1-18). Geneva: Author.

World Health Organization. (1985). *Women, health and development: A report by the director-general* (WHO Offset Publication No. 90). Geneva: Author.

World Health Organization. (1986). *Health implications of sex discrimination in childhood.* Geneva: Author.

World Health Organization/FAO. (1973). *Energy and protein requirements* (WHO Technical Report Series No. 522 and FAO Nutrition Meetings Report Series No. 52). Geneva: Author.

# 8

# Children Born from Unwanted Pregnancies: Prevention of Psychological Subdeprivation

## Zdenek Dytrych

In order to effect change in any physical, biological, mental, or social actions that influence the development of children, we need to know the basic factors that cause these actions. It is often possible to discern these factors from accumulated clinical experience, later making generalizations about individual cases. However, the more effective approach (even if not always automatically successful) is to conduct carefully thought-out and planned research that covers the complex interrelations that influence the development of a child in positive or negative ways.

For the last 20 years researchers associated with the Department of Social Psychiatry at the Psychiatric Research Institute in Prague, Czechoslovakia, have conducted a series of studies to identify factors that contribute to the adult well-being or later psychopathology of children born and living in various less favorable psychosocial conditions. The research presented in this chapter examines the Czechoslovakian approach to preventing later psychopathology in children and thereby improving the adult lives of these individuals by considering general theory, the findings of a longitudinal study on children born from unwanted pregnancies, and possible strategies for preventing unwanted pregnancies.

### Theoretical Approach

In addition to basic biological needs, there are basic psychological needs that must be adequately gratified if a child is to develop into a personality with good

AUTHOR'S NOTE: The study reported here was funded, at various times, by the Center for Population Research, (U.S.) National Institute for Child Health and Human Development (Grant HD-05569); the Ford Foundation; the World Health Organization; and the Czechoslovak State Research Plan. I am pleased to acknowledge the productive cooperation for more than 20 years of my American colleague, Henry P. David, and my Czech colleagues, Zdenek Matejcek, Vratislav Schüller, and Ludek Kubicka.

mental health. Psychological deprivation occurs when the subject is unable to satisfy these basic psychological needs for a considerable length of time. So far, five of these vital psychological needs have been well defined and experimentally verified:

(1) the need for a number, variety, and quality of external stimuli that motivate the individual to a desirable level of activity,

(2) the need for a degree of stability, order, and meaning in the external stimuli so that the child can turn experience into knowledge and working strategies (constitutes the fundamental prerequisite of any kind of learning),

(3) the need for positive emotional and social relations with primary caregivers and other educators (gives the child the feeling of security necessary for the internal integration of his or her personality),

(4) the need for social fulfillment and social value, which lay the foundation for the child's healthy consciousness of his or her own "I" or identity (includes the acquisition of useful social roles and valid personal goals in life),

(5) the need for an "open future" in which the child has the opportunity to make choices about his or her life (serves to stimulate and maintain the individual's life activity because "hope overcomes stagnation").

If the above needs are not met adequately, there may be lasting psychological consequences for the individual as an adult in any culture. However, research in this area is complicated by the fact that cultures interpret some types of behavior differently. From the beginning of our work, my fellow researchers and I have maintained professional contacts with American colleagues. This connection has demonstrated the need for evaluating the findings of our studies within our cultural context rather than generalizing them to all cultures. Our research was carried out in a country where the assessment of individual and small group behaviors, and the definition of what is and is not a norm, were fundamentally modified by the rules of the totalitarian system in which we were living. Being aware of our social situation, we tried to answer the following questions:

• What factors specific to Czechoslovak conditions handicap an individual's development?

• Do these factors have general validity extending beyond the society in which they were found?

One of the basic theoretical concepts that seems to have general validity across cultures is that of "subdeprivation" (Langmeier & Matejcek, 1975) or psychological deprivation. This concept is based on observations of the following groups of children: children born from unwanted pregnancies, children of alcoholic fathers, children born out of wedlock, children of divorced parents, and children born with a specific malformation (cleft palate and/or cleft lip) to young parents.

Our studies led us to hypothesize that there was a significant relationship between where a child fell on the continuum between acceptance and nonacceptance by parents (more commonly the mother, who, in Czechoslovàk culture, is the primary caretaker) and the degree of psychological deprivation. According to our concept of subdeprivation (psychological deprivation) the changes in the development of the child's personality are not striking and dramatic; rather, they systematically affect various spheres of the child's life, such as relations to important persons, efficiency, and personal satisfaction in life. No specific syndromes or symptoms have been found that predict whether a particular child is illegitimate or comes from a divorced family. However, if factors that can, by general consensus, be considered unfavorable to the social well-being of the child are combined into a summary score, these high-risk groups appear to deviate from the norm quite considerably.

The groups of study children had one common denominator—they all grew up in environments that were less stable, less affectionate, and less accepting than the usual. It is essential to add, however, that lack of emotional warmth and acceptance, especially from the mother's side, was not particularly apparent to the external observer.[1] This stands in marked contrast to the most important finding of our studies, that even these original inconspicuous deviations may have serious consequences in a child's future life.

## Study of Unwanted Children

Our study of children born from unwanted pregnancies suggests the conditions that are associated with children's well-being and protection from psychopathology. I shall describe the study briefly and present the basic findings (all details may be found in David, Dytrych, Matejcek, & Schüller, 1988).

### Background of the Prague Study

Abortion in the first three months, at the request of the pregnant woman on medical and social grounds, was legalized in Czechoslovakia in 1957. Early in the 1960s, when the children in the present study were born, the procedures had become comparatively stabilized—for every 100 births there were approximately 50 abortions. About 8% of abortion requests were denied by the district commissions, and 2-3% of these were upheld by the regional commissions to which some of the mothers appealed. This allowed us to define *unwanted pregnancy* operationally as one the mother was forced to complete after having twice requested an abortion and twice been refused.

Czechoslovakia's unified system of health care services and education, with centralized record keeping, permitted us to acquire comparable data, accumulated quite independently of the present research, on each child.

### Study Group

From 1961 to 1963, 24,989 women in Prague applied for abortions. The regional abortion commission denied 638 appeals. Of the appellants, 83 lived outside Prague or were aliens. Of the remaining 555, 43 were granted abortions by another commission. In 6 cases it appeared that the women were not pregnant, 80 women had "spontaneous" abortions (more than double what was then the Prague norm), 31 women moved from Prague, 9 gave false addresses, 8 were not found for other reasons, and in 62 cases no record about the termination of pregnancy was found, either in gynecology-obstetrics departments, prenatal counseling centers, or through the registry offices of the district national committees.

This left 316 women who gave birth to a child from an unwanted pregnancy and who lived in Prague. Of these children, 5 died in infancy and 1 died later (a lower percentage than the Prague average for the study period); 19 children were adopted by other families, a number far exceeding the nationwide average, considering the number of children in the group; 39 of the children moved with their parents from Prague or emigrated from the state; and 2 were placed in institutional care. Mothers of 7 of the children refused to cooperate in the study, and 6 children could not be examined for other reasons. In four cases the mothers stated that they did not now have nor did they ever have a child, although according to reliable evidence they had all delivered.

In sum, the Unwanted Pregnancy (UP) study group consisted of 220 children born to women twice denied abortion for the same unwanted pregnancy: 110 boys and 110 girls, pair matched with 220 Accepted Pregnancy (AP) control children born to women who had accepted their pregnancies. The study also involved all the children's mothers and, to a lesser extent, their fathers or father substitutes. At the time of first assessment, all UP and AP children were living in functionally complete homes.

### Control Group

Control over factors that by themselves may significantly influence the social development of a child was ensured by forming a control group on the basis of pair matching. The matching criteria included age and sex of the child, age of the mother, number of children in the family, ordinal position of siblings, and social status of the family as determined by its completeness and by the level of the father's education.

### Working Hypotheses

The principal hypothesis was that children born from unwanted pregnancies were at risk with regard to their personality development and, compared with children born from wanted, or at least accepted, pregnancies, would be a greater burden to society. The subhypotheses then postulated a greater frequency of health problems, school performance not in accord with actual intelligence, and less favorable behavioral characteristics in the group of "unwanted children."

A substantial percentage of women who were initially denied abortion finally managed to prevent the births of the children, whether legally or illegally. Therefore, those who did *not* succeed in preventing birth cannot, in all probability, be said to fall at the "negative" extreme on a hypothetical continuum of attitudes toward pregnancy ranging from happy expectation to peremptory, insurmountable resentment. Similarly, the control group does not include only wanted children; undoubtedly, it also contains a certain percentage of undesired births, even though the mothers did not apply for abortions. (In their interviews with a psychiatrist, 7.3% of the control mothers reported that they accepted the births of their children "without any pleasure.")

In order to prevent interpretations of those chance significant differences that occur if statistical tests are applied to a large number of variables, only a few "critical" items concerning individual hypotheses were selected, and predictions were made on the basis of theoretical reasoning and clinical experience. Only these items were used to test the hypothesis, other findings being considered supplementary. All of the items dealt with here are the "critical" ones.

### Data Sources and Examination Methods

The data on the children were obtained from health and school records and by means of questionnaires, interviews with the parents, rating scales, and direct pediatric, sociometric, and psychological examinations. The psychological methods used included the Wechsler Intelligence Scale for Children (WISC), Bene-Anthony Test of family relations, Aspiration-Frustration test, completion of stories, direct interview with the child, and rating scales of the personality traits of the child (for details, see David et al., 1988).

The teachers, psychologists, social workers, pediatricians, and others participating in the study were not told whether the children examined were part of the experimental group or the control group.

## Main Findings

### At Age 9 (Highlights)

Review of early childhood records showed that the UP and AP children began life under similar conditions. There were no statistically significant differences in birth weight or length, in the incidence of congenital malformation, or in signs of minimal brain dysfunction. However, more UP than AP subjects were either not breast-fed or breast-fed for only a short time. The UP children tended to be slightly, but consistently, overweight. At age 9, both groups obtained similar mean IQ scores on the WISC—102 for the UP subjects and 103 for the AP controls. However, the UP subjects received significantly lower school grades (except in math) and were rated less favorably in school performance, diligence, and behavior by their teachers and mothers. On sociometric scales, the UP subjects were significantly more often "rejected as friends" by their schoolmates than were the AP controls. Compared to the AP mothers, the UP mothers perceived their sons less favorably than they did their daughters.

The UP subjects scored significantly higher on the maladaptation score than did the AP controls. The highest scores were obtained by the 32 UP-"only" children, while the AP-only children had the lowest score. The male-only children among the UP had the highest scores of all.

In sum, although there were relatively few statistically significant differences at age 9, all the differences were consistently more negative for the UP children. The UP children appeared to be born into a potentially handicapping situation, a condition consonant with the concept of psychological subdeprivation.

### At Ages 14-16 (Highlights)

The second follow-up was conducted in 1977, when the children were 14 to 16 years of age. It was possible to locate 216 UP children and 215 AP controls, for a 98% follow-up rate. Previously nonsignificant differences in school performance had now reached statistical significance. This difference was not so much in UP children failing more often as in their being substantially underrepresented among students graded above average or higher. They rarely appeared on any roster of excellence. Similar findings were noted in teachers' ratings. Many more UP than AP children reported contentious relationships with their parents. In all the areas sampled, earlier differences not only persisted but had widened.

### At Ages 21-23 (Highlights)

A third follow-up was conducted in 1983-1984, when the study participants were young adults aged 21-23 years. At that time 50 UP and 50 AP subjects were married and 34 in each group had become parents. Data obtained from the population registers, from child-care councils, and from drug, alcohol, and criminal registers reflected a greater proneness to social problems among UP than AP subjects, tending to confirm the predictions of the maladaptation scores obtained at age 9. Some 73% of UP subjects and 70% of AP controls were available for individual structured interviews. Others were in military service, some had moved away from Prague, and a few were in prison. Of those interviewed, less than one-third as many UP as AP subjects said their lives had developed as expected and more than twice as many UP subjects stated that they had encountered more problems than anticipated.

Compared with the AP controls, the UP subjects reported less job satisfaction, more conflict with coworkers and supervisors, fewer and less satisfying relations with friends, and more disappointments in love. More UP subjects were dissatisfied with their mental well-being and actively sought or were in treatment. A larger proportion of UP subjects had had their first sexual experiences before age 15 and reported having had sexual relations with more than 10 partners. Among the married young adults in both groups, the UP subjects more often judged their marriages to be unhappy and significantly more often expressed the desire not to be married at all or not to be married to their present partners.

A Psychosocial Instability Score (PSIS) was constructed on the basis of structured interview responses to 37 items that, based on clinical experience, were considered indicative of unsatisfactory or problematic relationships within the psychosocial environment. An aggregate measure, the PSIS represents the sum of negative responses on each subscale. The differences in what the study participants said about themselves at ages 21-23 tended to be even greater than the differences in what parents, teachers, and schoolmates had said about them more than a decade earlier. However, the gap previously noted between UP boys and UP girls at age 9 diminished in young adulthood.

In both groups, 34 couples had become parents. While these samples were too small to allow for statistically significant results, the young UP mothers, more often than the young AP mothers, indicated that their pregnancies had not been welcomed. Moreover, UP subjects tended to list their physicians as their prime source of information about pregnancy and child development, whereas the AP women relied more often on their mothers.

### Summary

To summarize, findings from the longitudinal study of children born in 1961-1963 to Prague women twice denied abortion for the same pregnancy and pair-matched controls show that differences have continued and widened over time. While it is difficult to make predictions for individual children, there is considerable evidence that, on the whole, unwanted pregnancy and subsequent compulsory childbearing have a detrimental effect on psychosocial development, with socially undesirable long-term implications. Partially as a result of the study findings, abortion commissions were abolished in Czechoslovakia in January 1987. Abortions of unwanted pregnancies are now available on written request of the woman, provided her pregnancy does not exceed 12 weeks and there are no health-related contraindications.

In 1989 the World Health Organization European Regional Office in Copenhagen provided support for a further study. The purpose is to assess partner choice, marital relations, and reproductive behavior among the now adult UP and AP subjects, as well as the psychosocial situations of their firstborn children.

The results are expected to provide some initial indication of whether the risks of being unwanted continue into the third generation.

Funds are also being sought for a fourth follow-up wave in 1991, when the subjects will be approximately 30 years old. One objective is to determine whether previously observed differences between UP and AP subjects' social adaptation persist and are reflected in their parental behavior and in the development of their firstborn children. Another objective is to use newly collected data on adult UP and AP siblings to clarify to what extent the differences between the originally unwanted and accepted subjects can be explained by the specific effect of being unwanted as distinct from more general genetic or environmental factors.

### How to Prevent Psychological Subdeprivation

If young couples accepted the principles of planned and responsible parenthood, there would be no unwanted children. Although full acceptance of these principles seems to be far off, we have to work toward this goal. Ideally, young people would consider whether or not they want to have children, with whom they want to have them, and when they want to have them. However, even more important is the principle that children have the right to be born into conditions that guarantee their best psychosocial development. But what is to be done in cases when pregnancies arise in a rash, uncontrolled, casual way, without desire or plan on the side of the mother and/or father?

In the cities of Czechoslovakia, about 65-70% of newly married women are in their third or fourth month of pregnancy; most of these pregnancies are not planned. It would be naive to rely in such cases on a maternal instinct that unerringly would operate after the birth of the child—an instinct that, of course, exists as a biological phenomenon, but that has different intensity in individual mothers. Furthermore, it is likely that this instinct is weakened rather than intensified by the present cultural and social conditions in which the mothers live.

Even if the publication of our findings on unwanted children was an important factor in liberalization of the abortion law in Czechoslovakia in 1986, this does not mean that we have succeeded in finding a generally acceptable solution to the problem of being unwanted at birth. One can imagine an approach to counseling pregnant women that would change their expressed negative (or more frequently ambivalent) attitudes toward their expected children into more accepting ones. This would mean that in each case of diagnosed pregnancy in which there is a doubt about the woman's ability to accept the expected child, a therapist should step in to change her attitude and heighten the chances of the child's being positively accepted.

In our study there were at least three categories of mothers who did not accept their pregnancies. The first consisted of women who in the beginning of the pregnancy had more or less serious social problems; because of their pregnancies, they had to overcome certain social obstacles and give up what they had looked forward to in the near future. These mothers, in general, quickly adjusted to the fact of being pregnant and actively accepted their children after birth.

The second category consisted of women with highly ambivalent or negative attitudes toward their pregnancies due to complicated or hostile relationships with their partners—that is, the fathers of the children. If the relationship between parents was not resolved, the hostility toward the partner was transferred to the child—the child was not accepted.

The third, and most problematic, category consisted of those women who for some personality-related reason refused the roles of wife and mother. They hated becoming mothers; the children were foreign elements in their lives. These mothers were marked by perfectionistic but emotionally cold and alienated educational approaches.

If we could distinguish these categories of women, it would be possible to find more specific and effective forms of help. There is no doubt that in the first group it is enough to apply general educational "enlightenment," which means stressing the positive acceptance of the parental role as an integral part of one's own identity.

The parental role develops from early childhood to adulthood. However, Grossmann and Grossmann (1979, 1980) have shown clearly that after childbirth the greatest benefit from residence in the "rooming-in" department was derived by mothers whose pregnancies were planned, looked forward to, and fully accepted. On the other hand, those mothers whose pregnancies were unwanted and who had not developed positive maternal attitudes beforehand had practically no benefit from having their children with them in the rooming-in department.

What about secondary and tertiary prevention? If a child has already suffered from what we have defined as subdeprivation, it is most desirable to weaken or stop this process as soon as possible. There is some evidence that individual or family psychotherapy is effective, but the problem is how to diagnose subdeprivation in its early stages and then motivate the mother or the family to cooperate. As mentioned before, in cases of subdeprivation, defense mechanisms usually do not allow the mothers to realize that their children are not receiving as much acceptance as they need.

In Czechoslovakia, the Health Service is paying great attention to children's early development. A local pediatrician must see a child at least 10 times during the first year of life. Other very thorough preventive examinations follow at the ages of 3 and 5 years. For the last six years, these pediatric examinations have been supplemented by an evaluation of the social functioning of the family (the pediatrician must apply this now). Families are divided into four categories: eufunctional, problematic, dysfunctional, and afunctional. The pediatrician categorizes the family and can send the mother for specialized psychological or social assistance. (However, such special services are at the moment more envisioned than actually practiced.)

Secondary preventive programs that concentrate on more than the traditional analysis of the mother-child relationship need to be found. The role of the father must be emphasized. It is also important to expose children to the positive influence of peer groups, for they play an important role in the development of masculine or feminine identity of individuals as well as in development of parental postures (as has been shown in developmental studies of school-age children). The preventive effect of socializing procedures may be enhanced considerably by means of the so-called vertical biodromal aspect. This means that children are exposed to the influence of socializing factors in wider family circles by meeting both young adults and older adults.

The whole problem of psychological subdeprivation can be imagined as a floating iceberg. The peak above the surface is only the more serious social pathology to which deprivation contributes (aggression, alcoholism, drug use, criminality, and so on). Hidden below the surface is a much broader foundation, where, given "suitable" conditions, serious pathology originates. And emotional deprivation is especially fertile soil for the subsequent growth of asocial behavior.

Secondary prevention and tertiary prevention deal with that part of the iceberg that we see above the surface. Primary prevention aims to make the water in the ocean a little warmer, to melt that part of the iceberg under the surface and, ultimately, to dissolve it altogether.

## Note

1. *Editors' note:* We discussed with Professor Dytrych our concern that statements such as this appear to put all of the blame for the problems of the children on the mother. His rationale is that in Czechoslovak families, women have most of the responsibility for child care; the participation of fathers is minimal.

## References

David, H. P., Dytrych, Z., Matejcek, Z., & Schüller, V. (Eds.). (1988). *Born unwanted: Developmental effects of denied abortion.* New York: Springer.

Grossmann, K. E., & Grossmann, K. (1979). *Development of relationship patterns during the first two years of life.* Paper presented at the conference of the International Society for the Study of Behavior Development, Lund, Sweden.

Grossmann, K. E., & Grossmann, K. (1980). Die Entwicklung socialer Beziehungen in der ersten Lebens jahre. In M. Lukesh, M. Perret, & K. E. Schneewind (Eds.), *Socialization und intervention in der familie.* Bern, Switzerland: H. Huber.

Langmeier, J., & Matejcek, Z. (1975). *Psychological deprivation in childhood.* New York: Halsted.

# 9

# Making a Dangerous World More Tolerable for Children: Implications of Research on Reactions to Nuclear War Threat, War, and Disaster

**Milton Schwebel**

Superpower détente and subsequent events in many parts of the world set off an unfamiliar chain reaction. Suddenly, to everyone's astonishment, the world seemed on the edge of peace and free of survival problems. After years of the threat of nuclear holocaust, it is understandable that we should have gloried in the momentary euphoria. Not since an all-too-brief period following World War II had we experienced anything quite like it. Regrettably, all dreams must come to an end and, like the earlier one, this dream too has faded fast, as we have come to recognize that one set of world problems has replaced another. In any case, it is difficult to celebrate a new world of peace while a dozen or more regional wars are very much under way, ethnic violence is erupting widely, and terrorism and drug-instigated crime bring warfare to our streets.

What a pity the dream did not become a permanent reality, because a world without war and the threat of war would spare countless millions of children the nightmares they suffer about separation from parents, not to mention the very real experience of abuse, hunger, rape, injury, and death.

Even in the absence of war and its threatening shadow, children are confronted with an assortment of potential horrors. Nature itself offers up earthquakes, typhoons, hurricanes, tornadoes, and floods. Nature and society pose the possibility of an assortment of ecological disasters, and society itself is responsible for poverty, homelessness, unemployment, child abuse, and an assortment of crimes of unimaginable brutality. Fortunately, there is more to life than just its dark side. And after this litany of threats to the peace of mind and survival of children, it is heartening to remind ourselves of the other side of social reality: the countless people who have an enormous capacity for concern and compassion about the welfare of children. They go to great lengths, sometimes even to the point of sacrificing their own lives, for their children. And many devote themselves to studying the problems of growing up in this kind of world in order to be better able to improve children's lives.

The problems seem to be overwhelming. We can take it for granted that in the long foreseeable future the majority of children in the world will be faced with palpable threat of war, famine, drought, unemployment, poverty, or natural disaster, and many others will suffer the consequences of familial conflict. How is it possible to make a dent in all of these, or even in any one of them? It is discouraging enough to attempt to cope with problems of hunger when one takes note that the "poorest 400 million people [in the world] are so undernourished they are likely to suffer stunted growth, mental retardation, or death" and to learn that at the same time, ironically, Americans spend $5 billion each year on special diets for reduction of calorie consumption (Durning, 1990, p. 22). In the United States, some 20% of all children are in families whose incomes fall below the government-established poverty level. Yet, in the face of these painful facts, there is no national outcry that all children be given adequate diet and health care. Considering the quiet acceptance of poverty in this wealthy superpower, there is no reason to expect a significant change in the present worldwide circumstances under which children are reared and cared for. As realists, we must seek improvements in their lives under prevailing conditions even as we urge and strive for betterment in those conditions.

Under these circumstances, we are faced with the challenge of preparing children for inevitable hardship, especially by warding off, or at least reducing, the traumatic effects of anticipated and actual occurrences. To be concrete, what measures can help children in Armenia, San Francisco, and Tokyo to withstand the psychological strain of anticipated earthquakes and children in Cambodia, Northern Ireland, the Middle East, and Central America to cope with the stress of daily life in a war zone? The search for effective measures raises the following questions: Is it really possible to prepare children for such occurrences? Will such preparation actually minimize the potentially traumatic effects of earthquake, war, and so on? At what age level is it feasible and productive to provide that preparation? What conditions and kinds of preparation are effective at the various stages in child and adolescent development? Is it possible to develop an effective generic experience and set of conditions that prepare children for any kind of potentially traumatic life event? Or must prevention be limited to one potential trauma?

The remainder of this chapter is composed of several parts. In the first, I report on studies of how children constructed their reality in the nuclear age—how they conceptualized and reacted to the nuclear threat. From those studies I identify the major *coping cognitions* that children appear to rely upon in withstanding life's physical, cognitive, and emotional onslaughts. Next, studies about children's reactions to living in war-ravaged countries or experiencing natural disasters are examined to assess the importance of these coping cognitions to the children's psychological well-being. Finally, I propose features for prevention programs designed to make a dangerous world more tolerable for children.

## Contending with Nuclear Threat

Adult reactions to the new dangers of the nuclear age were studied as early as 1946, within a year after the bombing of Hiroshima (Woodward, 1948), but those of children not until 1961. Of course, the investigations of the 1960s did not come out of the blue. They were prompted by heated debates about installing bomb shelters in public schools. Opponents argued that since such shelters were useless, constructing them would have several unfortunate results: Children who were led to believe the shelters were safe havens would be left with a false sense of security, while children who regarded the shelters as worthless would lose confidence in their leaders. Furthermore, opponents argued, the construction would needlessly raise children's anxieties. Advocates insisted that the children were quite unconcerned, if not unaware, about it all, and therefore none of the arguments was valid. I decided to ask the children how they felt and what they thought about the possibility of war, its likely consequences, and their attitudes toward shelters. I did that in the fall of 1961 and again during the troubled Cuban missile crisis week, when the superpowers came closest to war (Schwebel, 1965). The 1961 study was the first of its kind and was followed by several others in the 1960s, before the period of détente initiated by a series of agreements between the United States and the Soviet Union; a small flood of studies subsequently appeared in the late 1970s and especially in the 1980s. A critical mass of research has emerged on what has been called the mental health implications of life in the nuclear age (Schwebel, 1986). From it one can construct a fairly clear and probably reliable picture of the course of the development of attitudes and reactions over part of the life span, starting with the late preschool years and extending on into adulthood. This conception of the construction of reality in the nuclear age (Schwebel, 1990) seems applicable also to other threats to survival.

The pilot study of about 20 children and youth that preceded the 1961 investigation revealed a pattern of response that was fairly typical thereafter. The questions I posed about the possibility of a war and its consequences aroused little reaction in some children, but strong emotion in many. Fear and anger predominated, with the latter directed at political leaders, "the old men," who the children felt were responsible for our being in a precarious situation that threatened to deny them a future.

Subsequently, I obtained written responses from about 1,900 junior and senior high school students, drawn nonrandomly from diverse socioeconomic groups in three states, to open-ended questions as to whether there would be a war, whether they cared, what would happen if there was, and their thoughts about fallout shelters. Analysis of the responses showed that most of the children anticipated the grim consequences associated with atomic warfare and many, like the pilot study subjects, expressed anger and fear. They were almost equally split in their expectation of war, with only about 6-9% uncertain. Two features of their written comments are especially relevant to our topic: The students (especially the younger ones) were concerned about separation from their families (e.g., "What if it happens when I'm in school?" or "I might come home and there's no home anymore—I'd rather be dead, too"). The youths (especially the teenagers) were concerned that they would have no future and be denied the opportunity for career, love, marriage, and family.

Within a year after my study, Escalona (1965) conducted one with a nonrandom sample of 311 10- to 17-year-olds. In this case, the words *war* and *atomic* were not introduced by the investigator; questions were limited to eliciting the children's fears about and wishes for the future. Nonetheless, the children revealed that concern about the danger of war was very much in their consciousness, with 70% of the sample spontaneously introducing fears about war and hopes for peace.

## A Longitudinal View

With these early studies as a background, we can examine the evolution of thinking about life in the nuclear age. The available data can be said to provide at least a tentative answer to the following question: How do children and adolescents construct reality as it relates to nuclear dangers and governmental safeguards? In the paragraphs below I address that question by reference to a few selected studies (for a more complete review, see Schwebel, 1990). It should be noted that most of the studies reported on below, and most in the so-called nuclear psychology literature, were conducted at times of crisis.

The process of constructing reality brings the child (and, later, the adolescent) into active involvement with an object or concept. The baby examines the rattle, shakes and listens to it, sucks and bites it, squeezes it, hits it against the crib, and throws it. That is how she develops her knowledge about "rattle" or, in other terms, how she constructs the mental reality of that object's physical reality. In a real sense, the same process is involved in constructing an individual's reality of the nuclear age.

### Preschool Years

One published study examined preschoolers. From four day-care centers, Friedman (1984) drew a sample of 92 4-year-olds whose families ranged, socioeconomically, from working-class to upper-class groups. She observed the preschoolers at play both before and after reading to them children's stories that involved conflict. At those two points in time she also obtained their associations to words and pictures, such as that of a collapsed building. Note that at no point did the investigator introduce the terms *war* or *nuclear*. Nevertheless, to the surprise of parents and teachers, 11 of the children referred to nuclear weapons, for the most part as an association to the picture stimuli, and in the cognitively limited form of their age. For example, commenting about his drawing, one child said: "This nuclear sub goes fast underwater—the missile on the bottom of the sub could blow your foot off if it was in the way."

Preschoolers absorb parental and older-sibling anxieties. They may fear something by imitation or by instruction that it is to be feared. Furthermore, they may associate the loud and fiery depiction of a mushroom blast with their generalized fears of life in a world of towering adults over whom they have so little control and who may people their nightmares.

From a mental health point of view we can speculate that preschoolers have not been *directly* affected by threats of nuclear holocaust; indirect effects are a different matter, however.

### 5- to 7-Year-Old Children

Children in this age range reveal an incipient sense of danger and a vague threat to family survival. Although available data are few, the family interviews and observational findings of Greenwald and Zeitlin (1987), involving 12 children aged 5 to 8, are illuminating and consistent with developmental expectations. For example, a 5-year-old, asked about the meaning of the word *nuclear*, said she did not know, whereas her 7-year-old brother said, "The school would be blown up." A 6-year-old said nuclear war meant "people shooting guns and all," and then, with further probing, that "the whole world is dead."

By their responses, these children show their cognitive developmental growth beyond preschoolers. They are struggling with the meaning of nuclear war, just as the baby struggles to make sense of the rattle, and in the process they show confusion between nuclear and nonnuclear war, for even a World War I bomb could cause the school to blow up. Nevertheless, their responses convey a sense of devastation, to their school and the whole world. And the emotional response associated with those destructive thoughts is very disturbing, at least as the 6-year-old quoted above put it, for when he has those fears "they [his parents] could tell me not to think about it . . . or find any easy way for me to get to sleep. . . . I can't think about it when I'm sound asleep." We see, then, that some children in this age group at least vaguely apprehend nuclear dangers and need assistance from their parents or parent substitutes to cope with their fears.

### 7- to 11-Year-Old Children

These children show marked changes over the younger groups in their constructions of reality. They have a greater capacity to understand at the same time as their environment (school, family, television, friends) confronts them with more realities, including those associated with the nuclear age.

More information is available on this age group than on younger ones, although no study has covered the full range of 7-11. From some sources (Escalona, 1965; Greenwald & Zeitlin, 1987; Schwebel & Schwebel, 1981; see also Carey's 1982 retrospective study), two features are evident. First, the children are aware and concerned. For example, an 8-year-old girl says, "I do something to put my mind off of it. . . . I'll go into my room, play with dolls and stuff." An 11-year-old boy who sees no solution says, "I don't want to think about it. I just want to live my life through." Second, their conceptions are still distorted. In 1962, one 10-year-old predicted that atomic war would have the result that "people would be different colors and have long feet and hands." Almost 20 years later, after the Three Mile Island nuclear accident, when asked what would happen if such an accident occurred near their homes, some said such things as "My father will take us in a car and drive fast to keep ahead of the radiation. Otherwise, the radiation would touch us and we would grow 10 feet tall."

This age group may be the most vulnerable. The children appreciate the dangers, probably even exaggerated versions of them, yet seem to have insufficient opportunities (at home and in school) to express and explore them. As a result, they are deprived of countervailing information, that is, information about what adults and even teenagers are doing to prevent catastrophes and to protect them. They are, themselves, in the process of developing their physical and mental capacities but not nearly enough to possess the kind of mastery characteristic of the older adolescent and young adult. And so if they worry secretly about the death of their parent(s) and their being left all alone, they must bear the weight of it without help.

### Age 12 and the Teens

Most of the psychological research, starting with the studies of the early 1960s referred to earlier (Escalona, 1965; Schwebel, 1965), covers the age range of 12 through the teen years. The following review of the recent studies (adapted from Schwebel, 1990) bears on issues relevant to the topic of this chapter.

Results of studies conducted in the 1980s, including those of Beardslee and Mack (1982), Solantaus, Rimpela, and Taipale (1984), Goldberg et al. (1985), Goldenring and Doctor (1986), Bachman, Johnston, and O'Malley (1989), and Chivian, Robinson, Tudge, Popov, and Andreyenkov (1988) (two of which— Solantaus et al. and Bachman et al.—used random or representative national samples), seem very much like extensions of the earlier ones. Teenagers, including inpatient and outpatient teenagers in psychiatric hospitals (Lowenthal, 1987), know and react in diverse ways. In the mid-1980s, about a quarter or more saw their future plans affected by the uncertainties. About a third were very concerned, another third somewhat concerned, and a third not at all. Yet between the early 1960s and the mid-1980s a change occurred. In 1961, 52% of the teenagers were unequivocal in saying there would be no war (Schwebel, 1965). In 1984, only about 14% of high school seniors were firm in their response that there would be no "world upheaval" in the next 10 years (Diamond & Bachman, 1986).

The recent studies, like the earlier ones, show that teenagers worry about the danger of nuclear war, and do so more than adults. Within this short age span of about eight years an important trend is detectable. The younger the subjects, the greater the proportion who worry often or a great deal, so that children and young teenagers worry more than mid-teenagers, and the latter worry more than older teenagers and young adults. There are at least three possible explanations for this change, the first two of which are self-evident. First, between the pre-teens and young adulthood, individuals acquire considerably greater sense of mastery in the physical, social, and psychological domains of behavior (which enables some of them to act on behalf of reducing the nuclear war threat, perhaps as members of organizations, in school, college, or elsewhere). Second, in this period individuals enter a stage of life involving greater personal responsibility and requiring them to direct much of their attention to jobs, postsecondary studies, or parenthood. Third, hypothetically they became more habituated to living with persistent danger, and the risk of war became less salient. This may happen because of the conscious realization that their worries and sleepless nights are all for naught, or it may result from recognition that while replete with crises, the nuclear age has been free of an exchange of nuclear weapons.

Further study may show that how young people fare and how salient the threat of war remains for them as they enter adulthood are related to several variables: social class (the condition of the job market will have more salience for a non-college-bound youth), age at times of heightened international tension (a 9-year-old is more vulnerable than a 4-year-old), physical and psychological status (an illness may heighten a child's feelings of helplessness), and familial experience (family stability and support for the child may decrease anxiety). All in all, whatever the reasons for the changes during the teen years and whether young people worry more or less, like their elders they are painfully aware of the probability of extinction should a nuclear war occur (Schwebel, 1990, pp. 521-552).

The fear and anxiety expressed by teenagers during heightened international tension do not add up to pathology. It is true that the small percentage of Finnish teenagers, especially females, who report frequent nightmares and conscious thinking about nuclear war (Solantaus et al., 1984) and the American high school seniors who show evidence of despair rather than worry or concern (Diamond & Bachman, 1986) are presenting symptoms suggestive of pathology. However, there is no evidence in the respective studies that nuclear war threats were responsible for these psychological experiences; in fact, Diamond and Bachman present some evidence to the contrary.

Rather than suffering from pathology, teenagers are trying to come to grips with the brutal realities of the nuclear age. During the 12 to 20 age span, as they become fully able to construct a mental reality consistent with the physical and social realities of the environment, they have the potential to be their own mediators. They have the capacity to appraise changing conditions, make a balanced assessment of both dangers and safeguards, and determine what position and action they will take. But they need help. During this span of about eight years, and all the more so at the younger end of it, as they are groping to establish their own identities and clarify their own values, they need some things that the adult world is not often prepared to provide them, namely, emotional support, objective information, and encouragement to be independent in their thinking.

## Implications of the Studies

From the point of view of prevention, the implications of the literature on the effects of nuclear war can be summarized as follows:

- A potentially traumatic event is not in itself stressful to preschool children, because they are incapable of perceiving the dangers entailed in it. They are stressed, if at all, by the reactions of their caregivers. Since those reactions are usually unavoidable and, therefore, an inevitable feature of the children's environment, it is important that caregivers provide the children with explanations appropriate to the children's level of cognitive development and with comfort and support.

- Children aged 5 to 7 have a growing awareness of what is objectively dangerous, at least a glimmer of it, as a result of their greater exposure to sources of information and their substantially increased capacity to recognize dangers in the environment. However, since the children are still very much subject to the possibility of gross distortion of objective reality—as received from their peers or stemming from their own developmental problems—teachers and parents need to be alert to implications of fear or anxiety and to be prepared to intervene.

- Children aged 7 to 11 are vulnerable because they know so much, yet a great deal of their knowledge may be deformed and incomplete. For instance, their knowledge of danger may not be counterbalanced by information concerning action to prevent war—that is, action to protect them. They need to be encouraged to talk about fears, as well as hopes and wishes, so proper correctives, as well as emotional support, can be provided if needed.

- Young teenagers know and understand more than younger children, but are lacking in the greater independence, skills, and emotional resources that enable older teenagers to do anything about it. Younger teens' fear, frustrations, and anger lead not only to suppression of their frightening thoughts, which can be a constructive defense mechanism under the circumstances, but also contribute to a tendency to avoid troubling problems. Consequently, it is better for youths to have opportunities to express their thoughts and feelings and be involved in discussion, if not action, the purpose of which is direct coping with the problem.

Not surprisingly, to varying degrees all children and teenagers require the security of knowing that they will not be left alone in the world, that someone will be there to love and care for them no matter what the future holds. They also need a belief in the future: that they will survive and have the chance to enjoy the satisfactions and pleasures of adult life. These objectives can be realized by youths' acquiring the practice of recognizing the dual aspects of a threatening reality, both the forces leading to danger and the countervailing ones. The latter consists primarily of preventive actions. In other words, and of course with variations according to age, an overarching implication of the literature on reactions to nuclear threat is that young people can be given opportunities to develop both cognitive competencies and affective reactions that enable them to cope with potentially frightening realities.

**Generalizability of Implications**

The 40 or so years of the nuclear age have been unique in several respects. World War III was a possibility at various points, but, unlike World Wars I and II, it was averted. Never before were the lives of so many people at stake, and never was the survival of life on the planet itself seemingly threatened. Despite the uniqueness of that period, the lessons learned about human reactions are probably useful in connection with countless other problems that arouse fear and even terror in children. Below, the wider applicability of those lessons is examined.

To assess the generalizability of the implications derived from studies about reactions to nuclear threat, one can start by abstracting major stress-reducing cognitions. These are the thoughts that were implicit in the reactions of children and teenagers who feared, more or less, the possibility of nuclear war:

(1) The dreaded event could occur.
(2) I will be separated from parents and family, by death or otherwise, and will be left alone, unloved, and uncared for.
(3) My way of life will be ended and I will have no future.
(4) I am powerless—there is nothing I can do about it.

Underlying all four cognitions is the child's *future orientation*. Children (and adults, for that matter) are fearful that the dreaded event will happen tomorrow, next week, or in a year—sometime in the immediate or distant future—and worry about the consequences of the event. They must cope *now* with something that has not yet occurred and may never occur (e.g., World War III), or that has already taken place and could be repeated (e.g., nuclear attack).

With that future orientation in mind it seems reasonable to consider that the implications of the nuclear war literature may be applicable to concern about earthquakes, tornadoes, hurricanes, and flooding in geographical areas where these events are predictable occurrences. The implications may also be generalizable to the all-too-many regions in the world where war, violence, and terrorism are part of life, the result of which is that children and their families may at any time become embroiled in conflict, usually as victims. The generalizations may apply, as well, to the ecological problems that are quickly becoming high priorities on the agendas of international and national organizations and that, very likely, as may be extrapolated from experience with children's reactions to nuclear fears in the early 1960s, are already arousing concern among children.

## Studies of Other Potentially Stressful Experiences

### Conventional War

It is commonly known that the death toll in World War II was about 50 million. It is not so well known that since that war about 20-25 million people have been killed and three times as many maimed or injured in armed conflict, most of it in the developing nations of Africa, Asia, Latin America, and the Middle East. The number of refugees (of both external and internal displacement) is estimated at 25 million. Most of the refugees as well as most of the dead and injured have been women and children (Grant, 1987).

The war literature reveals, obliquely at least, that the four cognitions listed above apply here as well. In the long subsection below on family and community cohesiveness, you will note that the children report fear that an attack will occur, their families will be split apart, and their way of life disrupted. The subsection below on active coping shows, besides the cognition of helplessness, the possibility of contending with those feelings through active involvement in struggle.

*Family and community cohesiveness.* Until recently, despite major conflicts in at least nine nations in Africa, no studies had reported on the impact of war on children on that continent, although research on children and war in Europe, Asia, and the Middle East had been reported (Kahnert, Pitt, & Taipale, 1983). Recently, published studies by a team of Ugandan and Norwegian scientists broke that silence and gave a sense of the children's experiences in recent years, after the brutal dictatorship of Idi Amin in the 1970s, his overthrow in 1979, soon followed by the violent government under Milton Obote, and his overthrow in 1985 by a new regime that in turn was toppled in 1986. Data for this study were gathered in 1985 (Raundalen, Lwanga, Mugisha, & Dyregrov, 1987).

The research includes four studies. I present here an examination of information from an evaluation of essays written by 450 schoolchildren of Kampala on war and violence and events that made them happy or sad. Grief and depression, stemming from the deaths of relatives or other significant persons, were the outstanding features in the essays. The kind of brutality these children experienced, observed, or learned about, as illustrated by the following excerpts from the essay of a "young girl" during the "1979 Liberation War," explains the intensity of the children's reactions. Her statement begins with the fact that when her family was about to bury her father, who had been killed, they were chased out of the village:

> My sister was lost in the war and my two brothers—we do not know their whereabouts now. My mother has checked everywhere, in the village where my grandmother stays and they are not there. When I think of my father I start crying; there is no peace, in Uganda. . . . After that we heard that my grandfather had died; a soldier shot him. I was afraid and we cried. We fear to go to the village because we hear it is dangerous these days. When I think of these problems, I feel very bad. (Raundalen et al., 1987, p. 89)

Six years later, at the time of the 1985 overthrow of the Obote government, the following occurred in the life of a 15-year-old boy who lived near Kampala:

> As soon as my mother turned her back on the soldier to get money from the house [so the soldier would free an innocent girl who had run into their compound], the soldier opened fire on her—a full magazine. We all fell down in the house. We cried, shouted, and the friend of our mother . . . came to our rescue. With that lady we took the body into the house and put it in a piece of cloth. We spent the whole night with it. (Raundalen et al., 1987, p. 91)

The investigators note that the essays refer very often to efforts to keep the family together. The children wrote of close bonds with their parents and the happiness generated by family life, but also that separation—caused by jailing, injury, and death—was much a part of their lives. The family, as the children saw it, was not powerful enough to give them assurance that they would be protected and cared for.

Under the circumstances, it was fortunate that the children found security outside their immediate families. In their essays they describe school as a haven and, as one subject reports, "an island of peace." One reason is that soldiers went to the homes, not to schools, to take a father or older brother or to pillage. Another reason is that the preoccupations of school activities protected them, at least for a few hours, from frightening thoughts about death of a parent and family dissolution. The children associated security most particularly with their grandparents' villages. When war broke out and shooting began (e.g., in 1979 or 1985), they fled from their town and ran to the nearest relative, usually a grandparent. There they felt safe and happy, at least until shooting began in the grandparents' villages, when they felt, as one of them said, that they had lost "the last shelter in Uganda" (Raundalen et al., 1987, p. 90).

The children and teenagers in the study experienced both war and the prospect of future war. They found some comfort and security in their immediate and extended families and in school. The finding of the importance of relatives and school, while not surprising, highlights the importance of an available and clearly designated support system in helping children cope with the terrifying fantasy of being left all alone, uncared for, and unloved.

Research in Israel involving Palestinian and Israeli children again highlights the crucial role of family and community. For example, Punamaki (1982) found that Palestinian and Israeli boys and girls were more fearful about their families' safety than about their own, a finding similar to frequent comments by young Americans in written statements made in 1961 about the possible effects of an atomic war (Schwebel, 1965). Punamaki's findings are also reminiscent of those of Freud and Burlingham (1943) during the World War II bombing of London, that young children who remained in London with a parent fared better psychologically than those who were safely housed with strangers in the countryside. Another Middle Eastern study compared anxiety level (as measured by the Children's Manifest Anxiety Scale) of Israeli children in shelled and nonshelled kibbutzim and found no difference (Ziv & Israeli, 1973). This finding has been attributed variously to the possibility that the children had become habituated to shelling, making it less of a threat, that it was the result of general efforts made to reduce anxiety, and finally that the institution of the kibbutz itself, by its very nature, provides the security that minimizes stress. This last, persuasive, argument is consistent with Milgram's (1982) proposal that children's reactions to war and disaster are influenced by the cohesiveness of their communities.

*Future outlook.* Considering that the Ugandan subjects, aged 13-15 years in 1985, had experienced warfare at least twice (1979 and 1985) and, in the intervening years, had known or suffered from actions that might have led to the jailing or death of relatives and friends, the tendency of many to write about the future in positive ways—about peace, justice, education, and jobs—may seem puzzling. There is no way of knowing from the reported data whether the subjects who were positive were different from others in intensity of anxiety and grief, or even in personal experience of loss. Such a positive outlook about the future is a constructive approach to coping with the immediate situation. It also represents the kind of balanced appraisal that seemed to be useful in coping with anxiety about nuclear war dangers. With such balance, one thinks: Horrible as life is now, look ahead to something positive. That is the cognitive message to convey in order to cultivate a habit of thought during troubling times. Another way to balance the negatives is by counterposing them with positives, as some of the Ugandan children did, at least momentarily, after each government was overthrown, and especially by taking a long-term view.

The Ugandan situation called for opportunities for children to release long pent-up feelings. In all probability the essay study provided a useful outlet, although presumably one not as effective as face-to-face interaction. In Uganda and other settings where warfare touches children sporadically, from the child's perspective danger is in the future—tonight, tomorrow, or next month. Children need the opportunity for expression, the assurance that they will not be left alone, and a balanced view of future positives and negatives.

*Active coping.* Intuitively, we expect that active coping is associated positively with mental health. In her study of Palestinian children in 1982 and 1985, Punamaki's (1988) findings were consistent with that expectation. Exposure to increased political hardships, violence, and perceived humiliation raised the level of active coping. That kind of response and adaptation is most likely to occur under conditions of community cohesiveness. Active coping was also found among Holocaust survivors who employed that mode more than a comparison group (Shanan & Shahar, 1983). These active coping modes were of both the overt behavioral and cognitive emotional types. The latter (cognitive coping) was initiated when the situation could not be modified and the best one could do was change one's perception of it and/or the affect associated with it. Although chance factors cannot be excluded, presumably survival depends to a considerable extent upon the survivor's ability to make realistic appraisals and to act on them. Concentration camp survivors' reports give dramatic evidence of the importance of both chance and rational coping strategies (Boehm, 1949/1985; Crome, 1989).

While it is painful to think in these terms, the fact is that we must seek ways to minimize the effects of long-term hostilities on children, such as those in Northern Ireland, the Middle East, Cambodia, and Central America. Studying 200 children's awareness of the connection between violence and death in Northern Ireland, McWhirter, Young, and Majury (1983) found that these 4- to 16-year-olds were not preoccupied with violent death. It appeared that they had become habituated during the more than 10 years of violence and that now, as the authors put it, the abnormal had become normal for the children. Documentary films of life in Belfast suggest that life does go on in a "normally abnormal" fashion: Children go to school, come home to their families (or substitute families, if they are orphaned), play, do their homework, and through it all feel the security provided by membership in a relatively cohesive community (whether Catholic or Protestant). In fact, life goes on so normally that children portray family conflict as more violent than community conflict (McWhirter, 1983). The normality may be explained by the fact that the children's lives are composed of the ingredients that the children in the nuclear studies feared they would lose: family, friends, school, play, and the continuation of life in what is now its normal way. These children have one other advantage. Unlike the children in Uganda, the Irish children benefit from the strength and cohesiveness of their communities; and the active resistance, in which they themselves play a part, probably counteracts potential feelings of powerlessness.

In brief, the literature on children's reactions to war and the threat of future war shows consistencies with the nuclear literature. Separation, aloneness, powerlessness, futurelessness, and loss of the regular way of life seem to be the major worries or mental terrors. The implications for intervention and prevention that were derived from the studies on reactions to nuclear cold war seem applicable to children in hot-war situations as well.

**Natural Disasters**

In one of the classic works on disaster, Baker and Chapman (1962) define three stages in the total disaster experience: anticipation, impact, and postimpact periods. According to Lazarus (1966), each stage calls for a different form of appraisal and of coping. Lazarus and Folkman (1984) suggest that in the *anticipatory* period people ask themselves questions such as whether and when the event (war, nuclear accident, tornado, divorce) will occur, what it will be like, whether it can be prevented and the feared consequences minimized, how they will manage it when it comes, and can they endure it. Answers to those questions will, of course, largely determine the nature of individuals' reactions as well as their choices of coping mechanisms. The latter include such tactics as avoiding thoughts about the threat and seeking information to improve coping. One general course of action is to modify the environment, if that is possible. Otherwise, one must rely on strategies to modify and regulate one's emotional reactions. The same processes of appraisal and choice of coping methods, though of different sorts, also characterize the impact and postimpact stages.

With a disaster experience now a matter of history, people have the future to contend with. What about the next one? What possibilities now exist to modify the situation and thereby avoid or reduce the consequences of the next threat? And if not that, how might it be possible to improve the regulation of one's emotions? While the disaster literature is extensive, particularly useful is research that includes a comparison group in its sampling. A study conducted by Dollinger, O'Donnell, and Staley (1984) on the effects of a lightning strike on children's fears is helpful. Children ages 10 to 13 were playing soccer when a lightning strike knocked down all the players and most of the children and adults on the sidelines. One boy never regained consciousness and died within a week, and two others were hospitalized for longer periods. The researchers selected control children from the same area in Illinois to be matched with the 29 in the lightning group, and all the children and one parent of each (mostly mothers) completed a fear survey form and were interviewed within a month or two after the disaster. As expected, the child-reported fears showed more than just a conditioning effect to storm-related fears. The lightning subjects showed a generalized fear to such other variables as sleep, noise, bodily penetration, death, and enclosed spaces. Furthermore, the correlation of the interviewer's ratings of lightning subjects' emotional upset and the children's fears of separation from parents was statistically significant at the .01 level.

After this natural disaster, the survivors' fears were evident behaviorally, too, as when during a storm one child put on a football helmet and ran down to the cellar, or another got into bed with parents. Fortunately, at least in the aftermath of this disaster, parents and professionals could confidently reassure the children that "lightning doesn't strike twice," or offer some statement about probabilities. Even such reassurances, as we know, do not quickly eradicate conditioned and generalized fears. By contrast, in disaster-prone areas or war-ravaged nations, or during long stretches of nuclear war crisis or in some future ecological crisis, that kind of reassurance cannot be offered because earthquakes, wars, and crises do recur.

Nevertheless, even for those living near active volcanoes or in war-prone regions, psychological as well as physical safeguards can be taken to reduce stress. As noted below, these safeguards can probably provide children with effective coping cognitions to deal with fearful realities.

## Psychoimmunization Against Trauma

From a biological perspective, the immune system protects the organism from foreign substances such as bacteria and viruses. The physiological process that brings this about is well understood. By comparison, the complex relationship between the psychological experience of stress and the biological processes involved in safeguarding the organism is not well understood. Nevertheless, there is considerable evidence demonstrating a relationship between stress and the immune function (Stein & Schleifer, 1985).

The concept of psychoimmunization is valuable shorthand for conveying the idea that psychological prevention is just as feasible as biological prevention. Its major shortcoming is the implication that a specialist, such as a psychologist, can use the equivalent of the medical doctor's injection needle and give a psychological inoculation to a recipient. This implies a passive state that is not at all necessary and usually is undesirable in any effective educational and therapeutic process.

It would be naive to suggest that psychoimmunization would enable children to endure war, disasters, parental unemployment (McLoyd, 1989), marital transitions (Hetherington, Hagan, & Anderson, 1989), and so on unscathed. However, the literature in this recently developed field does suggest the possibility of reducing negative effects and, in any event, of avoiding traumatic consequences.

For example, Meichenbaum's (1977) coping skill training procedures—calling for educational, rehearsal, and application phases—have been used to immunize individuals, in this case against learned helplessness. In an experiment involving undergraduates, the experimental subjects were given stress inoculation—coping skills training—after which they and control subjects were presented with the experimental problems. The inoculated students performed at a significantly higher level, presumably owing to the protection the skills afforded them against learned helplessness and some of the effects of stress (Altmaier & Happ, 1985). In another study, speech-anxious students were inoculated by providing them with experiences that raised their feelings of success. In the posttest situation they showed confidence levels superior to those of the nonanxious controls (Altmaier, Leary, Halpern, & Sellers, 1985).

### Stress-Reducing Programs

For our purposes, as we consider how to psychoimmunize children to enable them to cope more effectively with future trauma-producing events, it is helpful to return to the four major stress-producing cognitions presented above:

(1) The dreaded event could occur.
(2) I will be separated from parents and family, by death or otherwise, and will be left alone, unloved, and uncared for.
(3) My way of life will be ended and I will have no future.
(4) I am powerless—there is nothing I can do about it.

An effective program would help children transform these negative cognitions into positives—without, however, engaging in Pollyannaish fantasies. Of course, we would expect affective components to change along with the cognitive. The following list is illustrative of goals we might seek (these would vary, of course, according to the age of the child or teenager):

(1) The dreaded event might not occur, and if it does, the event will not be as bad as you imagine. We will see to it that we come through it safely. Efforts by us (your family) and by your community are under way to prevent it (e.g., ecological disaster) or to be prepared for it (e.g., flood).
(2) Here are all the steps taken to protect you from separation and to assure you that you will be loved and cared for.
(3) You do have a future, and chances are that your way of life will be pretty much the same, except insofar as there are inevitable changes both in our lives and in the world around us.
(4) You are not powerless. There are particular actions you can take, either as a member of a group (e.g., your family or your class) or by yourself, including

changing your outlook and, when appropriate, putting the frightening thought out of your mind.

Some stress theories and training procedures can be useful in modifying cognitions and feelings. Experience in applying guidelines in inoculating children by calling on concepts such as Meichenbaum's (1977) coping skill training procedures (educational, rehearsal, and application phases) and Lazarus's (1966) stage approach (anticipation, impact, and postimpact) suggests the following: First, as we would expect, different age groups require distinctly different emphases. Younger children need much more support in connection with the first cognition (the dreaded event could occur) and reassurance about the second (separation from family), whereas teenagers need reassurance about the third cognition (lack of a future) and encouragement about the fourth (powerlessness). Second, in inoculating children, content and affect vary with the nature of the dreaded event. In the case of a natural disaster, the dreaded future event is not instigated by a hateful enemy or perceived as the result of action (or inaction) by incompetent leaders. Furthermore, as in the case of earthquakes, floods, and tornadoes, once the disaster has passed (including aftershocks) there is respite for a while. By contrast, children in Northern Ireland, Cambodia, Central America, and the Middle East cannot count on a sustained break from danger.

Children probably learn to cope with the serious difficulties in life, including parental unemployment, divorce, and death, as they do with less significant events. For them to take control of their reactions and regulate their own behavior, one necessary step involves their acquisition of the metacognitive skills that enable them to monitor their thoughts and feelings about dreaded events. Another related step is when through "social learning" they model their reactions and behavior after those of another person, usually a parent or teacher. Consequently, the success of a psychoimmunization program depends upon parents and teachers themselves being prepared to confront future events in constructive ways. They can do that by scrutinizing their attitudes, conceptions, and habits of thought in reference to those events. Living in an earthquake-prone environment, they may find that they cope by denying that an earthquake could happen or that it could possibly affect them if it did occur. Or perhaps they cope by consciously putting threatening events out of their minds, even on those occasions when their children inquire about the danger. On the other hand, the adults may be so preoccupied with danger that they give themselves and their children no peace of mind.

A program designed for parents and teachers should seek to make them sufficiently secure that they can help children cope constructively with the four cognitions. Parents can be prepared to encourage their children to look realistically at the possibility that the dreaded event might occur and at effective ways of confronting it when it occurs, especially at the measures taken to safeguard the children, assuring them of being with adults who would love and care for them, and reassuring them about the future.

Of course, in some situations such flat reassurance cannot be offered. Ronstrom (1989), a Swedish children's ombudsman who has worked with Afghan refugee children in Pakistan and has been an observer in Central America, distinguishes between the European experience of war and that of Central America, where there is a blurring of the distinctions between civilians and combatants, enemies and friends. Many surviving children have been witness to mutilation, torture, massacres, and the disappearance of family members. Ronstrom claims that the psychological effects of these "irregular wars" are different from those of conventional wars. Her "therapeutic considerations" are useful; for purposes of this discussion it is noteworthy that she characterizes the family as being "absolutely basic" (p. 152) and stresses the importance of strengthening it in the interest of the children. In related fashion she proposes mobilizing the resources of the community in the interest of continuity for the children. The children would also be helped directly, through therapy groups in which they would have opportunities to release and share their anxieties, perhaps through play, drawing, and drama.

Bearing in mind age variations, programs for children should provide them ample and frequent opportunity to express their fears and anxieties and their hopes and wishes, preferably within a group of peers, with at least one secure adult present. There is no better way to know what correctives are necessary than by hearing children voice their concerns and hopes directly, as Greenwald and Zeitlin (1987) did in studying nuclear fears. The content of a program, whether an informal one at home or a formal one in school, should grow from the needs and age of the child. Moreover, consideration of "the future" may require special attention, since Hesse's (1986) review of nuclear fears and other available evidence in the mid-1980s suggests that many young people feel hopeless about the future.

Whatever the target area, inoculations are procedures to strengthen children through education and rehearsal in preparation for all the stages: anticipatory, impact, and postimpact. The program prepares them, through sensitive caring, education, and rehearsal, to deal now with the problems of anticipating a dreaded future, coping with that event when it occurs, and looking beyond it, to a future free of that dread. Most programs reported in the literature on traumatic events are introduced after the events have occurred and are intended to minimize the destructive consequences. Releasing pent-up emotion gets high priority, with verbal communication recommended for older children and teenagers and the use of play and art for younger children (Terr, 1983). Working with parents is also an agenda priority, because their own emotional state may lead them to give inadequate and confusing responses that only aggravate the situation for the children (Elizur & Kaffman, 1982). Experience on the Caribbean island of Montserrat in the aftermath of the destructive hurricane Hugo in 1989 highlights psychological needs in hurricane-prone areas. According to Carol Tuitt (personal communication, 1990), the only psychologist on the island, a majority of the adults were worried about another catastrophe as the 1990 hurricane season approached in June. The most worried were "single parents, persons with elderly relatives in their homes and those with very young children." Another variable related to level of concern was how safe the individuals felt during Hugo. Those who expected to perish were more likely to be among the subsequent worriers. Tuitt estimates that about 60% of the children and 35% of the teenagers were worried about the future hurricane. She reports that the disaster preparedness committee was about to launch a campaign to protect lives and to maintain psychological well-being. Besides that, she had plans to resume the kinds of group sessions with teachers that she had instituted immediately after Hugo. The groups' purpose was to enable teachers to encourage children's exploration of feelings through such means as discussion and poetry.

While lessons learned from experience with programs in war and disaster areas are useful, they do not speak directly to the nature of programs designed to inoculate children against future stress. Several efforts in Israel with this latter focus have led to new approaches. Children are provided with generic techniques to enable them to function effectively under stress. They learn to trust themselves so that they can tolerate conditions that are stress provoking and can develop new approaches when old ones no longer work (Ayalon 1983; Klingman, 1978). Lazarus and Folkman (1984) indicate that one can actively engage stress-producing conditions, first by seeking to modify the stressor or, if that is impossible, by modifying one's reaction to it, perhaps through some distraction. The Israeli program (Klingman, 1978), which was also used in a study of Lebanese children (Day & Sadek, 1982), emphasized such an active approach. Clearly, the aims of such programs are to counter feelings of powerlessness and to allow children to develop cognitions that include a future.

The four cognitions seem to be useful guides in parenting and teaching in general, and not just in anticipation of natural and social disasters. Partly, they are useful because most families endure at least one life event that is potentially traumatic to children, including such obvious ones as parental joblessness, divorce, and death. Partly, too, the four cognitions are useful because they provide a sound mental health basis for development and education in general. Children (and adults) should not go through life primed for some inevitable catastrophe. They should feel assured that their families and their communities care about them, and that regardless of what happens, they will be loved and cared for. They should be given every opportunity to develop a sense of competence and mastery over their environment and over themselves, including their thoughts, emotions, and impulses. They should feel confident that they will have a future.

Of course, having these cognitions serve as guides in homes and schools is not an easily achieved objective. Interventions aimed at psychoimmunizing children against stress in this dangerous world require the understanding, support, and direct involvement of parents and educators. Parents must themselves possess positive outlooks and be aware of their children's need for them. Schools must give high priority to the cultivation of feelings of personal mastery.

Some individuals will object to the introduction of anxiety-provoking topics, as they did in connection with the threat of nuclear war (Adelson & Finn, 1985), because of the possible effects on children. The hard reality is that children are not unaware of these topics (Klineberg, 1986; Schwebel, 1990), and it is generally in the children's interest to examine them in the presence of someone who can help them correct gross inaccuracies and provide support and reassurance. In connection with nuclear issues, several authors have provided helpful advice to parents (Greenwald & Zeitlin, 1987; Wetzel & Winawer, 1986).

The four major cognitions that I have proposed as a guide in developing programs and the few illustrative programs themselves are only a beginning. In a world that demonstrates in so many ways that it does not greatly value children, such beginnings are to be cherished.

## References

Adelson, J., & Finn, C. E. (1985). Terrorizing children. *Commentary, 79,* 29-36.

Altmaier, E. M., & Happ, D. A. (1985). Coping skills training's immunization effects against learned helplessness. *Journal of Social and Clinical Psychology, 3,* 181-189.

Altmaier, E. M., Leary, M. R., Halpern, S., & Sellers, J. E. (1985). Effects of stress inoculation and participant modeling on confidence and anxiety: Testing predictions of self-efficacy theory. *Journal of Social and Clinical Psychology, 3,* 500-505.

Ayalon, O. (1983). Teaching children strategies for coping with stress. *Bereavement Care, 2,* 2-3.

Bachman, J. G., Johnston, L. D., & O'Malley, P. M. (1989). *Monitoring the future, 1988.* Ann Arbor: University of Michigan, Institute for Social Research, Survey Research Center.

Baker, G. W., & Chapman, D. W. (1962). *Man and society in disaster.* New York: Basic Books.

Beardslee, W., & Mack, J. E. (1982). The impact on children and adolescents of nuclear development. In R. Rogers (Ed.), *Psychosocial aspects of nuclear developments* (Task Force Report No. 20) (pp. 64-93). Washington, DC: American Psychiatric Association.

Boehm, E. H. (1985). *We survived.* Santa Barbara: ABC-Clio. (Original work published 1949)

Carey, M. (1982). Psychological fallout. *Bulletin of Atomic Scientists, 38,* 20-24.

Chivian, E. P., Robinson, J. P., Tudge, J. R. J., Popov, N. P., & Andreyenkov, V. G. (1988). American and Soviet teenagers' concerns about nuclear war and the future. *New England Journal of Medicine, 319,* 407-413.

Crome, L. (1989). *Unbroken: Resistance and survival in the concentration camps.* New York: Schocken.

Day, R. C., & Sadek, S. N. (1982). The effect of Benson's relaxation response on the anxiety levels of Lebanese children under stress. *Journal of Experimental Child Psychology, 34,* 350-356.

Diamond, G., & Bachman, J. (1986). High-school seniors and the nuclear threat, 1975-1984: Political and mental health implications of concern and despair. In M. Schwebel (Ed.),

*Mental health implications of life in the nuclear age* (pp. 210-241). Armonk, NY: M. E. Sharpe.

Dollinger, S. J., O'Donnell, J. P., & Staley, A. A. (1984). Lightning-strike disaster: Effects on children's fears and worries. *Journal of Consulting and Clinical Psychology, 52*, 1026-1038.

Durning, A. (1990). Life on the brink. *World Watch, 3*(2), 22-30.

Elizur, E., & Kaffman, M. (1982). Children's bereavement reactions following death of the father: II. *Journal of the American Academy of Child Psychiatry, 21*, 474-480.

Escalona, S. K. (1965). Children and the threat of nuclear war. In M. Schwebel (Ed.), *Behavioral science and human survival* (pp. 201-209). Palo Alto, CA: Science and Behavior Books.

Freud, A., & Burlingham, D. (1943). *War and children.* New York: New York Medical Books.

Friedman, B. (1984). Preschoolers' awareness of nuclear threat. *Newsletter of the California Association for the Education of Young Children, 12*, 4-5.

Goldberg, S., LaCombe, S., Levinson, D., Parker, K. R., Ross, C., & Sommers, F. (1985). Thinking about the threat of nuclear war: Relevance to mental health. *American Journal of Orthopsychiatry, 55*, 503-512.

Goldenring, J. M., & Doctor, R. (1986). Teen-age worry about nuclear war: North American and European questionnaire studies. In M. Schwebel (Ed.), *Mental health implications of life in the nuclear age* (pp. 72-92). Armonk, NY: M. E. Sharpe.

Grant, J. P. (1987). Foreword. In C. P. Dodge & M. Raundalen (Eds.), *War, violence, and children in Uganda* (pp. ix-xvi). Oslo: Norwegian University Press.

Greenwald, D. S., & Zeitlin, S. J. (1987). *No reason to talk about it.* New York: W. W. Norton.

Hesse, P. (1986). Children's and adolescents' fears of nuclear war: Is our sense of the future disappearing? In M. Schwebel (Ed.), *Mental health implications of life in the nuclear age* (pp. 93-113). Armonk, NY: M. E. Sharpe.

Hetherington, E. M., Hagan, M. S., & Anderson, E. R. (1989). Marital transitions: A child's perspective. *American Psychologist, 44*, 303-312.

Kahnert, M., Pitt, D., & Taipale, I. (Eds.). (1983). *Children and war.* Geneva: Geneva International Peace Research Institute.

Klineberg, 0. (1986). Children and nuclear war: A methodological note. In M. Schwebel (Ed.), *Mental health implications of life in the nuclear age* (pp. 253-260). Armonk, NY: M. E. Sharpe.

Klingman, A. (1978). Children in stress: Anticipatory guidance in the framework of the educational system. *Personnel and Guidance Journal, 57*, 22-26.

Lazarus, R. S. (1966). *Psychological stress and the coping process.* New York: McGraw-Hill.

Lazarus, R. S., & Folkman, S. (1984). *Stress, appraisal, and coping.* New York: Springer.

Lowenthal, M. (1987). *Emotionally disturbed adolescents' reactions to the nuclear threat.* Unpublished doctoral dissertation, Rutgers University.

McLoyd, V. (1989). Socialization and development in a changing economy: The effects of paternal job and income loss on children. *American Psychologist, 44*, 293-302.

McWhirter, L. (1983). The Northern Ireland conflict: Adjusting to continuing violence. In M. Kahnert, D. Pitt, & I. Taipale (Eds.), *Children and war* (pp. 129-142). Geneva: Geneva International Peace Research Institute.

McWhirter, L., Young, V., & Majury, J. (1983). Belfast children's awareness of violent death. *British Journal of Social Psychology, 22*, 81-92.

Meichenbaum, D. (1977). *Cognitive-behavior modification: An integrative approach.* New York: Plenum.

Milgram, N. A. (1982). War related stress in Israeli children and youth. In C. D. Spielberger, I. G. Sarason, & N. A. Milgram (Eds.), *Stress and anxiety* (Vol. 8, pp. 656-676). Washington, DC: Hemisphere.

Punamaki, R. L. (1982). Childhood in the shadow of war: A psychological study on attitudes and emotional life of Israeli and Palestinian children. *Current Research on Peace and Violence, 5,* 26-41.

Punamaki, R. L. (1988). Historical-political and individualistic determinants of coping modes and fears among Palestinian children. *International Journal of Psychology, 23,* 721-739.

Raundalen, M., Lwanga, J., Mugisha, C., & Dyregrov A. (1987). Four investigations on stress among children in Uganda. In C. P. Dodge & M. Raundalen (Eds.), *War, violence, and children in Uganda* (pp. 83-108). Oslo: Norwegian University Press.

Ronstrom, A. (1989). Children in Central America: Victims of war. *Child Welfare, 68,* 145-153.

Schwebel, M. (1965). Nuclear cold war: Student opinions and professional responsibility. In M. Schwebel (Ed.), *Behavioral science and human survival* (pp. 210-224). Palo Alto, CA: Science and Behavior Books.

Schwebel, M. (1986). The study of stress and coping in the nuclear age: A new specialty. In M. Schwebel (Ed.), *Mental health implications of life in the nuclear age* (pp. 5-15). Armonk, NY: M. E. Sharpe.

Schwebel, M. (1990). Construction of reality in the nuclear age. *Political Psychology, 11,* 521-552.

Schwebel, M., & Schwebel, B. (1981). Children's reactions to the threat of nuclear plant accidents. *American Journal of Orthopsychiatry, 51,* 260-270.

Shanan, J., & Shahar, O. (1983). Cognitive and personality functioning of Jewish Holocaust survivors during the midlife transition (46-65) in Israel. *Archives of Psychology, 135,* 275-294.

Solantaus, T., Rimpela, M., & Taipale, V. (1984). The threat of war in the minds of 12-18-year-olds in Finland. *Lancet, 8380*(1), 784-785.

Stein, M., & Schleifer, S. J. (1985). Frontiers of stress research. In M. R. Zales (Ed.), *Stress in health and disease* (pp. 97-114). New York: Brunner/Mazel.

Terr, L. C. (1983). Chowchilla revisited: The effect of psychic trauma four years after a school-bus kidnapping. *American Journal of Psychiatry, 140,* 1543-1550.

Wetzel, N. A., & Winawer, H. (1986). The psychosocial consequences of the nuclear threat from a family systems perspective. In M. Schwebel (Ed.), *Mental health implications of life in the nuclear age* (pp. 298-313). Armonk, NY: M. E. Sharpe.

Woodward, P. (1948). How do the American people feel about the atomic bomb? *Journal of Social Issues, 4,* 7-14.

Ziv, A., & Israeli, R. (1973). Effects of bombardment on the manifest anxiety level of children living in kibbutzim. *Journal of Consulting and Clinical Psychology, 40,* 287-291.

# 10

# Endangered Children in Thailand: Third World Families Affected by Socioeconomic Changes

## Chok C. Hiew

A few years ago, in 1985, I was a participant at the Vermont Conference on the Primary Prevention of Psychopathology (VCPPP) to celebrate what was then a "Decade of Progress in Primary Prevention." After reviewing the history of prevention and the major models, research, and interventions for the prevention of psychological dysfunction in the United States and in Canada and Europe, key speakers and contributors boldly announced that primary prevention had finally arrived. Doubters and critics were served notice that there was strong evidence that primary prevention programs worked. There existed exemplary and substantive bodies of prevention programs and activities based on solid theories and methodologies, rigorously evaluated and unequivocally effective. Participants felt heartened that these accomplishments would continue with each passing year, with their further development and application in future prevention efforts.

I believe that we are now beginning a new decade in which prevention and promotion efforts must shift to a prominent global perspective. National and geographical boundaries are growing increasingly irrelevant as risk factors detrimental to the survival and health of the human species permeate the entire world. Human behaviors that lead to physical and mental disorders, that can ruin the environment and destroy the entire species, cannot truly be prevented or resolved solely on a local or national basis. As more countries join in the global economy and international trade in goods, services, and production, good and evil effects transcend national barriers and have direct implications for people's lives that are difficult to ignore. Without a global perspective, the success of primary prevention is illusory.

AUTHOR'S NOTE: My thanks go to Wanapa Intaprasert (Suan Prung Hospital, Chiangmai, Ministry of Public Health), Sombat Tapanya, and Suthi Intaprasert (Department of Psychiatry, Faculty of Medicine, Chiangmai University) for their assistance in the collection and translation of materials and information from Thailand.

In the last several years, I have had opportunities to be in Thailand and Japan, to learn about as well as to appreciate their fascinating cultures and histories and to observe some of the socioeconomic changes that have transformed the lives of their people. My motivation was to broaden the boundaries of community psychology to include Third World and Asian countries and to attempt to apply Western psychology to issues and problems relevant to them. Guided by my experiences as a community participant-conceptualizer, my purpose here is to present how preventive approaches are applicable to social problems and policies aimed at improving the well-being of children in Asian countries.

The central theme of this chapter is that rapid economic development in Asia has altered the family unit and that not all of the changes in family patterns are beneficial. Beginning in the 1960s, economic and industrial development have produced a steady proliferation of countries in Asia transformed from rags to riches and national prosperity. The Industrial Revolution in the Pacific Rim was set into motion only after World War II, with Japan leading the way. More recently, in the last decade, even a traditionally have-not nation, Thailand, is making the economic transition to unaccustomed prosperity. The impact of economic change is part of a global trend, unique in world history, in which a common set of social forces—specifically, industrialization and urbanization—has produced a similar family outcome. This phenomenon is the rise and increase of the nuclear family everywhere (Goode, 1963), in both East and West, as nations seek to meet and sustain their goal of economic growth. By the year 2000, according to U.N. estimates made in 1980, this will be a predominantly urban world, with two-thirds of the global urban population located in developing countries.

The nuclear family form per se is unrelated to quality of family functioning. For example, Bahr (1988) has recently challenged the notion that contemporary American nuclear families are in decay because of the disappearance of the traditional extended family associated with "the good old days." He argues that despite all the changes threatening the family today, it is a myth that traditional family life in previous generations was superior; in fact, families in the past were "far less democratic, healthful, loving, and supportive of individual growth than those of our own time" (p. 29). In the Asian context, while the increased incidence of nuclear families is part of, as well as beneficial to, the industrialization process, the reverse is not necessarily true. That is, many children in nuclear families as well as in fragmented Asian families are suffering adverse consequences that have created a variety of social problems.

Japan has become an industrialized nation faster than any other in the history of the world. While the usual family nuclearization and urbanization has occurred (in 80% of the population), Japan is also probably the only nation able to use its family system positively in the industrialization process. Japanese male employees are widely considered to be workaholics, devoting all their energies to their employers and work organizations. Their families or spouses obey by not letting family matters interfere with this devotion. Such a family system has aided in propelling

Japan to the position of the world's most productive economic superpower. Recently, however, the human costs of this ever-increasing emphasis on productivity and its relationship to mental health have begun to be recognized. The Japan Productivity Centre, for example, conducts occupational mental health and stress assessments at the request of work organizations, and psychiatrists and psychologists are involved in implementing organizational stress-reduction programs.

A new social problem involving children has also occurred (Hiew, 1990). Japanese families are not only nuclear; another pattern is the psychological and physical absence from the family of the father who is tied to work demands. As fathers become remote and ineffectual figures, mothers become devoted to their children's education, and children's lives are devoted to gaining entrance to top secondary schools and prestigious universities. Because of the fierce competition for admission, children and adolescents can be said to spend almost as much time in classrooms as their fathers do at work. Such family patterns have been blamed for the appearance of intrafamily violence perpetrated by young adolescent children (often boys). Parental abuse, school refusal or phobia, bullying, and delinquency are emerging social problems among young adolescents in Japan. These are normally good students, obedient, with good relations with their mothers. The precipitating event is the adolescent's sudden refusal to attend school. As worried parents and others attempt to coerce the child to return, the pressure mounts and the child turns on the parents and assaults them violently. The child usually shows remorse, as well as bizarre behaviors, but the violence continues. According to a National Police Agency report (cited by Hiew, 1990), family violence is considered the most serious national problem facing Japanese families today, with one out of five families estimated to show various forms of such child violence perpetrated on parents.

In contrast to North American nuclear families in transition, the rigidity of the Asian social system and the pace of sociocultural changes have meant that there are fewer available alternatives or established options to changes in the traditional family unit. More important, in North America the recognition of children's rights ensures that adequate institutional and state support and services exist to protect and safeguard the well-being of children independent of their families. In contrast, in Asian families, children are traditionally totally dependent on their families, and it is the responsibility of families to care for their children. Thus any changes in family patterns that alter the traditional family structure or reduce its supportive resources would inevitably make children suffer. In such family patterns, the lives of children are endangered. Such is the situation for many children in Thailand.

## The Endangered Child in Thailand

The cases of child neglect and exploitation described below are representative of the major problems faced by poor Thai children:

Neng is a six year old boy living in a slum near the port area in Bangkok. His parents are migrants and both parents had found work as laborers in cargo boats. The parents are often not at home and are away at work, a week at a time. Neng is left in the care of a relative when his parents are away. One day, the child was punished painfully (with cigarette burns on his hand) for tearing a book. When the parents discovered this, the child was placed in the home of a babysitter in the neighborhood. In that environment, the children's pastime was paint sniffing. Neng was initially forced to take part and soon became addicted. He lost weight and became slow in speech and responding. Neng came home to stay with his mother who was pregnant. He is now taken to school and given herbal medicine to recover. The child expressed the feeling that he is unloved and his parents do not care for him. (Khap-um, 1986, p. 24)

Sanan lived in a village with six siblings and parents who were farmers. At age 8 years, she could not read or write despite completing two years of elementary school. She was sent to Bangkok where she worked as a maid for five years. Hardly more than a child herself, she had to take care of her employer's toddler and do household chores until bedtime. When she was 13 years old, she began working in a mosquito net factory. Her parents would receive 3,000 Baht per year in her home village. Sanan and 45 other children under 15 years and 5 adults worked in the factory. Each child toiled for 18 hours per day (from 6 a.m. to midnight), seven days a week. They could not talk while working nor were they allowed to leave the factory at any time. They could expect three meals consisting of poor quality rice and little else. After a year, the police raided and closed down the factory. Sanan received help from social agencies. She suffered headaches, depression and had suicidal wishes. She wanted to return home as soon as possible. (p. 27)

Noog is 14 years old and has five brothers and sisters living in a village with her parents who were farmers near Chiang Rai. She has completed six years of school. Her parents sent her to Bangkok to work in a restaurant where a friend had gone earlier. Shortly after, she was taken to a brothel where she was told she must sleep with men in order to repay the 3,000 Baht given to her mother. For every customer she slept with, 800 Baht was paid to the establishment. She was not paid any wages but was able to remit 1,000 Baht to her parents three times during the eight months she worked in the brothel. After that she was moved into a low-class "tea-house" where the customer paid 80 Baht to the establishment for sexual services. She had to work from noon until midnight and was paid 50 Baht each day. Her parents in the village were not aware of what had happened. Soon after, the police closed down the "tea-house" and Noog was sent home. (p. 26)

In Thailand, the majority (80%) of the population lives in villages or rural communities. Children become victims as rural families migrate to urban centers, as parents relocate abroad or domestically for work purposes without their children, or when children separated from their families become exploited as child labor. Several factors account for the mass exodus of farmers in remote rural areas into urban centers as well as abroad.

## Rural Migration and Slum Children

By the mid-1960s, about 25% of all farmers in Thailand had lost their land and were farming rented land. Indebtedness combined with poor harvests from natural disasters such as floods and droughts forced farmers to migrate to the capital city, Bangkok, to look for work (Tangkananurak, 1987). The most recent census in 1983 found that over the previous 20 years, the proportion of farmers in the population had shrunk from 82.4% (in 1960) to 72.5%. The flow of migrants into Bangkok gained rapid momentum in the late 1960s and 1970s, with the new urban development policy and the expansion of industrial and commercial activities under the first National Economic Development Plan. With the Vietnam War, international trade expanded to supply Americans with their military needs. This led to an inflow in the labor sector and the spread of slums and squatters throughout the city. Basic infrastructure, such as housing, roads, waterworks, sewage disposal, and social and health services, became stretched to its limits. In the last decade, further expansion—global trade, manufacturing by multinational corporations, local and foreign investment, and the booming tourist industry since 1985—has led to two socioeconomic effects. One is the establishment of a small, well-educated urban middle class, with nuclear families working in the public sector or in private enterprises in white-collar or professional occupations. The second—less desirable, but more common—effect has been an increased demand for unskilled labor, producing a dramatic increase in land costs as well as rural migrants. Many of these laborers (70%) are young, single females (15-19 years) and males (15-24 years); the rest are nuclear families with young children (National Statistical Office, 1985). They have found work in dockyards, as street vendors, as mechanized ricksha drivers, as domestic servants, as shop assistants, and as food industry and factory workers. Still others resort to begging, stealing, peddling drugs, or prostitution. Again, slums and squatter areas have proliferated.

Government statistics in 1984 reported there were 556 slums and squatter areas housing a million people. Subsequently, between 1984 and 1985, some 84,000 persons migrated to Bangkok. Within the first six months of 1989 alone, the number escalated to more than 545,000 relocated from rural areas to Bangkok. A Mahidol University (Institute of Population and Social Research) survey (cited in "Come and See," 1989) indicates that in the last two years, 2 million migrants, predominantly from remote regions in the northeast, were residing in Bangkok, swelling the population beyond the official 5.8 million to 8 million people.

Slums and squatter areas are part of the urban structure in Bangkok. This is where most rural migrants would be settled. About 35% of the low strata work force live in these areas under the poorest conditions. Most of these settlements are located in illegal areas, such as public grounds, along canals and open sewer drains, and near railway tracks, highways, and port areas. For young children there is constant danger to health and life. There is no clean water, plumbing, or sanitation in the house, and no playgrounds or roads. There is little welfare assistance and few educational opportunities for the children.

Slum families have to be prepared to move constantly as they are evicted by landowners (Patpui, 1984). In one slum area called Klong Thoay, in the port vicinity, 42% are children and adolescents under 14 years old. Most people have low education—73.5% of household heads have completed fourth grade—and 9.9% have no education. Women's educational level is lower than the men's, with 18.8% being uneducated. Of children under 14 years, 30% are completely uneducated. The parents have no permanent or full-time jobs and work at whatever they can find on a daily basis, such as port labor or construction work. Children and old people also join in the work activities, doing manual chores on ships, painting, garbage screening, cleaning, and janitorial activities. Others work at home, making paper bags, flowers, or food for sale. Whether they will have any work on a given day is uncertain; there is no steady income.

Family life is clearly affected by this living situation. Children cannot go to school on a regular basis, because they may be needed to care for younger siblings if the parents find work. Formal schooling is considered a luxury for older children, who are expected to work alongside their parents. While elementary school is compulsory, enforcing attendance is left to parents. For many families there is no choice anyway, because many do not have possession of their children's birth certificates or did not register the births of their children, and without these documents children cannot be accepted in school. Additionally, many children are forced out of their homes or become runaways and live together with other street children.

Clearly, once industrialization begins, the need for labor means that rural family patterns are the first to change. Those in the rural population, with a desperate need for employment, sell their labor in the open market. They also need to become mobile and migrate to distant cities, where they rapidly lose their kinship ties and family networks. In the process, their children lose the traditional support of extended family and the basic stability and amenities of living. Their future is even bleaker, as they miss out on educational opportunities and their potential to reach healthy, productive adulthood becomes tenuous.

Urban and national authorities and planners in Thailand are overwhelmed by the excessive rural migration and overurbanization, which is well beyond the major cities' economic and social absorption capacity. In Bangkok, living conditions have declined for unemployed and underemployed families and children,

migrant as well as nonmigrant, as the physical environment and urban infrastructure has deteriorated. For slum and squatter families, efforts by city authorities to provide low-cost housing and slum upgrading have not been successful.
In fact, they quickly became absorbed by middle-class families also in need of
housing. For slum dwellers the crucial need is land ownership, not more com-
fortable housing, a difficult undertaking requiring structural changes in government policy and institutional support (Patpui, 1984).

In the long run what is needed is decentralization and dispersion of economic development and population and a wider distribution of employment opportunities
away from Bangkok. The current Fifth National Plan is aimed at correcting overurbanization by promoting innovative regional growth centers to counter the pull of
migrant workers to the capital. Fuller (cited in Koyano, 1985), however, reports that
research on growth policy indicates little success; in fact, rather than reversing the
urbanization process, the policy seems to have intensified and consolidated social
and economic inequality. For example, in Chiangmai, the capital city of the northern provinces, despite economic growth, the traditional dominance of Bangkok has
ensured that the lion's share of increased wealth flows out of Chiangmai to Bangkok. In employment terms, people who fill the upper and middle echelons are from
Bangkok, while local rural people commute from semiurban areas to fill the lower
stratum of the labor market.

Wungaeo (1985), a political scientist, has criticized macro-level economic
and social development and foreign aid projects and professionals as having
failed to take into account the realities and harsh world of poverty and scarcity.
There is a need for close understanding of the needs of people and communities
and how they perceive economic and social changes. Understanding such factors would strengthen individual and community competence to cope with mod-
ernization and would increase the effectiveness of social-economic policies. For
example, adoption of long-term social change programs requires the recipients'
self-help efforts, which depend on fuller understanding of the programs meeting
recipients' needs. There is also a need to integrate community resources such as
professionals and the middle-class strata into development projects. For example, Wungaeo points out that the nongovernment organizations that advocated
for and assisted children were supported by local resources. About 70% of the
funding and support of the Duang Prateep Foundation, which is active in slum
children programs, and 50% of the funding of the Foundation for Children
agency came from people in middle-class occupations.

**Migrant Workers in the Construction Industry**

Industrialization has produced a booming construction industry in the urban
centers, especially in Bangkok. For rural migrants with children, construction

work becomes attractive because only basic and manual work skills are required, both men and women are eligible, no intermediaries or references are needed, and, most important, rudimentary housing is provided within the construction site. In 1960, there were only 69,000 construction workers in Thailand's urban centers; by 1983 this had increased fivefold, to more than 370,000 workers nationally (Tangkananurak, 1988).

A survey by the Foundation for Children (1982) showed that 79% of the construction workers in Bangkok were formerly farmers. In 1989 the number of workers was estimated at 200,000 employed in more than 1,000 construction sites ("Come and See," 1989). These workers enjoy few benefits. They are paid the minimum wage, which is equivalent to a little more than U.S. $3.00 per day. Female construction workers are paid less than minimum wage. Further, wages are paid on an irregular basis, and sometimes not at all. There are no holidays or medical benefits. Living quarters are located within the building site, and home for an entire family typically consists of a single room, 3 × 3 meters in size, usually made of corrugated metal sheets and plywood. Work safety measures are almost nonexistent, and fatal accidents are common. In 1987 children of construction workers below 15 years of age numbered 30,000. A Foundation for Children survey reports that 74% of the children under 6 years of age suffer from malnutrition because of the lack of adequate food (Tangkananurak, 1987). There is no formal schooling, and no play areas. Parents work every day of the week and the children receive little care. Public health officials report that sickness is common and health conditions are bad enough for epidemics to break out in construction housing areas (Tangkananurak, 1988).

The children who live on these construction sites live in a physically dangerous environment; accidents resulting in injuries or death are common. Bangkok newspapers have frequently reported fatal mishaps—children falling into deep building shafts, falling from unfinished buildings, or being crushed by falling objects or collapsing buildings. In addition, once one job is completed, the family moves to another construction site, so that constant strain is experienced during relocation to the new environment.

The plight of these children has been taken up by nongovernment child welfare groups. The Foundation for Children began establishing educational centers within workers' housing areas in construction sites in 1979 (the Mobile Preschool Children Project). Project activities include (a) setting up early school centers in cooperation with construction companies to teach reading, writing, and arithmetic (as well as moral education for older children) daily; (b) providing lunches to halt malnutrition; (c) teaching vocational skills to older children in the evenings; (d) organizing field trips, educational tours, and camping trips monthly; (e) providing health care for workers and their families in cooperation with medical clinics and hospitals; and (f) organizing programs aimed at mothers that include home visits to provide information about child care, employment, and recreational activities; assisting mothers with infants; and organizing vocational courses.

However, several obstacles have been encountered in establishing this program. For one thing, frequent moves by workers looking for new employment make it difficult for families to become involved on a long-term basis. Inadequate funding means that programs have to be terminated at some sites in order for other sites to receive program services. There has also been lack of support from construction companies, with common excuses such as "no space" and "not our policy." Over the last eight years, a total of 42 centers have been implemented on a rotating basis. However, currently there are only three centers in operation, and funding is grossly inadequate to meet the needs of the 30,000 children under 15 years spread over the 1,000 construction sites ("Come and See," 1989).

## Migrant International Labor

Rural migrants have another channel of employment open to them: They can become part of the global labor pool abroad. Department of Labor statistics indicate that, in 1989 alone, there were 125,000 migrant Thai workers abroad, and that for each of the preceding five years there was a regular movement of more than 100,000 workers overseas to Middle Eastern, Asian, and European countries. In addition, a large but unknown number were working illegally in neighboring countries. Entire villages in Thailand's northeastern region have only children, women, and old people remaining, as the men have left to seek jobs. Most of these migrants leave their families behind for one to five years. They may also complete one contract, return home briefly, and sign on for another extended stay abroad. This movement has been widely seen as nationally beneficial, as remittances from overseas workers rank second in terms of national income (Singhanetra-Renard, Chaparnond, Tiyayon, & Prabudhanitisarn, 1988). In 1988, bank remittances from overseas Thai workers came close to U.S. $1 billion. However, international labor has mixed value for communities and individuals. It is common knowledge among Thais that marital and family problems are rife during these work-related separations. A well-known phrase reflecting the situation is: "Going over, land is lost; coming home, wife is gone."

Typically, a Thai villager going to work in a Middle Eastern country sells his land to pay often exorbitant sums to a recruitment and employment agency. Money earned is remitted home regularly, making the village spouse relatively wealthy, with a lot to spend and much idle time, as well as problems of loneliness. She may be preyed on by opportunists during vulnerable periods. The situation often ends with tragic results, family discord, divorce, or homicide and suicide. Children ultimately lose one or both parents this way. While there has been some research into the detrimental effects on rural community families of work-related separation of men from their families (see Singhanetra-Renard et al., 1988), there do not appear to be any published studies of intervention to prevent exploitation and to assist families in coping with the situation.

## Child Labor

Child labor, defined here as children's paid or unpaid work done outside the family under frequently exploitative conditions, is a common problem in many Third World countries and has recently gained prominent attention (Moore, 1983; Rodgers & Standing, 1981). Given the high rate of unemployment and poverty, and the production of labor-intensive goods for export, inexpensive child labor appears to be one unfortunate consequence. National governments are influenced by Western notions of child labor, so that official government statistics may be suspect. A low incidence of child labor could be the result of children frequently not being paid for their work. Governments may make child labor illegal, yet be reluctant to enforce the laws or to control abusive practices. As long as industrialists and entrepreneurs take advantage of normative low wages and use the surplus child labor work force to push costs even lower, and as long as families have insufficient income to survive otherwise, child exploitation will be tolerated by all parties and will be difficult to eradicate.

In Thailand, a dramatic increase in child labor is apparent under the conditions of poverty caused by industrialization and by exploitation-based changes in modes of production. Purisinsit (1988) cites a U.N. (ESCAP) survey in 1983 that estimated the child labor force at 2 million, mostly in illegal factories as well as working as street vendors and in eating places. These illegal factories are often small or medium in size, with poor ventilation and few safety measures. For example, one case involving a candy factory came to light when several children died because of mistreatment and constant work sitting on bare floors.

Child labor is illegal for children under age 12, yet the number of child workers younger than that is estimated at 200,000, with 60% working more than 11 hours per day and 50% working without holidays. For children between 12 and 15, work is legal provided that it is "light work," does not involve carrying more than 10 kilos, and is not dangerous to health and growth. However, child labor laws have not been enforced effectively and children continue to be exploited.

Several factors are linked to the prevalence of child labor: (a) There is uneven economic development occurring at a rapid pace in the urban centers while the rural sector has remained impoverished, (b) there is high unemployment in rural sectors such as the northeastern and northern regions, and (c) about 80% of the population live in the rural sector and have no more than elementary education. For children, primary education is not compulsory and secondary education is restricted and expensive.

It would be impractical to eradicate child labor immediately, but much should be done to improve working children's lives by firm regulation of working conditions. Children who work must continue to have access to educational, medical, and recreational facilities. Public attitudes need to be changed, from the position that parental rights permit sending children off to work to the viewpoint that children have the right to education and protection from exploitation. At the same time, poor families deserve resources from society to carry out this change. It would be helpful to identify incentives that will, for example, enable rural parents to send their children to school and keep them there, rather than at work.

### Child Prostitution and the Tourism Industry

The sexual exploitation of children has reached monstrous proportions, ironically tied to the expansion in the tourism industry in a number of developing nations, including the Philippines, Sri Lanka, and Thailand (Ekachai, 1990). In the Philippines, a conservative estimate by UNICEF of the number of child prostitutes is about 20,000, two-thirds of whom are street children and runaways used by pedophiles. In Sri Lanka, where ethnic violence has frightened most tourists away from big hotels, there is full occupancy in beach resorts frequented by pedophiles. It is estimated that roughly 10,000 "beach boys" aged between 8 and 16 are moved from resort to resort and are sexually as well as financially exploited (paid less than a dollar a day).

A government survey of child and adolescent development (cited in Purisinsit, 1988) reported the number of child prostitutes under 16 years of age in Thailand to be 30,000. This may be only the tip of an iceberg. Nongovernment agencies such as the Foundation for Children have recently estimated the number of child prostitutes to be as high as 800,000 for children under 15 years of age, working in some 60,000 brothels across the country as well as being exploited in child pornography (Ekachai, 1990). While the exact number may be in dispute, it is clear that Thailand has the largest proportion of child prostitutes in Asia. There has been an unprecedented explosion of child prostitution linked to poverty and the unregulated and massive expansion in the flesh trade in tourism. International tourism has increased every year in Thailand since 1985; a record 4.25 million tourists visited the country in 1988, and tourism is the nation's top source of income. Professor Prawase Wasi has blamed this tragic development on the global economy that exploits the inequities inherent among nations, on sexism, and on a tourist industry that blatantly caters to sexual and hedonistic desires.

A large number of foreign men come to indulge in sexual sprees with poor women. They have lots of money to spend, and this creates a heavy demand for prostitutes. And when the supply of young women falls short, the business goes to younger girls, leading to child prostitution. (Cited in Ekachai, 1990, p. 23)

However, another factor blamed for the tragedy is the country's often open acceptance of polygamy and prostitution. Open sex tourism has produced two local effects. One is that some of the traditional reservations about prostitution have been removed—that is, many now feel that what is good for tourist entertainment is good for the locals. Second, as traditional sources of adult females in the sex trade have shifted to cater to foreign tourists, a supply shortage has been created for local consumption. Additionally, prostitutes become less affordable to locals. Children are recruited to fill the gap, because they are cheaper and more plentiful. They include male children who are mainly runaways, victims of family abuse and neglect.

The majority of child prostitutes are female victims, however. Typically, recruiters descend on villages and persuade unsuspecting and poor farmers to allow their young daughters (and sons) to "work" in the cities (Purisinsit, 1988). Families are given 3,000-4,000 baht for three years of child work. At other times, migrants return to their home villages and entice their neighbors to let their children leave. Once these children are brought into the city, they are housed in cheap brothels frequented by the lower working class and subjected to the most inhumane conditions and health hazards. These children are also preyed on by perverted foreign tourists.

These sexually abused children are extremely vulnerable and at great risk of being directly infected with AIDS because of their sexual contact with men who belong to high-risk groups, such as homosexuals, drug addicts, and laborers (Intaprasert & Hiew, 1990). The Thai Ministry of Public Health, in June 1989, conducted an AIDS prevalence blood test in 14 large cities (Ungchusak, 1989). The major finding was that prostitutes, especially those in lower-class brothels, had become an important source of HIV transmission (exceeding even IV drug users). In another survey targeted at lower-class brothels in one popular tourist province (Chiangmai), prostitutes in the youngest age group (up to 19 years of age) had the highest proportion of HIV positives (44%).

While great concern has been expressed about child prostitution by children's rights groups and individuals, there is also a sense of helplessness about finding effective solutions. Like the illicit drug abuse problem, the solution requires dealing with both supply and demand factors. Consumers in the sex industry and perpetrators, both foreign and local, have to be reached. Where huge profits are being made in child prostitution, business and politics are in collusion and law enforcement becomes ineffectual.

## Primary Prevention in a Third World Country

Children in Thailand are adversely affected by urban migration, industrial changes, and unequal economic development that has led to the unplanned nuclearization and fragmentation of the family. Such untold suffering on the part of innocent children cannot be tolerated and must be halted by every means available. Countless children will continue to suffer in the future from multiple stressors springing from sociocultural origins beyond their control. For them, their environment has produced a host of life-threatening and health-damaging experiences, including (a) physically and emotionally damaging infant and childhood experiences; (b) poverty and degrading life experiences; (c) powerlessness, victimization, and loss of self--esteem; and (d) loneliness, social isolation, and social marginality. These factors have been clearly established, by epidemiological studies as well as by much of the research reported in VCPPP publications, to be related to all forms of human distress, psychopathology, poor health, and deviance. With so many personal tragedies, the nation of Thailand is losing a precious resource that it can ill afford to lose.

As a social science, in terms of aspirations, goals, and practice, preventive psychology has a unique role to play in the betterment of children. In the United States, primary prevention strategies directed at social change and enhancement of personal competence and coping have demonstrated their utility in contributing toward the goal of eradicating psychopathology (e.g., Joffe, Albee, & Kelly, 1984). The Canadian national health promotion policy is also based on a preventive framework (Epp, 1986). "Health for All by the Year 2000" is the theme promoted by the World Health Organization for its global member states. In Canada, health for all is to be achieved by facing certain challenges, through a number of health promotion mechanisms and strategies, specifically (a) by meeting social and behavioral health challenges (addressing inequities, increasing prevention, and enhancing coping), (b) through health promotion mechanisms (such as self-care, mutual aid, and healthy environments), and (c) through implementation strategies (fostering public participation and strengthening community health services and coordinated public health policy).

**Obstacles to Prevention Work**

As in other Third World countries with limited resources, in Thailand advanced training and support for applied research in human development and psychological health are practically nonexistent (Wagner, 1986). Despite the existence of a number of major universities, there are no doctoral programs in clinical or community psychology or other prevention-focused programs. Tapanya (1989) describes some attempts at community preventive interventions using indigenous resources, but points out that the obstacles to preventive interventions include the shortage of trained professionals, the overdominance of the medical model, and the complexities of entrenched social problems.

Another obstacle is the lack of appreciation of psychological factors in international aid and development agencies. Funds from these agencies are concentrated almost exclusively on technological intervention and economic development and production, with little attention to how the changes expected in the targeted population are influenced by motivational, attitudinal, and other human factors. Most administrators of international agencies are not psychologists, and they have little understanding of the application of psychology in solving community problems. Moreover, for most agencies, notions of mental or psychological health or well-being sound too much like privileged Western middle-class values, irrelevant to Third World problems and needs. For example, a Canadian government agency active in supporting research, the International Development Research Centre, does not provide research support for any project with "merely" mental health objectives. Yet psychology can contribute much to national development in Thailand, for example, through the application of behavioral principles to develop culturally relevant social incentives, to assist the population in making changes to more adaptive life-styles and alternative vocations, and to implement programs to eliminate environmental health hazards (Mikulas, 1983).

### Prevention and Children

In Thailand, effective implementation of primary prevention strategies could produce an innovative and comprehensive alternative to end the social problem of child victimization. The goal of improving children's lives requires not only understanding the economic and sociocultural factors and the basic needs for proper development of the child, but also changing those conditions that create inequities in resources, employment, education, and health. While the general goal to undertake prevention is clear, operationalizing prevention procedures to accomplish such objectives is complex. To do primary prevention, a collaborative model is needed that will bring together policymakers, administrators, professionals, nongovernment agencies, universities, and concerned people across different areas, including public health, education, social sciences, and economic and community development. While this is obviously more simply said than done, to do otherwise would perpetuate the problem (Hollnsteiner & Tacon, 1983).

As a developing country, Thailand needs much assistance from international agencies, children's groups, and professional associations to draw national and global attention to its problems and to develop and implement preventive interventions. A recent exemplar of such national and international collaboration came after Thailand's sudden awakening to the problem of AIDS. (Intaprasert & Hiew, 1990). A national AIDS policy, including strategies for prevention, has been developed and implemented by the Ministry of Public Health with the assistance of WHO. Government and nongovernment agencies and social action groups are working to complement one another's efforts. The voices and support of influential people, including health specialists, religious figures, and a member of the royal family, have all contributed to raising the consciousness of the people concerning the severity of AIDS in Thailand and the attitudinal and behavioral changes needed for its prevention.

### Poor Families and Children's Well-Being

The theme of the 1988 conference of the International Council of Psychologists was "East-West Dialogue: The Role of Psychologists in Promoting Health and Well-Being." During its regional meeting in Bangkok, the key symposium was on primary prevention and health promotion (Hiew, 1988). Professor Chancha Suvannathat (1988), an eminent developmental psychologist in Thailand, argued that the proper care and socialization of children by their families have been severely threatened by migration, urbanization, industrialization, and family nuclearization. She proposed that the essential vehicle to promote child health and well-being is the family unit, and further suggested that a national policy is needed to focus on strengthening the family as a top priority, by providing the institutional support necessary to improve parents' competence to care for their children and to provide the resources for children's basic needs and the enhancement of their future well-being and independence. It is also my belief that a focus on the family as a target population to operationalize primary prevention efforts to protect and improve children's lives in Thailand and elsewhere merits serious consideration. Theoretically, the various prevention strategies repeatedly articulated in Albee's (1986) prevention equation and variations of it (Elias, 1987) can be focused on family health.

In brief, healthier families can be fostered if we can enhance their health competence while at the same time eradicating their social and environmental stress (Albee. 1986). Specific strategies can be formulated to eradicate stressors and risk factors in the environment and to enhance family competence through increased socialization practices, social support resources, and opportunities for connectedness.

Culturally, the family concept certainly has appeal and will readily attract strong commitment by all strata of society. It may be easier then for society to care and to feel responsible for making the effort to assist the most disadvantaged groups in the country by redressing the root social and economic inequities. Such motivation is necessary to sustain a long-range agenda without which primary prevention efforts may not last (Albee, 1986). It will also be in tune with, and undoubtedly bolstered by, the recent U.N. General Assembly resolution proclaiming 1994 as International Family Year.

Whatever your professional expertise and concerns, I hope that you will actively support this movement and become one of the many who will be needed to join and pull together to search for lasting solutions to meet the basic needs of children, the most disadvantaged group in the Third World and elsewhere.

## References

Albee, G. (1986). Toward a just society: Lessons from observations on the primary prevention of psychopathology. *American Psychologist, 41,* 891-898.

Bahr, H. M. (1988). Family change and the mystique of the traditional family. In L. Bond & B. Wagner (Eds.), *Families in transition: Primary prevention programs that work* (pp. 13-30). Newbury Park, CA: Sage.

Come and see the Children's Centre in construction sites. (1989). *Thai Contractor News, 17,* 83-85.

Ekachai, S. (1990, May 8). Slaves of the modern world. *Bangkok Post, 45* (sec. 3).

Elias, M. (1987). Establishing enduring prevention programs: Advancing the legacy of Swampscott. *American Journal of Community Psychology, 15,* 539-553.

Epp, J. (1986). *Achieving health for all: A framework for health promotion.* Ottawa: Health and Welfare Canada.

Foundation for Children. (1982). *Industrial construction labor force.* Bangkok: Chulalongkorn University, Institute of Social Research.

Goode, W. J. (1963). *World revolution and family patterns.* New York: Free Press.

Hiew, C. C. (1988). Primary prevention plans for health promotion in Thailand. In *Proceedings of the Bangkok regional meeting of the International Council of Psychologists.* Khon Kaen University.

Hiew, C. C. (1990). *Separated by their work: Canadian and Japanese families with fathers living apart.* Symposium paper presented at the International Congress of Applied Psychology, Kyoto, Japan.

Hollnsteiner, M., & Tacon, P. (1983). Urban migration in developing countries: Consequences for families and their children. In D. A. Wagner (Ed.), *Child development and international development: Research-policy interfaces* (pp. 5-26). San Francisco: Jossey-Bass.

Intaprasert, W., & Hiew, C. C. (1990). *AIDS in Thailand.* Poster session presented at the Vermont Conference on the Primary Prevention of Psychopathology, Burlington.

Joffe, J., Albee, G., & Kelly, D. (Eds.). (1984). *Readings in primary prevention of psychopathology: Basic concepts.* Hanover: University Press of New England.

Khap-um, P. (1986). Reflections on children's life. *Thai Public Welfare, 29,* 23-27.

Koyano, S. (Ed.). (1985). *Sociological study of urbanization in Southeast Asia.* Tokyo: Japanese Ministry of Education, International Joint Team for Overseas Scientific Surveys.

Mikulas, W. L. (1983). Thailand and behavior modification. *Journal of Behavior Therapy and Experimental Psychiatry, 14,* 93-97.

Moore, F. (1983). Child labor and national development: An annotated bibliography. In D. A. Wagner (Ed.), *Child development and international development: Research-policy interfaces* (pp. 87-106). San Francisco: Jossey-Bass.

National Statistical Office. (1985). *The survey of migration into the Bangkok metropolis and vicinity.* Bangkok: Prime Minister's Office.

Patpui, S. (1984). *The rights of slum people.* Thammasat University, Faculty of Social Sciences and Humanities.

Purisinsit, V. (1988). *Sociological view of children and adolescent deviant behavior.* Chiangmai University, Faculty of Social Sciences.

Rodgers, G., & Standing, G. (1981). *Child work, poverty, and underemployment.* Geneva: International Labor Organization.

Singhanetra-Renard, A., Chaparnond, P., Tiyayon, P., & Prabudhanitisarn, N. (1988). *Economics and dynamics of recruitment for international contract labor.* Chiangmai University, Faculty of Social Sciences Abstracts.

Suvannathat, C. (1988). A Thai perspective on family and child socialization as the primary prevention base for health care and promotion. In *Proceedings of the Bangkok regional meeting of the International Council of Psychologists.* Khon Kaen University.

Tangkananurak, W. (1987). *Children of construction workers.* Bangkok: Rungsang.

Tangkananurak, W. (1988). *Forgotten children in Thai society.* Bangkok: Rungsang.

Tapanya, S. (1989). Community psychology in Thailand. *American Journal of Community Psychology, 17,* 109-119.

Ungchusak, K. (1989). AIDS: Situation, problem and tendency. *Serm Gan Patana* (Bangkok), *1,* 12-15.

Wagner, D. A. (1986). Child development research and the Third World. *American Psychologist, 41,* 298-301.

Wungaeo, S. (1985). Urbanization of Bangkok and national development. In S. Koyano (Ed.), *Sociological study of urbanization in South East Asia.* Tokyo: Japanese Ministry of Education, International Joint Team for Overseas Scientific Surveys.

# PART III

# Multilevel Systems Approaches to Prevention

Diversity in form and function mark those prevention efforts designed to improve children's lives around the world—from broad social and political systems-level initiatives to intimate, one-on-one foci, from formal regulatory efforts to informal network building, from individual to regional to international initiatives. Yet, whatever its structure, the effectiveness of a preventive intervention approach requires a fit between it and conceptual, cultural, methodological, geographical, and social-political targets. This section illustrates attempts to reach children through diverse approaches that carefully consider this fit, with the common theme of promoting constructive change in the lives of children by coordinating services across multiple levels within social-political systems.

The section begins with a historical account of primary prevention programs in Europe. Clemens M. H. Hosman, an associate professor in preventive psychology at the University of Nijmegen in the Netherlands, examines European developments in the field of mental health promotion and primary prevention of mental disorders. He presents recent initiatives of the World Health Organization (WHO) designed to stimulate Europewide prevention efforts in mental health. His analysis includes information about the progress made as well as the problems and obstacles confronted in developing and implementing prevention programs throughout Europe. By providing a history of prevention efforts in mental health in Europe, he illustrates both how European prevention efforts have evolved to their present state and the possibilities for their future development.

In Chapter 12, Wolfgang Stark, director of the Munich, Germany, Self-Help Resource Center, describes a project that is part of the Healthy Cities Program initiated by the WHO. Here the target group is specific and the methodology focuses on empowerment as a model for health promotion of children and youth in the city of Munich. Stark illustrates how the WHO started a networking system at the international level that encouraged more than 250 cities in Europe to start health promotion projects and to participate in national networks that have been developed by a group of core cities. The Munich program has been a joint effort of the Munich Self-Help Resource Center and approximately 50 other self-help and nonprofit organizations, together with a number of citizens' groups working toward active collaboration of citizens of all ages. Participants in the Munich

147

program agreed that improving the lives of children required that links be established among social policymakers, neighborhood projects, and community participation. A series of Future Labs with children, youth, and adults were created to develop perspectives on the city from the grass-roots level and to serve as planning instruments and tools to stimulate citizens to create and shape their own physical and social environments.

The authors of Chapter 13 are five individuals who have been active mental health workers in varied regions of the Netherlands: Henk Verburg, the national coordinator at the Dutch Union for Outpatient Mental Health Care; Hans Janssen, a youth preventive worker at RIAGG Zuidhage in the Hague; Marion Rikken, who works in the prevention section at the RIAGG Oost-Veluwe in Apeldoorn; Cees Hoefnagels, project manager and chief of the Prevention Team at the RIAGG in Utrecht; and Elsa M. van Willenswaard, who works as the project manager for the RNO RIAGG in Rotterdam. These authors describe the advantages of the Netherlands' 57 RIAGGs (Regional Institutes for Outpatient Mental Health Care) in providing a structure for mental health prevention programs on a regional level throughout the Netherlands. Brief descriptions of four Dutch prevention programs are presented: a home-based play guidance program, a program for children of parents with mental disorders, a child sexual abuse program, and a treatment program for child sexual abusers.

As Nomita Sonty illustrates in Chapter 14, the coordination of services for children is not limited to European countries. Sonty, a postdoctoral fellow in the Pain Management/Biobehavioral Program at the St. Louis University Hospital in St. Louis, Missouri, describes how India's Integrated Child Development Scheme (ICDS) arose out of a need to coordinate services among various government agencies for optimal utilization of resources and provision of services. The objectives of the program, its infrastructure, the services provided, its financial support, and its effects on services for children and women are reviewed. Evaluations of the program indicate that birth weight and immunization of infants have both increased, and the incidence of malnutrition and the infant mortality rate have decreased. In addition, not only has the program provided services for women, but it has served as a major employer for them as well.

Like Wolfgang Stark, the authors of the final chapter in Part III—Forrest B. Tyler, director of the Clinical/Community Psychology Program at the University of Maryland; Sandra L. Tyler, coordinator of the COPE Project; Anthony Tommasello, associate professor of clinical pharmacy at the University of Maryland School of Pharmacy; and Mark R. Connolly, regional coordinator for Street Kids International—take an empowerment approach in their work with children. They emphasize the importance of replacing the defect model with a competency orientation when working with street children. Using the story of Huckleberry Finn, these authors portray creatively and effectively the problems of devalued children who are treated as if they are property. Through interviews with street children in Bogotá, Colombia, and Washington, DC, they illustrate that these children want psychological supports, relationships, and a role in society, like any other children. By using a competency orientation, the authors were able to involve the street youth in defining themselves and their world so that all involved in the project became a part of the solution to solving the problems of street youth. The data presented support the hypothesis that adolescents who develop early autonomy and who live outside of families and adult authority are capable of making rational and positive choices in their lives.

# 11

# Primary Prevention of Mental Disorders and Mental Health Promotion in Europe: Developments and Possibilities for Innovation

## Clemens M. H. Hosman

This chapter focuses on European developments in the field of mental health promotion and primary prevention of mental disorders. An analysis is offered of progress to date and the innovations needed during the next decade. Priority must be given to solving some serious infrastructural problems that impede the progress so desperately needed in this field both within and beyond Europe. The available resources for prevention in the field of mental health are not only scarce, they are being used inefficiently. It is imperative that we combine resources, knowledge, and experience from different countries so that we can better position ourselves to make progress in prevention and thus promote a healthy future for children. Working for almost 18 years in this field, I have developed a deep conviction that the strengthening of international collaboration in the development of prevention programs, research and infrastructure, and exchange of information should be among our highest priorities at this time. In light of this statement, the organizers of the first worldwide Vermont Conference on Primary Prevention of Psychopathology (VCPPP) in June 1990 deserve to be complimented for their initiative in bringing people together from so many countries and providing them the opportunity to develop international cooperative networks.

It is not the purpose of this chapter to give a complete overview of promising preventive programs and policies in Europe. It may seem even a bit reckless to attempt a report on the developments in Europe. It is currently possible only to paint a very rough and incomplete picture. To date, no one has a clear overview of what is going on in the preventive mental health field within the 31 European countries, even if we restrict ourselves to efforts directed toward children. In fact, this is one of the first and most serious problems with which we must cope.

151

Nevertheless, some European countries present interesting examples of prevention programs and policies (some of which are described more extensively in other chapters of this volume). Of special interest are certain recent initiatives of the World Health Organization (WHO) to stimulate Europewide prevention efforts in the field of mental health. Being involved in this endeavor, I will present information about the progress made, and especially about the problems and obstacles we confront in promoting the development and implementation of prevention programs throughout Europe—problems and obstacles that demand innovative solutions so that we can progress with further international collaboration on program implementation, evaluation, and research (Hosman, 1989). I will start by giving you a bit of insight into the history of prevention efforts in Europe.

## History of Prevention in Mental Health in Europe

Although one is often under the impression that the prevention of mental disorders is a recent focus in mental health care, the truth of the matter is that the history of prevention of psychopathology in Europe goes back to the turn of the century. This period was characterized by several progressive social movements, such as the labor movement, actions against child labor, the antitrust movement, and the movement for women's rights. Many people at that time became conscious of societal evils that threatened the health and well-being of large groups within society. In this cultural climate of reform movements, the mental hygiene movement evolved both in Europe and in the United States. Yet we can trace the ideas of mental hygiene back even further, to many European and American publications throughout the nineteenth century (Gerards, 1984; Reimann, 1967).

### The Mental Hygiene Movement

The mental hygiene movement focuses upon (a) the improvement of the care and living conditions of psychiatric patients, referring to a more community-oriented type of care; (b) psychiatric prophylaxis, that is, prevention of mental illness both by trying to prevent the onset of new cases and by early treatment of mental problems in children; (c) the dissemination of knowledge concerning mental hygiene to the general public and community leaders to improve mental health; and (d) cooperation with social organizations that have influence upon the mental health of people (Meng, 1939; Pfister-Ammende, 1955; Reimann, 1967).

It appears that these goals were already formulated at the beginning of this century, in 1908 (Meng, 1939; Pfister-Ammende, 1955; Reimann, 1967). When we consider them carefully, we can conclude that they are almost identical to those of the recent prevention movement of the 1960s and 1970s, and even of the Health for All Strategy of the World Health Organization in the 1980s and 1990s (see WHO, 1985). Ideas about primary, secondary, and tertiary prevention, from perspectives of both prevention and mental health promotion, and even a plea for what is called, in current health policies, a "multisectoral approach" (WHO, 1985) were all present early in the 1900s. Similarly, the mutual influence and exchange of ideas among the continents that we saw at the June 1990 VCPPP meeting was already taking place at the beginning of the twentieth century.

In light of current theoretical models behind the Health for All program of the WHO (1985), the contribution of Adolf Meyer is especially worth mentioning (e.g., see Meyer, 1908/1973; Reimann, 1967). In 1892, this Swiss psychiatrist moved to the United States and became one of the leading personalities in American psychiatry and a strong protagonist of the mental hygiene movement. One of Meyer's unique contributions to the American Committee for Mental Hygiene was to shift its orientation more and more from the reform of psychiatric care to the prevention of mental diseases. Meyer's theory of psychobiology was a strong reaction to the static and dominantly somatic-oriented psychiatry that dominated at the end of the nineteenth century. He described mental diseases as a pathologic adaptation resulting from a dynamic interaction of physical, psychological, and social forces. Each of those forces, according to Meyer, could be influenced preventively, both by education and by changes in the social and physical environment, such as housing, neighborhoods, and workplaces.

This multicausal approach to mental health and mental illness was essential for the mental hygiene movement—"a healthy person in a healthy community," as the Swiss mental hygienist Meng (1939) phrased it in his classic textbook on mental hygiene. Mental hygienic work included multilevel interventions directed at individuals, couples, families, organizations, communities, and the general public. As is typical of interdisciplinary movements, mental hygiene associations were uniting people from a wide range of disciplines—psychiatrists, psychologists, sociologists, criminologists, educators, theologians, teachers, lawyers, and historians. This holistic, multicausal, and multilevel approach appears quite modern, as it resembles the principles of the current WHO (1985) Health for All program.

An example of the influence of the United States on Europe is embodied in Clifford Beers. He was a founder of the worldwide mental hygiene movement, one of the roots of the later mental health movement and the World Federation for Mental Health. In the early 1920s Beers visited several European countries to promote his ideas and to stimulate international collaboration. Most European countries founded associations for mental hygiene before the end of the 1920s, with Finland being the first in 1917.

Recently I came across the annals of the constitutive conference of the German Mental Hygiene Association, which took place 62 years ago in Hamburg (Roemer, 1929). The financial paragraph of the report on this meeting refers to a grant of 300 German marks offered by Clifford Beers himself. Wilhelm Weygandt, one of the founders of the German association, referred in his opening address to "the many psychiatrists and hygienists who have written in their textbooks a chapter on prophylaxis." As early as 1904, Weygandt himself published a book titled *Verhütung der Geisteskrankheiten (Prevention of Mental Diseases)*. Around the turn of the century there were many initiatives in mental hygiene and prevention coming from a diversity of backgrounds, but these initiatives had little impact, as Weygandt concluded in his opening address, because there was *no coordination* and *no concentration* of the existing forces. Today, more than 60 years later, this remains a crucial problem in the development of prevention in Europe and perhaps worldwide.

Quite modern, therefore, were the efforts of the early mental hygienists to develop a Europewide collaborative network. Already at the meeting in Hamburg in 1928 there were representatives of mental hygiene organizations from a wide variety of European countries, from Russia to the Netherlands and from Norway to Italy. During the 1920s and 1930s, the European mental hygiene movement succeeded in the organization of an international collaborative network with regular meetings and with prevention as one of the topics on the agenda. At the First International Congress on Mental Hygiene in Washington in 1930, there were more then 3,000 representatives from approximately 50 countries. For we who are now accustomed to the ease of international communication by telephone, fax, computer networks, and air travel, it is truly amazing to recognize that, decades ago, people with such limited resources and lack of supporting infrastructures were quite successful in creating international collaboration for the promotion of mental hygiene.

To summarize, the mental hygiene movement was strongly oriented to prevention, even advocating primary prevention. It was a movement with a multicausal and holistic approach, supported by many motivated scientists, professionals, and social organizations representing a large diversity of disciplines, a movement with quite modern ideas about possibilities for preventive strategies and successful in organizing collaborative networks in Europe, the United States, and even worldwide. Further, it was a movement very much dedicated to the improvement of the mental health of children.

### Successes and Failures of the Mental Hygiene Movement

This history should have served as a very favorable starting point, fertile soil for advancing preventive interventions. Nevertheless, looking back over the last 50 years, the success of the mental hygiene movement in Europe was not so much prevention. In most recent reports on the European history of mental health care since World War II, prevention—especially primary prevention—is mentioned only incidentally and often in a skeptical manner, if at all (Breemer ter Stege & Gittelman, 1987; Freeman, Fryers, & Henderson, 1985; May, 1976). The main success of the mental hygiene movement was the improvement of the quality of care for psychiatric patients, deinstitutionalization, and especially the development of facilities for outpatient community-oriented care, such as many child guidance centers. At the beginning of the 1980s in many European countries, mental hospitals and psychiatric departments of general hospitals were still dominating the mental health scene.

How was it possible that the mental hygiene movement in Europe had favored for such a long time the idea of primary prevention and mental health promotion and yet had not succeeded after World War II in making this task a substantial part of mental health care? This is an important question to answer because it will help us to estimate and perhaps improve our chances for success in the future. Undoubtedly there are many factors responsible, of which I would like to highlight four: (a) The scientific base of the mental hygiene movement was very weak, because the supporting sciences themselves (psychiatry, psychology, and sociology) were still in their infancy; (b) the movement did not succeed in translating its vague preventive goals into specific targets and long-term planning for systematic program development; (c) the preventive ideas of the movement were not translated into government responsibility, national public policy, or legislation; and (d) many countries had very low budgets for mental health care because mental health had a low priority, with prevention and mental health promotion frequently seen as a kind of luxury.

### Recent Developments in Europe

The overall picture of prevention developments in Europe was rather gloomy, at least until the early 1980s. For some countries, however, the picture was much brighter, and during the 1980s the situation in Europe improved. Generally speaking, prevention and mental health promotion are most developed in northwestern Europe, in countries such as the Netherlands, Norway, Finland, and Great Britain. Due to the influence of the WHO, more and more countries have become active in their preventive efforts. For the coming 20 years I hold a quite optimistic vision, with the presumption that we will succeed in overcoming some serious infrastructural problems. It is necessary to make quick progress because scenario studies point toward a significant increase in the demand for curative care during the next 20 years (Scenariocommissie Geestelijke Volksgezondheid, 1990).

#### Intercontinental Support

For the growth of prevention work in Europe we owe a great deal of gratitude to several well-known prevention experts from the United States. From the early 1960s to 1980, Gerald Caplan visited the Netherlands and other European countries several times, giving seminars and holding consultative meetings to spread his ideas. Several years later, Richard Price shared invaluable input for the improvement of the quality of our preventive work and initiated our efforts in the systematic evaluation of programs. The contributions of Price's (1983, 1988) four-domain model of prevention research and the "14 ounces of prevention" (Price, Cowen, Lorion, & Ramos-McKay, 1988) are spreading rapidly through the Netherlands as well as reaching other regions of Europe, as I was informed by one of my colleagues from Athens. Alexander Leighton (1987) made a similar contribution in supporting the Norwegians, as George Albee did for community-oriented psychologists in the Federal Republic of Germany. The organizers of the Vermont Conferences may be credited too, because their proceedings are used more and more as vital sources of knowledge on primary prevention of psychopathology and even more for mental health promotion in Europe.

### Prevention Programs

Notwithstanding the difficulties in obtaining information about prevention efforts in Europe, more and more examples are gradually becoming known. The present volume contains contributions on prevention programs for children from Great Britain, Norway, Germany, the Netherlands, Czechoslovakia, and Poland. Other examples could be added. Well known is the work of Rutter on protective factors and the influence of the school environment on children (e.g., Rutter, 1979). Very valuable for prevention, too, are the epidemiological studies of Brown and Harris in London on the social origins of depression in lower-class women (see Brown, Andrews, Harris, Adler, & Bridge, 1986; Brown, Bifulco, & Harris, 1987; Brown & Harris, 1978). Their epidemiological work of more than 20 years is now being translated into preventive strategies directed at girls at risk. In this respect, Jennifer Newton's (1988) recent book *Preventing Mental Illness* is also worth mentioning, as are the epidemiological studies of Tsiantis and Valavani in Greece on needs assessment of children at risk and their coping with severe life events. The investigators integrated their longitudinal research on risk and protective factors with the development of prevention programs in day-care centers and nursery, primary, and high schools (Soukou-Valavani, 1990). As a last example, note the day-care system that has been developed in Sweden, which nowadays gets much international interest because of its high quality.

### Volumes on Prevention

Having depended primarily on American publications for many years, I find it encouraging that several scientists and lecturers from various European countries have recently published their own volumes on prevention in mental health. There are volumes written by authors from Germany (Brandstädter & von Eye, 1982; Minsel & Scheller, 1981; Rudolf & Tölle, 1984; Stark, 1988), France (Chanoit & de Verbizier, 1987), Norway (Dalgard, 1987), the Netherlands

(Bosma & Hosman, 1990a; Hosman, Bosma, & Frazer, in press; Hosman, van Doorm, & Verburg, 1988), and Great Britain (Newton, 1988), as well as some by a combination of European authors (Cooper & Helgason, 1989). Of the many published articles, I would like to refer to two in English, both from German authors. Stark (1986) analyzes the different ideologies behind primary prevention and stresses the need for a theoretical basis. Cooper (1990) presents a critical discussion of the relationship between prevention and epidemiology and the value of contributions from community psychology.

### Legislation

Another promising development concerns the legislation that some European countries have accepted, favoring prevention and mental health promotion. An interesting example is the development that has taken place in the Federal Republic of Germany, where, during 1989, the *Gesundheits reformgesetzes* (Law on Health Reform) became operative (Wiche, 1990). An essential element of this law is the obligation of health insurance companies to finance and offer educational materials and programs in the field of prevention and health promotion and to search for determinants of health and disease. This law could have a very beneficial effect on the progress that needs to be made in prevention and mental health promotion.

Another example is the Paid Parental Leave Act that has been accepted recently in Sweden and allows either of the parents to leave work for up to 12 months after childbirth, with a continuation of 90% of salary. A third example of prevention-oriented legislation is offered by the Netherlands, where a law was passed several years ago requiring all primary schools to have a health education curriculum. Health education and mental health education are now a regular element of primary school programs in this country, and health education officials are lobbying for a comparable law for secondary schools. These examples show that stimulation of prevention-oriented legislation is a very productive strategy for increasing large-scale efforts in prevention and mental health education.

### Council of Europe

The Council of Europe plays a special role in the promotion of mental health for children. This council, made up of ministers from Western European countries, makes European policy, controlled by the European Parliament. With the growing unification of Europe, we may expect that this council will play an even more important role in the future in planning and financing Europewide prevention programs in mental health.

The Council of Europe recently published three valuable reports favoring mental health promotion for children. One report concerns the preparation of a European Convention on the Rights of the Child (Council of Europe, 1989b). This report reviews the many binding texts the council has published on various specific aspects of child welfare, the decisions of the European Committee on Human Rights, and the case law of the European Court of Human Rights. Another report strongly recommends the increase of day-care facilities for children (Council of Europe, 1988). It is estimated that within the European Economic Community there is a need for day care for 12 million children under the age of 3, in contrast to the 1 million places available. An overview on methods of child rearing in Europe and the role of family services is presented in another report of the council that describes many preventive measures and services that have been realized in the various European countries and policies for the 1990s (Council of Europe, 1989a). Examples of a more innovative nature include schools for parents; self-help groups for single parents, foster parents, and adoptive parents; regular magazines and television programs to present preventive messages; telephone call-in services; a youth ombudsman; and the creation of meeting places for children and parents according to the "Green House" model of Francoise Dolto in Paris.

The Council of Europe (1989c) also has specified additional priority items and target groups for mental health promotion and prevention directed toward young people:

(1) Psychosocial support to mothers suffering from serious mental disorders related to severe alcohol and drug dependency throughout their years of child rearing

(2) Help for children confronted with marital separation or parental death

(3) Promotion of psychosocial skills and adequate coping mechanisms through health education in schools, to address the increasing burdens on the ability of youths to solve problems because of rising expectations and requirements of children and especially adolescents, coinciding with less opportunity for them to rely on traditional norms and values

(4) Development of effective social networks and special housing programs for adolescents who are not supported adequately by their parents

(5) Special programs for children of ethnic minorities, immigrants, and refugees

Other problems needing preventive interventions include child abuse, suicide and parasuicide, depression, and school failures.

I would like to add to this list the mental health consequences that pollution has on children, a dramatic example being the nuclear disaster at Chernobyl. Now, three years after this tremendous accident, children in the area have to stay at home day after day and are not allowed to play in their gardens or on the streets. And what about nuclear plants with leakages resulting in a higher incidence of leukemia and cancer? What does it mean for children and their parents to live for years with the uncertainty of being victims of nuclear radiation?

**Role of the World Health Organization**

A strong incentive to the development of prevention in Europe has been presented by the WHO. While long interested in prevention, the WHO formerly had been quite skeptical about primary prevention of mental disorders. This has changed since the European Office of the WHO (1985) developed its Targets for Health for All by the Year 2000. The original draft of the European Health for All strategy, containing 38 targets, had been criticized for its limited emphasis on mental health. Since this criticism, special attention has been given to the mental health aspects of the program. Progressively, the European Office of the WHO is taking a lead in the stimulation of international cooperation in the development and implementation of effective preventive measures and mental health promotive interventions. As one of the results, the European countries represented in the World Health Organization accepted a policy document titled *Prevention of Mental, Psychosocial and Neurological Disorders in the European Region* (WHO, 1988). It specifies a broad range of measures to be implemented to promote mental health and prevent mental disorders, based on current scientific knowledge. The document lists primary, secondary, and tertiary preventive interventions, both general and more specific preventive measures, differentiated by their appropriateness for various age groups. The proposed interventions are directed at a broad range of biological, psychosocial, environmental, and social risk factors and protective factors. In addition, special attention is given to the development of standardized indicators for monitoring progress in implementation, and for promoting epidemiological and evaluative research.

The existence of such a European document, accepted by all the European governments, is a tremendous step forward. Yet, it is still just a paper of 80 grams lying on the desks of government officials and officers of national associations. So, the WHO is now preparing a strategy on how to implement those preventive measures throughout Europe, how to stimulate the needed infrastructures for prevention and research in this field, and how to integrate and make the best use of those activities that are ongoing in different European countries. For example, the WHO is preparing a European Task Force for Prevention of Mental Disorders, which will commence its work in 1991.

In 1989, just before the major political shifts in Eastern Europe, other members of the World Health Organization and I met at the German Hygiene Museum in Dresden with 25 experts from 10 European countries to start a European WHO Task Force on Mental Health Promotion and Education. For the short run this task force has chosen two priorities, both directed at the improvement of mental health in children. The first is the selection and implementation of preventive measures by primary health care centers to improve psychosocial development in children. Accordingly, the European Office of WHO recently organized a first international meeting on this subject in Athens (Soukou-

Valavani, 1990). The experts involved are searching for a feasible program of preventive measures for children under 5 years old, to be implemented by primary health care centers in the European countries. The second priority is the strengthening of psychosocial competence and coping skills education in the schools. A group of European experts was invited to convene in October 1990 to discuss their own experiences and to attempt to identify the most effective programs and the conditions for their successful implementation (Bosma & Hosman, 1990b). The recent volume of the VCPPP concerning school programs (Bond & Compas, 1989) was very valuable in supporting this effort.

The WHO Health for All strategy and the related Healthy Cities Project (see Stark, Chapter 12, this volume) are fostering the development of a new public health movement (Stark, 1986). They also may be the start of a new mental health movement that differs from the mental hygiene and first mental health movements in significant ways: This new mental health movement is oriented toward well-defined targets, scientifically based programs, and evaluation, and it includes formal agreements with the national governments that make it their responsibility to implement the Health for All program.

## The Future:
## Problems and Possibilities for Innovation

The main barriers to progress in preventive mental health care in Europe are not so much the lack of knowledge or programs. Rather, they are infrastructural problems and obstacles, at both national and international levels, that are clearly in need of innovative solutions: (a) the lack of shared information, (b) the lack of collaboration and coordination, and (c) the lack of management and planning.

### Lack of Shared Information

One of the main problems in Europe is a lack of communication about ongoing programs and research projects. There is a paucity of knowledge both within and across countries about which prevention programs have been developed and implemented, who the experts and leading organizations are, and which research institutions are conducting particular kinds of prevention research. Although I am very grateful to the organizers of the 1990 Vermont Conference on Primary Prevention for the networking opportunities that meeting provided, I find it bizarre that I have to travel to a small place called Burlington, Vermont, on another continent, 4,000 miles away, to meet several of my European colleagues in prevention for the first time—some even from my neighboring countries!

There is almost no systematic exchange of information about prevention work in Europe. Except for the work of a few people, such as Dan Olweus, there is not even a tradition of international publishing on prevention programs in

Europe. In part this is not surprising, given that we have to cope with approximately 25 different languages. If someone in San Francisco has written a high-quality article, there is a great likelihood that a colleague with similar interests in Washington, D.C., will come across the article in less than a year. If someone in Yugoslavia, however, writes an article on an interesting prevention program in his native language, it could take more than 10 years for this information to reach the other side of Europe, if it arrives at all. Thus the exchange of information is extraordinarily difficult.

My own country, the Netherlands, is a good example of the information problem. We have more than 20 years of experience with the development of prevention programs and numerous experts in our nation. Despite this situation, it is infrequent that we make international presentations or publish prevention articles in international journals. So I would like to make a plea to the non-English-speaking countries to write in, or have their publications translated into, English.

*New strategies for information exchange.* To deal with this lack of communication, we urgently need to develop a *European "Who's Who"* in this field and a continental and even intercontinental *network of clearinghouses* connected to well-informed sources in the different countries. Another important solution is the creation of a *European newsletter* on prevention and mental health promotion and the organization of *exchange markets for prevention programs*, as is done in industries and businesses. Stimulated by their contact during the 1990 Vermont Conference on Primary Prevention, a group of European prevention experts took the initiative to begin preparations for a first European Conference on Prevention and Mental Health Promotion, planned tentatively for 1992.

*Improved tracking of available knowledge and expertise.* A special problem in obtaining relevant information is that not all of the pertinent work and knowledge is labeled as *prevention* or *mental health promotion*. These labels produce only a minority of the relevant information available in the literature, as we had to conclude from our Prevention Evaluation Research Project at the University of Nijmegen after several computer searches. Many scientists and program directors do not recognize their work as prevention. The available resources and information needed to make more progress in the area of prevention are probably much more plentiful than we are aware.

How could we solve this problem? First, we could create a special *international thesaurus for prevention and mental health promotion* to make better use of the existing on-line information systems. Second, it is imperative that we *involve new relevant organizations and disciplines* in this new mental health movement, such as economists and experts in business, management, and legislation. To get more external support we need to make much clearer the *social and even economic value of mental health* and the social and economic benefits that could be expected from preventive programs.

*Health indicators and classification of programs.* To improve the exchange of information, at least two other conditions need to be met: increased availability of a set of useful mental health indicators, and a classification system to describe preventive programs and measures. We need indicators on the mental health status of population groups, risk and protective factors, implemented programs, and available infrastructures. A common set of indicators could play a significant role in helping to set priorities for prevention and in providing necessary feedback on the progress made in achieving our goals. Having comparable indicators will significantly enhance international collaboration in developing effective prevention programs and research. Among the current list of indicators added to the European Health for All program, indicators for mental health are quite meager (de Girolamo, 1989; WHO, 1981). The improvement of valid and useful indicators needs to be a topic for international collaboration.

Meaningful international exchange of information on programs and their effects requires a kind of international classification. The WHO in Copenhagen is developing an International Classification System of Mental Health Care. Parallel to this, an *International Classification of Preventive Care* will be prepared describing both the organization offering the program and the preventive program itself.

### Coordination and Collaboration

Another serious problem in Europe is the nearly complete lack of international collaboration and coordination in the field of preventive mental health, which leads to an inefficient use of our scarce resources. Even within a small country such as the Netherlands, it has become clear that there has been a waste of energy and money due to an inefficient planning of preventive efforts. Prevention teams in many different locations have been inventing, independent of one other, the same wheel. This enormous waste is magnified when repeated on a continentwide basis. A more efficient use of resources could be promoted by international agreements to concentrate on shared priority items and common problems and on a careful distribution of developmental tasks across the different expert centers or networks of centers.

Coordination and collaboration are needed at different levels. First, the collaboration among the Council of Europe and the European Offices of the WHO and the World Federation of Mental Health needs to be strengthened considerably. At this moment these organizations are operating quite independently. It is crucial that we achieve international agreement and wide support regarding a policy on prevention development. Second, we need a strong collaboration between the WHO and key persons in the different countries. This could be enhanced very much if every country would create some kind of national coordinating group for preventive action in mental health.

Further, it is imperative that *all* the European countries translate the Health for All program into national health policy. Another strategy is for us to become more involved in the already existing WHO network of the Healthy Cities Project. Although there are some good examples of mental health promotion programs within the Healthy Cities Project, especially programs focusing on children (Stark, 1986), overall the mental health involvement in this project is very meager.

I make a special plea for the creation of *international topic-specific collaborative networks* between centers for program development and prevention research. When professionals throughout Europe and other countries are working collaboratively on a shared topic, such as the development of a similar school program, the prevention of depression, or the prevention of psychiatric problems in children of mentally disturbed parents, it is my experience that progress can be made far more easily by a quick exchange of experiences and programs and by combining research efforts. In this respect, the WHO will select approximately 10 pilot areas throughout Europe to experiment collaboratively with the implementation of the WHO document on prevention of mental disorders.

### Management and Planning

The third main problem concerns the difficulties in management and planning of both program development and the development of a prevention sector at local, national, and international levels. Who should be involved at each of these levels? Who needs to be responsible for the development of programs and infrastructures, and which institutions are able to carry out this responsibility successfully? Who will take care of the continuity of program implementation and efficient use of the scarce resources for prevention? The main question is: How should we *manage* the development of prevention at the different levels? This topic has received only minor attention in the prevention literature, yet the answers are crucial if progress is to be made over the next 10 to 20 years.

The following examples demonstrate the complexity of this problem. The development and large-scale implementation of effective prevention programs could take 10 years or even longer. Funding is frequently provided only for a couple of years, and sometimes is heavily dependent upon short-term political priorities. If there is no guarantee of continuity, we run the risk that our investment of resources will be wasted, if not only used inefficiently. This emphasizes the importance of long-term planning of research, program development, and dissemination. It seems crucial, as well, to have small, permanent staffs available at local, state, and national levels to provide continuity independent of changing administrations and short-term grants.

Another problem arises from the large variation of infrastructures among the European countries—large differences in health systems, legislation, and financial regulations. Some countries have long-term health policies (i.e., Finland,

Sweden, the Netherlands) and others do not; some have specialized prevention and health education experts (i.e., Germany, the Netherlands), but most do not. Sometimes the prevention of mental disorders is seen as a task principally of primary health care centers, general practitioners, and district nurses (e.g., in England). Sometimes primary prevention is considered a task of politicians or nonprofessional organizations rather than of the health system.

Another important question is: Should we first develop effective prevention programs within the context of university research programs, and then look for possibilities to disseminate these products? Or should we link ourselves from the beginning with the support and involvement of service organizations that have the power and resources to implement programs on a large scale? Or should the development of new programs first and foremost be the responsibility of mental health centers or public health services, with research institutions following up on these initiatives to support the improvement of the most promising programs?

Because of large differences among European countries, we need to gain more insight into the possible models for prevention development and the available strategies to attain preventive goals. It would be very helpful if we could begin by creating an *inventory of the models of and pathways to prevention initiatives* that are currently used at different regional levels in Europe and on other continents. Subsequent to the inventory, we need to study the relative advantages and disadvantages of the different developmental models, and the ways in which the effectiveness of each may vary with cultural and economic climate. We are urgently in need of *theories* on the development of prevention and the needed infrastructures for progress. These issues need regular and more central positions on our agenda. Given their great importance for the future of prevention, they deserve to be central subjects in international conferences during the next decennium.

In summarizing my views, I am reminded of the title of a textbook that our clinical psychology students used about 10 years ago: *The Disorganized Personality* (Kisker, 1977). The situation of our field today seems most suitably characterized as *disorganized prevention*. The prevention field must be reorganized if it is to have a healthy future and be able to contribute significantly to a mentally healthy future for children.

### References

Bond, L. A., & Compas, B. E. (Eds.). (1989). *Primary prevention and promotion in schools.* Newbury Park, CA: Sage.

Bosma, M. W. M., & Hosman, C. M. H. (1990a). *Preventie op waarde geschat: een studie naar de beinvloedbaarheid van determinanten van psychische gezondheid.* Nijmegen: Beta.

Bosma, M. W. M., & Hosman, C. M. H. (1990b). *Primary prevention and mental health promotion in schools: Programs for competence* (Report for the European WHO Task Force for Mental Health Promotion and Education). Nijmegen: University of Nijmegen.

Brandstädter, J., & von Eye, A. (Eds.). (1982). *Psychologische Prävention: Grundlagen, Programme, Methoden.* Bern: Huber.

Breemer ter Stege, C., & Gittelman, M. (Eds.). (1987). Trends in mental health care in Western Europe in the past 25 years [Special issue]. *International Journal of Mental Health, 16*(1-2).

Brown, G. W., Andrews, B., Harris, T., Adler, Z., & Bridge, L. (1986). Social support, self-esteem and depression. *Psychological Medicine, 16,* 813-831.

Brown, G. W., Bifulco, A., & Harris, T. O. (1987). Life events, vulnerability and onset of depression. *British Journal of Psychiatry, 150,* 30-42.

Brown, G. W., & Harris, T. O. (1978). *Social origins of depression: A study of psychiatric disorder in women.* London: Tavistock.

Chanoit, P. F., & de Verbizier, J. (Eds.). (1987). *Sectorisation et prevention en psychiatrie.* Toulouse: Editions Eres.

Cooper, B. (1990). Epidemiology and prevention in the mental health field. *Social Psychiatry and Psychiatric Epidemiology, 25,* 9-15.

Cooper, B., & Helgason, T. (1989). *Epidemiology and prevention of mental illness.* London: Routledge.

Council of Europe. (1988). *Forms of child care.* Strasbourg: Author.

Council of Europe. (1989a). *Methods of child upbringing in Europe today and the role of family services.* Strasbourg: Author.

Council of Europe. (1989b). *The need for a European convention on children's rights.* Strasbourg: Author.

Council of Europe. (1989c). *Preliminary draft recommendation on the protection of the mental health of certain vulnerable groups in society.* Strasbourg: Author.

Dalgard, O. S. (Ed.). (1987). Preventive psychiatry, methods and experiences. *Acta Psychiatrica Scandinavica, 76,* 1-82.

de Girolamo, G. (1989). *Indicators for mental health programs.* Geneva: World Health Organization.

Freeman, H. L., Fryers, T., & Henderson, J. H. (1985). *Mental health services in Europe: 10 years on.* Copenhagen: World Health Organization Regional Office for Europe.

Gerards, F. M. (1984). *Psychosociale educatie: een strategie voor preventie.* Unpublished doctoral dissertation, University of Utrecht.

Hosman, C. M. H. (1989). Toekomst en innovatie van de preventieve geestelijke gezondheidszorg. *Tijdschrift Gezondheidsbevordering, 10,* 184-207.

Hosman, C. M. H., Bosma, M. W. M., & Frazer, W. (in press). *Effectiviteit van preventieve interventies: effecten en voorwaarden.* Nijmegen: University of Nijmegen, Department of Clinical Psychology.

Hosman, C. M. H., van Doorm, H., & Verburg, H. (Eds.). (1988). *Preventie In-Zicht.* Lisse: Swets & Zeitlinger.

Kisker, G. W. (1977). *The disorganized personality.* Tokyo: McGraw-Hill.

Leighton, A. H. (1987). Primary prevention of psychiatric disorders. *Acta Psychiatrica Scandinavica, 76* (Suppl. 337), 7-13.

May, A. R. (1976). *Mental health care in Europe.* Geneva: World Health Organization.

Meng, H. (1939). *Seelicher Gesundheidsschutz.* Basel: Schwabe.

Meyer, A. (1973). The role of mental factors in psychiatry. In T. Millon (Ed.), *Theories of psychopathology and personality.* Philadelphia: Saunders. (Original work published 1908)

Minsel, W. R., & Scheller, R. (Ed.). (1981). *Brennpunkte der Klinische Psychologie (Band 2): Prevention.* Munich: Kösel Verlag.

166 Clemens M. H. Hosman

Newton, J. (1988). *Preventing mental illness.* London: Routledge & Kegan Paul.

Pfister-Ammende, M. (Ed.). (1955). *Geistige hygiene, forschung und praxis.* Basel: Schwabe.

Price, R. H. (1983). The education of a prevention psychologist. In R. Felner, L. Jason, J. Moritsugu, & S. Farber (Eds.), *Preventive psychology* (pp. 290-296). New York: Pergamon.

Price, R. H. (1988). The prevention enterprise in mental health: History, state of the art and future prospects. In C. M. H. Hosman, H. van Doorm, & H. Verburg (Eds.), *Preventie In-Zicht.* Amsterdam: Swets & Zeitlinger.

Price, R. H., Cowen, E. L., Lorion, R. P., & Ramos-McKay, J. (Eds.). (1988). *14 ounces of prevention: A casebook for practitioners.* Washington, DC: American Psychological Association.

Reimann, H. (1967). *Die Mental Health Bewegung.* Tübingen: Mohr/Siebeck.

Roemer, H. (Ed.). (1929). *Bericht über die Erste Deutsch Tagung für psychische Hygiene.* Berlin/Leipzig: de Gruyter.

Rudolf, G. A. E., & Tölle, R. (Eds.). (1984). *Prävention in der Psychiatrie.* Berlin: Springer.

Rutter, M. (1979). Protective factors in children's responses to stress and disadvantage. In M. W. Kent & J. Rolf (Eds.), *Primary prevention of psychopathology: Social competence in children.* Hanover, NH: University Press of New England.

Scenariocommissie Geestelijke Volksgezondheid. (1990). *Zorgen voor geestelijke gezondheid in de toekomst.* Utrecht: Bohn, Scheltema & Holkema.

Soukou-Valavani, I. (1990). *Summary report of the WHO Child Mental Health Meeting on Preventive Aspects for the Under Fives.* Athens: Aghia Sophia Children's Hospital, Department of Psychological Pediatrics.

Stark, W. (1986). The politics of primary prevention in mental health: The need for a theoretical basis. *Health Promotion, 1*(2), 179-185.

Stark, W. (Ed.). (1988). *Lebensweltbezogene Prävention und Gesundheitsförderung: Konzepten und Strategien für die psychosoziale Praxis.* Freiburg: Lambertus Verlag.

Wiche, E. (1990). Zum Stand der Gesundheitsförderung durch die Krankenkassen nach der Gesundheidtsreformgesetzes. *Zeitschrift für Gesundheitsförderung, 13*(1), 3-7.

World Health Organization. (1981). *Development of indicators to measure progress towards health for all by the year 2000.* Geneva: Author.

World Health Organization. (1985). *Targets for health for all.* Copenhagen: WHO Regional Office for Europe.

World Health Organization. (1988). *Prevention of mental, psychosocial and neurological disorders in the European Region.* Copenhagen: WHO Regional Office for Europe.

# 12

# Empowerment and Social Change: Health Promotion Within the Healthy Cities Project of WHO—Steps Toward a Participative Prevention Program

**Wolfgang Stark**

The concept of empowerment (Rappaport, 1981, 1987; Stark, 1989) as a model for health promotion has far-reaching implications for our professional activities, especially in the area of primary prevention. If taken seriously, empowerment means basic changes in the ideas and methods of the field in both practice and research, for it leaves behind a view of professionals and researchers in social and health science as parental. To illustrate such change, we look at a health promotion project for children and youth in the city of Munich. This project is part of the Healthy Cities Project initiated by the European office of the World Health Organization (WHO). The Healthy Cities Project networks more than 30 cities (Rotterdam, Stockholm, Barcelona, Milan, and London, among others) throughout Europe, all trying to get health promotion efforts started on the urban level. While these 30 cities form an international exchange network, the Healthy Cities Project, since its start in 1986, has also encouraged more than 250 cities in Europe to start health promotion projects and to participate in national networks that have been developed by the core cities of the international program. The Munich Healthy Cities Project reflects our notion of primary prevention and our professional work within the Munich Self-Help Resource Center.

In recent years, most intervention programs attempting to prevent physical or mental health problems have been aimed at individuals. To protect these individuals from health risks, their habits (e.g., smoking), their behavior (e.g., ways of coping with life events), or their social environments were to be changed. As I have noted in an earlier paper, these conceptions of primary prevention are based on unexplicated assumptions and often are transferred from professional and scientific contexts so that they relate marginally and sometimes not at all to

167

the issue of primary prevention (Stark, 1986). Historical analyses of primary prevention efforts show the impact of these "value preoccupations," and the analyses are still true for the present situation (Cumming, 1972; Spaulding & Balch, 1983). These assumptions are summarized in the following statements (for a more thorough analysis see Stark, 1986, 1989):

(1) There are two groups of people: persons at risk and persons not at risk. If there is no etiological knowledge of specific disorders, try to find genetic or behavioral risks attributable to individuals. This public health model of prevention is aimed at classifying people or populations and prescribing interventions following this categorization.

(2) Reducing risks and promoting "healthy behavior" or habits will enhance both physical and mental health and thereby reduce costs for (mental) health care. (Individuals are held responsible for their own health status and are taught how to change their habits individually by various forms of health education.)

(3) Institutions, organizations, and communities will present problems in the same way individuals do. Social and community interventions, therefore, are a promising way of changing behavior patterns on a large scale. Since the above two models will not cover the full range of problems in a population because of limited capacities, the activities of professionals should be extended to a higher level of intervention.

Assumptions about prevention and intervention are strongly influenced by the traditional models of (mental) health care: The professional is the expert who solves the problems of a client. This "parenting view" toward individuals in need (Rappaport, 1981) adds to the power of health and human service agencies rather than changes them to promote health. Rappaport (1981) puts it this way:

> This is what underlies much of prevention: Find so-called high-risk people and save them from themselves if they like it or not by giving them, or even better, their children, programs which we develop, package, sell, operate and otherwise control. Teach them how to fit in and be less of a nuisance. Convince them that a change in their test scores is somehow a change in their lives. (p. 13)

The picture here is of a human being who is run by techniques, controlled and controllable, calculated and predictable. This picture reproduces the traditional medical model in our health and social policies. Instead, if we take seriously the ideas of health promotion discussed by the WHO (1986) and in the context of projects such as Healthy Cities (Hancock, 1990), we must develop an independent theoretical background for our endeavors.

## Health Promotion as an Empowerment Process

The World Health Organization has been considered a promoter of preventive approaches oriented toward individual behavior change. The Ottawa Charter on Health Promotion, which has been signed by experts and representatives of more than 60 countries, has changed the politics of the WHO considerably: The concept of health promotion discussed in the Ottawa Charter has far-reaching implications that go way beyond health in the common sense. Health promotion no longer is achieved only by advocating healthful food, physical exercise, or early medical examinations. Instead, health promotion "aims at reducing differences in current health status and ensuring equal opportunities and resources to enable all people to achieve their fullest health potential" (WHO, 1986, p. 3). Here *health* is seen as a synonym for a better quality of life, and improving health means improving the way working, living, and environmental conditions are organized in our society in order to make it a source of health and not a source of illness. Ilona Kickbusch (1985), one of the architects of the Healthy Cities Project in Europe, states:

Health promotion redirects thinking about health:—by reasserting its social and political aspects—by ensuring the people the power to define their own health concerns—by placing health more clearly in the context of other aims in life. (p. 5)

The Ottawa Charter on Health Promotion expresses a wide array of perspectives on promoting health through public policy. Specifically important are the active role of the public and the call for social action and community participation from the very beginning. Together with a multisector approach, these perspectives are essential for health promotion, fostering the strengths and the resources of people and settings in order to overcome deficits and weaknesses. In other words, they initiate empowerment processes and social change.

The concept of empowerment (Rappaport, 1987; Stark, 1989; Swift & Levin, 1987) is a model for our future prevention efforts and serves as the conceptual background of our work in Munich. *Empowerment* means reversing and reinterpreting traditional goals and concepts of social and health care, so that the focus is no longer on deficits of people or settings to be cured or prevented. A social policy of empowerment (Rappaport, 1981) emphasizes quite the opposite. It focuses on processes that enhance the strength of people and their ability to control their own lives and their situations in a social environment. If one important premise for emotional and psychosocial well-being is the ability of a person to control his or her own life (Gronemeyer, 1988; Hohner & Hoff, 1983; Illich, 1982; Kieffer, 1984), then empowerment provides the appropriate theoretical background and knowledge base for all our efforts to promote health. It is not easy to define empowerment, for we are used to the semantics of needs, weaknesses, and deficits: powerlessness, learned helplessness, alienation, loss of sense of control over one's life. Empowerment requires a radical change in our conception of psychosocial and health issues. Focusing on the strength of (re)gaining control over one's life, empowerment

> (1) refers both to the phenomenological development of a certain state of mind (e.g. feeling powerful, competent, worthy of esteem, etc.) and to the modification of structural conditions in order to reallocate power (e.g. modifying the society's opportunity structure)—in other words, empowerment refers both to the subjective experience and the objective reality; and (2) is both a process and a goal. (Swift & Levin, 1987, p. 73)

Empowerment does not aim at any specific outcome or at normative goals. The process for a single elderly person resisting placement in a nursing home may look very different than that for a young single mother struggling through life, or for people in a mutual-aid group on chronic diseases, or for a group of citizens trying to protect their homes from a new housing development plan. Empowerment processes are not run or controlled by professionals; they occur in everyday life with any kind of people, groups, or structures, although there are situations and conditions that either foster or hinder the process.

From a community study on the empowerment process of poor citizens, Kieffer (1980) derived the following dimensions of empowerment:

> 1. Development of a more positive and potent sense of self (self-concept) 2. Construction of knowledge and capacity for more critical comprehension of the web of social and political relations which comprise one's experienced environment, and 3. Cultivation of resources and strategies, or more functional competence, for efficacious and protective attainment of personal and collective socio-political goals. (p. 18)

It is necessary to distinguish the kinds of questions relevant to psychosocial phenomena—questions that enhance the empowerment process of people, settings, and structures or that tend to pacify. These different types of questions can be called "needs questions" and "resources questions": The needs question leads to a society of needs and quick fulfillment. What are the needs of a person or a situation? is at the same time a pacification question. It implies that we must satisfy the needs and, if we are successful, the process comes to an end. The person in need is "waiting"—which most often means passivity. On the other hand, if we ask resources questions, we are asking about resources inherent in a person or a situation, asking about things useful for the future. If we ask about situations causing scarcity and lack of resources, making life hard for people or preventing the enhancement of their potential, we are not only asking about what is, but also for the causes and the background. And, most important, we start a process without controlling the outcome. Here, the corresponding action type is "searching." We are starting a process that is expanding, because searching cannot be restricted to one individual, but instead involves contact with people and settings.

### Healthy Cities: The Munich Approach

Initiating a process of empowerment within the context of health promotion was our very first idea when we heard about the Healthy Cities Project that was about to start in some European cities. The program matched the goal of our Self-Help Resource Center in Munich, which was not only to serve as a clearinghouse for self-help groups but also to network self-help groups of various kinds (e.g., citizens' groups on the grass-roots level and related organizations) to gain influence by concerned citizens on public policy and to foster community participation.

Spring 1987 marked the starting point of the Healthy Cities Project in Munich. In the beginning, the Munich Self-Help Resource Center, together with some 50 self-help groups and nonprofit organizations, discussed possibilities for health promotion in the city. Concerned by multiple social and health problems affecting especially children, we agreed to focus on health promotion for children and youth. Soon we approached members of the City Council, and, after some reluctance, the city established a steering committee chaired by one of the mayors to prepare the project. The Self-Help Resource Center agreed to network citizen groups and nonprofit organizations and to set up an office to coordinate these efforts.

In order to integrate a major part of the city's administration, the Health Department coordinates the activities of other departments participating in the project (Planning and Developmental Department, Youth Department, Department for Cultural Affairs, School Department, and Department of Environmental Protection). Since last year two special project clearinghouses—one to network the citizens' groups that are part of the Munich Self-Help Resource Center, the other at the Health Department to coordinate the activities of the administration—have been established. These offices are working together closely in order to provide information and newsletters for people interested in the program. They are also trying to get more groups and departments involved in the program.

One of the first effects of this new type of collaboration between citizens and administration has been the decision of the City Council to declare the Ottawa Charter on Health Promotion as the basis for the future policy of the city. All participants and the City Council agreed upon "health promotion for children and youth" as the main focus of the Healthy Cities Project in Munich. There are two reasons for this choice: (a) Social and ecological problems in the city have a stronger impact on the lives of children, and (b) children are always struck harder by environmental or social constraints that basically affect all people. Therefore, enhancing health and living conditions for children in Munich would have far-reaching effects in the long run for all citizens.

Munich is more and more becoming a city designed for young urban professionals; children and families in the context of this development are becoming marginal. To ensure a good quality of life for the city, it is important to think about the part of the population who will be in charge in the future: the children and youth of today.

The citizens' groups, together with members of the administration, established six task forces on health promotion in Munich to address the following: health care and nutrition, social environment and living conditions in the neighborhoods, environmental protection, schools, advocating for children (Kids' Lobby), and establishment of Future Labs. Another task force on economics, labor, and health will be formed soon. In the process, all participants agreed upon the overall goals described below as the goals of the Munich Healthy Cities Project, and agreed to work to put them into action.

First, health promotion at an urban level is efficient only when it is a vital part of the basic policy of the city—which means it is an overall goal and criterion influencing all administrative decisions and planning strategies. The special emphasis of the program—improvement of the living conditions of children and youth—put two major goals on the political agenda: the issue of health promotion regarding the weaker part of the population and the understanding that developing a healthy public policy means talking about the future of the city, and especially the future of the people.

The development of the project already shows the particularity of the Munich program, especially in comparison with programs in other cities. This specific program has been a joint venture of the Self-Help Resource Center and a number of citizens' groups working toward an active collaboration of citizens of all ages with professionals and city officials. The program therefore could develop an active and perhaps ongoing cooperation between, and equal status for, city officials and concerned citizens. This clearly is an effect of the bottom-up strategy. It has the potential to benefit from both the administration's strengths (continuity, financial and human resources, planning competence) and the strengths of informal groups (flexibility, innovative power, sensitivity for and sense of the community); the two groups can support each other's efforts while not blurring contradictions in interests and goals.

The second step following joint planning of health promotion efforts was to activate and integrate the public and the people in the neighborhoods—especially children and youth. Special attempts were made to achieve this goal: Most of the 17 projects that are part of the Munich Healthy Cities Project are, or will be, carried out together with citizens in specific neighborhoods or all over the city. For instance, parents from various advocacy groups for children with chronic diseases formed a parents' advisory board concerning health care delivery for children, which in the meantime has gained official status within the city's administration. In another project, specific neighborhoods with environmental or social problems have been selected as models for the improvement of the social environment, especially regarding the living conditions for children. In one neighborhood parents and other community activists, with the support of the city's garden department, began converting abandoned lots into temporary playgrounds and parks. Elsewhere, community activists organized neighborhood kids to conduct their own research on opportunities for playing safely in the neighborhood, tying that to proposals for traffic reduction and building their own playgrounds.

We started a series of laboratories with children, youth, and adults to develop perspectives on the city from the grass-roots level. These Future Labs are both planning instruments and tools for envisioning, an attempt to stimulate the social fantasy of citizens in order to encourage them to create and shape their own (physical and social) environment. A central part of the Munich Healthy Cities Project, Future Labs help to monitor ongoing activities and projects and to generate new ideas. As a start, last year we organized five Future Labs and a contest on the future of the city with children and youth. In addition, some Future Labs have been organized specifically for adults—for example, Perspectives of Being a Parent in Munich or Collaborative Planning for Health Promotion with city officials, politicians, members of citizen's groups, mental health professionals, and other public organizations (Stark & Haberland, 1990). The results of the Future Labs have included a variety of detailed proposals and innovative plans for a healthier city developed by both kids and adults. They have been displayed and discussed during a four-week exhibition and conference on the future of the city. The conference program included talk shows, excursions to industrial plants and research labs, various workshops, and radio and television programs, culminating in the city's first Kids' Forum in Munich's City Hall, all performed by children and youth. They took the leading part during the conference (adults have been admitted only as resource persons), discussing their issues with politicians and city officials. These discussions will continue regularly, and have led to an official Kids' Council in the city of Munich.

Other parts of the program are still struggling due to lack of support by large parts of the city's administration. Projects in the areas of environmental protection or schools, although well designed and of high priority, do not get adopted by officials. Citizens who put a large amount of time and energy in various types of voluntary action then do not feel valued, and officials get the feeling of being criticized or underestimated by active citizens. In addition, ideas and proposals presented by kids often are not valued as serious contributions to the solution of so-called grown-up problems. This shows the sometimes huge cultural gap between those "in charge" and those "in need," who apparently are to be kept in need within our bureaucratic structures. Bridging this gap and achieving collaboration in health promotion and the improvement of the living conditions of the children in the cities is one of the most challenging tasks of the Healthy Cities Project in the future. We started addressing this issue by organizing Future Labs on collaboration, bringing people together who usually do not meet or even plan projects together. In addition, the Healthy Cities Project used already existing community boards in the neighborhoods, or formed new ones where necessary. These groups designed their own health and health promotion needs and processes in their area. Crucial for the near future, however, is to convince the Munich City Council to provide the financial or organizational resources that turn out to be necessary to get projects off the ground, for continuing education, and for events or meetings in the neighborhoods.

Despite all barriers we are optimistic. Although the Healthy Cities Project by definition is a five-year program, the goal of developing a city that is becoming a healthier and more promising place for Munich's children, and all other parts of the population, will remain on the political agenda of the future.

**Lessons We Learned**

What we learned from the program, but also from our broader work within the Munich Self-Help Resource Center, is that it is necessary to work on linking three different areas to initiate empowerment processes and social change: sociopolitical impact, neighborhood projects, and community participation. The combination of the three creates unique resources and enhances the strengths of each. It also helps to prevent the weaknesses and restrictions connected with specific types of action or research—be it political work, grass-roots activism, or conducting a scientific study.

Community participation in this sense is a very fragile yet durable and challenging process. It requires specific types of support, providing space for reflection and discovery, and also a structure of everyday life that allows us to shape situations, physical environments, or social institutions. If we want everybody to be an active and reflective member of his or her community (and, once again, this seems to be one of the important premises to prevent health and mental health problems), there have to be various kinds of resources to rely on—financial, interactive, and emotional. We still do not know very much about the processes and conditions that foster or hinder community participation and empowerment; obviously, these processes and conditions constitute one of the most crucial and most difficult parts of the entire Healthy Cities Project. The Munich Self-Help Resource Center therefore recently started a small study on community participation among the member cities of the National Healthy Cities network in the Federal Republic of Germany (Bobzien, Geislinger, Hillenbrand, & Stark, 1990).

Perhaps the first and most important task for professionals, if they want to adopt an empowerment perspective in their work, is to learn to ask questions, not to give answers, to develop a sensitivity for strengths in people and settings. In order for these strengths to be enhanced and expanded, connections are necessary among individuals, groups, institutions, and the social environment. There have to be opportunities to shape these connections and linkages, for this will change and enhance both people and settings. Professionally, there are two ways to support empowerment processes: (a) by providing and fostering opportunities to link people and groups in order to start a process through which they can share experiences as well as organize and shape their own lives and social environments; and (b) by emphasizing especially those intermediary lines between the different levels of empowerment. Initiating exchange between these levels, making it possible for them to influence each other, is one of the most important ways to foster empowerment processes. Establishing linkages between these different levels also means enhancing community participation. In sum, professional work on empowerment often means a very indirect way of working with people. It is working with people, but with people in context.

Humankind, until now, has spent an incredible amount of time and energy on controlling and exploiting our natural resources. Maybe now, at the turn of the century leading to the year 2000, the time has come to develop and foster primarily human resources. Human resources and power will be productive under the conditions of freedom and promotion. This requires the courage to initiate processes that are not totally predictable. Perhaps this challenge constitutes the future role for professionals in the human services: to be infectious for empowerment and sometimes even to cause epidemics.

## References

Bobzien, M., Geislinger, R., Hillenbrand, W., & Stark, W. (1990). *Über die Schwierigkeit, sich einzumischen. Partizipationsprozesse in der Gesundheitsförderung.* Unpublished manuscript, Munich.

Cumming, E. (1972). Primary prevention: More cost than benefit? In H. Gottesfeld (Ed.), *The critical issues of community mental health* (pp. 161-174). New York: Behavioral.

Gronemeyer, M. (1988). Die Macht der Bedürfnisse. *Reflexionen über ein Phantom.* Reinbek: Rowohlt.

Hancock, T. (1990). Developing healthy public policies at the local level. In A. Evers, W. Farrant, & A. Trojan (Eds.), *Healthy public policy at the local level.* Frankfurt: Campus.

Hohner, H. U., & Hoff, E. H. (1983). Prävention und Therapie. Zur Modifikation von objektiver Kontrolle und Kontrollbewusstsein. *Psychosozial, 20,* 30-48.

Illich, I. (1982). *Vom Recht auf Gemeinheit.* Reinbek: Rowohlt.

Kickbusch, I. (1985). *Health promotion: The move towards a new public health.* Unpublished manuscript, Copenhagen.

Kieffer, C. (1980). *Empowerment: An alternative approach to prevention.* Unpublished manuscript, University of Michigan, Ann Arbor.

Kieffer, C. (1984). Citizen empowerment: A developmental perspective. *Prevention in Human Services, 3,* 9-37.

Rappaport, J. (1981). In praise of paradox: A social policy of empowerment over prevention. *American Journal of Community Psychology, 9,* 1-25.

Rappaport, J. (1987). Terms of empowerment/exemplars of prevention: Toward a theory for community psychology. *American Journal of Community Psychology, 15,* 121-144.

Spaulding, J., & Balch, P. (1983). A brief history of primary prevention in the 20th century: 1908-1980. *American Journal of Community Psychology, 11,* 59-80.

Stark, W. (1986). The politics of primary prevention in mental health: The need for a theoretical basis. *Health Promotion, 1,* 179-185.

Stark, W. (1989). *Empowerment, health promotion and the competence for social conflict and change.* In J. W. Salmon & E. Goepel (Eds.), *Community participation and empowerment strategies in health promotion: Symposium papers.* Bielefeld: University of Bielefeld.

Stark, W., & Haberland, C. (1990). *Future laboratories: A tool for visioneering.* Unpublished manuscript, Munich.

Swift, C., & Levin, G. (1987). Empowerment: An emerging mental health technology. *Journal of Primary Prevention, 8,* 71-94.

World Health Organization. (1986). *Ottawa charter for health promotion.* Copenhagen: Author.

# 13

# The Dutch Way of Prevention

**Henk Verburg**
**Hans Janssen**
**Marion Rikken**
**Cees Hoefnagels**
**Elsa M. van Willenswaard**

## Prevention: An Integral Part of Outpatient Services in the Netherlands

Henk Verburg

The Netherlands is a small and very crowded country in Western Europe with roughly 15 million inhabitants. The country is divided into 12 provinces, which together are divided into more than 700 municipalities. In the Netherlands there are 57 Regional Institutes for Outpatient Mental Health Care (RIAGGs, for short), each servicing about 250,000 people. In a big city such as Amsterdam, there are five RIAGGs; in a big but less populated province such as Friesland, there is only one. The regions of the RIAGGs together cover the whole country. A RIAGG is comparable to a community mental health center. It can be described as a service somewhere between a place for general health care (the family doctor) and a psychiatric hospital. Each RIAGG has departments for children, juveniles, adults, and elderly people. The activities of the RIAGGs are paid for by a national government insurance system: Every Dutch citizen has the right to be helped free of charge by a RIAGG when he or she needs it.

Considering the prevention of psychopathology in the Netherlands, it is important to know that every RIAGG has not only a therapeutic task, but also a preventive task. Every RIAGG has one or more prevention workers. This means that there are more than 200 prevention workers in the Netherlands. Together they run more then 400 big and small regional prevention projects. Some 70% of these projects are aimed at roughly the same 10 topics: parental education, the school system, sexual violence and incest, work and unemployment, divorce, ethnic groups, women, elderly people, suicide, and social functioning. All the projects are run on a regional scale. There are virtually no national prevention projects. On the other hand, there is more and more cooperation among different regions.

For the last 15-20 years a systematic development of mental health care prevention (MHC prevention, as we call it) has been established. During the 1980s a national prevention policy was developed within the Netherlands Association for Outpatient and Community Mental Health Care (the union of the RIAGGs). This policy has had a big influence on the development of the prevention efforts of the RIAGGs.

There is a lot of agreement about the definition of this kind of prevention: It works toward the systematic averting—in a broad sense—of serious mental health problems. Because these problems are often developed or preserved under the influence of a combination of factors on individual and social levels, prevention activities are usually, directly or indirectly, aimed at individuals and groups as well as at organizations and social structures. Within a preventive approach one can work from a problem-oriented perspective as well as thematically. Health promotion activities also fit in a preventive approach. There is also agreement about the way this type of prevention must be designed and carried out: as projects, based on a good analysis of the problem and a well-designed and well-described strategy and supported by evaluation research.

Mental health care prevention in the Netherlands has several interesting features that people from other countries may find useful. First, with RIAGG prevention there is an established regional structure in the Netherlands for MHC prevention—a structure that covers all ages and every part of the country. Second, an important element of this structure is that the prevention function does not stop the moment a prevention project is implemented in the region. The prevention worker just carries on with another project. This means that a body of knowledge and experience builds up in the RIAGG that guarantees continuity in the prevention function.

A third advantage of this structure is that it has allowed the development of a shared prevention policy for the whole mental health care sector. This policy is supported by the RIAGGs and has been translated into concrete activities. A fourth point of interest is the close relationship between prevention and therapeutic work done by the RIAGGs. The result is that the RIAGG prevention activities include a range of topics and approaches: primary, secondary, and tertiary prevention as well as mental health promotion. Many prevention programs combine the different approaches. The prevention activities are based on specialized knowledge about mental health present in the RIAGGs and are partly carried out by therapeutic workers. The prevention workers are often the coordinators of the projects. In the four presentations about prevention projects in the Netherlands presented below, you will see how these characteristics work out in practice.

This leads to my fifth point: Through this close relationship with therapeutic work, prevention clearly functions as an innovator within the mental health system.

Examples are mental health care aimed at women, at the perpetrators and victims of incest and child abuse, and at those who manifest mental health problems connected with work or unemployment. This means that the therapeutic work done by the RIAGG deals more than before with relevant community problems.

A final point is that MHC prevention work in Holland is backed by a supportive national structure. This allows successful projects to be exported to other regions. Currently a number of national model programs are being developed.

A disadvantage of the present system in the Netherlands is that there is much diversity in the work done. Each region sets its own priorities. Too often, projects that have already been carried out in one region are developed again in another region. This is not a very efficient way to use the existing capacity. Another disadvantage is that prevention in the Netherlands still has more structure than content at this time. There is more quantity than quality. This is shown, for example, by the fact that little in-depth prevention research has been done. Third, strangely enough, in the Netherlands there is a rather strong separation between "health education" and "mental health prevention."

These disadvantages may surprise you in a country where prevention in mental health care seems to be so well structured, but they are a logical result of the way in which prevention was developed in the Netherlands. It began at a very basic practical level, without much theoretical and methodological support. Each prevention worker started in his or her own way and tried to build up prevention programs from scratch. This is totally opposite to the situation in some other countries, where much money, energy, and expertise is put into the development and testing of an effective prevention program, often one that is thereafter not repeated because there is no structure to implement the project elsewhere.

It is clear that prevention work in the Netherlands has strong and weak points. We hope, through international contacts, to learn from others and to share our experiences. Our structure and your programs could be a winning combination. This description of the Dutch situation provides you with a context for the four examples of prevention projects in the Netherlands that follow.

## Play Guidance at Home

**Hans Janssen**

In the major cities in the Netherlands, such as Amsterdam, Rotterdam, and the Hague, large numbers of immigrants from Turkey and Morocco have settled during recent decades. In certain areas 15-20% of the population are immigrants. In some elementary schools 98% of the children are immigrant children. For most of the immigrants from Morocco and Turkey, the new life in the Netherlands is a hard life. Apart from all the problems caused by living in a strange environment with a different language and a different set of values, there are specific problems such as housing, employment, health, mental health, and the education of children.

Immigrant children often start their school careers with a certain developmental retardation and other arrears that are hard to make up and that cause new problems for them in school and later in the labor market. Many of these children demonstrate lack of social skills, especially in playing together with other children. They also have very short concentration spans, moving from one plaything to another as soon as they come in contact with playthings in the elementary school.

That, at least, was the signal we received at the RIAGG in the Hague, where I work, from a few worried school social workers, about seven years ago. This signal corresponded perfectly with similar signals: The government and the local authorities and the RIAGG staff had decided almost at the same time to give priority to the increasing mental health problems of immigrants and top priority to the problems of immigrant children.

When we started this project, my colleague Ineke Wienese and I did some exploratory research, mainly by interviewing schoolteachers, school doctors, health visitors, and other professionals in the area. We found out that immigrant children with these kinds of problems all had two factors in common:

- The mothers of these children all lived very isolated lives. They were all Muslim women, and they had practically no contacts whatsoever, with Dutch women or with women of their own nationalities.
- In the houses of these families there also seemed to be no toys or games of any kind available for the children. In addition, parents did not seem to pay much attention to stimulating their children to play. Instead, their major parental educational task seemed to be to try to keep the children quiet.

Combine these two factors and you get the picture: mothers and children, sitting in a poorly furnished room, all day long, every day, doing nothing exciting, nothing that is fun or that stimulates communication. That is boring, believe me. Certainly it is boring for children, who have a great need for stimulation and discoveries of any kind. When children get bored, they get restless, and become—in the eyes of the parents who try to keep them quiet—disobedient. They have to be punished more and more, simply because they do not keep quiet.

The boredom of the children not only frustrated their own development, it influenced all of family life. Quite often we met, in the project, immigrant mothers who were getting more and more depressed. They not only felt homesick and isolated, they also felt a certain incapacity to raise their children well. While we were interviewing in the area, the juvenile police of the Hague did some research among runaway youngsters. When children run away from home, that is always a signal that there is something wrong within the family. The police in the Hague found that most of these runaways were immigrant kids. Their main complaint was that they had no contact, no communication whatsoever with their parents. Of course, there was a language problem—these children, growing up and going to school in Holland, were learning to speak Dutch, while their parents still spoke Moroccan and Turkish. Yet language was not the biggest problem—the biggest problem was the lack of communication of any kind.

How could we intervene? How could we demonstrate to these parents the importance of playing with their children instead of constantly trying to keep them quiet? Organizing parents' groups would make no sense at all: These parents would not come to such groups. Distributing brochures and leaflets promised to be even less successful: Many parents—and that goes certainly for the mothers—could not read, either Dutch or their own language.

Instead, we created a form of home training and a perfect network of participating professionals: a health visitor, a school social worker, and others. We especially searched for professionals who had access to the families because they knew the families personally, through professional contacts. We also contacted the College for Professional Youthwork. Students at this college get a very good theoretical education and also have to fulfill a year of practical assignment. Additionally, these students are the perfect age for this project (20-21 years old). They are enthusiastic about working and playing with children, and they adopt a more and more professional attitude during their college years, which is of great importance for methods such as home training and modeling.

We made an agreement with the College for Youthwork: Each year we get 20-25 students. Only female students are recruited, because we work with Muslim families. Each student works in the project for a year, spending 150-200 hours in the project.

After a one-week training program, each student is introduced into one Moroccan or Turkish family, which is carefully selected for the project. The families are informed a few weeks in advance by the health visitor or the school social worker. They are not only informed, but also asked if they really agree with the introduction of (as it was announced) "a girl who comes every week to play with your children." When parents hesitate, no persuasive power is used, but practically all parents have said yes from the very start of the project.

Each student is introduced into one family by the health visitor. After the introduction, she visits "her" family every week on a regular day. Each time, she brings toys, games, and so on for the children from the toy library (which, by the way, participates in the project, too). She spends an hour or so playing with each child individually, to give them each personal attention. Then she plays with all the children together, when that is possible. In the first weeks all students are confronted with real civil wars within the families. Children can cause a big fuss over one toy, many times destroying the toy meanwhile. These children are not used to toys, and they are certainly not used to sharing them with their brothers and sisters. The students must use their educational skills to help the children to solve their own fights and find ways of playing together and, at the same time, to be good models for the parents, who are mostly eager to solve the fights with their bare hands.

When there is time left and the weather is okay (which is not always so in Holland), the student might ask the parents' permission to take the children out, to go to a recreation ground, the zoo, the beach, the library, or the toy library. Before she goes home, she tries to have a short conversation with the parents. (This is one of the biggest problems in the project—most of the fathers speak at least some Dutch and can understand it, but most of the mothers do not.) Talking with the mothers usually is talking with hands and feet, smiling, showing interest in her cooking and embroidery, and—at the end—laughing together.

The selection of toys and games always demands great care. After a few weeks of observation the student formulates specific goals for each child in the family (by the way, some of these families, especially Moroccan families, are quite large, with six or more children). For one child the specific goal could be improvement of the concentration span; for another child in the same family goals may involve the learning of social skills and how to play together with others. Games and toys are always selected carefully, with these specific goals in mind.

The student also visits the schoolteachers of the children from time to time, to discuss these specific goals and—later—the children's progress, as perceived by their teachers.

This project has now run for more than five years in the Hague. In one area in the Hague we reached about a hundred families, with altogether about 450 children. What effects did we perceive?

- There was great improvement of the atmosphere in the families: better contact between parents and children, decreased tension, fewer fights and quarrels between parents and children, less punishment necessary to keep the children quiet. Instead, many parents bought or borrowed playthings for their children and spent more time playing with their children.

- There was some improvement in the concentration spans and social skills of the children, demonstrated at school.

- Last, but not least, the students all reported that they had learned a lot from this practical year. They got insight into the problems of Turkish and Moroccan families, their way of life, their habits and customs, their beliefs, norms, and values. This is rather important: Later on it is very likely that these students will have to work professionally with Turkish or Moroccan children and parents.

In the last two years our example has begun to be followed in more and more other cities in Holland. Currently, the project runs in at least 15 other cities. Local authorities are getting interested and are ready to subsidize these projects—at least partly.

## A Primary Prevention Program
## for Children of Parents With Mental Disorders

Marion Rikken

In the Netherlands in recent years specific attention has been given to the children of parents with mental illness. It gradually became clear that the various signals these children manifested might point to serious underlying problems. In order to gain a better insight into the character of these problems, some RIAGGs, in close cooperation with the University of Nijmegen, started a program for this group of children. (In the Netherlands most preventive mental health workers are employees of RIAGGs.)

In the case of children of mentally disturbed parents, we first did a review of the current scientific literature and discovered several related American investigations. We then did several complementary studies in order to apply the findings to the Dutch situation. Our own investigations comprised a Delphi study with a panel of 20 experts in the field, a register research, and in-depth interviews with 19 young adults (20-30 years of age) who had grown up in families in which one of the parents had a psychiatric diagnosis. We also did several preventive interventions on an experimental basis, monitored by program evaluation research. Before considering in more detail some of these preventive interventions, I would like to mention some results of the preliminary Dutch studies.

The Delphi panel consisted of 20 mental health professionals who had direct or indirect contact with these children and their families. The risk factors and support factors they selected as the most relevant were the following:

(1) *Regarding the parent:* the seriousness and the chronicity of the disturbance
(2) *Regarding the family:* problems in the relationship of the parents, the parent-child interaction, and the health of the remaining parent
(3) *Regarding the child:* organic vulnerability, age, and competence
(4) *Regarding the surroundings:* the level and quality of sustenance of the social network

Of these factors, the parent-child interaction scored highest, followed by the seriousness and the chronicity of the disturbance of the parent, and the age and the competence of the child. It seems possible to protect these children by enhancing their assertiveness, raising their competence, and giving them better social support. It is also possible to influence the parent-child interaction, the health of the remaining parent, and the problems in the relationship of the parents with each other.

The group of young adults that was interviewed consisted of children of families in which at least one parent was hospitalized and diagnosed by an expert as mentally ill.

(1) Some 25% of the children said that they had broken off their school education under the influence of the parent's illness.

(2) All of the children, except one, said they had no contact whatsoever with a mental health worker during the time of the parent's illness.

(3) Most of the children were not informed about the nature of the parent's illness. They would have liked to have had information from the remaining parent, from the family doctor, or from someone they could trust.

(4) Most of the children were socially isolated. They did not talk about the parent's illness with other children because they felt a taboo around mental illness.

As to their experiences, they said that they felt a great need for someone to support them, for someone who could talk with them about the parent's illness and about the family situation, and with whom they could relax and do nice things as well. They needed someone to share their problems with, someone who could give them support and attention.

On the basis of these studies, we saw as separate targets for intervention the child, the parent with the illness, the "healthy" parent, the family and its surroundings, the mental health worker, the school, and the families and friends of mental patients.

I will describe one of the interventions that I myself developed and tried out in my own institute. It was monitored by program evaluation research by the University of Nijmegen. It is one element of a program that covers several activities, such as presenting new supporting persons to children of mental health patients, activity support groups for these children, parent support training, and interviews with the children held by the parent's therapist. The program was developed in cooperation with the psychiatric division of a general hospital and the mental hospital. The intervention I shall describe aims at supporting children from 6 to 18 years of age and their parents after a crisis hospitalization of one of the parents in the psychiatry division of a general hospital or in a mental hospital. We chose the moment of hospitalization because then the family is most willing to talk. We made a protocol for the mental health workers of the crisis section in our RIAGG, the most important aspects of which are as follows:

- At the moment of hospitalization of a parent with children ages 6-18, the involved mental health worker informs the "healthy" parent that the hospitalization also has a significant effect on the child.

- Following that, the mental health worker has an interview with the child and the healthy parent. The latter receives information about what it means to a child when a parent is hospitalized and about what the specific needs of the child are in this period.

- The child is informed of the mental illness of the parent, and is told what a mental hospital is, what happens in the clinic, and what the roles of the different mental health workers around the family are. He or she is also given information on how to deal with the parent's illness. In these interviews the child is given many opportunities to express his or her emotions. The mental health worker then leaves a checklist with the "healthy" parent on which he or she can score the behavior of the child, so that possible problems can be identified.

- Finally, after a period of three weeks, a mental health worker from the youth section in our RIAGG visits the family to discuss the checklist and to see if more interventions are necessary (for example, further help may take the form of placing the child in a children's group, providing the child with someone to talk to outside the family, assistance and/or training for the remaining parent, or treatment of the child at the RIAGG).

The evaluation research showed that part of this program can be integrated in the regular procedures of the RIAGG. According to the mental health workers, there is clear evidence in the case of hospitalization that this procedure met the needs of the healthy parents and the children. It turned out to be fruitful also to supply information about the other possible interventions mentioned above.

The support of these children will be more effective when they can be shown a video about the mental hospital and receive an information brochure especially designed for them. We are planning to extend the program in the future, in our institute, to all parents in treatment diagnosed as mental patients.

An important side effect of this program has been that the mental health workers get a view of the position of their patients' children. In the past they often did not even know if there were children involved.

Finally, a hint at two more activities in the field of prevention. One of them concerns an information program in high schools (developed by a mental hospital), which includes two lessons, one for students and another for teachers. Different aspects of psychiatry, views on "abnormal" and "normal" behavior, prejudices toward (mental) patients, and so on are dealt with. A second program comprises activity groups for children from the age of 15 years and older (developed by a national self-help organization). Themes for discussion in these groups include role reversal, recognizing one's own emotions, fear of mental illness, and handling feelings of guilt and shame, as well as facing taboos.

I hope I have succeeded in showing you how important this subject is and how large groups of children can be helped to reduce the chance that they, too, will become mental patients in later stages of their lives.

## Prevention of Child Sexual Abuse in the Netherlands

### Cees Hoefnagels

During the last five years many activities have been undertaken to prevent child sexual abuse in the Netherlands. Usually they are done by professionals, working in various organizations that differ in perspective—that is, they have different backgrounds from which they approach the subject of child sexual abuse. These perspectives include human sexuality, child abuse in general, mental health, health education, child sexual abuse within the family, and sexual violence against girls and women.

Since the "discovery" of child sexual abuse, with the resultant public indignation about it, child sexual abuse has become a serious issue in the Netherlands. Many organizations—whether they deal with human sexuality or health education, with sexual violence or child abuse in general—have had to answer questions on child sexual abuse. Questions come from professionals, counselors, doctors, teachers, and ordinary people. In the Netherlands, in general, the nature of the prevention of child sexual abuse consists of two parts:

(1) *Education of adults who work with or help children professionally, such as teachers and counselors:* The main purpose is to teach them about a child's behavior when there is a suspicion of sexual abuse, what the needs of a child are, how to talk with sexually abused children, how to report suspected incidents of abuse, what help is available, and where to get it.

(2) *Development and distribution of materials that can be helpful for professional workers in case of child sexual abuse:* These include maps of mental health services and lists of abuse signals.

In order to give you some idea, I would like to present a few figures. In 1988 in the Netherlands 2,000 instructional and educational seminars on child abuse were given by 200 professional workers. The materials mentioned above are distributed at these seminars. Nowadays a massive preventive effort in the Netherlands is aimed at these activities. I estimate these efforts cover more than 80% of the total preventive effort on child sexual abuse. A remarkable fact is that most interventions are actually not aimed at preventing child sexual abuse; that is, they are not perceived as primary prevention.

Let me tell you something about the other 20% of preventive efforts:

(1) *In-school projects with theater play and role playing for children ages 9 to 12, supporting teachers and parents at the same time:* These projects are aimed at increasing children's self-defense skills, to prevent sexual abuse or to teach the children to tell somebody if they are abused. Most of you know these projects quite well, because we have more or less copied them from projects in the United States.

(2) *Projects with perpetrators:* A very interesting project of this type is presented below by my colleague Elsa van Willenswaard.

(3) *A project, using a video and exercises, that helps a teacher to initiate a discussion about sexual violence with boys and girls in the classroom:* This is aimed especially at preventing boys from violating girls.

(4) *A project with a booklet for mothers who know or suspect that their children are being sexually abused by their husbands:* The booklet aims to help the mother in her difficult situation and to support her decision making.

I would now like to mention three new developments in the Netherlands. First of all, we are trying to find ways to implement programs that will take advantage of recently gained expertise and new preventive strategies. For example, one obvious way of prevention is to teach a teacher to cope with suspected cases of abused boys or girls. This could be called the first level of implementation. A second level of implementation would be to incorporate a prevention program on child sexual abuse in the school curriculum. Part of this strategy would be to develop materials useful for this purpose. A third level would be to implement a preventive and didactically acceptable program on child sexual abuse in teachers' training colleges. A fourth level would be to incorporate these subjects as mandatory ones at all teachers' training colleges. In the Netherlands we are developing strategies mainly on the first level, because at the higher levels there is a serious lack of theoretical notions about necessary conditions and possible strategies.

A second important development is that we are widening our scope geographically. We do not limit ourselves to regions we actually work in, but work together to develop nationwide preventive interventions. Two national community awareness campaigns are under preparation at the moment. The first is a campaign for victims of abuse. Children who are abused physically, emotionally, or sexually will be stimulated to tell somebody and to try to get help. The main slogan of this campaign is "Some secrets you have to talk about." A second campaign that is being prepared now is aimed at boys and men from 15 to 35 years old and at people who work with these boys and men. Its purpose is to change the mentality and attitudes of boys and men in order to diminish their sexually violent behavior. This kind of campaign reflects a change from potential victim-oriented to potential perpetrator-oriented preventive programs. More and more we are coming to the conclusion that sexual violence is basically a male problem—and that is where we have to attack it.

The last important development in the Netherlands, which is also the main focus of this conference, is the stimulation of the primary prevention of psychopathology. I will restrict myself to the primary prevention of child sexual abuse, which causes a lot of pathology. I must admit we have difficulties in the Netherlands with executing primary preventive interventions, as you may have gathered from what I have told you. We are convinced these difficulties do not occur only in the Netherlands. I did some research in the Netherlands and asked professional workers whose daily work is to prevent child sexual abuse what makes it so difficult to do primary prevention in this field. Here are some of their answers:

(1) At first we didn't know better alternatives.

(2) Things we do are generally received enthusiastically; there is a great demand for materials and information we have developed and have distributed. Therefore we feel compelled to remain in the phase that we only wanted to be a temporary one.

(3) The indignation over, and the urge to *deal with*, child sexual abuse is greater than the support we can actually mobilize in order to *prevent* child sexual abuse.

(4) We are restricted by mental health services, whose primary goal is to care and cure and, in turn, they are not exactly prevention oriented. Secondary prevention is "the best we can do."

(5) The subject of primary prevention of child sexual abuse is felt to be complex, tricky, touchy, and delicate. The choice of which "cause" to attack is partly ideological and will meet resistance.

## Treatment of Child Sexual Abusers
## as Part of a Prevention Strategy

Elsa M. van Willenswaard

I would like to tell you about a project we developed in Rotterdam for the treatment of incest offenders. Rotterdam is a city of 650,000 people of 23 different nationalities. It is the biggest port in the world. This means that most of its citizens are laborers, and that leads to a culture of "Don't waste words, let's do it." That is why it is not surprising that after only a year of preparation a very complicated project could be started on a subject that generally meets with a lot of resistance and opposition. Why is this project so complicated?

First of all, you have to know that in the Netherlands no one has a duty to report a case of child abuse. As this implies, there is no regular cooperation network between police and justice on one side and the mental health system on the other. In our society these two are totally different sectors. They are not familiar with each other in their ways of working, thinking, and talking. And what we have learned from experiences in treating sex offenders in the United States is that, on a voluntary basis, these treatments are almost impossible. This is mainly because offenders are rarely motivated for treatment. They deny that there has been a problem on their part for many years, which makes it inevitable that a severe and confrontational treatment situation would be created. Treatment of sex offenders stands a chance only if the power of a judge is behind it.

After many years of therapeutic work with children who were victims of sexual abuse, and giving other children information on how they can prevent becoming victims, I started to think about what would be a better way to prevent child sexual abuse. I changed my scope, and focused on the offenders. I did some research and decided that, considering the situation in Rotterdam, treatment could be a first step in developing prevention programs. This meant a bridge had to be built between the mental health care system and the justice system. It took some effort, but I had the good fortune to come across a prosecutor who was prepared to listen and to interpret. Thus a cooperation network started.

Today, the Department of Justice, the courts, the District Psychiatric Service, the Department of Rehabilitation, and the three Institutes of Outpatient Mental Health Care in Rotterdam are participating in this project. We developed a plan that all parties eventually agreed upon, although some compromises could not be avoided. A total of 100 people play an active role in this project now.

A second complication in this project is the opposition against sex offenders. As you know, it took some time to open the eyes of society to the problem of child sexual abuse, but making clear how much the victims suffered finally got the message across. Mental health care workers were prepared to face the problem and to talk with victims—but facing the offenders or even treating them was out of the question. The commitment to the victim and the negative emotion against the offender were so strong that it prevented therapists from sitting down with offenders, analyzing their situations and their motives. It just was not possible, the time was not ripe. I felt this resistance very strongly in my negotiations with the general managers of institutes, the Ministry of Health, and other therapists. So at every opportunity I again explained my point of view, that by treating the offenders we could help current victims and prevent new child sexual abuse. My view is supported by American surveys that show that most sex offenders have several victims, that recidivism after imprisonment is high, and that recidivism after treatment is very low.

A third complication I want to mention is that of the differing viewpoints held on the problem of child sexual abuse. In the Netherlands it was mainly the women's liberation movement that brought attention to the problem of sexual violence in general and child sexual abuse in particular. This, in addition to the fact that most victims are female. The effect was that mainly female workers dealt with this problem. They made analyses and developed methods of working with the victims. The basic female point of view is that the basis for the sexual abuse of young girls by men is found in the structural inequality in our society between women and men. As a result of the specific male socialization, males have few ways of dealing with their emotions. Sex is their main outlet for expressing and communicating their emotions. That is why sex becomes an instrument in abuse. As you can imagine, this point of view is still the subject of many discussions among psychotherapists, but because in practice mostly women are working with the victims this has been no problem. Things took a different course, however, when men took on working with the offenders. Mostly they analyzed the situation as a sexual deviation that required a behavioristic training program. No power inequalities were suggested, no structural problem in our society was mentioned—they saw sexual abuse as simply a deviation in behavior some men seem to have. This latter point of view also dominates the literature and conferences on treating offenders we know from the United States. For the Rotterdam project we needed a treatment program that was based on the female point of view of this matter, which was not available. The solution was to develop a new handbook, and so we did. In a few months this handbook for treating child sexual offenders will be published in the Netherlands.

It took a year to solve the problems I have just described for you and to develop a plan of execution. I shall describe this plan in short:

(1) After an incest victim informs the police, the accused is arrested
(2) A judicial, psychological, and social inquiry is made
(3) Within three months the accused stands trial
(4) If the accused wants to be treated
(5) And the judge agrees to it
(6) The offender is dismissed from imprisonment, at which time special conditions can be made (e.g., no contact with the victim, prohibition from entering certain areas), and
(7) The treatment is started.

Special criteria have been developed to decide if someone is suitable for treatment (adequate command of the Dutch language, no IQ below 80, no alcohol or drug addiction, no severe psychopathology). The treatment takes about a year and a half and consists of one individual session a week, with the offender doing a lot of homework between sessions. If the results are good, this is reported to the prosecutor, the judge holds court, and the case is closed. If the offender does not cooperate, he is imprisoned at once. The project started in September 1989; six offenders are in treatment now and 17 are awaiting trial. We plan to treat about 40 offenders and then evaluate our experiences. I did not mention that this project is part of a multiple-systems approach. This means that we work together with the therapists of the victim and other people involved in the incest situation.

The main goals of the project are, first, the prevention of recidivism of incest offenders and the functional improvement of the individuals affected, and second, to make a contribution to the development of a general method for the treatment of incest offenders. For that purpose, the progress and results of the treatment are being observed and analyzed as part of a parallel scientific research project on the subject.

With this research we also try to discover more about the offender: What are his motives, the social circumstances, his personality, his attitude toward women and girls, and so on? There are quite a number of items that will be collected and processed in this research. We hope that this research will produce a lot of material for developing more and more effective primary prevention programs.

# 14

# A Multimodal Approach to Prevention: A Review of India's Integrated Child Development Scheme

**Nomita Sonty**

Community-oriented programs have shifted their focus from secondary and tertiary prevention to primary prevention. This has occurred over a protracted period of time, finally reflecting acknowledgment of the adage "An ounce of prevention is worth a pound of cure." Today, preventive efforts are being considered necessary in almost all walks of life, including health, industry, education, and community development. It is being recognized, although gradually, that prevention is the *modus operandi* in the promotion of health and reduction of psychopathology. The success of community-based efforts at prevention is often dependent on the following factors:

(1) Preparation of the target population and that population's readiness to accept such programs (Timing of programs is a significant factor in readiness for participation.)
(2) Involvement of members of the target population in the planning and implementation of the program (Clarke, 1981)
(3) Acceptability to the target population of the ideologies on which the programs are based (Omprakash, 1989)
(4) Costs and benefits incurred in participating in such programs
(5) Long-term financial and political support for such programs

Many countries have been involved in planning, implementing, and evaluating intervention programs with an emphasis on prevention. In India, efforts at prevention have focused on meeting the basic needs of the people, including adequate nutrition, clean drinking water, health care and prevention of communicable disease, family planning and population control, and education. Some community development projects in the country have attempted social change by improving the economic standards of people by providing them with the opportunity to engage in communal agriculture, to organize cooperative societies for marketing dairy and poultry products, and/or to participate in cottage industries.

Development programs that improve the socioeconomic standards in a community do not necessarily reach children, nor do they result in improving the environment in which these children live. In recent years, agencies working for the welfare of children have recognized the need for special social policies for children, based on the premise that "child development programs can become catalytic agents for social change and serve as entry points for improving the quality of life of present and future generations of the disadvantaged" (Sadka, 1984, p. 3). The existence of such policies provides programs with the political support necessary for maintaining the delivery of services and ensuring continuity of the program. The Integrated Child Development Scheme (ICDS) is one such program; it was introduced by the government of India as a comprehensive effort at prevention and the promotion of healthy child development.

This chapter is a review of the ICDS as an example of a multimodal attempt at prevention. It is of special significance because it targets vulnerable sections of society: women and children. The chapter is divided into two parts: First, a brief description of India, especially as it pertains to the child population, is offered, and then a review of the ICDS program is presented.

### Description of India

India is the second most populous nation in the world. With only 2.4% of the world's land area, it supports more than 15% of the world's population. India's estimated current population is more than 833 million, with a preponderance in the younger age groups. As of 1981 estimates, 39% of the Indian population consisted of children up to 14 years old and 16.67% of the total population was 6 years old or younger. The high percentage of infants and children has resulted in a high dependency ratio in which a large proportion of the population is vulnerable to illness and death. Some 40% of all deaths occur in the birth to 4 age group. Of the 8.6 million deaths per year, three million are those of infants. Although this trend has decreased over the last 60 years, the current infant mortality rate is still approximately 96 per 1,000 live births and continues to be significantly higher than that of developed countries.

India is a country of great diversity. It consists of 25 states, each of which has its own local government, language, and culture. Vast differences exist between rural and urban areas, and approximately 78% of the total child population lives in rural and tribal areas. Disparities in child-rearing practices, patterns of socialization, economic status, and available amenities are a few of the resultant consequences.

Both the government and the voluntary sector have made efforts to organize programs that affect the welfare of children in India. Before India obtained its independence, voluntary organizations played the major role in child welfare programs. Notable among them were the Indian Council for Child Welfare, the Indian Red Cross Society, the All India Women's Conference, and the Children's Aid Society (National Institute of Public Cooperation and Child Development, 1984). After independence, the central government assumed the major responsibility for continuation of these programs. In keeping with the Indian constitution, the government introduced social policies that stipulated free and compulsory education for children between 6 and 14 years of age, prohibited child labor, and prevented the cruel treatment of children. A number of expert bodies were organized to collect information on the needs of children, assess the effectiveness of existing programs, and provide recommendations for improvement.

Government departments such as Health and Family Planning, Nutrition, Education, Social Welfare, and Recreation organized their own independent projects for the welfare of children. A major obstacle in the implementation of these programs was the shortage of resources. Although experimentation with these programs continued, it became evident that a fragmented approach was not an effective one. An integrated, comprehensive, and coordinated effort for the welfare of children was recognized as being a necessary and secure investment in the future of the country.

## The Integrated Child Development Scheme

In 1972 the Ministry of Planning suggested a scheme that would integrate existing child-care services. In 1974 a national policy for children was introduced; it proved to be the cornerstone in the development of the Integrated Child Development Scheme. The policy required the state to provide adequate services for optimal social, physical, and mental development of children before and after birth.

The ICDS, founded on the premise of the National Policy for Children, was inaugurated on October 2, 1975. The first year was the experimental phase, during which 33 projects, distributed across many states, were initiated. Of these states, 19 were rural, 10 were tribal, and 4 were urban. In 1977, 100 more projects were sanctioned. The target for 1985 was a total of 1,000 projects. The objectives of the ICDS include the following:

(1) Improvement of nutritional health status of children from birth to 6 years old
(2) Laying the foundation for social, psychological, and physical growth of children
(3) Reduction in the incidence of mortality, morbidity, malnutrition, and school dropouts

(4) Achievement and implementation of a coordinated policy among various government departments for child welfare

(5) Provision of support for mothers and enhancement of their ability to care for their young

### Services Provided by the ICDS

The ICDS provides services such as immunizations, supplementary nutrition, growth monitoring, informal preschool education, and nutrition and health education. Projected targets for the 1980-1985 Five-Year Plan estimated that coverage in the above-mentioned services would include 1-2 million women and 6-10 million children.[1]

### Project Areas

The ICDS is the end result of a series of preparatory activities at the central and state levels of the government. Projects are sanctioned annually and are allotted on the basis of need, capability to implement the project, and commitment to the project. States with greater resources may introduce and support additional projects. There are three types of projects: rural, tribal, and urban. Since the composition of the child population in each area varies, the number of villages subsumed under a project area also varies. In each project area there are child-care centers unique to the ICDS that are called Anganwadi Centers. In rural and urban areas, a "project" includes 100 Anganwadi Centers, while in a tribal area it includes 50.

### Structure of the ICDS

On sanctioning a project, the state government identifies the site for the Anganwadi Center, recruits and trains Anganwadi workers (AWWs), a supervisor, and a child development project officer (CDPO). The field staff (CDPO, supervisor, and AWWs) of the project are usually women. In some instances where this is not possible, males are selected. The CDPOs and the supervisors are trained at the National Institute of Public Cooperation and Child Development (NIPCC), which develops training aids, conducts training programs, organizes regional orientation courses, and provides feedback on training issues to the Ministry for Social Welfare.

The AWWs are grass-roots workers, directly responsible for the delivery of the various services. They are usually selected from the village where the center is going to be established based on recommendations by the village community. The AWW is usually a young girl who is a high school graduate. Once selected, she is trained for three to four months and is paid a nominal honorarium during training and on the job. Her responsibilities include organizing preschool activities for about 40 children between the ages of 3 and 5 years; organizing supplementary nutrition for pregnant and nursing mothers and children aged 6 months to 5 years; imparting health and nutritional education to mothers; educating the community through home visits; obtaining community support; and assisting the primary health center staff in carrying out immunizations, health checkups, and delivery of family planning information. In addition, the AWW is expected to maintain and submit records to her supervisor and to act as a liaison with other agencies in her area.

The supervisor is responsible for 20 Anganwadi Centers. She makes frequent field visits to the centers, is a liaison between AWWs and the CDPO, and assists the CDPO in implementing the project.

The CDPO is responsible for one project area. She or he is often a graduate in humanities. As the coordinator of the ICDS, she or he conducts periodic field visits and group meetings. The CDPO collaborates with the primary health center staff and the block development officer. Submission of statistics to the Ministry of Social Welfare at the state and central levels of the government is one of the CDPO's responsibilities.

### Financial Support for the ICDS

The ICDS is predominantly the responsibility of the Ministry of Social Welfare, which provides funds for initial nonrecurring expenses directly to the center. The state government assumes responsibility for the supplementary feeding program. An evaluation of the cost-effectiveness of the ICDS in 1984 revealed that all children in India could enjoy the benefits of the ICDS at the price of less than 1% of the gross domestic product.

From 1975 to 1982, UNICEF assisted the Indian government in financing this program. Since 1982-1983, several other agencies, notably the World Food Program, Cooperative America Relief Everywhere (CARE), the Norwegian Agency for Development, and U.S. Agency for International Development, have provided varying degrees of assistance.

### Impact of the ICDS

In assessing the impact and trends of the ICDS, the most critical issues are as follows: Does the ICDS meet its objectives? If so, in what ways? Has the program helped integrate the independent services that, in the past, were provided for women and children? Has it led to discernible changes in the lives of children? Finally, has it brought about any social changes? Some of these questions are fairly direct and simple to evaluate; others are not.

Evaluations of the program have indicated that a majority of the beneficiaries have been poor, from rural and tribal areas, and in the age group of birth to 3 years. Women who have received prenatal care are also from the poorest socioeconomic class. On several important parameters, the impact of the ICDS on children can be seen. Some of these are increased birth weight, reduced incidence of malnutrition, increased coverage with immunization, and decreased infant mortality rate.

Sadka (1984) cites a study by Bhatnagar et al., who conducted a survey in 15 of the original 33 projects. These researchers demonstrated that in children exposed to the ICDS over a 21-month period, the incidence of severe malnutrition in the birth to 6 age group had decreased from 21.9% to 5.4%. In the moderate malnutrition group there was a decrease from 23.3% to 17.2%. The most significant decrease observed was in the incidence of severe malnutrition in the birth to 3 age group, which fell from 29.9% to 6%.

Immunization coverage doubled over a span of two years in areas served by the ICDS. In a 1982 survey conducted by the All India Institute of Medical Sciences (cited in Sadka, 1984), it was found that the coverage with BCG (vaccination against tuberculosis) and DPT immunization (vaccination against diphtheria, pertussis, and tetanus) in non-ICDS areas was 25.5% and 18.3%, respectively, while these figures were 45.6% and 43.4% in ICDS project areas.

Infant mortality rate is one of the most sensitive indicators of the quality of health care. According to the 1984 estimates, improvement was also seen in this index in ICDS and non-ICDS areas. The estimated infant mortality rate in ICDS areas was 83.3 per 1,000 live births, while the national rate in 1984 was 127 per 1,000 live births.

It appears that more children attending ICDS programs enter the primary school system, although few studies have assessed this issue formally. A systematic assessment of the effect of the ICDS on the cognitive and educational development of children would be a very important contribution to the area of early educational intervention, especially in light of the evidence that these very heterogeneous intervention programs "work" (Barnett & Escobar, 1989).

Although community participation in the ICDS program has gradually increased, the amount and nature of participation has varied from center to center. The community often contributes the land on which the Anganwadi Center is built, or a house that may be used as a center. Some families may help with building materials and free construction work, while others may send fresh vegetables and grains to the center to add to the supplementary nutrition provided there. The success and continuity of the ICDS program, after a five-year period, often depends on the community's ability to integrate the program into the community and support it financially, with minimal assistance from the state.

Coordination between ministries providing services to children has increased, and this has resulted in the integration of services. Initially, the Ministry for Social Welfare played a major role in the implementation of the ICDS, assisted to some degree by the Ministry of Health. Subsequently, technical ministries such as the Ministry for Works and Housing and the Ministry for Information and Broadcasting have started contributing significantly to the program.

Similar trends are seen at the state government level as well. The ICDS has assumed the role of main advocate for the cause of children, especially to those government agencies that in the past had lesser involvement in the welfare of children. Special daytime radio and television programs for women and children are aired at the ICDS Center, making it a central place for the dissemination of information.

The ICDS seems to have had an effect on women, partly in its capacity as an employer of a large force of women. According to estimates, in 1985 approximately 207,500 women were employed by the ICDS program. Projected figures for the end of the Seventh Five-Year Plan (in 1995) indicate that these numbers will double. It is speculated that the creation of employment opportunities for such a large force of women has the potential for producing significant social change. Increased awareness of the Anganwadi worker in the areas of health, nutrition, child-rearing practices, and the development of children is likely to have an impact on her life as a woman, spouse, and mother. Yet another indirect effect of the ICDS program may be seen in the area of family planning and the subsequent change in birthrate. Most of the AWWs are young women in their reproductive years; their improved understanding of family planning issues and contraception could, in the future, lead to smaller and planned families.

Outcomes influenced by health and nutrition education are likely to have long- and short-term effects. Long-term effects will be contingent not only on community education, but also on ongoing attitudinal changes and the overall development of the community. Therefore, it is crucial that the expectations of such educational programs be limited by the facilities available in the community. For example, if the health educator lectures on clean drinking water for infants, he or she needs to make sure that the community has a constant supply of running water. Therefore, the AWW may also have to be the liaison between the community and the block development officer in order to improve facilities so that her educational program can be effective.

Care for pregnant women in the prenatal and antenatal periods is instrumental in creating a society of healthy women and children. It is also crucial in the prevention of congenital diseases and malnutrition, and in the reduction of infant mortality. AWWs play a significant role in meeting this goal in their collaborative work with the primary health centers. In addition, they are strategically placed for the early identification of mental or physical handicaps among children in the community or among those attending the preschool. In order to optimize this task, the Rural Community Mental Health Center in Sakalwara experimented with training AWWs in early identification of mental handicaps and in the provision of minimal intervention through early stimulation programs. Although the results of the training were not studied systematically, the AWWs were able to identify severely and moderately retarded children. Because of time constraints, they had difficulty with the intervention programs.

## Conclusion

Although ambitious, the ICDS is a well-conceptualized program. A large force of nonprofessionals have played a pivotal role in its implementation on a nationwide basis. Decentralization of responsibility has led to the involvement of state governments in this program. Targeted at disadvantaged populations, the ICDS provides services that might significantly affect the lives of women and children.

Every program, however well conceptualized, runs the risk of facing some difficulties once implemented. Not being an exception to this rule, the ICDS needs to contend with the following issues so that its success as a program will not be jeopardized:

(1) The cornerstone for the delivery of the ICDS program is the AWW, and the success of the program depends to a great extent on how well she executes her responsibilities. The AWW has been assigned numerous tasks, and constraints on her time are a major problem.

(2) AWWs are educated up to the high school level. Not only is their level of comfort with maintaining extensive records limited, the task is also time-consuming and stressful.

(3) The status attributed to AWWs by the community will influence the degree to which they are accepted as agents of change. Some of the variables that might influence this are AWW age, sex, marital status, caste, self-esteem, popularity, and ability to make decisions.

(4) The AWWs are considered to be volunteers. They are paid a rather small honorarium, considering the responsibilities assigned to them. This can lead to lowered motivation, the formation of unions, and protest.

(5) The CDPO and supervisor are often the liaisons between the ICDS and other departments of the government. Adequate support for these workers is crucial.

(6) Ongoing political support for this government-sponsored program is vital for its continuation. Changes in policies and budgets may pose a threat to such programs. Therefore, increasing the involvement of local community leaders and obtaining their support for this cause is necessary.

Trends from initial evaluations have indicated that the ICDS has contributed to the improvement of the lives of children (at least on a few parameters) in socioeconomically deprived areas. To optimize the benefits of this program, it might be worth introducing a community development aspect into the scheme so as to facilitate economic growth in the community.

In conclusion, the ICDS serves as a model for multimodal, preventive, and developmental programs for the welfare of women and children. Ongoing research is needed to provide further information on the effects of the program, important variables in the success of the program, and difficulties encountered by the program.

## Note

1. India establishes policies in five-year periods, a procedure that began after India gained its independence in 1947. The ICDS program began in 1975, during India's Fifth Five-Year Plan.

## References

Barnett, W. S., & Escobar, C. M. (1989). Research on the cost-effectiveness of early educational intervention: Implications for research and policy. *American Journal of Community Psychology, 17*, 677-704.

Clarke, B. D. (1981). The concept of community: A re-examination. In P. Henderson & T. N. David (Eds.), *Readings in community work* (pp. 32-38). London: George Allen & Unwin.

National Institute of Public Cooperation and Child Development. (1984). *Manual on integrated child development services.* New Delhi: Author.

Omprakash, S. (1989). Toward a synergism of rural development and community psychology. *American Journal of Community Psychology, 17*, 121-132.

Sadka, N. L. (1984). Integrated child development services in India. In N. Chawla (Ed.), *Integrated child development scheme.* New Delhi: UNICEF.

**15**

# Huckleberry Finn and Street Youth Everywhere: An Approach to Primary Prevention

**Forrest B. Tyler**
**Sandra L. Tyler**
**Anthony Tommasello**
**Mark R. Connolly**

One of the great classics of American literature is Mark Twain's *The Adventures of Huckleberry Finn*. As children, we idolize Huck as a symbol of boyhood, integrity, and rugged individualism. As professionals, we may also see him as a street youth, a runaway, a delinquent, or, as our bureaucracies sometimes put it, a PINS (a person in need of supervision, subject to arrest and incarceration for being out unaccompanied by an adult). Early in Huck's story, his absent father returns to make a claim because Huck has been given some money. He goes to court to take Huck away from Judge Thatcher and the widow. They, in turn,

> went to law to get the court to take me away from him and let one of them be my guardian; but it was a new judge that had just come, and he didn't know the old man; so he said courts mustn't interfere and separate families if they could help it; said he'd druther not take a child away from its father. (Twain, 1979, p. 30)

The new judge fails to reform the old man, who continues to harass Huck and seek control of his money. Much later in the story Huck runs away and joins Jim, an escaped slave. Huck first decides to turn Jim in, but recants, concluding:

> They [men looking for escaped slaves] went off and I got aboard the raft [where Jim was hidden], feeling bad and low, because I knowed very well I had done wrong, and I see it warn't no use for me to try to learn to do right; abody that don't get *started* aright when he's little ain't got no show—when

the pinch comes there ain't nothing to back him up and keep him to his work, and so he gets beat. Then I thought a minute, and says to myself, hold on; s'pose you'd 'a done right and give Jim up, would you felt better than what you do now? No, says I, I'd feel bad—I'd feel just the same way I do now. Well, then, says I, what's the use you learning to do right when it's troublesome to do right and ain't no trouble to do wrong, and the wages is just the same? I was stuck. I couldn't answer that. So I reckoned I wouldn't bother no more about it, but after this always do whichever come handiest at the time. (pp. 95-96)

At the end of the book Huck leaves, saying, "But I reckon I got to light out for the territory ahead of the rest, because Aunt Sally she's going to adopt me and sivilize me, and I can't stand it. I been there before" (p. 283).

Huck's story provides a graphic illustration of how society defines children as property. That is, children "belong" to parents, their perspectives are devalued, and they are considered incapable of responsible judgment or conduct. As long as children are portrayed as flawed and poorly socialized property, society can be involved only in secondary and tertiary prevention, continuing to minimize its damage. Our experiences have led us to a quite different view. Children are neither small adults nor property. Rather, they are resourceful humans. Like adults, they are capable and caring and need caring relationships and support.

## A Competency Orientation

To practice primary prevention, society needs an approach in which adults can accept children's caring and incorporate ways for them to express that caring. As George Albee (1980) put it more than a decade ago, we must build a competency model to replace the defect model. The competency orientation of our cross-disciplinary, cross-cultural group underscores our solid agreement with Albee's directive. It has led us to emphasize four important points: the impact of definitions and labels, the fact that children are not property, the possibility that family structure may not be the only way to go, and the impact of a shift in professional perspective. We have integrated four interrelated models to guide our work; these are described below.

The *resource collaborator* model (Tyler, Pargament, & Gatz, 1983) embodies the notion that we all have resources as well as limitations, and that we gain from as well as give to each other when we interact. We have used this model as an organizing approach to involve youth, agency people, and research staff as collaborators.

The *ethnic validity* model (Tyler, Sussewell, & Williams-McCoy, 1985) stresses the notion that there is no one profession, culture, or status that defines everyone's reality. Everyone's terms of existence and participation are accorded legitimacy and respect. This model's value for us has been its demand that we understand others from the contexts of their life situations, not ours.

The *facilitator/activator* model (Barbarin, Tyler, & Gatz, 1979) embodies the idea that helping others is two-faceted. It involves assisting people's efforts to solve their current problems while at the same time working to activate their problem-solving capabilities. This approach has forced us to figure out how to help society's representatives and street kids work together to improve the kids' lives without undermining their resourcefulness.

The *psychosocial competence* model (Tyler, 1978) assumes that each of us is organizing and leading his or her own life on the basis of an acquired sense of self-efficacy and self-worth, a sense of a relationship to the world, and a characteristic way of negotiating life events. Further, those characteristics are shaped by the supports and threats in our lives and vice versa. We have used this framework to gather information about street youth and their lives, to interpret our findings, and to plan and evaluate intervention approaches.

## Projects

Two of our projects with street youth may serve to illustrate the consequences of using a competency approach. One project was in Bogotá, Colombia; the second was in the Washington, DC, area. Both were developed in response to requests from individuals in frontline agencies who were working directly with street youth.

### Bogotá Study

In 1982, Sandy Tyler was working with an organization providing health care to kids on Bogotá's streets. The workers asked us to help them document the lives of street youth from the point of view of the youth, not that of organized society. Over the next five years we collaborated to build a structured interview schedule, train street workers to conduct interviews, analyze the results, and build a training guide for use with the workers.

The kids answered a series of open-ended questions about their lives and experiences. They also rated themselves on the five-point scales we used to measure psychosocial competence and environmental variables on which the research and intervention was focused (see Table 15.1). The youth rated their perceptions of their own self-efficacy, trust, and level of coping in four settings: in general, at home, in institutions, and on the street. They also rated the personal and physical supports and threats in those settings. Scale scores are the sum of the ratings in each category.

### Washington Study

In 1987 a Washington, DC, organization invited us to help develop an outreach program for street kids from Latin America. We expanded our approach

**Table 15.1** Scales Used to Measure Psychosocial Competence and Environmental Variables

|  |  |  |
|---|---|---|
| *Psychosocial Competence Scales* | | |

| Self-Efficacy (S-E) |  | Self-World (S-W) |
|---|---|---|
| self-respect |  | sense of belonging |
| control of life |  | cooperation |
| happiness |  | respect for authority |
| self-honesty |  | concern for others |
| self-trust |  | sharing |
|  | Behavioral Attributes (B-A) |  |
|  | resourcefulness |  |
|  | planning |  |
|  | independence |  |
|  | work |  |
|  | leadership |  |

| *Environmental Scales* | | |
|---|---|---|
| Psychosocial Supports |  | Physical Supports |
| affection |  | clothing |
| assistance |  | food |
| protection |  | shelter |
| fellowship |  | health care |
| respect |  | hygiene facilities |
| trust (friends) |  |  |
| Psychosocial Threats |  | Physical Threats |
| danger from people |  | chance of accidents |
| danger from authorities |  | danger from infections |
| revenge from victims |  | and disease |

and adapted our interview to look more closely at substance use and the life context of these youth. For purposes of comparison, we interviewed 21 non-Latino youth in a runaway shelter in the Washington suburbs. There were 14 girls and 7 boys, with an average age of 16.

## Findings

### Bogotá

Our Bogotá interviews included 94 boys under age 18 who live on the streets. On the average, they were age 13 and had left home at the age of 8. Most of them were first- and second-born sons, highly valued children in Colombian society. Many had been sexually or physically abused, shot, or stabbed.

They lived by a combination of legal and illegal activities. They did not fit stereotypes of immature, greedy, self-centered, antisocial delinquents. Rather, many were responsible for someone else. When asked about home and institutions, they valued being cared for and having opportunities to contribute and/or to learn. They disliked abuse and betrayal. In fact, that is why they left their homes and institutions—they were not family or institutional rejects. When asked what they wished for, only 7 of 258 wishes were antisocial or destructive. They wanted psychological supports, relationships, and a role in society. Less frequently, they wished for biological necessities, such as food and shelter.

The youth reported that, when not working, they enjoyed a wide range of activities, including destructive ones such as drinking and taking drugs. A substantial number were sexually active. They were also children who made their own toys, played soccer and other games in the parks, splashed in the public fountains, and slipped into the movies.

### Washington, DC

We are now analyzing the Washington, DC interviews and finding some interesting similarities and differences with the Bogotá sample. We interviewed 49 males and 8 females; 68% were from El Salvador. They were older than the Bogotá youth, with an age range of 13 to 21 years and an average age of 17.7. Those who had left home did so, on the average, at age 15. Of the sample, 49% were first- or second-born children, and they were not as unlinked from their families as the Bogotá kids. Some 65% reported that others were responsible for them, including parents, friends, and siblings. Only 7% reported being responsible for others. These kids were involved in a wide range of jobs to support themselves. A small number also stole, borrowed or begged, and did odd jobs. During free time they enjoyed sports, movies, television, talking with friends, and "hanging around." What they liked best about home and institutions were family, friends, and learning; they disliked "problems," discipline, and rules.

Many of these kids are immigrants, some without papers. After seeing friends and relatives killed, they came to the United States with their families or on their own to escape that violence. They may be living with relatives or parents, but are still responsible for themselves. In any case, they must deal with being caught between two cultures, often feeling they belong to neither. About life in the United States, they liked work, freedom, and opportunities for education; they liked least discrimination, drugs, and crime.

### Psychosocial Competence Patterns

In these groups we looked at self-efficacy, self-world (trust), and behavioral coping scores as well as the perceptions of personal and physical supports and threats. They rated themselves in their overall lives, their homes, schools, insti-

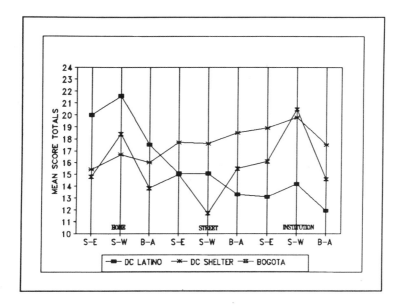

**Figure 15.1.** Psychosocial Competency Scores

tutions, and the streets. The importance of context as a determinant of psychosocial competence patterns is illustrated in Figure 15.1.

The D.C. Latino youth reported themselves at home to be highly trusting, somewhat less self-efficacious, and even lower on active coping, but overall rated themselves most competent there. From home to the streets to institutions, it was downhill. The D.C. shelter youth gave almost the opposite picture, except that their ratings of active coping tended to be higher than their ratings of self-efficacy, at least on the streets and in institutions. The Bogotá youth rated themselves most self-efficacious at home and in institutions; on the streets, where they were on their own, they were substantially more active copers and least trusting.

All of these youth readily differentiated among these settings in ways that reflected their realities. Regression analyses showed that for all three groups, levels of self-efficacy, trust, and coping were related primarily to perceived levels of personal supports. The exceptions were as follows: For the Bogotá youth in institutions, levels of trust were *negatively* related to the presence of *physical* threats and positively related to *physical* supports. For the D.C. Latino youth in institutions, psychosocial characteristics were related to *physical* supports, not personal supports. For the shelter youth at school, ratings of self-efficacy and levels of coping were *negatively* related to personal *threats*.

Overall, in spite of their hard lives, these street youth were amazingly less bitter than we had any reason to expect. They wanted to love and be loved, to have a role and to contribute. Their senses of self, of the world, and of how to negotiate their lives reflected their realities and the supports in them. They were aware of threats and dangers, but not driven by them.

## Discussion of Competency Models and Primary Prevention

The points made at the beginning of this chapter provide a framework for integrating our experiences and those of others with a competency model perspective and a focus on primary prevention.

### The Impact of Definitions and Labels on Children

We forget how much the words we use to express our thoughts also shape our thoughts. For example, when I refer to "my" children, I am using a shorthand way of indicating which children, but I also suggest ownership and property. Without recognizing this dual meaning, I do not keep my meaning clear. When I use the words *street youth, delinquents,* and *alienated kids* to describe these youth, I am also separating them from society by words that become labels. Such labels are often inaccurate, stigmatizing, and damaging not only to the children's self-esteem, but to their survival. For example, street children in Honduras are known as *resistoleros*; *Resistol* is the brand name of a popular glue product (shoe cement) that some children inhale. Most of the children on the Honduran streets do not sniff glue, yet all are labeled as glue sniffers and addicts. In Brazil, Guatemala, and Colombia, street children have been targeted for extermination by extrajudicial "security" forces (death squads). In Mexico City, children and youth found to be seropositive for HIV have been referred to as *sidosos* ("ones with AIDS") and face discrimination and persecution.

A recent study in Brazil showed that the majority of 80 street children stated that they do *not* like the label "street children." Many felt that they had much more in common with (as opposed to differences from) children who live at home (de Oliviera, 1989). As professionals, we cannot truly speak of preventing problems until we recognize the problems' interrelationship with our entire social structure. Until street youth are considered a part of society instead of delinquents or fringe elements, they will remain someone else's kids and responsibility. Their views of society and their world will remain separated, making efforts to reach and work with them difficult and frustrating. We cannot change our approach unless we change our frame of reference. The competency framework has provided us a basis for changing to a primary prevention orientation. By using it, we were able to involve kids and street workers with us in defining themselves and their world. We all became part of the solution instead of different aspects of the problem.

### Children Are Not Property

By looking at several cultures through the lenses of our mixed disciplines, our group has been able to see more clearly the overriding self-defeating nature of adult-controlled "ownership" of children. While the nature and forms of conventional societies may differ, the common constraint in relation to kids is that they are property. The situation of street children simply dramatizes the more general condition of all children.

Children must learn society's standards. It is our contention that to attain a sense of personal integrity, we must all acquire a personal code that, at times, differs in important ways from society's conventional standards. Huck made this abundantly clear as he sorted out his dilemma involving Jim. If we are to launch an effective primary prevention approach to the factors that bedevil children's lives—all children, not just street children—we must recognize that children react negatively to being considered property. Children also react positively to being treated like valued human beings; this seems to us an important starting point.

These same ideas are reflected in our society around the issue of illegal use of drugs and alcohol. Data sets compiled through the National Household Survey (National Institute on Drug Abuse, 1989b), Monitoring the Future (Johnson, O'Malley, & Bachman, 1989), and DAWN (National Institute on Drug Abuse, 1989a) have chronicled the drug use practices of Americans since the early to middle 1970s and throughout the 1980s. What emerges is a pattern of illicit drug use (primarily marijuana) that peaked in 1979 and 1980 and has been declining since that time (Kozel & Adams, 1986). In the 1980s we witnessed a cocaine abuse epidemic and a growing public disdain for illicit drug use. During this time, self-reported alcohol use in all age groups has remained relatively stable or has declined. The currently popular but questionably effective (Strasburger, 1989) "Just Say No" campaign is a simplistic approach to a very complicated issue. Unfortunately, this campaign has also been exported to Latin American countries, where it has met with very limited, if any, success. As one Guatemalan street youth stated, "It's hard to 'say no' when you have nothing." However, its popularity demonstrates the lack of tolerance on the part of adults for any drug experimentation by adolescents. It has been said that the campaign in effect tells adolescents: "You have no identity of your own. We know what is best for you. You will do as we say." In short, adults continue to operate on the assumption that Twain highlighted, namely, children are property to be molded to our liking.

The basic premise that drug use exposure begins a straight line toward deviance has been effectively questioned by Shedler and Block (1990). Their data indicate that adolescents who had never experimented with any illicit drug,

**Table 15.2** Comparison of Washington, DC, Latino and Household Survey Figures of Substance Use Among Street Youth (rates per 100)

| Age Group | Marijuana Ever Used | Marijuana Past Year | Marijuana Past Month | Alcohol Ever Used | Alcohol Past Year | Alcohol Past Month | Cocaine Ever Used | Cocaine Past Year | Cocaine Past Month | Total Illicit Drug Use[a] Ever Used | Total Illicit Drug Use[a] Past Year | Total Illicit Drug Use[a] Past Month |
|---|---|---|---|---|---|---|---|---|---|---|---|---|
| *Total*[b] | | | | | | | | | | | | |
| DC (N = 57) | 57.9[c] | 29.8[c] | 26.3[c] | 78.6[c] | 58.9 | 50.0 | 19.3 | 8.8 | 8.8 | 61.4[c] | 33.3 | 29.8[c] |
| Household[d] (N = 1,217) | 26.3 | 16.2 | 8.5 | 60.5 | 54.1 | 38.9 | 9.9 | 6.9 | 3.3 | 32.9 | 20.9 | 10.7 |
| *12-17* | | | | | | | | | | | | |
| DC (N = 20) | 40.0[c] | 20.0[e] | 20.0[e] | 73.7[c] | 36.8 | 36.8 | 25.0[c] | 15.0[e] | 15.0[e] | 45.0 | 25.0 | 20.0[e] |
| Household (N = 763) | 16.9 | 12.8 | 5.2 | 47.1 | 42.5 | 25.4 | 4.6 | 3.6 | 1.3 | 24.3 | 16.3 | 7.3 |
| *18-25* | | | | | | | | | | | | |
| DC[f] (N = 37) | 67.6[c] | 35.1 | 29.7[c] | 81.1 | 70.3 | 56.7 | 16.7 | 5.4[e] | 5.4[e] | 70.3[c] | 37.8 | 35.1[c] |
| Household (N = 454) | 42.0 | 22.1 | 13.8 | 83.2 | 73.7 | 61.4 | 18.7 | 12.6 | 6.7 | 47.6 | 28.7 | 16.8 |

a. Includes use of marijuana, cocaine, and any other illicit substances. Excludes alcohol use.
b. Rates for totals are unadjusted.
c. Indicates that the Washington, DC, Latino youth figure is significantly greater ($p < .05$) than Household Survey figures.
d. Refers to the National Household Survey conducted by NIDA. These figures are for the Latino sample only.
e. Values are too low for reliable estimates to be made.
f. Washington, DC, data in the 18-25 age category are based on respondents between the ages of 18 and 21, inclusive.

followed from age 3 to age 18, were less well psychologically adjusted than their cohorts who had. They state: "It may be wrong to pathologize adolescents who experiment with drugs by assuming that they fall between nonusers and drug abusers on a continuum of psychosocial adjustment" (p. 613). Some who read their report may assume that this statement applies only to mainstream youth. That is, they may assume that any drug use is pathological if the youth are homeless, runaways, or precociously independent.

Our DC data suggest a different interpretation. We compared our Latino youth with an age- and ethnicity-matched sample from the National Household Survey (National Institute on Drug Abuse, 1989b). Our Latino youth were more likely to have experimented with marijuana, alcohol, and cocaine, but there is *no* suggestion that the 12- to 17-year-olds were more likely to have used any of these substances in the past month (see Table 15.2). This comparison supports our existing hypothesis that adolescents who develop early autonomy and choose to live outside the realm of adult authority are capable of making rational choices in their lives.

### Families Are Not the Only Way to Go

Despite the increased frequency of child abuse cases being made public in our country, we still assume the benevolence of the family. In the United States, the nuclear family is perceived to be the natural organization of humans, while any other structures are labeled pathological. Most psychological and other professional literature supports this view. For example, Hartup (1983) concludes his review of peer relations in the *Handbook of Child Psychology* by saying, among other things:

> Secure family relations are the basis for entry into the peer system and success within it. Family breakdown tends to interfere with adaptation to the peer culture, and good family relations are needed throughout childhood and adolescence as the basis for peer relations. . . . Dissonance may be considerable when adolescents are alienated from their parents and associate with agemates who endorse misconduct. (p. 172)

The implication is that the adolescents are responsible for the dissonance. There is no consideration that they might be looking for the acceptance they are not getting at home. Hartup's reference list does not include materials about street youth, nor does his review seem to allow for the resilience of children from dysfunctional families. He gives no suggestion that children can create alternative constructive networks that provide belonging and a framework for constructive psychosocial development. Hartup's point seems to be that if it isn't adult modeled, it isn't any good.

We are not opposed to healthy families, nor are we arguing for the positive values of dysfunctional ones. What we strongly disagree with is the assumption that families are the *only* vehicle for healthy socialization. For example, a former street girl of our acquaintance said, "My parents don't say that my morals are different from theirs; they say that I'm immoral." She also said that to her, "home" means having a space into which her parents cannot intrude. She, like Huck, had developed a sense of morality that includes respect for the individuality and rights of others; her parents had not—at least as far as she was concerned. Another street youth was more graphic. He responded to the question, "What would your dream house be like?" by saying, "It would be the same house that I left, except that my parents would have their hands tied behind their backs and tape over their mouths." You may not like the way this youth expresses himself, but it is clear that he wants some rights of his own, and he wants his home.

Children in developing countries such as Colombia and Guatemala also leave home to escape extreme poverty. They often want to return home only after making enough money to improve the quality of life in the household and the community.

Rather than sending these youth to an institution or back home, we could help them with their goals and simultaneously help to strengthen society. We suggest considering other ways of providing them with rights and a home. Alternatives to families include group homes, community youth organizations, and noninstitutional support programs.

### Impact of a Shift in Perspective

We have seen many street youth programs in a number of places and countries. Some are clearly more effective than others; some are not effective at all. Those that work share an important element, namely, they deal with the context as well as the kids. That is, they recognize the interplay among youth, family, peers, and society and make that recognition explicit to the kids by acknowledging the reality, humanity, and point of view of the youth. Peer networks are an important source of care and companionship for these kids. Further, youth leadership and involvement as well as community participation are essential elements in successful efforts. "Charitable" programs that limit youth participation in the planning, implementation, and evaluation of program activities, and/or do not allow children to earn an income, are less popular with the children and often detrimental to their personal and vocational development.

An example of a successful primary prevention program that began with a focus on children is in Barranquilla, an industrial city in Colombia. Zona Negra is a collaborative project among residents of the area, university participants, and community businesspeople. It was established when the businesspeople found they were losing trained workers because of the poverty and disorganization in the neighborhoods. Cross-disciplinary teams from the university started by establishing a day-care center in the home of a volunteer in the community. Parents attended classes to learn about child development, nutrition, health, and culture. Eventually, a clinic was added, roads were paved, and houses and other structures were improved as the community worked for them. University participants and businesspeople provided consultation, support, and supplies, but the men and women in the community did the work. The Zona Negra project began with an assumption that the community people were competent and then appealed to their strengths. Barranquilla now has better workers, less crime, and children who are part of the community (Amar, 1986).

Another successful project is Integracion Juvenil (Youth Integration) in Puerto Plata and Santiago, Dominican Republic. The same sectors of society are involved with the program (businesspeople, community residents, university students, and youth), yet their perspective is quite unique. Most important, the children are collaborators in the program, not objects of adult interventions. The children who spend most of their time on the streets, participating very little in program activities, are known as "engineers," for they work hard to survive. Kids who are involved in vocational training or income-generating activities are "scientists," for they are studying. The "wise men" and "super wise men" are those who attend formal schools or have jobs in the so-called formal sector. Perhaps the most impressive impact of such positive labeling is that the children are proud of their identities. When asked by one of the authors if he was a street kid, a young boy responded, "Some of the others are, but I am an engineer."

## Summary

Central to our perspective is the way we have approached these projects. All of them were developed by cross-disciplinary groups using competency models to bridge the inevitable differences that arise in such mixed groups. No one of us could lay claim to having all the right concepts, perspectives, and approaches. Thus our assumptions were constantly challenged and, even though we did not always take it gracefully, we learned to question and expand our own disciplinary boundaries in ways that added creativity to our problem solving— an ingredient we see as essential to primary prevention.

Most of this work has been cross-cultural. From seeing street youth in several contexts, we began to see their central integrity. In stressful situations, children survive the best they can in whatever way they can. They then learn how to define what is meaningful to them and establish personal codes of ethics and morality and views of society that fit their situations. Their commonalities result from living under highly stressful conditions with very limited options for survival, few of which have social approval.

Programs that expect to be successful with street youth must start by learning the youths' perspectives on their situations and on society, including their criticisms. Doing so will enable participants to establish a shared basis from which to change the reality that has isolated youth and involved professionals in perpetuating the problems they have been trying to solve. Then both will be on the road to creating a society in which the Huck Finns of the world will *want* to be civilized. That is what primary prevention should be about.

## References

Albee, G. W. (1980). A competency model must replace the defect model. In L. A. Bond & J. C. Rosen (Eds.), *Competency and coping during adulthood* (pp. 75-104). Hanover, NH: University Press of New England.

Amar, J. A. A. (1986). *Los hogares communales del niño: Teoria y experiencias.* Barranquilla: Ediciones Uninorte.

Barbarin, O., Tyler, F., & Gatz, M. (1979). *Individual and community competence: Developing and integrating strategies over time.* Washington, DC: Administration on Aging.

de Oliviera, W. F. (1989). *Street kids in Brazil: An exploratory study of medical status, health knowledge, and the self.* Unpublished master's thesis, University of Minnesota.

Hartup, W. (1983). Peer relations. In P. H. Mussen (Ed.), *Handbook of child psychology: Socialization, personality, and social development* (Vol. 4, pp. 103-196). New York: John Wiley.

Johnson, L. D., O'Malley, P. M., & Bachman, J. G. (1989). *Monitoring the Future: Drug use, drinking, and smoking—national survey results from high school, college, and young adult populations, 1975-1988* (NIDA, DHHS Publication No. ADM 89-1638). Washington, DC: Government Printing Office.

Kozel, N. J., & Adams, E. H. (1986). Epidemiology of drug abuse: An overview. *Science, 234,* 970-974.

National Institute on Drug Abuse. (1989a). *Data from the Drug Abuse Warning Network (DAWN): Annual data 1988* (NIDA Statistical Series 1, No. 8, DHHS Publication No. ADM 89-1634). Washington, DC: Government Printing Office.

National Institute on Drug Abuse. (1989b). *National Household Survey on Drug Abuse: 1988 population estimates* (DHHS Publication No. ADM 89-1636). Washington, DC: Government Printing Office.

Shedler, J., & Block, J. (1990). Adolescent drug use and psychological health: A longitudinal inquiry. *American Psychologist, 45,* 612-630.

Strasburger, V. C. (1989). Prevention of adolescent drug abuse: Why "just say no" just won't work. *Journal of Pediatrics, 114*(4), 676-681.

Twain, M. (1979). *The adventures of Huckleberry Finn.* New York: Signet Classics.

Tyler, F. B. (1978). Individual psychosocial competence: A personality configuration. *Educational and Psychological Measurement, 38,* 309-323.

Tyler, F. B., Pargament, K. I., & Gatz, M. (1983). The resource collaborator role: A model for interactions involving psychologists. *American Psychologist, 38,* 388-398.

Tyler, F. B., Sussewell, D. R., & Williams-McCoy, J. (1985). Ethnic validity in psychotherapy. *Psychotherapy, 22,* 311-320.

# PART IV

# Educational Systems Interventions

Around the world, educational orientations are key to prevention efforts. They empower individuals, groups, and communities to be more actively engaged in and able to make effective decisions regarding their lives and needs. The focus upon individual and collective competence and growth are integral to the educational perspective. Whether incorporated in formal educational systems or in more broadly based day-to-day activities, educationally oriented prevention efforts are essential to engaging people more fully in the course of guiding their futures.

This section presents interventions that have been implemented in the United States, India, and Poland. While quite varied in their goals and structures, they all focus on educating children and families in an effort to enhance their competencies for supporting their own lives and those of the people around them. The majority of nations around the world engage children in a formal educational system at some point in their first 10 years, thus educational institutions provide early, ready, and regular access to a major portion of the population. Less developed in most nations are broad-based mechanisms for systematic, continued education of the public, outside of the formal education system. As the following chapters reveal, this is a problem that needs to be considered as we work toward constructing systems for improving children's lives.

In Chapter 16, the authors discuss two successful U.S. school-based approaches to promoting children's social competence. Authors Maurice J. Elias and Leslie R. Branden-Muller have worked with the Improving Social Awareness-Social Problem Solving (ISA-SPS) Project, which was honored with the 1988 Lela Rowland Prevention Award, and more recently approved by the National Diffusion Network as a federally validated substance abuse prevention program. Elias is codirector of the project and associate professor of psychology at Rutgers University, where Branden-Muller is a doctoral student in clinical psychology and a project consultant. Author Victor A. Battistich, senior research associate at the Developmental Studies Center in San Ramon, California, has conducted extensive research on the Child Development Project, a comprehensive elementary school program designed to enhance children's prosocial development. This intensive classroom program is supported and extended by a variety of school-wide and family components.

Battistich, Elias, and Branden-Muller carefully consider the commonalities and distinct characteristics of the two school-based programs, taking us step by step through the goals and structure of each. It becomes clear that the strength of their projects is linked to the investigators' attention and sensitivity to close integration of theory, data, program design, and detail in implementation. The chapter provides insights into effective program implementation and institutionalization that are critical to preventive intervention efforts that go well beyond school-based programs.

In Chapter 17, K. V. Kaliappan describes two intervention projects, related to the improvement of academic performance, that he has conducted in the schools of India. A professor of clinical psychology at the University of Madras, India, Kaliappan has been concerned with preparing schoolchildren to manage home, personal, and academic stress, positing that the main objective of education is personality development. But he questions whether the current education system in India may be counterproductive, actually generating more stress than it manages. Kaliappan summarizes the research that he and his colleagues have conducted on training children and families to manage stresses and enrich student personality and academic development. He details two of his investigations, which compare the effectiveness of specific training techniques (and their combinations). Kaliappan argues that broad-scale integration of such training into ongoing educational programs is essential to reduce stress and to promote healthy personality development among India's youth.

The final two chapters of Part IV discuss the need for family-oriented intervention that is set well beyond the formal educational system. The first of these examines quality of life in families with mildly mentally retarded children and a combined intervention and prevention program to improve the lives of these families. Author Irena Obuchowska is professor and head of the Department of Psychopathology of Children and Special Education at Adam Mickiewicz University in Poznan, Poland; Michael Obuchowski is in the Department of Medical Genetics, New York State Psychiatric Institute. They describe a program of implementing and evaluating the external family member (EFM) intervention, which is aimed at fostering mentally retarded children's independence from and acceptance by their parents and the well-being of the family. In the EFM program, graduate student home visitors met with parents of retarded children over a 10-month period and discussed problems of independence and emotional acceptance and their meaning for the psychological development of individuals. Not only was the intervention successful at fostering independence and acceptance of the mentally retarded children, but it served as a beneficial preventive intervention for siblings as well.

In the final chapter of this section, Helena Sek, professor of psychology at Adam Mickiewicz University, Poznan, Poland, and her coauthors, Agnieszka Bleja and Aleksandra Sommerfeld, address the need to foster broad and basic parental competencies in order to improve children's lives. While extrafamilial support persons and institutions are extraordinarily important, they also have the potential to suggest a diminished importance of parents' direct responsibilities and capabilities—disempowering and undermining the confidence of those parents. Sek and her colleagues summarize four significant developmental contexts: the period immediately following birth, creative parent-preschool play, school start, and parent-adolescent interactions. They conclude that we must emphasize educationally oriented programs for parents that engage them in understanding and contributing more effectively to their children's developmental processes in these and other contexts.

# 16

# Two School-Based Approaches to Promoting Children's Social Competence

**Victor A. Battistich**
**Maurice J. Elias**
**Leslie R. Branden-Muller**

Marion Dewar's keynote address at the 1990 Vermont Conference on the Primary Prevention of Psychopathology emphasized needs for realism, commitment, and action on behalf of children. In this chapter, we describe two school-based programs that have responded to these needs. Although there are clear differences between the programs in the nature, scope, and duration of their interventions, they also have much in common. Each is directed toward the goal of promoting positive social development, and each attempts to achieve this goal through systematic efforts to enhance children's personal and interpersonal competencies, and to create supportive school environments that are responsive to children's needs. As such, the programs are illustrative of a small but growing number of longitudinal, developmentally sensitive, and comprehensive school-based approaches to primary prevention (see Schaps & Battistich, in press).

AUTHORS' NOTE: Principal authorship of this chapter was determined through a sophisticated social decision-making and problem-solving strategy (i.e., we drew lots). Support for the ISA-SPS Project has come primarily from the Schumann Fund for New Jersey, the William T. Grant Foundation, and the UMDNJ-CMHC at Piscataway's Social Problem Solving Program. The contributions of a talented action-research team, the collaboration of numerous school districts in New Jersey, and the inspiring vision of Gary Lamson, Virginia Brinson, and Thomas Schuyler are gratefully acknowledged. The Child Development Project has been supported through a grant from the William and Flora Hewlett Foundation. The project was initiated as a result of the ideas and efforts of Dyke Brown, and has been planned and carried out by a large number of talented educators and social scientists, under the direction of Eric Schaps, Daniel Solomon, and Marilyn Watson. Correspondence regarding this chapter should be addressed to either Victor Battistich, Developmental Studies Center, 111 Deerwood Place, Suite 165, San Ramon, CA 94583, or Maurice Elias, Department of Psychology, Rutgers University, Livingston Campus, New Brunswick, NJ 08903. Inquiries about the Child Development and ISA-SPS projects should be addressed to Victor Battistich and Maurice Elias, respectively.

217

At a previous Vermont Conference focused on school-based programs (see Bond & Compas, 1989), a recurrent theme was the need to move away from exclusively "person-centered" intervention programs to "systems-level" interventions that attend to the influence of the social environment of the classroom and school on children's adaptive functioning. This call is predicated on the recognition that development is a complex and dynamic process involving multiple interacting systems of influence, and thus that intervening at any one level of a system in isolation is unlikely to be effective. It is worth noting here that the dynamic and multifaceted nature of development is reflected not only in the relationship between person and environment, but within the individual as well (i.e., in the interrelationships of cognitive, affective, and behavioral systems). Social competence is not simply a matter of understanding others' needs and intentions or knowing how to respond effectively in a problem situation, but also of having the ability to perform necessary actions and being motivated to do so. Both of the programs described are therefore multilevel interventions that attempt to affect all of these domains. Although different in their specific elements, both programs combine a number of practices into coherent, mutually reinforcing systems of positive influences designed to foster children's cognitive, affective, and behavioral growth, and to provide an environment that will support and maintain positive social development.

In addition to being comprehensive, the two programs share another important feature: They regard children's social and emotional development as an educational goal that is as essential and important as their intellectual growth (Battistich, Schaps, Solomon, & Watson, in press; Elias & Clabby, 1984). The programs are therefore designed to be integral to the functioning of the school. Although schools frequently serve as sites for prevention and social development programs, interventions in the vast majority of cases are implemented as short-term, independent, or "add-on" units to the curriculum. Such ephemeral interventions are isolated from students' general learning experiences and therefore have little chance of producing widespread and enduring effects (Greenberg & Kusche, 1988). In contrast, the programs discussed below are systematically incorporated into the "normal" activities of the classroom. This helps to ensure that students' experiences are coherent and integrated, and that students have extensive and varied opportunities to practice skills and apply them in the context of their daily lives.

These underlying commonalities may help to explain why both programs, although quite different in orientation and approach, have been found to be effective not only at enhancing children's social skills (e.g., cognitive perspective-taking and problem-solving abilities), but also at improving their behavioral adjustment (e.g., relationships with peers, and the ability to cope with stressful social situations). Briefer, less comprehensive and systematic approaches to promoting social competence, although far more typical of school-based primary prevention programs, generally have not been found to produce significant improvements consistently in *either* cognitive problem-solving skills or behavioral adjustment (for reviews see Durlak, 1983; Rubin & Krasnor, 1986; Urbain & Kendall, 1980).

Despite the considerable gains made in the last decade in our understanding of the etiology of problem behaviors and in the sophistication of our models of prevention, the gap between knowledge and effective practice is still unacceptably large (Foege, 1990). There is widespread concern with issues of implementation. If we are to be effective in our efforts to improve children's lives, programs must be implemented with fidelity, and must continue to be implemented after their initial, "demonstration" phase. Both of the programs described in this chapter have 10-year histories, marked by a theory-based action research tradition that has involved intensive monitoring of implementation processes and a concerted effort to ensure that the programs become institutionalized in the settings where they have been implemented. After describing each of the programs, we will describe the model that has guided our approaches to implementation and discuss some of the lessons we have learned about achieving effective and enduring implementation of school-based programs.

## The Improving Social Awareness-
## Social Problem Solving Project

The Improving Social Awareness-Social Problem Solving (ISA-SPS) Project began in 1979, when parents and educators in Middlesex Borough, New Jersey, began looking for a way to address the difficulties their children were having in making the transition from elementary to middle school, and in dealing with the increased responsibilities and demands of the middle school environment. The school district entered into collaborative arrangements with the Community Mental Health Center of the University of Medicine and Dentistry of New Jersey and with Rutgers University to try to develop an effective prevention program. Converging evidence from the research literature, program practices, educational philosophy, and common sense led project staff members to expect that considerable benefits could result from teaching students flexible strategies to promote their everyday decision-making, problem-solving, and overall coping skills (Elias & Clabby, 1989).

The ISA-SPS program is a developmentally sequenced curriculum that is provided to students by their teachers as a regular part of classroom instruction. The curriculum currently in use was developed during the course of several years of action research, and consists of a cumulative series of lessons implemented in four successive phases: the Readiness Phase, the Instructional Phase, the Application Phase, and Reviews of Readiness and Instructional Phases. Generally, formal lessons are taught for 20 to 30 minutes weekly, with follow-up activities taking place two to three times per week.

The Readiness lessons are designed to prepare children to work together effectively and help promote positive interpersonal relationships in the classroom by teaching two sets of basic skills: self-control, and social awareness and group participation. Self-control lessons help prepare children to learn in a group setting. They teach children how to listen carefully, how to follow directions, how to recognize and manage their feelings so that they can engage in effective problem solving, and how to converse in an appropriate way with peers. Social awareness and group participation lessons emphasize understanding others' feelings and perspectives, and engaging in rewarding exchanges with others. These lessons teach children to communicate their own feelings and listen to other people's feelings as part of a group, to give and accept praise, to understand the qualities that go into a good friendship, and to know when to ask for help. Children in kindergarten through second grade and in special education classes usually spend the entire year on the Readiness Phase of the curriculum.

The Instructional Phase teaches students to use an eight-step decision-making and problem-solving strategy when faced with problems, choices, or stressful decisions. It is designed to be carried out over a period of years. In order to meet the changing personal, interpersonal, and intellectual needs and capabilities of children as they mature, the curriculum presents the same set of core ideas at each grade level, but introduces the concepts through activities and applications that are age appropriate. In the Instructional Phase, children learn to think through problems and to assume an active role in problem solving. They learn things they can do to solve their own problems, thereby gaining confidence in themselves as problem solvers. Children also learn to work together as a team, to listen to each other, and to learn about each other.

The eight steps that make up the social decision-making and problem-solving strategy are as follows (Elias & Clabby, 1989):

(1) Look for signs of different feelings.
(2) Tell yourself what the problem is.
(3) Decide on a goal.
(4) Stop and think of as many solutions to the problem as you can.
(5) For each solution, think of all the things that might happen.
(6) Choose your best solution.
(7) Plan it and make a final check.
(8) Try it and rethink it.

While the steps, by definition, are presented in a sequential fashion, their interdependence and interrelatedness are stressed throughout. The stepwise presentation is merely an instructional procedure intended to help students learn the components of good problem solving. Lessons are crafted to have personal relevance to children's lives through the use of role plays and both commercial and student-prepared videotapes.

The Application Phase of the program promotes the generalization and transfer of problem-solving skills by helping students to relate the strategies learned in the Instructional Phase to academic material and everyday social situations. It is this phase of the curriculum that is most directly concerned with integrating the program with the regular academic curriculum. The ISA-SPS approach is applied, for example, to creative writing, language arts, and social studies lessons, and to topics such as thinking about what we see and hear in the media, recognizing and changing interpersonal weaknesses, finding alternatives to stereotyping and prejudice, and solving the problem of moving to a new grade or school.

An additional phase of the program is the Readiness Review and Instructional Review. Typically used at the beginning of the school year as a review of what was learned the prior year or to aid children new to the school in understanding the key elements of the program, the Review is conducted by eliciting from students their recollections of basic skills. This serves many functions, such as promoting instructional continuity, keeping teachers focused on the children's levels of understanding, facilitating retention and application, and preventing any skill deficiencies of slower learners or new students from going unnoticed.

A number of features are common to all the lessons. They typically begin with a "sharing circle," a circular seating formation that encourages group interaction. In the circle, shared information moves from the impersonal to the personal, thereby allowing each child to contribute without having to reveal personal information if he or she feels uncomfortable doing so. "Testimonials," children's recounting of when they used or could have used a problem-solving skill since the last lesson, are a formalized "peer modeling" feature of the ISA-SPS program.

Four retention aids are integral to the lessons: review, repetition, reinforcement, and reminders. Lessons begin with a *review* of the previous lesson. *Repetition* of the material through different modalities (such as singing, reading, and writing) and different sources (such as peers, teachers, and aides) helps children remember the lessons. *Reinforcement* in the form of rewards and praise also aids retention. Ideally, children's efforts are acknowledged each time they attempt to employ a skill, and they are given specific feedback about other circumstances in which the skill could be used. *Reminders* to children to use their new skills at various points throughout the day are another effective tool. These reminders may come from bus drivers, teachers, aides, or administrators, or from posters and prompts.[1]

Another integral part of the curriculum is its malleability. It is assumed that teachers will be flexible and competent at planning lessons and selecting and shaping the material presented in the ISA-SPS curriculum. Teachers and administrators first learn the program elements and then may adapt the project's approach to fit their particular teaching styles and students. Student, colleague, and observer feedback can provide valuable information about how best to shape the lessons to capture student interest in a given class or school. Modifications or innovations that work at communicating the lessons and intent of the ISA-SPS program are welcomed because they enrich the curriculum. For example, the Readiness Phase grew out of a need by special education teachers to modify the Instructional Phase for their students.[2]

The ISA-SPS program and its components have been evaluated over the course of the last decade, primarily through a controlled multiyear study involving all fourth- and fifth-grade classes in a suburban blue-collar community in a central New Jersey school district. The extent to which teachers implement the curriculum has been examined using data from a variety of sources—consultants' feedback, videotaped ISA-SPS classroom sessions, observers' reports, teachers' lesson books, and principals' notes. The findings indicate that teachers generally have followed the curriculum and attempted to apply the basic tenets in their classrooms. The level of satisfaction of users of the program also has been evaluated. Teachers, administrators, and students have given very supportive responses to satisfaction surveys. For example, teachers felt the program contributed to their understanding of their students and provided them with a strategy for dealing with problems.

Research also has examined the degree to which students learned social decision-making and problem-solving skills from participation in the program. Using the individually administered Social Problem Situation Analysis Measure (Elias, Larcen, Zlotlow, & Chinsky, 1978) and the knowledge and application sections of the Group Social Problem-Solving Assessment (Elias, Rothbaum, & Gara, 1986), all phases of the program have been shown to make a difference in how children deal with a variety of situations. For example, children who had Instructional Phase lessons improved significantly in knowledge of problem-solving concepts, sensitivity to others' feelings, willingness to take the initiative to solve problems, and capacity to understand and consider the consequences of their actions (Elias & Clabby, 1989). Children who had been trained in the Readiness Phase showed marked skill acquisition when compared with matched controls. For example, 63% of the program children were able to identify several ways that their bodies signaled to them that they were upset, compared with only 27% of the control group (Elias & Clabby, 1989). All of the program children, 100%, said that the lessons helped them to solve problems more effectively and made them happier. Furthermore, 95% were able to name specific times when they had used problem solving. Of these, 35% mentioned times when they used problem solving at school, and 60% named times when they used it with friends and siblings (Elias & Clabby, 1989).

Finally, the most solid evidence of the program's effectiveness to date comes from a study of the effect of exposure to the curriculum on students' coping with the transition to middle school. It was found that students who had received the program in elementary school were better able than control students to handle a variety of stressors in the middle school environment (Elias, Gara, et al., 1986). A full report of the current findings supporting program effectiveness may be found in Elias and Clabby (1989).

The ISA-SPS curriculum has been extended to encompass all grade levels from elementary through high school, in both regular and special education classes, and the program currently is being implemented in a number of school districts in the eastern and midwestern United States. With the assistance of a grant from the U.S. Department of Education's National Diffusion Network, the program is being disseminated to schools throughout the country by providing educators with the training, materials, and consultation they need to implement the approach effectively.

### The Child Development Project

The Child Development Project (CDP) is a comprehensive elementary school program (K-6) designed to enhance children's prosocial development, that is, the development of attitudes and motives that reflect a sincere concern for the rights and needs of others as well as the self, the knowledge and skills necessary for mutually beneficial and productive social relationships, and a personal commitment to fundamental democratic values (Brown & Solomon, 1983; Solomon et al., 1985). The program is derived from a theoretical model that integrates elements of traditional, authority-based models of socialization with constructivist, cognitive-developmental theory (see Battistich, Watson, Solomon, Schaps, & Solomon, in press; Watson, Schaps, Battistich, Solomon, & Solomon, 1989). Children are viewed as actively striving to understand the social world, to develop the skills they need to function autonomously and effectively, and to form positive relationships with others. However, because children often lack the skill, knowledge, or self-control to integrate egoistic and prosocial concerns on their own, adults must facilitate prosocial development by establishing an environment that meets children's needs for competence, self-determination, and social connectedness, and by providing children with moral guidance. Theoretically, an environment that meets these conditions would be a caring community (see Solomon, Watson, Battistich, Schaps, & Delucchi, 1990) in which children are active participants and come to understand the importance of prosocial values to social life through personal experience.

The CDP program consists of an intensive classroom component that is supported and extended by a variety of schoolwide and family components. Collectively, these elements are designed to create a caring and participatory school community in which children are given numerous opportunities to learn about others' needs and perspectives; to collaborate with one another and to engage in a variety of prosocial actions; to discuss and reflect upon their social experiences as they relate to values of fairness, kindness, and social responsibility; and to exercise autonomy and participate in decision making about their activities and their school environment. Although the program does include specific "lessons" (e.g., a literature-based language arts curriculum), it is not a separate "social development" curriculum; rather, it is an approach to schooling that regards academic and social development as inseparable, and that regards students as autonomous and important contributors to their own education and their own socialization.

The classroom program consists of four major elements:

(1) *Developmental discipline:* This is an approach to classroom management that promotes the internalization of prosocial norms and values and the development of self-control by building positive interpersonal relationships within the classroom, involving students in class rule setting and decision making, emphasizing understanding of the principles underlying rules, and using nonpunitive control techniques that center on induction (Hoffman, 1983) and mutual problem solving.

(2) *Cooperative activities:* Students work together in small groups toward common goals on academic and nonacademic tasks, are explicitly encouraged to strive for fairness, consideration, and social responsibility, are given training in relevant group interaction skills, and are provided with opportunities to reflect upon how these values and skills are applied in social relations through discussions of group process.

(3) *Activities to enhance interpersonal understanding and prosocial values:* Exemplary works of literature, class meetings, and discussions are used to enhance sensitivity to and understanding of the feelings, needs, and perspectives of others, and to heighten students' awareness of the importance of prosocial values to social life,

(4) *Opportunities for prosocial action:* Students take responsibility for doing classroom chores, help other students in class, help maintain and improve the school environment, and perform charitable community service activities.

For more extensive descriptions of these four elements, see Solomon, Watson, Schaps, Battistich, and Solomon (1990) and Watson et al. (1989).

Schoolwide activities, such as a "buddies" program in which older students tutor and care for younger students, help to extend the sense of community throughout the school, and provide additional opportunities for enhancing social understanding and engaging in actions to benefit others. Family activities, such as cooperative family projects and "family homework," are designed to enhance both family-child and family-school relationships. The bond between family and school is further strengthened through school "coordinating teams" of teachers and parents that take responsibility for the operation of schoolwide and family-school activities.

The initial field trial of the CDP was conducted in a suburban, largely middle-class community in Northern California. Research was focused on a longitudinal cohort of children who began the program in kindergarten at three elementary schools in the fall of 1982 and completed sixth grade in the spring of 1989. A corresponding cohort of children who attended three other elementary schools in the same school district served as a comparison group. The study was based on a quasi-experimental design in which the six schools were formed into two groups (matched on size, student achievement, family SES, and teacher interest in the program) that were then randomly assigned to program or comparison status. Assessments of a cross-sectional random sample in the year prior to the start of the program indicated that students at program and comparison schools were equivalent with respect to a large number of social attitudes, values, skills, and behaviors.

Extensive observations in program and comparison classrooms each year (conducted by observers who were unaware of the intervention) consistently indicated that implementation of each element of the classroom program was substantially higher in program than in comparison schools (Solomon, Watson, Delucchi, Schaps, & Battistich, 1988). These differences have been corroborated by teacher and student reports. For example, program students regularly reported more autonomy in the classroom, greater involvement in the development of class rules, and more participation in classroom decision making than did comparison students.

Analyses of student outcome data for kindergarten through sixth grade revealed several strong and consistent program effects. Classroom observations repeatedly revealed that students in program classrooms engaged in more spontaneous prosocial behavior (e.g., helpfulness, cooperation, giving of affection, support, and encouragement) than did students in comparison classrooms (Solomon et al., 1988). Program children also scored significantly higher than comparison children on questionnaire measures of the extent to which their classrooms were like a "caring community" in fourth through sixth grades (Solomon, Watson, Battistich, et al., 1990).

Other findings indicate that the program has had positive effects on students' social competencies, acceptance by peers, and social adjustment. From first through fifth grades, a variety of interview measures of conflict resolution and social problem-solving skills consistently indicated that program children had greater perspective-taking skills and showed more consideration of the other person's needs as well as their own in problem situations, were more likely to consider the consequences of their actions and anticipate obstacles to effective resolution, and used more prosocial and cooperative strategies (e.g., discussing the problem, explaining their positions, sharing or other compromise solutions) than did comparison children (Battistich, Solomon, Watson, Solomon, & Schaps, 1989). Program students also scored significantly higher than comparison students on sociometric measures of peer acceptance in both third and fifth grades, and scored significantly lower than comparison students on questionnaire measures of loneliness and social anxiety in sixth grade (Battistich, Solomon, & Delucchi, 1990).

Program children also appeared to be more committed to democratic values than did comparison children. In third grade, program children scored higher than comparison children on a questionnaire measure of assertion responsibility (i.e., the belief that one has a responsibility to state one's position even if it seems unlikely to prevail). In fourth grade, in addition to assertion responsibility, program children also scored higher than comparison children on a measure of equality of representation and participation (i.e., beliefs that all members of a group have a right to influence group decisions and to be involved in group activities; Solomon, Schaps, Watson, & Battistich, 1987).

Finally, there is some preliminary evidence suggesting that the program may have positive effects on academic as well as social competencies. Program students scored significantly higher than comparison students on a measure of "higher-order" reading comprehension (i.e., understanding of the meaning of a poem or short story, rather than simple recall of the content of the text) administered in sixth grade (based on a measure developed by the Educational Testing Service).

Overall, the findings from the initial field trial of CDP indicate that the program was effective in creating a caring and supportive school environment, and had beneficial effects on children's interpersonal skills, social adjustment, behavior in the classroom, and commitment to democratic values. Several of these effects involve a combination of appropriate self-assertion and concern for others, suggesting that the program may help children acquire the kind of balance of individualistic and communalistic motives that lies at the heart of our definition of prosocial behavior. Research on the program is currently proceeding on two fronts. In order to determine longer-term effects of the program, follow-up assessments of the original longitudinal cohorts will be conducted through at least eighth grade. At the same time, the program is gradually being introduced at two elementary schools in an ethnically and socioeconomically diverse community, and dissemination to several additional school districts throughout the United States is planned to begin in 1991. Careful evaluations at each of these diverse sites will help us determine the kinds of settings in which the program can be effectively implemented, as well as broaden our understanding of the program's effects on children.

## Turning Program Ideas into Enduring Realities:
## A Pragmatic, Ecologically Sensitive, Action-Research Approach
## to Implementation and Institutionalization

The findings from careful evaluations of the programs described above clearly indicate that they have been effective at enhancing children's social competencies. What is equally important, however, is that both programs have endured in their initial settings and have been implemented in additional settings.

Too often in the past, promising educational innovations have neither been continued in their original settings nor successfully disseminated to new sites (Berman &
McLaughlin, 1978; Elias, 1987; Sarason, 1982). Although a detailed account of the
implementation of either program cannot be provided here (but see Elias & Clabby,
in press; Watson et al., 1989), it may be useful to describe a general model of the
development of effective school-based programs, and to elucidate some of the important principles that have emerged in the course of both projects about what is required to establish and maintain meaningful programs in schools.

The operation of both projects is consistent with the conceptualization of prevention-
oriented action research presented by Price and Smith (1985). Innovative programs
in this model pass through four interrelated cycles of development. *Problem analysis* involves the identification of a needed service or setting-oriented problem, and
the delineation of a theoretical model of the key factors governing the phenomena
of interest and the proposed change process. This is followed by the phase of *innovation design*, in which the likely effects of various program technologies on the
factors identified as contributing to the problem are critically examined, and a specific intervention program is designed. This program is then subjected to *field trials*,
during which it is carefully implemented in one or more settings and subjected to
both formative monitoring (to ensure that the program is actually being implemented as intended) and summative evaluation (to determine whether or not the
program is having its intended effects). Finally, assuming that the findings from
field trials are positive, the program enters the cycle of *innovation diffusion*. During
this cycle, procedures for disseminating the program to a larger number of settings
are developed, but typically under implementation conditions that involve considerably less direct monitoring and scrutiny by program staff, and less rigorous evaluation than during the preceding cycles.

The reality of school-based action research is that this cyclic process of program
development is virtually continuous. Once a program is introduced into a setting,
redesign is necessary to adapt program practices to changes in the social ecology of
the setting and to make certain that the program retains the appeal to implementers
that fostered its initial adoption. Further complicating matters is that the innovation
is repeated in different school buildings, at different grade levels, and with different
student and staff populations, and each change in context requires reanalysis and
potential redesign. Field trials should be conducted in each different context so that
necessary modifications and adaptations to the original innovation design can be incorporated before the program is more widely disseminated. Even so, a given program may be applicable only to certain classes of settings and populations. For
example, the CDP and ISA-SPS programs may be most effectively disseminated to
elementary schools that not only perceive a need for addressing the problems they
were designed to prevent, but also share the programs' underlying philosophies and
have the commitment, organizational structures, and resources required to achieve
meaningful and long-lasting changes in school practices.

There is now a vast literature on the implementation of innovations (e.g., Harvey, Kell, & Drexler, 1990; Hord, Rutherford, Huling-Austin, & Hall, 1987; Huberman & Miles, 1984; Yin, 1979) that can be drawn upon to fill in much of the detail in the phases of program development outlined by Price and Smith. Recently, considerable attention has been paid to a final stage in the life cycle of a program, which has been referred to as the *institutionalization* of an innovation (Commins & Elias, in press; Hord et al., 1987). The importance of this stage is that it extends thinking and research beyond the consideration of factors that promote adequate implementation of a program to the identification of factors that help to ensure that innovations are maintained at their implementation sites after their initial demonstration phases, and that they retain both their essential features and their effectiveness. Table 16.1 presents an integration of factors considered important to the institutionalization of a program, with the principles underlying effective program implementation outlined by Weissberg, Caplan, and Sivo (1989).

Implementing a program is not a linear process. In practice, the rather linear portrayal in the table must be woven into the cyclic model of Price and Smith. What is perhaps most critical and daunting about the tasks in the table is that unremediated difficulties in any of them can place long-term utilization and effectiveness of a program in jeopardy. With this in mind, we have attempted to isolate several factors that, in our collective experience, we have found to be essential to achieving enduring and effective program implementation (for a more extensive discussion of these and related issues, see Commins & Elias, in press; and Schaps & Battistich, in press).

### Some Lessons Learned

*A program's effectiveness is limited by the organizational "soundness" of the host environment and collaborating groups.* This must be considered when choosing a setting for a program, selecting collaborating groups or agencies, or attempting to diagnose why a program is not being carried out as designed. An implicit part of successful implementation is sound organizational functioning over time, and the action research team must actively work to bolster overall organizational health for all involved groups.

*Successful programs engender investment and "ownership" on the part of participants.* Programs endure to the extent that participants come to see them as "their" programs. From the earliest stages of program development, change agents must continuously determine what criteria of success are meaningful to implementers and other stakeholders (administrators, policymakers, parents), and reach consensus with these groups on the indicators to be used and the nature and timing of desired feedback. This task will be greatly aided by the presence of an on-site leadership group responsible for monitoring progress, gathering feedback information, suggesting refinements or other program adaptations, and seeing that needed changes are carried out properly.

**Table 16.1** Tasks Required for Effective and Enduring Implementation of Programs

| (1) Program conceptualization | (a) Use existing theory, research, and intervention information at both person and environmental levels to specify main program concepts, assumptions, and goals. |
|---|---|
| (2) Program design | (a) Identify and review potentially appropriate intervention materials and practices. |
| | (b) Examine materials and practices for developmental appropriateness and cultural relevance, and modify as necessary. |
| | (c) Define key elements needed for successful long-term implementation. |
| | (d) Prepare training materials, procedures, and guidelines for implementation. |
| | (e) Specify organizational linkages and conditions that will allow integration of the program with the mission and existing operations of the host setting(s): for example, creation of a program committee or group supervision structure, coordination with school resource committees or similar group. |
| (3) Program implementation | (a) Conduct a pilot study and adapt the program to recipients, implementers, and ecological realities. |
| | (b) Fine-tune training, supervision, and consultation procedures. |
| | (c) Develop a system to ensure high-quality implementation. |
| | (d) Articulate procedures for providing more intensive, alternative, and/or supplemental services to recipients who are not responsive to the program; consider alternative program designs. |
| | (e) Develop contacts at various organizational and community levels to ensure ongoing support of the program and the resources needed to carry it out. |
| (4) Program monitoring and evaluation | (a) Identify valid, viable approaches to measuring the extent and quality of implementation; changes in focal attitudes, knowledge, skills, relationships, and mediating factors; and implementer and consumer receptivity and responsiveness. |
| | (b) Design and carry out an appropriate data collection and analysis plan. |
| (5) Program diffusion | (a) Conceptualize how the program can be implemented elsewhere, by others, with varying degrees of involvement by program developers. |
| | (b) Produce transportable materials and clear, specific training and replication guidelines. |
| | (c) Determine procedures for baseline level of program monitoring and evaluation in new sites, and provide relevant materials and training. |

SOURCE: Adapted from Weissberg et al. (1989).

*Careful and continuous monitoring and evaluation are essential to effective programs.* There are no "pure" programs and no "precise" replications; adaptations to the local ecology of the setting are inevitable and therefore essential to effective implementation. Nevertheless, these adaptations must not stray from the key program elements or the underlying principles on which the program is based. Thus the quality and integrity of program implementation must be monitored in each setting. This "quality control" is achieved through formal and informal assessment procedures, and through the establishment of appropriate organizational structures and procedures for supporting and maintaining the "essential" program within the larger context of the setting (e.g., to ensure that program implementation is not adversely affected by competing demands, or that other practices within the setting are not incompatible with program practices or principles). In the absence of careful assessment of program implementation, evaluations of effectiveness can be quite misleading.

*It takes time for implementers to understand a program thoroughly and to become genuine collaborators in program development.* Meaningful change is a difficult process that requires "active" learning, repeated practice, and careful reflection. In our experience, it usually is not until the end of a full year of implementation (typically, the end of the second year of the program, since the first year usually consists of a pilot program) that program implementers have developed a genuine understanding of the program and can therefore provide informed input to the course and nature of program adaptation in their setting. Extensive consultation with program staff is used to "fine-tune" the program during one or more additional years of implementation, when the program can truly be said to be functioning. Actual institutionalization of the program generally requires about five full years of implementation, by which time a core of staff has had sufficient experience with the program to have developed the expertise and comfort to use it effectively, and for program practices to have become an integral part of the staff's overall approach to schooling.

### The Role of School-Based Approaches to Promoting Social Competence in the Global Prevention Effort

Considered in light of the fact that many children around the world face daily threats to their physical survival, the goal of promoting children's social competence may seem to lose much of its urgency. Even in the wealthiest and most technologically advanced nations, there are large numbers of children whose most basic needs are not being met adequately. In the United States, for example, the number of children living in substandard conditions has increased dramatically since the 1970s, to the point that children under 5 years old have the highest percentage living in poverty of any age group in the population (Preston, 1984). Clearly, massive efforts are needed worldwide to see that children are fed and clothed, given adequate shelter, and protected from psychological abuse and physical harm.

At the same time, school-based programs such as the ISA-SPS Project and the Child Development Project have considerable global relevance, and there is reason to believe that their cross-national and cross-cultural generality will increase in the future. Ultimately, this is based on the recognition that the kinds of competencies identified and discussed in this chapter are characteristics that are essential to effective functioning in an increasingly complex and technological world (Gardner, 1983; Sternberg & Wagner, 1986). If children are to experience healthy relationships and occupy meaningful and productive roles in society as adults, they must be competent at communicating and working cooperatively with others. They need to be able to express their own opinions and beliefs; to understand and appreciate the perspectives of others who differ from them in background, needs, or experiences; and to become skilled at reasoned disagreement, negotiation, and compromise as methods of solving problems when their own needs or interests conflict with those of others. Indeed, in the face of decreasing resources and increasing global interdependence, it can be argued that such qualities are essential to our survival.

The question, then, is not *whether* we must enhance children's social competencies, but rather *how* to accomplish this goal. Until this century, most of the world's children grew up in tight-knit, cohesive communities where the responsibility for their education and socialization was shared by the family, the neighborhood, and social institutions. In much of the so-called developed world this already is no longer the case, and it is becoming increasingly true in less developed nations as well. James Coleman (1987) has described how the social, economic, and political changes that accompanied increasing industrialization led to the decline of the family and community as socializing institutions, with the result that much of the extensive "social capital" that was once devoted to child rearing has been lost. If for no other reason than by default, the school *must* take on much of the responsibility for children's social development, for, increasingly, the school is the only institution that is capable of doing so.

There also is a growing recognition that changing schools to meet children's social and emotional needs more effectively and to promote their social competencies may not only help to prevent a wide variety of behavioral and psychological disorders, but may be essential for improving academic achievement as well (Coleman, 1987; Linney & Seidman, 1989; Tharp, 1989). The narrow focus of the educational system on the development of basic academic skills has contributed to the development of an educational underclass composed primarily of the poor and certain cultural minorities, whose difficulty in school leads them to lose hope and drop out, and thereby alienates them from the economic and political mainstream of society. The kinds of changes to schooling represented by the ISA-SPS and Child Development Projects are desirable for all children, but they may be imperative for those whose economic circumstances or sociocultural backgrounds put them most at risk of school failure.

The climate of concern for the children of the world has perhaps never before been so intense and forward-looking. Although there are a great many obstacles to be overcome (see Kramer, Chapter 1, this volume), hope was expressed at the Vermont Conference that through worldwide ratification of the United Nations Convention on the Rights of the Child, the nations of the world would "turn the corner" and begin to realize that the phrase "Children are our future" is not a cliché but an affirmation of converging humanitarian, economic, and political realities (see Sochet, 1990). One essential part of the global effort to improve children's lives is to enhance the capacity of socializing agents and institutions to provide children with the full range of knowledge, skills, and experience they will need to function effectively as adults. Schools are a logical and necessary base for such work. It is our hope and belief that the result of these combined modest but steady efforts will be a gradual and inexorable improvement in children's competencies that will enable future generations to meet the challenges of leadership, social responsibility, and global interdependence with skill, wisdom, and sensitivity.

## Notes

1. A prompt is a concept that is distilled into one word or phrase that cues the child to think of the overall skill and all its components. The child need only hear the prompt and he or she is thereby reminded to engage in a series of steps or to demonstrate some behavior. For example, "Keep calm" is a signal to the child to regain self-control; "VENT" reminds the child to behave in a polite, socially acceptable way. These and other self-control and social awareness prompts are an integral part of the curriculum and of the broader social decision-making and problem-solving climate that becomes established in project schools.

2. These modifications are disseminated to a large network of people using the ISA-SPS approach through the *Problem Solving Connection* newsletter. For more information about this newsletter, contact John Clabby at the University of Medicine and Dentistry of New Jersey, Community Mental Health Center at Piscataway, ISA-SPS Unit, 240 Stelton Road, Piscataway, NJ 08854.

## References

Battistich, V., Schaps, E., Solomon, D., & Watson, M. (in press). The role of the elementary school in prosocial development. In H. E. Fitzgerald, B. M. Lester, & M. W. Yogman (Eds.), *Theory and research in behavioral pediatrics* (Vol. 5). New York: Plenum.

Battistich, V., Solomon, D., & Delucchi, K. L. (1990, August). *Effects of a program to enhance prosocial development on adjustment.* Paper presented at the annual meeting of the American Psychological Association, Boston.

Battistich, V., Solomon, D., Watson, M., Solomon, J., & Schaps, E. (1989). Effects of an elementary school program to enhance prosocial behavior on children's cognitive-social problem-solving skills and strategies. *Journal of Applied Developmental Psychology, 10,* 147-169.

Battistich, V., Watson, M., Solomon, D., Schaps, E., & Solomon, J. (in press). The Child Development Project: A comprehensive program for the development of prosocial character.

In W. M. Kurtines & J. L. Gewirtz (Eds.), *Handbook of moral behavior and development: Vol. 3. Application.* Hillsdale, NJ: Lawrence Erlbaum.

Berman, P., & McLaughlin, M. W. (1978). *Federal programs supporting educational change: Vol. 8. Implementing and sustaining innovations.* Santa Monica, CA: RAND Corporation.

Bond, L. A., & Compas, B. E. (Eds.). (1989). *Primary prevention and promotion in the schools.* Newbury Park, CA: Sage.

Brown, D., & Solomon, D. (1983). A model for prosocial learning: An in-progress field study. In D. Bridgman (Ed.), *The nature of prosocial development* (pp. 273-307). New York: Academic Press.

Coleman, J. S. (1987). Families and schools. *Educational Researcher, 16*, 32-38.

Commins, W., & Elias, M. J. (in press). Institutionalization of mental health programs in organizational contexts: The case of elementary schools. *Journal of Community Psychology.*

Durlak, J. (1983). Social problem solving as a primary prevention strategy. In R. D. Felner, L. A. Jason, J. N. Moritsugo, & S. S. Farber (Eds.), *Preventive psychology* (pp. 31-48). New York: Pergamon.

Elias, M. J. (1987). Establishing enduring prevention programs: Advancing the legacy of Swampscott. *American Journal of Community Psychology, 15*, 539-554.

Elias, M. J., & Clabby, J. F. (1984). Integrating social and affective education into public school curriculum and instruction. In C. Maher, R. Illback, & J. Zins (Eds.), *Organizational psychology in the schools: A handbook for professionals* (pp. 143-172). Springfield, IL: Charles C Thomas.

Elias, M. J., & Clabby, J. F. (1989). *Social decision making skills: A curriculum guide for elementary grades.* Rockville, MD: Aspen.

Elias, M. J., & Clabby, J. F. (in press). *School-based enhancement of children's and adolescents' social problem solving skills.* San Francisco: Jossey-Bass.

Elias, M. J., Gara, M., Ubriaco, M., Rothbaum, P. A., Clabby, J., & Schuyler, T. (1986). Impact of a preventive social problem solving intervention on children's coping with middle-school stressors. *American Journal of Community Psychology, 14*, 259-275.

Elias, M. J., Larcen, S. W., Zlotlow, S. F., & Chinsky, J. M. (1978, August). *An innovative measure of children's cognitions in problematic interpersonal situations.* Paper presented at the annual meeting of the American Psychological Association, Toronto.

Elias, M. J., Rothbaum, P. A., & Gara, M. (1986). Social-cognitive problem solving in children: Assessing the knowledge and application of skills. *Journal of Applied Developmental Psychology, 7*, 77-94.

Foege, W. (1990). Closing the gaps: Ensuring the application of available knowledge in the promotion of health and prevention of disease. *Journal of School Health, 60*, 130-132.

Gardner, H. (1983). *Frames of mind.* New York: Basic Books.

Greenberg, M. T., & Kusche, C. A. (1988, March). *Preventing pathology and promoting social competence: A developmental model.* Paper presented at the annual meeting of the American Association of Orthopsychiatry, San Francisco.

Harvey, G., Kell, D., & Drexler, N. (1990, April). *Implementing technology in the classroom: Paths to success and failure.* Paper presented at the annual meeting of the American Educational Research Association, Boston.

Hoffman, M. L. (1983). Affective and cognitive processes in moral internalization. In E. T. Higgins, D. N. Ruble, & W. W. Hartup (Eds.), *Social cognition and social development: A sociocultural perspective* (pp. 236-274). New York: Cambridge University Press.

Hord, S., Rutherford, W., Huling-Austin, L., & Hall, G. (1987). *Taking charge of change.* Alexandria, VA: Association for Supervision and Curriculum Development.

Huberman, M., & Miles, M. (1984). *Innovation up close: How school improvement works.* New York: Plenum.

Linney, J. A., & Seidman, E. (1989). The future of schooling. *American Psychologist, 44,* 336-340.

Preston, S. (1984). Children and the elderly. *Scientific American, 251,* 44-49.

Price, R., & Smith, S. (1985). *A guide to evaluating prevention programs in mental health* (DHHS Publication No. ADM 85-144). Washington, DC: Government Printing Office.

Rubin, K. H., & Krasnor, L. R. (1986). Social-cognitive and social-behavioral perspectives on problem solving. In M. Perlmutter (Ed.), *Cognitive perspectives on children's social and behavioral development* (pp. 1-68). Hillsdale, NJ: Lawrence Erlbaum.

Sarason, S. B. (1982). *The culture of the school and the problem of change* (2nd ed.). Boston: Allyn & Bacon.

Schaps, E., & Battistich, V. (in press). Promoting healthy development through school-based prevention: New approaches. In E. Goplerude (Ed.), *A practical guide to substance abuse prevention in adolescence.* Washington, DC: Government Printing Office.

Sochet, M. (1990, June). *Kids meeting kids: Bringing children together to promote international understanding.* Paper presented at the Vermont Conference on the Primary Prevention of Psychopathology, Burlington.

Solomon, D., Schaps, E., Watson, M., & Battistich, V. (1987, April). *Promoting prosocial behavior in schools: A second interim report on a five-year longitudinal demonstration project.* Paper presented at the annual meeting of the American Educational Research Association, Washington, DC.

Solomon, D., Watson, M., Battistich, V., Schaps, E., & Delucchi, K. (1990, September). *Creating a caring community: A school-based program to promote children's sociomoral development.* Invited presentation at the International Symposium on Research on Effective and Responsible Teaching, Fribourg, Switzerland.

Solomon, D., Watson, M., Battistich, V., Tuck, P., Schaps, E., Solomon, J., Cooper, C., & Ritchey, W. (1985). A program to promote interpersonal cooperation and consideration in children. In R. Slavin, S. Sharan, S. Kagan, R. Hertz-Lazarowitz, C. Webb, & R. Schmuck (Eds.), *Learning to cooperate, cooperating to learn* (pp. 371-401). New York: Plenum.

Solomon, D., Watson, M. S., Delucchi, K. E., Schaps, E., & Battistich, V. (1988). Enhancing children's prosocial behavior in the classroom. *American Educational Research Journal, 25,* 527-554.

Solomon, D., Watson, M., Schaps, E., Battistich, V., & Solomon, J. (1990). Cooperative learning as part of a comprehensive classroom program designed to promote prosocial development. In S. Sharan (Ed.), *Cooperative learning: Theory and research* (pp. 231-260). New York: Praeger.

Sternberg, R., & Wagner, R. (Eds.). (1986). *Practical intelligence: Nature and origins of competence in the everyday world.* New York: Cambridge University Press.

Tharp, R. G. (1989). Psychocultural variables and constants: Effects on teaching and learning in schools. *American Psychologist, 44,* 349-359.

Urbain, E., & Kendall, P. (1980). Review of social-cognitive problem-solving interventions with children. *Psychological Bulletin, 83,* 109-143.

Watson, M., Schaps, E., Battistich, V., Solomon, D., & Solomon, J. (1989). The Child Development Project: Combining traditional and developmental approaches to values education. In L. Nucci (Ed.), *Moral development and character education: A dialog* (pp. 51-92). Berkeley, CA: McCutchan.

Weissberg, R. P., Caplan, M. Z., & Sivo, P. J. (1989). A new conceptual model for establishing school-based social competence promotion programs. In L. A. Bond & B. E. Compas (Eds.), *Primary prevention and promotion in the schools* (pp. 255-296). Newbury Park, CA: Sage.

Yin, R. (1979). *Changing urban bureaucracies: How new practices become routinized.* Lexington, MA: Lexington.

# 17

# Personality Development and Academic Improvement for Schoolchildren in India

## K. V. Kaliappan

Stress has become an inevitable part of modern life. From preschool age, children seem to be exposed constantly to academic stress. Some of the major factors contributing to academic stress in India include multilingualism among a population of more than 850 million, half of whom remain illiterate, a greater than 50% dropout rate from primary and middle school, scores of educated youth remaining unemployed, and memory-based examinations. Hence the 1986 National Policy on Education (Government of India, 1986) advocated certain remedial measures, such as delinking degrees from jobs in selected areas, examination reforms, the creation of more open universities, institutes of distance education and rural universities, continuous training of teachers at all levels, compulsory primary education, and strengthening adult education as a mass movement. Although the Indian educational system is undergoing thorough changes as detailed in the National Policy on Education, it nevertheless seems necessary to prepare students to manage home, personal, and academic stresses.

The main objective of education is personality development, but only research can answer the question of whether the present-day educational system in India helps in promoting students' personality development or instead places them under too much stress. If the students are in stress, then it is necessary to design special personality development programs to alleviate stress and enable students to perform more efficiently in their academic pursuits. Will such programs be effective?

What are the specific stresses confronted by schoolchildren in India? Examinations seem to produce severe stress. Newspapers in India have reported a few students committing suicide due to failure in examinations. In addition, creative students appear to face stress, as revealed by Pradeep (1983). He investigated

AUTHOR'S NOTE: I very much appreciate the sincere work of Dr. R. Rajendran and Dr. T. J. Kamalanabhan, junior research fellows in the UGC career award project, and all my other research scholars.

the relationship of creativity, intelligence, and motivation to academic performance among 80 male and 80 female eleventh-standard students. The correlation between academic performance and creativity was negative and highly significant (boys, $r = -0.52$, $p < .01$; girls, $r = -0.44$, $p < .01$) when motivation and intelligence were partialed out. Many Indian studies also support this finding (e.g., Paramesh, 1972; Rebecca, 1985). Commenting on the examination system in India, Pradeep (1983) asserts that because "the examinations act as a filtering system in which all creative students are filtered out and only intelligent students get through, the country is really missing their service, which should be considered as a serious drawback" (p. 105).

With my research students, I have undertaken many studies in personality development and academic improvement of school students. A few relevant studies will be presented here before a discussion of my University Grants Commission's career award research project.

Effects of relaxation and placebo therapies on anxiety, tension, feelings of inferiority, insecurity, attention, concentration, and memory were studied by Sitharthan (1980). Each treatment group consisted of 25 students of the fifth standard. Both therapy groups reduced feelings of inferiority, insecurity, tension, and anxiety after two months of implementation. The students also improved in immediate and associative memory. Concentration improved only for the relaxation therapy group. No improvement was obtained for either group in attention. Relaxation therapy proved better in reducing insecurity and improving immediate memory and concentration, whereas placebo was better in improving associative learning.

Chitra (1985) studied the effect of systematic desensitization and cue-controlled relaxation combined with study skills training with 20 test-anxious students belonging to sixth through eleventh standards. Academic performance was assessed through self-reports and teachers' reports. Though both the groups improved, the systematic desensitization approach proved more effective than cue-controlled relaxation in reducing test anxiety and improving academic performance.

Kanchana (1986) carried out a research investigation to reduce test anxiety and improve academic performance of high school girls. The sample consisted of 144 ninth-standard girls, aged 14-17 years, belonging to a corporation school. Sarason, Davidson, Lighthall, and Waite's (1958) test anxiety scale for children and Kanchana's (1986) study skills questionnaire were used to select students with high test anxiety and poor study skills. Relaxation therapy, systematic desensitization, and transcendental meditation groups formed the three therapy groups. Study skills training was combined with each of the three experimental groups.

Relaxation and systematic desensitization therapies were equal and better in reducing the test anxiety and improving the academic performance than was transcendental meditation. Study skills training improved study habits and contributed significantly to improving academic performance (path coefficient 0.62). The reduction in test anxiety also contributed significantly to the improvement of academic performance (path coefficient 0.56). A significant negative relationship was found between study skills and test anxiety (path coefficient 0.37).

Nithyakala (1987) studied 29 underachieving students (4 girls and 25 boys) with an intellectual capacity above the ninetieth percentile. They were 12-18 years old and studying in seventh, eighth, ninth, and plus one (eleventh) standards. These students were failing in one or more subjects prior to the study. A seven-week psychological training course was given during which three to four sessions of behavioral counseling were conducted for the specific problems of the students. In addition, students were divided into groups of four to six members and given human relations training. Skills were taught through group discussions, exercises, and games, with the use of learning contracts. The interpersonal skills taught to these students were knowledge of self and others (strengths and weaknesses), communication skills, how to express and accept compliments and criticism, appropriate emotional expression, and conflict resolution. Students were also given study skills training for a total of seven weeks. The psychological training brought a significant change in 7 of the 14 personality factors. Study skills and academic performance also improved. Although teachers had originally anticipated that all the students who were referred would be detained in the final examination, all but four showed marked improvement in their academic performance and were promoted.

Murugadhoss (1989) studied the effect of behavioral training on parents in enriching the family environment and modifying student personality, as well as the relationship between these changes and improved academic performance. Participants were 40 students (30 boys and 10 girls) belonging to sixth to tenth standards who had failed in one or more subjects and their single parents (15 mothers and 25 fathers).

Parent training improved family environment, as reflected by changes in six factors: parent-child interaction, parental involvement, parents' aspirations, discipline, parental attention, and parents' motivation. Behavioral training led students to become more enthusiastic, venturesome, self-assured, and relaxed. They also improved in study skills and academic performance. Training of parents was also associated with improved academic performance of the children. This improvement was equal to the improvement of students who were trained with the behavioral package. Training of both parents and students improved the academic performance still more.

A sample of 35 delinquent boys who were admitted to an approved home and were studying in a public school were given relaxation and systematic desensitization therapy for four months by Kannappan (1989). The Jesness (1972) inventory was administered four times: during (at two months) and after treatment (at four months), and at a three-month follow-up. The comparison between pre- and postassessments of the students showed that social maladjustment, value orientation, autism, alienation, withdrawal, and social anxiety were significantly reduced. A significant moderate rise in repression and denial was also found for both therapy groups as rated by the teachers. The systematic desensitization appeared superior, resulting in quicker improvement and greater maintenance of the improvement.

With this research as background information, I conducted a University Grants Commission career award project consisting of two experiments: The first managed academic stress to improve academic performance, and the second examined personality development and improvement in academic performance.

## Experiment 1

### Method

*Subjects*

Subjects included 285 male high school students 12-15 years old studying seventh to ninth standards in an English medium school. The majority belonged to middle socioeconomic status. Of this sample, students were selected for the main study who scored in the top quartile in one of three areas of academic stress: personal inadequacy ($n$ = 40), fear of failure ($n$ = 40), and interpersonal difficulties ($n$ = 40). Equal numbers of students in each of these three groups were randomly assigned to experimental (treatment) and control groups.

*Measures*

A student academic stress scale was developed especially for the investigation reported here. The final form of the scale consisted of 67 items describing the sources of student academic stress in the 12-15 age group. Respondents rated each item on a five-point scale ranging from "no stress" to "extreme stress." Factor analysis of the scale revealed four factors, which were labeled *personal inadequacy, fear of failure, interpersonal difficulties,* and *inadequate study facilities.* The raw score for each item was multiplied by its corresponding factor loadings to give a weighted score for each item. The weighted scores of all items that loaded on each factor were summed to create a total score for each factor.

*Personality Development Training*

Over a period of six months, the three experimental groups were given well-designed behavioral programs suitable for their respective stress areas, as shown in Table 17.1.

*Relaxation training.* Jacobson's (1938) deep muscle relaxation training was taught to the personal inadequacy group within four sessions. Each training session lasted for 45-50 minutes. Students were motivated to practice relaxation at home in addition to during three supervised sessions per week at school.

*Study skills training.* A six-week training program in study skills was conducted to improve the study habits of students. In discussion, a few factors were identified, such as difficulties in organization of time and in concentration during

**Table 17.1** Behavioral Treatment Programs for the Three Experimental Groups

| Experimental Group (Stress Area) | Treatment Program |
|---|---|
| Personal inadequacy | relaxation training<br>study skills training |
| Fear of failure | relaxation training<br>systematic desensitization |
| Interpersonal difficulties | assertiveness training<br>communication program |

study, motivation to study, and personal problems. Training was provided in the following areas (Kanchana, 1986):

(1) How to organize study time

(2) How to use a time table

(3) How to get started and concentrate on study

(4) Steps in learning a chapter

(5) How to read more effectively and quickly

(6) How to prepare for an examination

(7) How to tackle an examination

*Systematic desensitization.* Students with high stress regarding fear of failure were given relaxation and systematic desensitization training. Hierarchy on examination fear was used for group systematic desensitization (Wolpe, 1958). The program lasted for 12 weeks.

*Assertiveness training.* The interpersonal difficulties group was trained in assertiveness training to reduce stress. Nine types of responses were used: assertive talk, feeling talk, greeting talk, disagreeing passively and actively, asking why, talking about oneself, agreeing with compliments, refraining from justifying opinions, and looking people in the eye (Lazarus, 1973).

*Program on effective communication.* A film on "fear of talk" was shown to a group of students who were having interpersonal difficulties with parents, teachers, and peers. Training was given in various aspects of communication for three weeks.

### Design of the Study

All experimental and control subjects completed the student academic stress scale before and after the training program. The mean scores were subjected to *t*-test analyses. In a similar way, examination marks (indicators of academic performance) were also collected for statistical analysis.

**Table 17.2** Stress Reduction and Exam Improvement Following Training as a Function of Experimental Group

| Experimental Group (Stress Area) | Pre-Post Stress Reduction (S.E.) | t | Pre-Post Exam Improvement (S.E.) | t |
|---|---|---|---|---|
| Personal inadequacy | 10.67 (1.47) | 7.16* | 5.45 (0.21) | 6.72* |
| Fear of failure | 8.60 (1.89) | 6.19* | 6.05 (1.02) | 5.93* |
| Interpersonal difficulties | 5.90 (1.01) | 5.84* | 5.15 (1.09) | 4.72* |

*$p \leq 0.01$; $df = 19$.

### Results

Results confirmed the curvilinear relationship between stress levels and academic performance. Performance was best at moderate levels of stress. The quadratic component ($F = 7.69$) is significant at the 0.01 level. As seen in Table 17.2, there was a significant reduction in stress and improvement in academic performance among all three experimental groups of students after they completed the personality development training programs. The control groups did not show significant reduction in stress areas or improvement in academic performance.

In summary, seven to eight years of schooling in the educational system has led to personal inadequacy, fear of failure, and interpersonal difficulties contributing to high stress among one-third of the children included in this study. Personality development programs consisting of behavioral techniques such as relaxation, assertiveness training, and systematic desensitization are effective in reducing the stress and improving the academic performance of students. Continuous training in such personality development programs for the welfare of the students should be included in the educational system.

## Experiment 2

The second experiment was conducted to examine personality change and academic improvement associated with personality development training.

### Method

*Subjects*

The experimental groups included 54 boys and 20 girls 12-15 years old belonging to a middle socioeconomic status school; 54 boys and 15 girls were also included in the control groups. Age, sex, school, education level, intelligence, memory, and creativity were controlled across groups.

**Table 17.3** Change in Personality Factors Following Training

| Sex | Personality Factors | Mean Difference | S.E. | t |
|-----|--------------------|-----------------|------|------|
| Boys | dominance | 0.93 | 0.40 | 2.33* |
| | uncontrolled adequacy | 1.13 | 0.43 | 2.63* |
| | low ergic training | 1.15 | 0.48 | 2.40* |
| Girls | dominance | 1.30 | 0.58 | 2.24* |
| | low ergic training | 0.45 | 0.23 | 1.96* |

*$p \leq .05$.

### Measures

Cattell's Junior-Senior High School Personality Questionnaire was used to assess personality (see Cattell & Cattell, 1969). In addition, examination marks were used to reflect academic performance before and after training.

### Training

Relaxation, assertiveness, and study skills training were provided to the experimental group for a period of six months (see the section above on Experiment 1 for a description of the training programs).

### Results

As can be seen in Table 17.3, personality development training was effective in fostering personality change toward dominance (more assertive, aggressive, competitive, and stubborn), uncontrolled adequacy (more self-assured and calm), and low ergic tension (more relaxed and composed). In addition, both the boys and girls who received training showed significant improvement in academic performance (boys $\overline{X} = 2.83$, $t = 6.02$, $p \leq .01$; girls $\overline{X} = 4.55$, $t = 5.06$, $p \leq .01$), with girls showing greater improvement than boys ($t = 3.69$, $p \leq .01$).

## Overall Discussion

From 1980 to 1990, 10 years of continuous action research and personality development school outreach programs by myself and my research students for the benefit of schoolchildren, teachers, and parents have provided insight into various issues relevant to primary prevention. School education in India, particularly its examination system, produces stress in one-third of students, leading to personal inadequacies (Chitra, 1985; Kanchana, 1986). Academic stress also may produce interpersonal difficulties among schoolchildren, with the result that these children are not able to maintain good relations with teachers, parents, and classmates and also suffer from feelings of inferiority, insecurity, and fear of failure (Sitharthan, 1980). Academic stress leads to failure in examinations not only among children with average intelligence but also among children of high intellectual capacity (Nithyakala, 1987). Urban schoolchildren at every socioeconomic level suffer from examination fear (Kanchana, 1986). Research is needed to study the differences between rural and urban children in academic stress. This prevailing condition in India should be ameliorated by including personality development programs in the educational system. But the topic should not become another curricular subject and add stress to students. The training method should be creative, interesting, and based on experiential learning. Moreover, training of parents and teachers significantly promotes personality development of their wards (Murugadhoss, 1989).

Study skills training (Kanchana, 1986) seems to be an effective method for helping children perform better in their academic pursuits. Behavior modification techniques such as relaxation procedures (Jacobson's deep muscle relaxation, autogenic training), assertiveness training, communication and human relations skills training, desensitization procedures, and cognitive restructuring have proved effective in personality development and have led to better academic performance. Average students, low achievers, and delinquent children have benefited equally. Yoga and transcendental meditation can also be utilized for personality development.

Interesting and innovative techniques such as "know yourself better—who am I?"; "ship building and aspiration games"; "Micro-lab as icebreaking"; "know the reality skits"; and "pictorial feedback" are found to be highly effective in providing children with experiential learning (Akhouri, Mishra, & Sengupta, 1989). Our studies have also shown that female students have benefited more than males and also fare better in examinations as a result. Similarly, Indian women are better in adopting family planning methods, using hybrid seed varieties in agriculture, and so on, and much less likely to experience the problems of drug addiction and smoking than are Indian men. It may be that Indian culture provides more effective prevention and promotion in these areas for females.

## Prevention Strategies for India

One-third of the schoolchildren in India need personality development programs to manage academic stress. Parents and teachers should be trained to help provide personality development programs to schoolchildren. Parents may also be trained in child-rearing practices to foster personality development in their wards (Nizamuddin, 1984).

Mass movement is needed to change the prevailing stress-producing conditions of Indian schools. Popular articles in regional local languages, newspapers, weekly magazines, and television and radio programs on prevention may reach the masses. Formation of family counseling action groups such as the one started by *Mangaiyar Malar* (Ramesh, 1990), a Tamil monthly, may serve effectively toward primary prevention.

The National Service Scheme, National Cadet Corps, and Scouts are cocurricular schemes in India for developing the youth toward citizenship. Though special camps are being conducted under these schemes, they do not include well-designed personality development training programs. Such programs could usefully be incorporated in the activities of ongoing youth organizations. Such broad-scale integration of efforts to reduce stress and promote personality development are essential to supporting the development of India's youth.

## References

Akhouri, M. M., Mishra, S. P., & Sengupta, R. (1989). *Trainer's manual on developing entrepreneurial motivation.* New Delhi: New Statesman.

Cattell, R. B., & Cattell, M. D. (1969). *Handbook for the Junior-Senior High School Personality Questionnaire* (Publication No. 1602-04). Champaign, IL: Institute for Personality and Ability Testing.

Chitra, V. (1985). *Behavior therapy in reducing test anxiety of school children.* Unpublished master's thesis, University of Madras, India.

Government of India. (1986). *National policy on education.* New Delhi: Department of Education.

Jacobson, E. (1938). *Progressive relaxation.* Chicago: University of Chicago Press.

Jesness, C. F. (1972). *Manual of Jesness Inventory.* Palo Alto, CA: Consulting Psychologists Press.

Kanchana, M. (1986). *Effect of behavior modification techniques in reducing test anxiety and improving study skills on academic achievement of high school girls.* Unpublished master's thesis, University of Madras, India.

Kannappan, R. (1989). *Efficacy of behavior therapy techniques in improving the personality characteristics of delinquent boys.* Unpublished doctoral dissertation, University of Madras, India.

Lazarus, A. A. (1973). On assertive behavior: A brief note. *Behavior Therapy, 4,* 667-669.

Murugadhoss, R. (1989). *Behavioral training package for parents to enrich the family environment and for students to modify their personality in improving academic performance.* Unpublished doctoral dissertation, University of Madras, India.

Nithyakala, K. (1987). *The effect of psychological training on personality, study skills, and academic achievement of underachieving students with an intellectual capacity of 90th and 95th percentile.* Unpublished master's thesis, University of Madras, India.

Nizamuddin, S. (1984). *Effect of child-rearing practices on the relationship of children's intelligence, creativity and personality.* Unpublished doctoral dissertation, University of Madras, India.

Paramesh, C. R. (1972). *Creativity and personality.* Madras, India: Janatha.

Pradeep, T. (1983). *Academic performance in relation to achievement motivation, creativity and intelligence.* Unpublished master's thesis, University of Madras, India.

Ramesh, M. (1990, April). *Family counseling action group, Mangaiyar Malar.* Madras, India: Bharathan.

Rebecca, I. R. (1985). *The relationship of creativity, need for academic achievement and self-contempt to academic performance among high school students.* Unpublished master's thesis, University of Madras, India.

Sarason, S. B., Davidson, K. S., Lighthall, F. F., & Waite, R. R. (1958). A test anxiety scale for children. *Child Development, 29,* 105-113.

Sitharthan, T. C. (1980). *A study of the effects of relaxation and placebo therapy on school children.* Unpublished master's thesis, University of Madras, India.

Wolpe, J. (1958). *Reciprocal inhibition therapy.* Stanford, CA: Stanford University Press.

# 18

# Quality of Life in Families With Mentally Retarded Children: Promoting Independence and Acceptance

**Irena Obuchowska**
**Michael Obuchowski**

Mildly retarded children constitute about 80% of the mentally retarded population. They and their families are a group that may especially benefit from primary prevention efforts. Most of the mildly retarded have no neurological symptoms, and almost 75% of them are found to be linked to various low socioeconomic environmental factors. In about 25% of families with mildly retarded children, home life is quite positive and the children's basic physical needs are adequately met (Robinson & Robinson, 1976). However, the parents' educational level is often low and they usually do not know how to satisfy their children's psychological needs. Such families are promising targets for psychological intervention.

This study investigates two aspects of quality of life in families with mentally retarded children. *Quality of life* is difficult to operationalize. In order to define it, we assumed the goals that are most important to all people are those that, in the history of humankind, have motivated people to strive for, and even to sacrifice their lives for: freedom and love. In each of these two areas of human activity, a factor directly relevant to family life was chosen: (a) independence given children by parents, and (b) acceptance of children by their mothers.

The study reported here investigated the effectiveness of an external family member (EFM) intervention program in improving the quality of life in families with mildly mentally retarded children. The purpose of the intervention program

AUTHORS' NOTE: This study was conducted with help from several graduate students in the Child Psychopathology and Special Education Program at Adam Mickiewicz University, Poznan, Poland. Requests for reprints should be sent to Michael Obuchowski, New York State Psychiatric Institute, Box 58, 722 West 168th Street, New York, NY 10032.

was primary prevention directed toward the younger siblings living in the same household with mildly mentally retarded children. The intervention was not directed toward the children, but toward the children's psychological situation in the family. Family was understood as a system (Baumeister, 1988; Radochonski, 1984). The hypothesis of the investigation was that psychological intervention promoting independence and acceptance within the family would positively influence children's psychological development, particularly that of the younger siblings.

## Method

### Subjects

A total of 78 Polish families, each with a mildly retarded child, participated voluntarily in the study. Each family had to meet the following inclusion criteria: The families had to be intact; the mildly mentally retarded children could have no neurological symptoms; and the retarded children were attending Special School. All the selected families had at least one other younger preschool-age child. All families were living in a Polish city of about 600,000 inhabitants. The economic and educational statuses of the families were low.

Families were randomly assigned to an experimental group (MR-EXP) or a control group (MR-CTRL). There were 39 families in each group, and all families cooperated fully throughout the study. There were 22 boys and 17 girls in each group (mean age was 12.5 in the experimental group and 12.1 in the control group).

### Procedure

The MR-EXP group was subject to the external family member intervention; the MR-CTRL group did not receive any intervention procedure. The study was divided into three phases, which are described below.

*Phase 1.* Trained graduate students assessed two areas of interest. First, the independence of the mildly retarded children from their parents was evaluated by interviewing the children. Independence was understood as the right to make decisions. To determine to what extent the children made their own decisions, the interview focused on the following areas of independence in family life:

(1) Self-service
(2) Going out and coming back home
(3) Appearance
(4) Behavior
(5) Home duties
(6) School homework

(7) Interests
(8) Control of belongings (toys and so on)
(9) Contacts with playmates
(10) Leisure-time activities

The second area of interest was the acceptance of the mentally retarded children by their mothers. The graduate students evaluated maternal acceptance by interviewing the mothers of both experimental and control groups. The interview included questions on biographical memory of pleasant (PE) and unpleasant experiences (UE) in family life related to the retarded child.

*Phase 2.* The EFM intervention program was initiated for the experimental group. A specially trained graduate student entered the family for four hours each week over a 10-month period and played the role of an "additional" family member. The graduate student interveners were trained in familial interpersonal cooperation and nondirective discussion skills. Discussion topics were the issues of independence of the mildly retarded children, emotional acceptance of these children by their mothers, and the meaning of independence and acceptance for the psychological development of individuals.

*Phase 3.* Both the independence of the retarded children and mothers' acceptance of these children were assessed again for both groups. Additionally, information about the type of school, normal or special, the younger siblings began to attend was collected. The investigation was conducted from 1987 through 1989.

## Results

### Independence of Mildly Retarded Children From Their Parents

*Scoring.* The independence ratings in each area were scored from the interview on a three-point scale: high independence (two points), moderate independence (one point), and low independence (zero points). Scores for all 10 areas of independence were totaled to obtain the Index of Independence for each child. The independence data were analyzed using a repeated measures ANOVA (group × time). There was a significant group × time interaction, $F(1, 76) = 137.23, p < .001$ (see Figure 18.1).

Post hoc analyses (Fisher's LSD) did not show any significant differences in independence scores between the two groups at the beginning. The change in independence scores across time for the control group was also nonsignificant.

There was a significant change in independence scores for the experimental group after the EFM intervention procedure, $t = 20.2, p < .001$. The difference between the two groups at Phase 3 was also significant, $t = 16.2, p < .001$ (see Table 18.1).

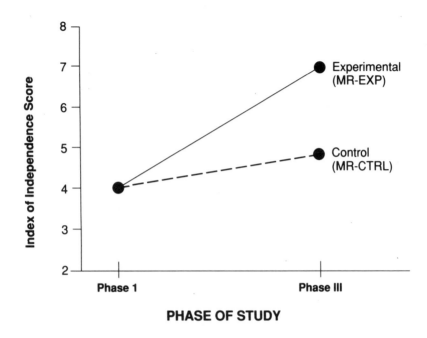

**Figure 18.1.** Change of Independence Scores Before and After EFM Intervention (MR-EXP) and After 10 Months (MR-CTRL)

### Acceptance of Mentally Retarded Children by Their Mothers

The index of acceptance was calculated as the proportion of pleasant to unpleasant experiences in family life as reported by mothers related to the mentally retarded child. The related experiences were categorized into PE and UE by two independent judges. The acceptance data were analyzed using a repeated measures ANOVA (group × time). There was a significant group × time interaction, $F(1, 76) = 110, p < .001$ (see Figure 18.2).

Post hoc analyses revealed a significant increase in the index of acceptance scores for the experimental group at Phase 3, $t = 17.3, p < .001$. There was no significant change in the index of acceptance score for the control group. The difference between groups at Phase 3 was also significant, $t = 15.4, p < .001$ (see Table 18.2).

### Primary Prevention Effect

In Poland, children customarily enter school at age 7. Prior to entering school, children attend the "zero class," which serves as a transition between kindergarten

**Table 18.1** Change of Index of Independence Scores at Phases 1 and 3

| Phase of Study | Study Group | |
|---|---|---|
| | *MR-EXP* | *MR-CTRL* |
| Phase 1 | 4.10 | 4.05 |
| Phase 3 | 6.90 | 4.80 |

and a more structured classroom. The decision concerning the type of education (normal or special) the child will subsequently receive is made during this year by a team of experts. All mentally retarded subjects belonging to the MR-EXP group and to the control group attended Special School. Their younger siblings were 5 or 6 years old at the beginning of Phase 1 (1987). There is a significant difference between the groups in the proportion of younger siblings who started normal school (at Phase 3: see Figure 18.3).

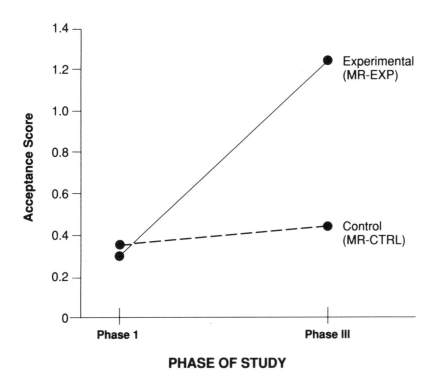

**Figure 18.2.** Change of Acceptance Scores Before and After Intervention (MR-EXP) and After 10 Months (MR-CTRL)

**Table 18.2** Change of Index of Acceptance Scores at Phases 1 and 3

| Phase of Study | Study Group | |
| --- | --- | --- |
| | MR-EXP | MR-CTRL |
| Phase 1 | 0.28 | 0.35 |
| Phase 3 | 1.22 | 0.43 |

## Discussion

The results suggest that the EFM intervention program is a promising primary prevention and family intervention technique. It was found that, as a result of EFM, mentally retarded children scored significantly higher on measures of self-perceived independence and maternal acceptance. In addition, a higher proportion of younger siblings began normal school in the experimental families than in the control families. From these results it can be inferred that psychological stimulation inside the family initiates a process of positive modification in family life that may influence school maturity and competence. The experiment will be repeated on a larger scale.

The psychological situation of the child as a factor in the prevention of mild mental retardation is largely underestimated. Primary prevention studies usually focus on environmental factors, such as poverty. In comparison with environmental factors, the psychological situation of the child within the family seems to resist quantification. Our study attempts to investigate the efficacy of psychological interventions by operationalizing and measuring two aspects of the psychological situation of families with mildly mentally retarded children. It appears that variables such as independence and acceptance can be measured and that significant changes may occur in these variables as a result of psychological intervention.

Methodological problems that arose in regard to the definition of the psychological variables of independence and acceptance included cultural and class-specific biases. These were resolved in the following manner. Ratings of "independence" were based on children's self-reports rather than parents' reports in order to avoid cultural bias. The role of independence of children in family education in Poland is quite different from in most Western European countries. The tradition is to restrict children's independence, but, in the opinion of the parents, children *are* independent. In another study, physically disabled children rated their independence as more restricted than that of normal children, and mentally retarded children rated their independence as more restricted than that of either physically disabled or normal children (Obuchowska, 1990). Caution should be exercised in interpreting children's self-ratings, especially concerning

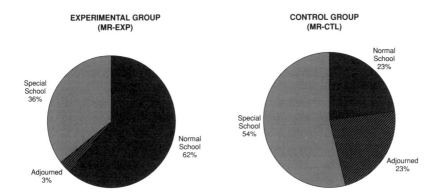

**Figure 18.3.** Kind of School Younger Siblings of MR-EXP (After EFM) and MR-CTRL Began to Attend: Normal or Special

NOTE: The third category was adjourned. It is important to mention that *adjourned* means that a definite decision was not made about the type of school, and the child was kept for one more year in the zero grade, for later re-evaluation. At this time we do not have information about the final decisions for the adjourned children.

the linearity of this relationship. The findings do strongly support the view that independence plays a crucial role in children's development.

In designing a measure of mothers' acceptance of the children, we took into consideration the possible bias introduced by the families' low SES and the mothers' low educational level. In comparison with questionnaires, an interview directed toward remembered experiences seemed to provide a more valid measure.

Our conclusion that, in these families, EFM was an efficacious intervention should be qualified in two respects. Although more siblings of MR-EXP children entered normal schools, the meaningfulness of this measure as an indicator of positive outcome or prevention of retardation is contingent on the ability of these siblings to stay in the normal school system on a long-term basis. Follow-up will be necessary to determine long-term outcome. However, we are optimistic that these children will profit from starting their education in a situation that is highly motivating to their psychological development.

In addition, although the intervention in this study was defined by a particular EFM procedure, it is possible that its efficacy was based on the general increase in attention, interest, and acceptance offered by the visiting graduate students. Future research might investigate the efficacy of methods employing those more general psychological interventions that do not require special training. If more general interventions have positive outcomes, then the range of practical interventions in psychological family systems and the possibilities for primary prevention will be greatly improved.

252    Obuchowska, Obuchowski

## References

Baumeister, A. A. (1988). Prevention and research: Behavior aspects—maximizing the quality of life for individuals with mental retardation and other developmental disabilities. In President's Committee on Mental Retardation, *Twentieth anniversary symposium.* Washington, DC: Government Printing Office.

Obuchowska, I. (1990). Rodzinne konflikty mlodziezy niepelnosprawnej zwiazane z realizacja potrzeby autonomii [Family conflicts of mentally retarded children related to the need for autonomy]. In M. Tyszkowa (Ed.), *Rodzina a rozwoj jednostki.* Poznan, Poland: Adam Mickiewicz University Press.

Radochonski, M. (1984). *Structural family therapy.* Rzeszow, Poland: Teachers University Press.

Robinson, N. M., & Robinson, H. B. (1976). *The mentally retarded child.* New York: McGraw-Hill.

# 19

# Fostering Parental Competence in Poland

Helena Sek
Agnieszka Bleja
Aleksandra Sommerfeld

Having analyzed the importance of various environments in affecting children's lives and development, we have concluded that we should focus on the level of the family and its conditions. Influences last longest in the natural family context and are probably of greatest strength. We believe that the present level of knowledge of parents' child-rearing and educational competence is insufficient.

Experiences during the most recent history of our country have shown that strong interference in different situations (nursery schools, kindergartens, schools, organizations, and so on) in the process of children's development and education sometimes poses a great threat. This is particularly true when educational systems mirror features of macrosystems (state, social, and political organizations) that play a negative part in human development. We are therefore now facing an important problem: how to reinforce natural parental competence.

## Parental Competence:
## A Developmental-Interactive Approach

We understand *parental competence* to be the skills adults have to meet effectively the requirements of parental roles and their own personal development in the process of the family's growth. We believe that only those parents who personally develop apart from their parental roles are able to further their educational competence in interaction with their growing children.

The perspective of our theoretical, empirical, and practical thinking is thus strictly interactive and developmental. We have also assumed that parent-child interaction takes a dual direction, and the developing child constantly places before his or her parents new tasks that enhance parental development and provide incomparable positive experiences. All of this, of course, takes place in the complex context of family living, in quite varied ecological, economic, political, cultural, and social conditions.

Competent parents are able to create a healthy life circle for their children and for their own development. Parents should possess adequate effectance and prosocial motivation, as well as the knowledge and experience to support effectively their children's development in the various periods of their lives—from conception through adolescence.

In our particular Polish social and economic conditions, and under the influence of a different cultural tradition (concerning the role of the family), the general scientific rule of psychology will mirror also that specific reality.

We have chosen the following phases in the development of parents, children, and the whole family to be the subject of our inquiry: (a) the couple in the unstable period following the birth of the first child, (b) creative activity in parent-preschooler interaction, (c) school start, and (d) parent-adolescent interactions. Preventive work is of particular importance at these periods, and empirical data must test these critical situations. We shall now present the most important findings concerning those studies.

## Study 1

Most often young adults in Poland conceive and give birth to their first child between the ages of 20 and 35 years. At this period of their lives, the young parents must undertake to fulfill many tasks pertaining to their own individual development. These are connected to career, social position, meeting the material requirements of their families, as well as prolonging the intimacy of their marital/partnership bonds and, finally, undertaking the role of parents and guardians of small children. The couple's bond seems to us to be of particular importance to the creation of an appropriate emotional climate for the newborn. From the psychological point of view, an appropriate emotional climate within the family, apart from the mother's protective competence, creates the healthiest life conditions. It is well known, nevertheless, that pregnancy and the birth of the first child, and the mother's concentration on that child, do not always enhance the growth of the parents' own emotional bond. The birth of the first child is a critical event in the parents' and the child's lives, and it carries both a great potential for development for all concerned as well as great risk.

The marital bond was tested in the realms of mutual contact, understanding, and cooperation using a sample of 30 married couples between the ages of 20 and 35, each with a child at least 3 months old. Levels of education differed. The following factors were seen as important for the marital bond:

- Motives for having a child
- Childbirth and parenthood preparation

- Attitudes toward the conceived child
- The process of delivery
- Interpretation of delivery
- The lying-in period
- The material condition

It was found that age, sex, and education did not play an important part in the evaluation of the couple's bond. Correlation and cluster analyses pointed to a different structure of the links between the variables of mothers and fathers. On the whole, the level of the evaluation of the marital bond was in both groups strictly connected to the level of "psychological readiness for parenthood"—that is, it depended on the conscious, responsible decision of both parents to conceive a child, their active preparation in birth and parenthood, a full acceptance of the child conceived, their life-style during pregnancy, and the interpretation of the delivery as a task for both. The above factors are strictly interconnected and influence the developmental passage through the crisis of the first child's birth.

In the case of men, however, the factors mentioned are much more strongly interconnected (high and very high correlations, .60-.70). Further, young fathers generally find the period directly succeeding the delivery much more difficult to cope with (the period depends on the temperament and condition of the baby as well as the parents' own condition and competence), particularly when they did not take part in birth preparations.

The evaluation of the couple's bond in the case of women is greatly dependent on the mother's attitude toward the conceived child, preparation for the birth and parenthood, and the interpretation of the delivery. The delivery and postdelivery period as physiological processes are not of such great importance.

Both fathers and mothers reached the conclusion that their material situation did not have any bearing on their bond in the new conditions. It is the only variable that is not linked to the other independent variables.

This and further studies provide clear postulates for preventive work with young adults in active birth centers, marriage and family counseling centers, and phone-in counseling. It should be stressed at this point that regardless of the material situation, particular attention must be paid to the appearance and stimulation of the so-called readiness for parenthood condition in prospective fathers and prospective mothers.

## Study 2

Play is a central activity for 3- to 6-year-olds. Creative activity is also of particular importance in this period. There is abundant research on the creative activity of preschoolers in our center. The research has shown that those teachers who are particularly able in stimulating creative activity are those who themselves exhibit much creative invention, and not those who only put good programs into practice. We believe that the effects of the programs employed are measured not in terms of their technology but of those who implement them.

Observations of the preparation of children's guardians at a nursing home to animate creative play brings to light a number of difficulties they possessed in that area. We also lack knowledge of the abilities and competencies of parents in this area. But it is parents, nonetheless, who are mainly responsible for the animation of the creative activity of their children. We are concerned with activities that possess the feature of novelty, that are motivated from within, and that include personal involvement. Such activities thus provide a great deal of pleasure in themselves.

We can differentiate two models of creating such activities. First, the *task model*, in which the adult concentrates on the specific aim or goal to be attained, selects situations and stimulation techniques corresponding to the child's abilities, and follows the rules of behavior (e.g., an open style of interaction with the child). Activities of this type are proposed to both parents and children every day on a television program called *Home Preschool*. Second, there is the *interactive model*, in which the parent and the child experiment together, seeking and choosing the goals and means of the game or other activity. Proposals may come from either partner. The adult does not stick to any fixed program, but only follows the child and his or her wishes. Our research with parents of 5-year-olds is aimed at showing if and in what forms of parent-child interaction creative activity appears, what its character is, and how it is estimated by parents and children. What further interests us is to determine what mode of animating creative activities is most common among parents. We believe that such studies will bring us closer to understanding the conditions stimulating the natural competencies of parents—both educational and preventive.

## Study 3

Much of our research concerns the promotion/prevention influences of the school start situation. In Poland the problem is particularly important because of the state of the educational system and the constant reforms it has undergone. Regardless of region-specific features, it has been shown that the school start in the life of a child contains as many chances for development as risks of failure. The school start is thus a critical event in the lives of both the child and the parents; it bring great changes in the life-style of the child and of the family. It magnifies expectations and pressures, limits the child's own preferences, introduces the principle of duty and concentration, and puts before children the necessity of social adjustment.

Many promotive programs for preschoolers have been arranged that are aimed at stimulating the child's competence for passing over the barrier of the school start. The parents' role in arranging such programs was slight. Our research has shown that parents' consciousness of such problems can actually hinder a program's preparation.

Our studies were concerned with the knowledge and opinions of parents concerning the risk factors of the school start. The scale of risk factors we developed consisted of 33 items concerning the child's traits, the family environment, and the school context. These factors were generated by competent judges among school psychologists. A total of 125 parents were tested, and, by way of comparison, 62 teachers (of first through third grade) and 55 psychologists working with children experiencing school difficulties. All those who were tested estimated the probability of difficulties at school for each of the 33 risk factors.

It was clear that both parents and teachers showed a tendency to underestimate many factors of school difficulties; this tendency was much stronger on the part of parents. Parents estimated the risk arising from the child's traits as only slightly above insignificant. Most often, parents underestimated the risk embedded in traits of children such as poor physical abilities, perceptive and cognitive problems, the tendency to squabble and fight, and the difficulties in making contact with adults. As the greatest risks, parents listed features of the educational system and the family climate, whereas teachers named family factors, school factors, and those connected to the children themselves. Psychologists found high-risk factors in all of these spheres.

The results show the difficult task facing those advisers who would like to improve children's situation at school through furthering parental competence. The question arises whether we should magnify the awareness of risk in parents. What result would this bring? Further, we are dealing with falsification of the parents' awareness (perhaps a defensive one) and that of teachers as well, only the falsification is of opposite tendencies. Thus at the moment we are facing a serious dilemma—where to start and, in particular, how to deal with parents. We think that one should first and foremost provide more adequate communication between parents and teachers. This seems particularly important in view of the new "social schools" (not-for-profit independent schools organized by parents) and the new Parents' Committees functioning in state schools.

## Study 4

The results of our studies on parental communication and supportive competence (in the case of children undergoing adolescent crises) proved to be very important from the perspective of cooperation with parents. In Poland, adolescents named parents alongside their peers as important sources of support. A random sample of 30 families with 16-17-year-olds attending secondary school were tested (analogical methods were used in the case of the father, the mother, and the teenager undergoing an adolescent crisis). A special Adolescence Discomfort Questionnaire was designed for this purpose.

Communicative competence was analyzed both in families where the parental mid-life crisis occurred simultaneously with the adolescent one and in other families where the former did not appear. The frequency of communication, the level of its openness, the symmetry/partnership, and scale of understanding with regard to the needs of identity, autonomy, dreams, and heritage were all estimated.

Somewhat better results were obtained by parents who were not undergoing their own crises; their results with regard to the symmetry of communication and agreement about the need of autonomy, identity, and heritage were all above average. Parents with mid-life crises obtained poorer results, and were at the same time more like each other. Mothers in both groups were more competent in communication. Fathers not undergoing a crisis talked with their children very rarely. Those experiencing their own crises talked much more frequently, and were more open and partnerlike.

These results show that the problems of communicative competence in the case of parents with a mid-life crisis is modified by their own developmental problems. This is seen particularly in fathers.

Parental competence with relation to adolescents does not only imply an effective agreement as to the most important developmental needs of teenagers and the acceptance of their independence and readiness to be partners, but also the ability to provide timely support.

Apart from the developmental crises questionnaires, a scale of social support was used, to be filled in by all three parties—the mother, the father, and the adolescent. The adolescents and their parents reported similar average estimates of the effectiveness of support, but the scale of effectiveness varied from 90% to 50%. Such variability is seen also with regard to the various forms of support.

An analysis of variance with repeated measures also found that effectiveness and agreement versus disagreement with regard to it depends on the particular form of support. Forms of support include expression of respect for the child's virtues and abilities, patient and attentive listening to the child's confidences, expression of feeling, information offered by parents about how they themselves coped, other information helping adolescents to cope with their problems, and explanations about what to expect in the future.

We found that parents overrated their competence in giving emotional and cognitive support. There was much more agreement between parents and teenagers in their opinions about material and instrumental support.

The main value of the above-described studies is that they make preventive thinking concerning the period of adolescence much more sensitive to variety and draw the work with parents closer to reality, instead of just echoing the stereotypes about the educational difficulties of adolescence.

One thing is certain: The cooperation of professionals and parents in that period should first and foremost be directed at perfecting communicative competence and negotiating conflict situations offering simultaneous competent support.

## Application and Conclusions

Our studies have proved how different parental competence should be depending on the developmental phases of the adult, the child, and the family. This in turn requires both parents and professionals who wish to foster those competencies to exhibit extremely elastic thinking and behavior.

There arises the question of what is common in all those childhood periods—what central abilities bind the whole together? All our studies have shown that what is most important is the ability to communicate with children (parental communicative competence), together with the parental trait of accurate social perception.

The reinforcement of competence on the whole should have the character of training. The spreading of training in educational skills in Poland seems to be an answer to that demand. This training is mainly conducted by professional tutors. Parents, overburdened by hardships of everyday life, and by force of habit used to believing that a professional guardian in school will take their place, seldom manifest the wish to develop their parental competence. On the other hand, attempts at interference with the natural homeostatic family environment (undertaken by local social workers and so on) are met with ill will.

Hence the most difficult problem arises: how to encourage and organize health and developmental counseling and support programs for parents. We believe it would be worthwhile to make use of the experiences of the more and more numerous active birth centers (the so-called schools of birth) organized by the state health care system and the church for pregnant women and their husbands. Our studies show that the programs of these schools can become popular among fathers too. They should introduce, apart from relaxation techniques and information on the care of babies, a purely psychological preparation for parenthood; that is, they should make use of all those factors that are so strongly connected to the crises of the first baby's birth.

Various self-help (support) groups and organizations are also very effective. Currently, however, they mainly group parents at risk and "problem" children, those who are somatically ill or disabled, and those threatened by some form of social pathology.

At the time when the child becomes a member of educational institutions, parents should perhaps receive attractive opportunities (as far as timing and their psychological comfort is concerned) in place of the dull talks and insipid meetings of parental committees. The growing social schools movement is a ray of hope in this respect.

Radio and television programs could also include discussions of the above-mentioned problems, as a way of propagating developmental and healthy life-styles. The propagation of knowledge and abilities via mass media is still a complicated matter in Poland, however, because of the threat of indoctrination and resultant loss of credibility.

Hence our main problem is how to implement our results into social practice, so that they will truly be beneficial to our children *and* improve the quality of our life. The results of our studies point to many complex and difficult factors to be overcome, including the falsified risk awareness we found on the part of parents and teachers.

As our studies bring out not only general social and developmental rules but also the specific features conditioned by socioeconomic and cultural factors, they invite cross-cultural research; such research should seek both universal data and the specific nature of geographic, economic, and cultural realities.

# PART V

# Prevention and Reduction
of Aggression and
Conduct Disorders

In many parts of the world, children increasingly appear to be exposed to physical aggression and a variety of acts of antisocial behavior. Millions of children around the world are victims of such actions daily. Even more children observe abundant models of such behaviors in their homes, communities, and through the media. In a great many cultures, youth is also a period for experimentation with aggressive and antisocial behavior—a time when children test various patterns of social interaction, observing and experiencing their consequences, and developing personal styles of expressing and communicating thoughts and feelings. Aggression and conduct disorders *among* children are recognized as an increasing problem in a number of countries around the world. The chapters in this section consider approaches to preventing or reducing aggression and conduct disorders among children.

In Chapter 20, Max W. Abbott, director of the Mental Health Foundation of New Zealand and president elect of the World Federation for Mental Health, describes a long-term nationwide campaign to reduce television violence in New Zealand. The extremely high incidence of violence on television is clearly documented, and many data suggest that prolonged exposure to televised violence fosters aggressive behavior in child viewers. The Mental Health Foundation of New Zealand, a national, nongovernment organization, has pursued a systematic course for dealing directly and assertively with this problem.

After summarizing the research that links television violence and child behavior, Abbott describes the various phases of the foundation's campaign to reduce television violence. As he illustrates so clearly, effective community campaigns require much more than a sound scientific base; dealing with the complex sociopolitical processes of the system is also essential.

In Chapter 21, Dan Olweus examines victimization among schoolchildren and a large-scale preventive intervention program for dealing with this problem in Scandinavia. Currently professor of personality psychology at the University of Bergen, Norway, Olweus previously taught at the universities of Stockholm and Umea and served as vice president of the Swedish Psychological Association.

His long and award-winning record of scholarship on aggression led to his current leadership in a nationwide program, coordinated with Norway's Ministry of Education, to reduce and prevent bullying and victimization.

In his chapter, Olweus illuminates the nature and scope of the bullying/victimization problem among Scandinavian schoolchildren. He then outlines the goals and components of his preventive intervention program, summarizing his careful evaluation of its effectiveness and addressing the program's subgoals. In so doing, Olweus provides us with a model that can be generalized to a host of other problems—a model of how to move from the definition and analysis of a problem to a framework for a preventive intervention.

In the final chapter of this section, Doreen Spilton Koretz and Joyce Barham Lazar summarize the state of the art in the prevention of child conduct disorders in the United States. As they explain, while many children show antisocial behavior at certain times in their lives, those who do so intensely and persistently may lead quite dysfunctional lives and be at significant risk for adult antisocial behavior as well. Defining the significance of the problem, and the risk and protective factors most pertinent to conduct disorders, Koretz and Lazar describe the major child- and family-focused preventive interventions that have been implemented in the United States. Moreover, they apprise us of current initiatives of the U.S. National Institute of Mental Health (NIMH) that have highlighted the prevention of conduct disorders as a national priority.

Koretz and Lazar are particularly well qualified to present us with this state-of-the-art snapshot, for they have been instrumental in fostering NIMH's support of preventive intervention research on conduct disorders. Koretz is currently Assistant Chief of the Prevention Research Branch, Division of Clinical Research, of NIMH, where she has been responsible for developing the Prevention Research Branch portfolio on the prevention of conduct disorders. Lazar has a long history of service and leadership at the institute also, as the chief of the Epidemiology Training Section, of the Social Sciences Research Section, of the Research Planning and Evaluation Branch, and, most recently, through the fall of 1990, as the chief of the Prevention Research Branch.

# 20

# Television Violence:
# A Proactive Prevention Campaign

**Max W. Abbott**

This chapter describes a proactive primary prevention program conducted over an eight-year period by the Mental Health Foundation of New Zealand. The main objective of this program has been and remains to reduce the amount of violence screened on New Zealand television.

The Mental Health Foundation is a national, nongovernment organization, with some similarities to the national mental health associations of the United States and Canada. In contrast to these bodies, the Mental Health Foundation is much younger, dating from 1977. Perhaps because of its recent origin, many of the organization's activities in the areas of advocacy, public and professional education, research, program development, and funding have been concerned with mental health promotion and the prevention of mental health problems (Abbott, 1986).

Ironically perhaps, given the chapter topic, the Foundation's origins are closely linked to television. Without a nationwide 24-hour mental health telethon that raised more than $2 million for the Foundation during its first year, it would have gotten off to a very slow start. I should add that senior television executives take some pleasure in reminding us of this at times when our critical gaze is focused on their programming habits. But more of this later.

From its outset in 1977, the Foundation was concerned about violence and its consequences for individuals and the wider community. Although low by international standards, there had been an upturn in the official rate of violent crime. At the same time, there was also a growing awareness that most violent crime goes unreported, especially that taking place in domestic settings. The plight of victims was starting to be recognized. Apart from short-term emotional and physical trauma, research was showing that violence typically trails in its wake long-term mental health problems, distorted personal relationships, and a diminished quality of life for victims. Thus what was traditionally either largely ignored or addressed as a matter of law and order was increasingly perceived as both a major public health and mental health issue (Abbott, 1983; Haines & Abbott, 1983).

**Table 20.1** The Prevention of Violence: Causal Relations

| | |
|---|---|
| Factors that develop attitudes favoring the use of violence | Childhood experience of family violence; traditional male sex roles; public attitudes toward violence; lack of empathy toward others; poor anger management strategies; inability to tolerate frustration; rewards for aggression |
| Factors leading to frustrations that could be expressed violently | Low self-esteem; educational failure; poor communication skills; family discord; poor conditions in institutions; racism; unemployment; poor housing; powerlessness; poverty |
| Factors reducing control of violence or facilitating its expression | Biological factors; alcohol and some drugs; environmental toxins; lack of neighborhood intervention; inadequate policing; availability of weapons; knowledge of violent tactics; interpersonal factors leading to conflict escalation |

During its first few years the Foundation was heavily involved in helping to set up support groups for victims of violence, such as Women's Refuge and Rape Crisis Centers, and organizations dealing with child abuse. At the time of my appointment as director in 1981, the Foundation's governing board was concerned with identifying major factors that lay behind violence between individuals with a view to moving further upstream with some of its interventions. From the scientific literature it was clear that the situation is multicausal. Some of the more significant factors are outlined in Table 20.1. This is a summary of a model developed by Hilary Haines, until recently the Foundation's deputy director, and an important figure in our television violence campaign. The model was subsequently adopted by a special ministerial committee to provide the framework for a major report on violence in New Zealand (Committee of Inquiry Into Violence, 1987).

The Foundation has programs under way that target a number of the factors outlined in the model. Furthermore, we are completing a report that critically examines the degree to which each of the more than a hundred recommendations of the Committee of Inquiry Report have been implemented by government and other organizations. From this it should be evident that the Foundation does not believe, and has never suggested, that entertainment violence in general or television violence in particular is the only or principal cause of violence in real-life situations. It would be wrong, naive, and counterproductive to think this.

Television violence was selected as an area for attention for a variety of reasons. We knew from surveys that by the time they leave school most New Zealand children will have spent more time watching television than they will have sat in classrooms. The generation reaching maturity in the early 1980s was the first to have lived with the small screen since infancy. A 1975 survey found an average rate of seven episodes of violence screened per hour (Ginpel, 1976).

This was very high by international standards. Indeed, it appeared that New Zealand's two public channels were a close second to U.S. private networks at the time. In other words, New Zealand children and New Zealanders generally were being exposed to very high levels of television violence, among the highest in the world. We were also aware that a large body of research addressed the link between television violence and real-life aggression. Although initially skeptical that this literature would be definitive, after reviewing it carefully we were satisfied that sufficient evidence had been established to support a policy decision.

## Television Violence and Behavior in Real Life

More than 3,000 published research reports have examined ways in which watching television violence influences behavior and attitudes. A major concern has been to determine whether, and under what circumstances, viewing violent programs leads to violent and criminal behavior in other settings. Most of this research has been conducted during the last 15 years, although it has a very long history, dating back to the introduction of television. This body of research has been reviewed a number of times by academics and practitioners. It has also been assessed together with other information by a variety of official committees and inquiries in a number of countries. Reviews are provided by Eysenck and Nias (1980), Friedrich-Cofer and Huston (1986), Huesmann (1986), Huesmann and Eron (1986), the National Institute of Mental Health (1982), and Rule and Ferguson (1986), among others.

Research in this area is of four major types: case histories, laboratory studies, surveys, and field experiments. In the early days there was debate about the interpretation of the research findings, much as there was with the early studies of lung cancer in relation to smoking. Today, apart from a few tobacco company executives, some scientists employed by the tobacco industry, and a number of heavy smokers, the claim of a causal link is no longer questioned. Research has gone on to look at other health consequences and is examining the effects of lower exposure levels, as in passive smoking, for example.

The situation with television violence is similar, with the various commissions of inquiry and research reviewers agreeing that there is a definite link. Typical of conclusions reached is that taken from the 1982 National Institute of Mental Health report. This report reviewed literature subsequent to an earlier 1972 report by the U.S. Surgeon General's Scientific Advisory Committee on Television and Social Behavior:

> After ten more years of research, the consensus among most of the research community is that violence on television does lead to aggressive behavior by children and teenagers who watch the programs. This conclusion is based on

laboratory experiments and field studies. Not all children become aggressive, of course, but the correlations between violence and aggression are positive. In magnitude, television violence is as strongly correlated with aggressive behavior as any other behavioral variable that has been measured. The research question has moved from asking whether or not there is an effect to seeking explanations for the effect. (National Institute of Mental Health, 1982, p. 6)

Laboratory and field studies have converged in pinpointing the most harmful kinds of depiction (Belson, 1978; Comstock, 1976). In summary, these portrayals are as follows:

(1) There is reward, or at least lack of punishment, for the perpetrator.
(2) The violence is presented as "justified."
(3) Identification with the perpetrator is encouraged.
(4) The violence is portrayed realistically (although its consequences may not be shown realistically).

Some of the earlier studies did not find an effect for girls, but more recent research is showing that although the link is weaker, girls are also influenced. There is a strong indication that middle childhood, ages 8-10, is a time when children are particularly susceptible to the effects of violent programs. Quite high doses appear to be necessary. Longitudinal studies show that these childhood effects persist into adulthood, with heavy viewers at age 8 to 10 committing more serious and violent criminal offenses in their 20s than their peers. Although women who have a heavy diet of television violence as children have not been found to commit more crimes, they are more likely to use physical punishment with their children and to permit their children to watch more television violence. Some of the soundest research in this area, methodologically, has been conducted by Leonard Eron and his collaborators in Poland, Finland, Australia, the Netherlands, and Israel (Eron & Huesmann, 1987; Huesmann & Eron, 1986).

**Other Effects**

In addition to influencing real-life aggressive behavior, television violence has been shown to have two other major effects on children. One well-established finding is that children who watch large amounts of violence become desensitized to the effects of violence when they encounter them in other situations. Not only do they tend to be less aroused while watching violent scenes, they are less likely to empathize with or help victims of actual violence. Also, heavy viewers of violence, both children and adults, have been shown to have an exaggerated fear of violence and mistrust of people.

### Early Relationships With Broadcasting Authorities

At the time the Foundation became involved in the area of television violence, New Zealand had two public television channels, both under the control of a corporation consisting of government-appointed members. As with its British equivalent, on which it was modeled, the Broadcasting Corporation of New Zealand (BCNZ) has, by statute, editorial independence from government.

Standards and rules governing programs and advertising, including the portrayal of violence, are laid down by a committee of BCNZ, and there are both informal and formal complaint procedures for people who consider that these rules have been breached. Although a public corporation, BCNZ in recent years has become increasingly dependent on revenue from television advertising.

At the time the Foundation was assessing the international literature and considering possible interventions, the director general of BCNZ was reported to have said in an address to a political party meeting that evidence shows violence on television causes a viewer reaction against violence. He claimed that Japanese television was violent, yet violent crime had decreased in Japan and concluded by saying that BCNZ would be concerned if there was the remotest possibility of young children being affected. Taken overall, there was little doubt that the message being conveyed was that television violence is at worst innocuous and at best beneficial.

These assertions from the head of BCNZ were so much at variance with the technical literature and conclusions from independent commissions that we felt obliged to challenge them. We issued press statements and sent copies of a literature review to various organizations, including the Broadcasting Corporation. Correspondence was entered into with both BCNZ and the minister of broadcasting. To sum up a lengthy and complex series of events, there was a sharp exchange of comment, publicly through the mass media and in private correspondence. Some of the heat was taken out of the dispute through a meeting between Foundation representatives and senior Broadcasting Corporation and Television New Zealand (TVNZ) representatives. While there was some clarification of the concerns of our respective organizations, BCNZ would not accept two major points: (a) New Zealand screens a large amount of violence and (b) a link has been established between television violence viewing and violent behavior.

As the only objective assessment of screened violence in New Zealand had been conducted seven years prior to this meeting with BCNZ executives, we acknowledged that more contemporary data were required. At the meeting, one BCNZ representative said he would be surprised if New Zealand was high on violence because in the previous year the Program Standards Department had made 151 cuts for violence and 74 for weapons display. Following the meeting we decided to prepare a comprehensive report that would include (a) a more extensive review of the relevant social science literature on television violence, and (b) a survey of violence currently screened on New Zealand television.

## Media Watch Survey:
## Phase 1 of the Campaign

From November 6 to November 12, 1982, trained volunteers rated violence in all dramatic programs shown on both channels. All programs except news, documentaries, sports, and variety shows were rated using a system developed by George Gerbner (1972), a pioneer of television monitoring. The basic unit of violence according to this system is the "episode." Multiple, conceptually related acts are rated as a single episode. This means, for example, that a fistfight in which several punches are thrown is rated as one episode. See Haines (1983) for methodological details.

During the 92 hours of dramatic programs viewed, 528 episodes of violence were recorded, giving a rate of 5.7 per hour. Two people rated each program, and the reliability measure of 0.9 was acceptable. As might be expected, violence was unevenly distributed across programs. A third of all programs had no violence in them, and 15% contained more than 10 episodes. Table 20.2 lists programs that contained more than 5 episodes of violence.

Programs intended for children screened violence at a rate of 8.5 episodes per hour, compared with the adult program average of 5.0. While the rate was high during children's hours, violence of a less serious kind was screened. The report provides a detailed account of the way in which violence was portrayed on New Zealand television, who the perpetrators and victims were, and what effects the violence had. In summary, the vast majority of violence perpetrators and victims are males. Violence was usually portrayed as being effective, especially for heroes (77% of cases) rather than villains or neutral characters. Hero violence was also more serious. Heroes caused deaths in 14% of their violent actions, compared with villains' 7%.

Extrapolating from the week suggested that perhaps 25,000-30,000 episodes of violence were screened per year on New Zealand television. A child who was drawn to violent programs could thus probably see as many as 10,000 episodes in a year. It did not seem probable that the 225 cuts made by Program Standards would make much impression statistically.

The methodology used in Media Watch was similar to that used in the previous 1975 study and was also comparable to rating systems used in other countries. Thus it appeared that there had been a slight reduction in the overall rate. This was largely a consequence of fewer violent cartoons being screened during the 1982 Media Watch week.

**Table 20.2** Programs Screened During Media Watch Week With More Than Five
Episodes of Violence

| Name of Program | Place of Origin | Duration in Minutes | Total Number of Violent Episodes |
|---|---|---|---|
| Man Behind the Gun | United States | 85 | 41 |
| Chisum | United States | 115 | 41 |
| Chic Chat (Monday) | contains U.S. cartoons | 30 | 20 |
| Pink Panther | United States | 20 | 19 |
| Dracula | United States | 90 | 18 |
| Fly Away Home | United States | 100 | 18 |
| Dukes of Hazzard | United States | 60 | 16 |
| Mannix | United States | 55 | 16 |
| Superbug | Europe | 100 | 16 |
| Baretta | United States | 55 | 15 |
| Help It's the Care Bear Bunch | United States | 25 | 13 |
| Fat Albert & the Cosby Kids | United States | 20 | 13 |
| The Incredible Hulk | United States | 60 | 13 |
| Magnum, P.I. | United States | 60 | 12 |
| Muppet Show | United States | 25 | 11 |
| It's a Wonderful Life | United States | 125 | 11 |
| The Lazy Ace | United States | 95 | 11 |
| Bret Maverick | United States | 60 | 11 |
| Escape | United Kingdom | 50 | 11 |
| Trapper John, M.D. | United States | 55 | 10 |
| Prisoner (Monday) | Australia | 55 | 10 |
| Bus Stop | United States | 90 | 9 |
| Rentaghost | United Kingdom | 30 | 9 |
| Target | United Kingdom | 50 | 8 |
| Evita Peron | United States | 110 | 8 |
| Code Red | United States | 50 | 8 |
| Professionals | United Kingdom | 55 | 8 |
| Kwicky Koala Show | United States | 25 | 8 |
| Rentaghost | United Kingdom | 30 | 7 |
| The Virgin Queen | United States | 90 | 6 |
| Prisoner (Tuesday) | Australia | 55 | 6 |
| Prisoner (Wednesday afternoon) | Australia | 55 | 6 |
| Dallas | United States | 50 | 6 |

It could be concluded that New Zealand television was the most violent public television in the world (where data were available), although it was slightly
less violent than some private networks elsewhere, particularly in the United States.
The report, in addition to the results of the Media Watch survey and a case study of
a 9-year-old boy's detailed viewing patterns during the week, also contained a
review of the literature and a list of recommendations addressed to broadcasters,

**Table 20.3** Recommendations to the Broadcasting Corporation of New Zealand

(1) BCNZ should acknowledge that social science research has established with a reasonable degree of certainty that viewing large quantities of television violence results in increased aggression in children, adolescents, and possibly adults.

(2) BCNZ should work rapidly toward a substantial reduction of violence on New Zealand television, particularly during children's viewing hours. A reduction in violence will be achieved only by changes in purchasing policy. Fewer programs in the action-adventure category should be purchased, and no increases should be made in the present quantity of cartoons screened.

(3) Overseas markets should be searched more thoroughly, so that we become less dependent on the United States for our television drama. Programs from the United States are higher on violence than programs from elsewhere, and they dominate our programming. Concurrently, the production of New Zealand-made drama should be encouraged.

(4) BCNZ should clearly express its distaste for high levels of violence to those from whom it purchases programs.

(5) BCNZ, when considering which programs to purchase, should take into account the violence level. Violence levels are calculated for new seasons' shows by the American organization, the National Coalition on Television Violence.

(6) BCNZ should fund independent monitoring of television violence. Standard measures of violence should be used, to enable comparisons with other countries and comparisons over time in New Zealand. The results of such annual surveys should be made public.

(7) BCNZ should substantially reduce violence in previews of forthcoming programs. In these previews far too much violence is shown totally out of context.

(8) BCNZ should recommend that its advertisers avoid using violence to sell products.

(9) In conjunction with reducing the quantity of violence on television, BCNZ should pay careful attention to the kinds of violence screened, bearing in mind the more harmful program features discussed in Chapter Four. The program standards department should keep abreast of current social science literature on the most harmful types of television violence.

(10) BCNZ should recognize its responsibility to viewers, and not attempt to shift the responsibility to parents.

SOURCE: Haines, H. (1983).

educators, and parents (Haines, 1983). A summary of the recommendations that were sent to the Broadcasting Corporation is provided in Table 20.3.

## The Response of Broadcasting Authorities

We considered that the report met BCNZ's request for more up-to-date information and that our recommendations were consistent with the conclusions drawn from the research and survey. The report was sent to the Broadcasting Corporation as a courtesy, prior to public release, with an agreement by both parties that no comment would be made until the release date a few days later.

Breaking the agreed-on embargo, BCNZ skillfully stole the march on us, completely distorting the report's findings and claiming that the Foundation's concerns were directly primarily toward such beloved Muppet characters as Miss Piggy and Kermit. The 83-page report was reduced to a front-page newspaper headline, "TV Keeping an Eye on Muppets." The national morning radio news began: "The TV Muppets have been labeled 'violent' by the Mental Health Foundation. Now Kermit, Fozzie, Miss Piggy and the gang, with some other television cartoons like the Pink Panther, are among the programs to be reviewed by the Broadcasting Corporation for their scenes of violence. The Mental Health Foundation report claims that they contain high levels of violence likely to cause violence in society." In reality, the Muppets were not listed in the body of the report. It was stated explicitly that one should be cautious about condemning any particular series from information based on one week's program— sound advice in the case of the Muppets, which is not usually high on violence, although Miss Piggy does have an outburst from time to time. It was also stated that while violent cartoons do have an influence on the behavior of very young children, cartoon violence is not as strongly implicated as other forms of television violence. Furthermore, the recommendations addressed to BCNZ did not ask for a reduction in cartoons because they had already made substantial reductions in the past. The Foundation made it clear in the report that its major concern was with more realistic portrayals of violence by heroes in police, crime, and action-adventure programs. We did manage to get subsequent media coverage that presented the material in a more accurate and balanced way. This coverage also exposed the Broadcasting Corporation's ploy. This response to the report and our efforts to assume a less confrontational approach to our dealings with the BCNZ led us to conclude that the organization had no intention of discussing our concerns openly and even less interest in reducing levels of screened violence. Subsequent media comments by senior BCNZ officers, correspondence, and meetings reinforced this assessment.

**Prevention Campaign: Phase 2**

At this stage we were forced to reassess our strategy. Clearly our past assumptions were naive, to say the least. We were assuming that the world is populated by "reasonable" people concerned with the well-being of others and a respect for socially relevant research findings. We were assuming that if we documented the negative effects of certain forms of programming, broadcasters would, in the public interest, make changes. Reality, as we experienced it, was clearly not consistent with this viewpoint.

We realized that if television violence levels were to be reduced other approaches would be required. It was also evident that it could be quite some time before this terminal goal would be reached. Further communication with the Broadcasting Corporation was considered pointless in the short term. Instead, we shifted our focus to politicians, professional and community organizations, and members of the general public. A number of intermediate goals were formulated, including the following:

(1) Getting as many organizations as possible to inform their members about the effects of television violence and the need to reduce violence levels
(2) Getting these same organizations to formulate a policy calling for less violence on television and conveying this to politicians and the Broadcasting Corporation
(3) Increasing public opposition to high levels of television violence
(4) Stimulating an official inquiry into television violence

A wide variety of activities were undertaken with regard to these goals and more specific objectives. They included annual repeats of the 1982 Media Watch survey and associated publicity, regular media releases on the topic, and cooperation with sympathetic journalists, including television directors and reporters, papers at professional conferences, public addresses, teaching units for schools, pamphlets, bumper stickers, and a range of overt and covert lobbying activities.

While the BCNZ remained resistant to our efforts to induce a change in programming policy, during the early years of our campaign public opinion polls showed a considerable increase in the percentage of the adult population who reported wanting less violence on television. Prior to the campaign a national poll (conducted in May 1981) indicated that 62% of the adult population wanted to see less violence. Two years later the Foundation commissioned a repeat of the poll using the same polling agency and repeating a number of the questions. This poll was taken two months after the release of the Foundation's report *Violence on Television* and the Muppets incident. There was a great deal of media coverage of the topic at that time. This media interest is reflected in the fact that the 1983 poll and its successor in 1984 were largely funded by the *Auckland Star*, a major Auckland newspaper.

The 1983 poll showed that 71% of the public believed that there was too much violence on television, compared with 62% in the survey two years before. It is interesting that the shift of approximately 10 percentage points occurred across all of the major age and gender categories (see Table 20.4).

The poll was repeated again, just over 18 months later, near the end of 1984. The findings were very similar to those of the previous poll, suggesting stability in public opinion on this topic. Interestingly, the only subgroup that showed a change was young adults with children. More people in this category favored a reduction in screened violence in the 1984 poll. Given the apparent stability of

**Table 20.4** Responses to National Polls on Attitudes Toward Television Violence on Three Different Occasions: 1981-1984 (in percentages)

| | Amount of Violence Television Should Show | | |
| --- | --- | --- | --- |
| | May 2, 1981 | May 28, 1983 | December 1, 1984 |
| Much more/a little more | 3.3 | 3.6 | 2.7 |
| About the same | 19.7 | 15.9 | 18.3 |
| A little less/less | 30.3 | 34.7 | 33.2 |
| Much less | 31.7 | 35.7 | 37.4 |
| Support for less | 62 | 71 | 71 |
| *Individuals Favoring Violence Reductions* | | | |
| Male | 53 | 61 | 59 |
| Female | 72 | 80 | 81 |
| Young (under 35) with children | 56 | 67 | 72 |
| Older married (grandparents) | 75 | 86 | 86 |

opinion in favor of a reduction and the belief that attitude shift had plateaued, further polls were not conducted by the Foundation.

In addition to the attitude shift, during 1983 a number of national organizations made public statements calling for reductions in television violence. Examples include the New Zealand Committee on Children, the Peace Studies Foundation, the New Zealand Psychological Society, the Parent-Teachers' Association, and Monitor. Most previously had no policy on the topic or had not taken a public stand. Interestingly, TVNZ's controller of programming claimed in a December 1983 radio interview that viewers were fairly satisfied with locally screened programs and that he did not believe there was growing opposition to television violence. At that time TVNZ did, however, introduce a video clip of a well-known children's television host advising parents of 7:30 p.m. and 8:30 p.m. watersheds in programming and that programs after 8:30 p.m. might not be suitable for children. The Foundation repeated its Media Watch survey in 1983. A summary of the results is provided in Table 20.5. Both the 1983 and the following 1984 surveys show increases in violence levels, the 1984 rate of 9.5 per hour being the highest ever recorded in New Zealand and on a par with the more violent commercial networks in the United States.

## The Royal Commission on Broadcasting

In response to requests from the Foundation and other organizations, the minister of broadcasting included the topic of television violence in the terms of reference of the Royal Commission on Broadcasting and Related Communications.

Table 20.5 Media Watch Surveys, 1982-1989

| Year | Hours of Dramatic Programs | Episodes of Violence | Episodes per Hour |
|------|----------------------------|----------------------|-------------------|
| 1982 | 94 hours, 18 minutes | 535 | 5.7 |
| 1983 | 107 hours, 38 minutes | 724 | 6.7 |
| 1984 | 89 hours, 30 minutes | 846 | 9.5 |
| 1986 | 121 hours, 20 minutes | 781 | 6.4 |
| 1988 | 114 hours, 15 minutes | 693 | 6.1 |
| 1989 | 170 hours, 50 minutes | 742 | 4.3 |

The Commission received written and oral submissions throughout 1985 and 1986. A total of 56 submissions were received from a very wide cross section of the community. Both the Foundation and the Broadcasting Corporation made substantial written submissions and spoke before the commissioners. The Commission report, published in September 1986, outlines the Foundation's submission at length and notes that with few exceptions other submissions were consistent with those of the Foundation. It states, "Many referred to and supported the conclusions and recommendations of the Mental Health Foundation's Media Watch Surveys, and recommended a reduction in the number of violent programs screened" (Royal Commission of Inquiry into Broadcasting and Related Telecommunications, 1986, p. 418). In its summing up, the Commission report says, "The large number of submissions received on this term of reference . . . indicates to us a high public awareness of the problem of violence on television and an increasing belief that this is connected with the level of violence in the community" (p. 421). The Commission concluded that there was sufficient established knowledge and public concern to warrant a reduction of violence on New Zealand television. In short, the Commission found against the Broadcasting Corporation and endorsed virtually all of the recommendations put to it, and the BCNZ some years before, by the Foundation.

## The Ministerial Committee of Inquiry Into Violence

While the final verbal submissions were being heard by the Royal Commission, the minister of justice established a special committee to examine violence and violent crime and to recommend measures to reduce their incidence. On the topic of television violence the Ministerial Committee of Inquiry Into Violence received 425 written submissions and an unspecified number of oral submissions at public meetings. More submissions were received on this topic than any other aspect of violence considered by the Committee. As mentioned previously, the Foundation made a submission that addressed many different aspects of violence and a variety of preventive measures that could be taken. In addition, the Foundation provided the Committee with copies of its television violence submission to the Royal Commission and related reports and surveys. I also had informal discussions with Committee members and was asked for advice on drafting the television violence section of the report.

The Roper Report, as it has come to be known, was released in March 1987 (Committee of Inquiry Into Violence, 1987). It was critical of the Broadcasting Corporation for its stance and endorsed the conclusions of the Royal Commission. It also endorsed most of the Commission's recommendations and was even stronger in its call for reduced violence levels. It questioned the value of "watershed commercials" and the need for further research. Instead, it requested a reduction in violent viewing "across the board" and said that the Commission's recommendation concerning more research would "delay implementing remedies which present research indicates are required now" (p. 133).

### Change in the Corporation

In early 1986, both the chairman of the Broadcasting Corporation and the chief executive of Television New Zealand were replaced by the new Labor government. The new appointees took a different stance on the matter of television violence from that of their predecessors. Indeed, the new head of Television New Zealand asked the Royal Commission if he could make a late and additional submission to the substantial report already presented on behalf of the BCNZ by TVNZ's controller of programming. While still reluctant to accept the link between television violence and real-life violence, he acknowledged widespread public concern and, in marked contrast to the Broadcasting Corporation's earlier evidence, undertook to reduce what he euphemistically termed "hard action" programs through a changed purchasing policy using a wider range of program sources. He subsequently amplified these commitments through the media and also agreed to advise international contacts within the industry that BCNZ wanted to see less violence in programs being planned and made.

What effect has there been on levels of screened violence? An important part of our public education and advocacy efforts revolved around further Media Watch surveys. The findings, summarized in Table 20.4, also provide a measure of success with regard to our terminal objective—reducing levels of screened violence. These findings indicate that the policy changes announced by the new TVNZ head in 1986 have been translated into program changes. This appears to have been achieved mainly by dropping some of the more violent action/thriller programs that originate predominantly in the United States. However, the great majority of violence appearing on New Zealand television continued to come from that country. The last Media Watch survey, conducted during November

1989, found that the average rate of violent episodes per hour was just over four. This is a substantial change from the situation five years before, when the rate was more than double at nine. However, the 1989 figure is still quite high by international standards, especially for public television.

It is of course not possible to infer a causal relationship from a case study of the type outlined. While that might frustrate us as scientists, as practitioners our major concern is to achieve results. As of the end of 1989 the outcome was satisfactory. I also have a hunch that our program, sustained over nearly a decade, had something to do with it. It certainly helps to flesh out the lean reward schedule that is often the lot of the proactive preventionist to think this way.

There is one other occasion where a nationwide campaign was shown to be followed by a reduction in levels of violence on television. During the mid-1970s, U.S. organizations such as the American Medical Association, the American Psychiatric Association, the American Psychological Association, and the National Parent-Teacher Association actively lobbied for programming changes. Some large corporations refused to be involved with or have their products advertised during violent programs. This pressure was effective in reducing overall violence levels. It also played a part in the decision of the leading networks to introduce two-hour "family" viewing periods each evening. However, the effects were short-lived and by the end of the 1970s violence levels rose again and continued to increase throughout the following decade. The introduction of additional private companies and cable networks contributed further to violent programming. For accounts of the 1970 campaign in the United States, see Carter and Strickland (1977), Comstock (1976), and Mankiewicz and Swerdlow (1978).

At the time of this writing, major changes are occurring in New Zealand television. Legislation has been passed deregulating television and allowing the establishment of private channels. The first private network has recently been established, and additional subscriber channels will be introduced shortly. It remains to be seen whether public pressure and the newly established Broadcasting Standards Authority will be sufficient to sustain reductions in levels of television violence. The U.S. experience during the 1970s and our earlier dealings with television industry representatives do not provide grounds for optimism.

Given the international focus of the present volume, it is important to note that the United States is the major producer of violent television programs for the international market. The great majority of high-violence programs screened in New Zealand originate in the United States, and New Zealand is probably typical of English-speaking countries in this regard. The United States is a particularly violent society, with very high homicide rates. It is perhaps not surprising that this is reflected in cultural "products" such as television programs and movies. The culture also has an unusual emphasis on individual, as opposed to collective, rights and on the market economy. These factors may help to explain why concerted efforts to reduce violent programming and encourage more prosocial programs have had little long-term success. Given the connections between viewing violent television and real-life violent behavior, it is difficult for people with a different social heritage to understand how a court of law could rule that a voluntary television industry code on violence portrayals is not in the public interest. I am referring to the U.S. Justice Department's suit against the National Association of Broadcasters code. The suit, which was supported by a district court of appeals in 1979, contended that the code violated antitrust provisions (Landers, 1988).

Many countries, especially socialist states and most non-English-speaking countries, have very low rates of television violence. Some, such as Sweden, have such low rates that efforts along the same lines as our Media Watch surveys have been abandoned because there was insufficient violence to rate (Haines, 1983). However, this situation is changing. The International Coalition Against Violent Entertainment (1990) has announced that U.S. distributors have recently signed contracts with Eastern European counterparts that will result in an influx of some of the most violent television programs and films produced in the United States and other Western nations. The increased availability of satellite technology also makes the matter of television violence increasingly a global issue, requiring international as well as national and local responses.

# References

Abbott, M. W. (Ed.). (1983). *Child abuse prevention in New Zealand.* Auckland: Mental Health Foundation of New Zealand.

Abbott, M. W. (1986). The Mental Health Foundation's Primary Prevention Programme: 1981-1985. *Mental Health in Australia, 16*, 12-21.

Belson, W. (1978). *Television violence and the adolescent boy.* Hampshire: Saxon House.

Carter, D., & Strickland, S. (1977). *TV violence and the child: The evolution and fate of the Surgeon-General's Report.* New York: Russell Sage Foundation.

Committee of Inquiry Into Violence. (1987). *Report of Ministerial Committee of Inquiry Into Violence.* Wellington, New Zealand: Government Printer.

Comstock, G. A. (1976). The role of social and behavioral science in policymaking for television. *Journal of Social Issues, 32*, 157-178.

Eron, L., & Huesmann, L. (1987). Television as a source of maltreatment of children. *School Psychology Review, 16*, 195-202.

Eysenck, H. J., & Nias, D. K. B. (1980). *Sex, violence and the media.* London: Granada.

Friedrich-Cofer, L., & Huston, A. C. (1986). Television violence and aggression: The debate continues. *Psychological Bulletin, 100*, 36-71.

Gerbner, G. (1972). Violence in television drama: Trends and symbolic functions. In G. A. Comstock & E. A. Rubinstein (Eds.), *Television and social behavior: Vol. 1. Media content and control.* Washington, DC: Government Printing Office.

Ginpel, S. (1976). Violent and dangerous acts on New Zealand television. *New Zealand Journal of Educational Studies*, pp. 152-187.

Haines, H. (1983). *Violence on television.* Auckland: Mental Health Foundation of New Zealand.

Haines, H., & Abbott, M. W. (1983). *Proceedings of the National Seminar on Rape.* Auckland: Mental Health Foundation of New Zealand.

Huesmann, L. R. (1986). Psychological processes promoting the relation between exposure to media violence and aggressive behavior by the viewer. *Journal of Social Issues, 42,* 125-140.

Huesmann, L. R., & Eron, L. D. (Eds.). (1986). *Television and the aggressive child: A cross-national comparison.* Hillsdale, NJ: Lawrence Erlbaum.

International Coalition Against Violent Entertainment. (1990, June 8). *Mass media watchdog group protests introduction of violent entertainment into the Eastern Bloc.* Press release.

Landers, S. (1988, July). Watching TV violence shapes people's values. *APA Monitor.*

Mankiewicz, F., & Swerdlow, J. (1978). *Television and the manipulation of American life.* New York: Time Books.

National Institute of Mental Health. (1982). *Television and behavior: Ten years of scientific progress and implications for the eighties* (DHHS Publication No. ADM 82-1195). Washington, DC: Government Printing Office.

Royal Commission of Inquiry into Broadcasting and Related Telecommunications. (1986). *Report of the Royal Commission on Broadcasting.* Wellington, New Zealand: Government Printer.

Rule, B., & Ferguson, T. (1986). The effects of media violence attitudes, emotions and cognitions. *Journal of Social Issues, 42,* 29-50.

Surgeon General's Scientific Advisory Committee on Television and Social Behavior. (1972). *Television and growing up: The impact of televised violence* (Report to the surgeon general, U.S. Public Health Service). Washington, DC: Government Printing Office.

# 21

# Victimization Among Schoolchildren: Intervention and Prevention

## Dan Olweus

Victimization or bullying among schoolchildren is certainly a very old phenomenon. The fact that some children are frequently and systematically harassed and attacked by other children has been described in literary works, and many adults have personal experience of it from their own school days. Though many are acquainted with the bully/victim problem, it was not until fairly recently—in the early 1970s—that efforts were made to study it systematically. So far, these attempts have largely been confined to Scandinavia. In the 1980s, however, bullying among schoolchildren received some public attention also in other countries, such as Japan, England, Australia, and the United States. There are now clear indications of an increasing societal as well as research interest in bully/victim problems in several parts of the world.

This chapter gives an overview of some recent research findings on bullying or victimization among schoolchildren in Scandinavia. I will mainly confine myself to the effects of a large-scale intervention program designed to deal with bully/victim problems, which has been evaluated in 42 schools in Bergen, Norway (Olweus, 1990). I will also briefly describe the content of the program and some of the principles on which it was based.

A number of findings concerning developmental antecedents of bullying problems, characteristics of typical bullies and victims, and the veracity of some popular conceptions of the causes of these problems are presented only briefly or not at all in this context, since these results have been described in detail in

AUTHOR'S NOTE: The research reported here was supported by grants from the William T. Grant Foundation, the Norwegian Research Council for Social Research, the Swedish Delegation for Social Research, and, in earlier phases, the Norwegian Ministry of Education. Several of the ideas presented were developed while I was a fellow at the Center for Advanced Study in the Behavioral Sciences, Stanford, California. I am indebted to the University of Bergen, the Spencer Foundation, the Norwegian Research Council for Social Research, and the Center for Advanced Study in the Behavioral Sciences for financial support of my year at the Center.

previous publications (e.g., Olweus, 1973a, 1978, 1979, 1980, 1981, 1983, 1984, 1986, 1987, 1990). It should be mentioned, however, that the findings from this earlier research have generally been replicated in several different samples and were obtained with a number of different methods, including peer ratings, teacher nominations, self-reports, grades, projective techniques, hormonal assays, and mother/father interviews about child-rearing practices. Most of these results were derived from my Swedish longitudinal project (comprising approximately 900 boys), which started in the early 1970s and is still continuing.

Before embarking on the main theme of my presentation I will give a brief definition of terms. In addition, I will draw a portrait of typical victims and bullies as a background for the intervention program. (For a more comprehensive overview, see, e.g., Olweus, 1986, 1990.)

## Definitions

I define *bullying* or *victimization* in the following general way: A person is being bullied or victimized when he or she is exposed, repeatedly and over time, to negative actions on the part of one or more other persons. The meaning of the expression *negative actions* must be specified further. A negative action takes place when someone intentionally inflicts, or attempts to inflict, injury or discomfort upon another—basically what is implied in the definition of aggressive behavior (Olweus, 1973b). Negative actions can be carried out by physical contact, by words, or in other ways, such as making faces or obscene gestures or refusing to comply with another person's wishes.

It must be stressed that the terms *bullying* and *victimization* do not apply when two persons of approximately the same strength (physical or psychological) are fighting or quarreling. *Bullying* applies to situations in which there is an imbalance in strength relations (an asymmetric power relationship): The person who is exposed to the negative actions has difficulty in defending him- or herself and is somewhat helpless against the person or persons who harass.

It is useful to distinguish between *direct bullying*—with relatively open attacks on the victim—and *indirect bullying*, which may take the form of social isolation and exclusion from a group. It is important to pay attention also to the second, less visible, form of victimization. In this chapter the expressions *bullying, victimization,* and *bully/victim problems* are used interchangeably.

## Prevalence

In connection with a nationwide campaign against bully/victim problems in Norwegian comprehensive schools launched by the Ministry of Education in 1983, data were collected with a questionnaire measuring different aspects of victimization from more than 700 schools all over Norway (Olweus, 1985, 1986, 1990).[1]

On the basis of this survey, one can estimate that some 84,000 students, or 15% of the total in the Norwegian comprehensive schools (568,000 in 1983-1984), were involved in bully/victim problems "now and then" or more frequently (autumn 1983), as bullies or victims. This percentage represents 1 student out of 7. Approximately 9%, or 52,000 students, were victims, and 41,000, or 7%, bullied other students "now and then" or more frequently. Some 9,000 students were both victims and bullies.

It can thus be stated that bullying is a considerable problem in Norwegian comprehensive schools, a problem that affects a very large number of students. Data from other countries such as Sweden (Olweus, 1986), Finland (Lagerspetz, Björkqvist, Berts, & King, 1982), England (Smith, 1989), and the United States (Perry, Kusel, & Perry, 1988) indicate that this problem exists also outside Norway and with similar or even higher prevalence rates.

### Characteristics of Typical Victims and Bullies

The picture of the *typical victim* emerging from the research literature is relatively unambiguous (see Olweus, 1978, 1986). Victims of bullying are more anxious and insecure than students in general. They are often cautious, sensitive, and quiet. When attacked by other students, they commonly react with crying (at least in the lower grades) and withdrawal. They have a negative view of themselves and their situation. They often look upon themselves as failures and feel stupid, ashamed, and unattractive. Further, victims are lonely and abandoned at school. As a rule, they do not have a single good friend in their class. They are not aggressive or teasing in their behavior; accordingly, one cannot explain the bullying as a consequence of the victims themselves being provocative to their peers (see below). If they are boys, they are likely to be physically weaker than boys in general.

In summary, the behaviors and attitudes of the victims seem to signal to others that they are insecure and worthless individuals who will not retaliate if they are attacked or insulted. A slightly different way of describing typical victims is to say that they are characterized by an anxious personality pattern combined (in the case of boys) with physical weakness.

This is a sketch of the most common type of victim, whom I have called the *passive* or *withdrawn* victim. There is also another, smaller group of victims, *provocative* victims, who are characterized by a combination of both anxious and aggressive behavior patterns. (See Olweus, 1973a, 1978, for more about this kind of victim.)

A distinctive characteristic of *typical bullies* is their aggression toward peers; this is implied in the definition of a bully. They are, however, often also aggressive toward teachers, parents, and siblings. Generally, they have more positive attitudes toward violence and use of violent means than do students in general. They are often characterized by impulsiveness and strong needs to dominate others. They have little empathy with the victims of bullying. If they are boys, they are likely to be physically stronger than boys in general, and victims in particular.

In contrast to a fairly common assumption among psychologists and psychiatrists, I have found no indication that aggressive bullies (boys) are anxious and insecure under a tough surface. Data based on several samples and using both direct and indirect methods such as projective techniques and hormonal assays all point in the same direction: The bullies had unusually little anxiety and insecurity or were roughly average on such dimensions (Olweus, 1981, 1984). And they did not suffer from poor self-esteem. In summary, the typical bully can be described as having an aggressive personality pattern combined (in the case of boys) with physical strength.

Bullying can also be viewed as a component of a more generally conduct-disordered, antisocial, and rule-breaking behavior pattern. From this perspective, it is natural to predict that youngsters who are aggressive and who bully others in school run a clearly increased risk of later engaging in other problem behaviors such as criminality and alcohol abuse. Several recent studies confirm this general prediction (Loeber & Dishion, 1983; Magnusson, Stattin, & Dunér, 1983). In my own follow-up studies I have also found strong support for this view. Approximately 60% of boys who were characterized as bullies in grades 6-9 had at least one conviction at the age of 24. Even more dramatically, as much as 35-40% of the former bullies had three or more convictions at this age, while this was true of only 10% of the control boys (those who were neither bullies nor victims in grades 6-9). Thus as young adults the former school bullies had a fourfold increase in the level of relatively serious, recidivist criminality. It may be mentioned that the former victims had an average or somewhat below-average level of criminality in young adulthood.

### A Question of Fundamental Democratic Rights

The results obtained in my research demonstrate convincingly that bullying is a considerable problem in Scandinavian elementary and junior high schools, that teachers (in 1983) did relatively little to counteract it, and that the parents knew too little about what their children were exposed to or engaged in. The victims of bullying are a large group of students who are to a great extent neglected by the school. We know that many of these youngsters are the targets of harassment for long periods of time, often for many years (Olweus, 1977, 1978). It does not require much imagination to understand what it is to go through the school years in a state of more or less permanent anxiety and insecurity and with poor self-esteem. It is not surprising that the victims' devaluation of themselves sometimes becomes so overwhelming that they see suicide as the only possible solution.

Bully/victim problems have even broader implications than those suggested in the previous paragraph. They really concern some of our fundamental democratic principles: Every individual should have the right to be spared oppression and repeated, intentional humiliation, in school as in society at large. No student should be afraid of going to school for fear of being harassed or degraded, and no parent should need to worry about such things happening to his or her child.

Bully/victim problems also relate to a society's general attitude toward violence and oppression. What kind of view of societal values will a student acquire who is repeatedly bullied by other students without interference from adults? The same question can be asked with regard to students who, for long periods of time, are allowed to harass others without hindrance from adults. Refraining from actively counteracting bully/victim problems in school implies tacit acceptance.

In this context, it should be emphasized that it is of great importance to counteract these problems also for the sake of the aggressive students. As reported above, school bullies are much more likely than other students to follow an antisocial path. Accordingly, it is essential to try to redirect their activities into more socially acceptable channels. There is no evidence to suggest that a generally "tolerant" and permissive attitude on the part of adults will help bullies outgrow their antisocial behavior pattern.

### Main Goals and Components of the Intervention Program

Against this background, it is now appropriate to describe briefly the effects of the intervention program developed in connection with the campaign against bully/victim problems in Norwegian schools. The major goals of the program were to reduce as much as possible existing bully/victim problems and to prevent the development of new problems. The main components of the program, which was aimed at teachers and parents as well as students, were the following:

(1) *A 32-page booklet for school personnel describing what is known about bully/victim problems (rather, what was known in 1983) and giving detailed suggestions about what teachers and the school can do to counteract and prevent the problems* (Olweus & Roland, 1983). Efforts were also made to dispel common myths about the nature and causes of bully/victim problems that might interfere with adequate handling of them. This booklet was distributed free of charge to all comprehensive schools in Norway.

(2) *A 4-page folder with information and advice to parents of victims and bullies as well as "ordinary" children.* This folder was distributed by the schools to all families in Norway with school-age children (also free of charge).

(3) *A 25-minute videocassette showing episodes from the everyday lives of two bullied children, a 10-year-old boy and a 14-year-old girl.* This cassette could be bought or rented at a highly subsidized price.

(4) *A short questionnaire designed to obtain information about different aspects of bully/victim problems in the school, including frequency and the readiness of teachers and students to interfere with the problems.* The questionnaire was completed by students individually (in class) and anonymously. Registration of the level and nature of bully/victim problems in the school was thought to serve as a basis and starting point for active intervention on the part of the school and the parents. A number of the results presented earlier in this chapter were based on information collected with this questionnaire.[2]

Another component was added to the program as used in Bergen, the city in which the evaluation of the effects of the intervention program took place. Approximately 15 months after the program was first offered to the schools (in early October 1983), we gave, in a two-hour meeting with the staff, individual feedback information to each of the 42 schools participating in the study (Manger & Olweus, 1985). This information, derived from the students' responses to the questionnaire in 1983, focused on the level of problems and the social environment's reactions to the problems in the particular school as related to data from comparable schools obtained in the nationwide survey (October 1983). At the same time, the main principles of the program and the major procedures suggested for intervention were presented and discussed with the staff. Since we know from experience that many (Norwegian) teachers have somewhat distorted views of the characteristics of bullying students, particular emphasis was placed on a discussion of this topic and on appropriate ways of handling bullying behavior. Finally, the teachers rated different aspects of the program, in particular its feasibility and potential efficacy. Generally, this addition to the program and the program itself were quite favorably received by the teachers, as expressed in their ratings.

## Subjects and Design

Space limitations prevent detailed presentation here of methodological information, including sampling scheme, definition of measuring instruments and variables, and significance tests, so only summary descriptions and main results will be provided.

Evaluation of the effects of the intervention program is based on data from approximately 2,500 students originally belonging to 112 grade 4-7 classes in 42 primary and junior high schools in Bergen (modal ages at Time 1 were 11, 12, 13, and 14 years, respectively). Each of the four grade/age cohorts consisted of 600-700 subjects, with a roughly equal distribution of boys and girls. The

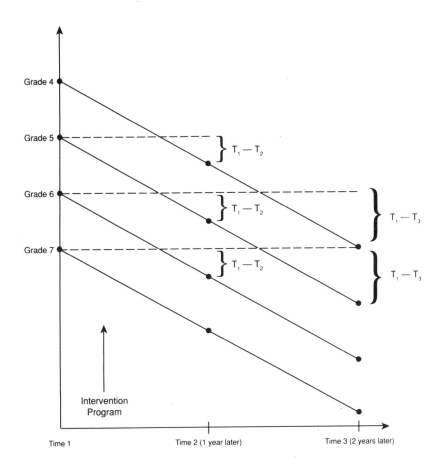

**Figure 21.1.** Design for Evaluation of Effects of Intervention Program

NOTE: These are fictitious data, but they do to some extent reflect the general trend of the empirical findings.

first time of data collection (Time 1) was in late May (and early June) 1983, approximately four months before the initiation of the campaign. New measurements were taken in May 1984 (Time 2) and May 1985 (Time 3).

Since the campaign was nationwide, it was not possible to set up a strictly experimental study with random allocation of schools or classes to treatment and control conditions. Instead, a quasi-experimental design (sometimes called an "age cohort" or "selection cohort" design; see Cook & Campbell, 1979) was chosen, making use of "time-lagged contrasts between age-equivalent groups." In particular, for three of the cohorts data collected at Time 1 (see Figure 21.1) were used as a baseline with which data for age-equivalent cohorts at Time 2 could be compared. The latter groups had then been exposed to the intervention program for about 8 months. For example, the data for the grade 5 cohort at Time 1 (modal age 12 years) were compared with the Time 2 data for the grade 4 cohort, which at that time had reached the same age as the baseline group. The same kind of comparisons were made between the grade 6 cohort at Time 1 and the grade 5 cohort at Time 2, and between the grade 7 cohort at Time 1 and the grade 6 cohort at Time 2.

Comparisons of data collected at Time 1 and Time 3 permit an assessment of the persistence or possible decline or enhancement of the effects over a longer time span. For these comparisons data for only two of the cohorts could be used as a baseline, those of the grade 6 and grade 7 cohorts, which were contrasted with data collected at Time 3 on the grade 4 and grade 5 cohorts, respectively. The latter groups had been exposed to the intervention program for approximately 20 months at that time.

An attractive feature of the design is the fact that two of the cohorts serve as a baseline group in one set of comparisons and as a treatment group in another. This is the case with the grade 5 cohort at Time 1, the data for which are used as a baseline in comparison with the grade 4 cohort data collected at Time 2 (after 8 months of intervention). In addition, the grade 5 cohort data obtained at Time 2 serve to evaluate the possible effects of 8 months of intervention when they are compared with the data for the grade 6 cohort at Time 1. The same situation applies to the grade 6 cohort in comparisons with the grade 5 and grade 7 cohorts, respectively.

The advantage of this aspect of the design is that a possible bias in the sampling of the cohorts (selection bias) would operate in opposite directions in the two sets of comparisons, thus making it much more difficult to obtain consistent (apparent) intervention effects across cohorts as a consequence of such bias. There are, however, no grounds for expecting such bias, since the classes/schools were distributed on the different cohorts by a basically random procedure. Accordingly, the cohorts should be essentially equivalent in important respects at Time 1. This aspect of the design would provide the same kind of protection against faulty conclusions in case the baseline data for one or both of these cohorts were unusually high or low simply as a function of chance.

To avoid erroneous conclusions caused by possible selective attrition (more extreme or deviant individuals may be more likely to drop out in longitudinal studies), analyses were restricted to students for whom there were valid data at both time points in a particular comparison (both for the baseline and the intervention groups). In the present research, however, the results were basically the same whether we controlled or did not control for such attrition.

It should also be noted that since selection of the subjects was not based on some kind of "extreme score" criterion, the problem with "regression toward the mean," which looms large in many evaluation studies, is not at issue in the present research. By using the present design the common and serious problem of attempting to adjust statistically for initial differences between nonequivalent groups is also avoided.

## Statistical Analyses

Since classes rather than students were the basic sampling units (with students nested within classes), it was considered important to choose a data-analytic strategy that reflected the basic features of the design. Accordingly, data were analyzed with analysis of variance (ANOVA), with students nested within classes nested within schools nested within times/occasions (Time 1 versus Time 2, Time 1 versus Time 3). Sex of the subjects was crossed with times, schools (within times), and classes (within schools). Since several of the cohorts figured in two comparisons, the analyses had to be conducted separately for each combination of cohorts (for further information, see Olweus, in press).

For several of the variables (or derivatives of them, such as percentages), less refined (and, in some respects, less informative) analyses with *t*-tests and chi-square were also carried out. The findings from these analyses were in general agreement with those obtained in the ANOVAs.

Properties of the outcome variables analyzed are discussed elsewhere in some detail (Olweus, 1990). Generally, it was concluded that the evidence available attests to the adequacy and validity of the data employed.

## Results

Results for the variable "being exposed to direct bullying" are presented separately for boys and girls in Figures 21.2 and 21.3. (Due to space limitations, only the results for this variable are shown graphically; see Olweus, 1990, for a more complete presentation.) Since the design of the study is relatively complex, a few words about how to read the figures are in order.

The panel to the left shows the effects after 8 months of intervention, while the one to the right displays the results after 20 months. The upper curves (designated Before) show the baseline data (Time 1) for the relevant cohorts (the grade 5, grade 6, and grade 7 cohorts in the left panel and the grade 6 and grade 7 cohorts in the right). The lower curves (designated After) display data collected at Time 2 (after 8 months of intervention) in the panel to the left and at Time 3 (after 20 months of intervention) in the right-hand panel for the age-equivalent cohorts (the grade 4, grade 5, and grade 6 cohorts at Time 2 and the grade 4 and grade 5 cohorts at Time 3).

It should be noted that there are minor differences in the baseline data (Before) for the grade 6 and grade 7 cohorts when presented in the left and right

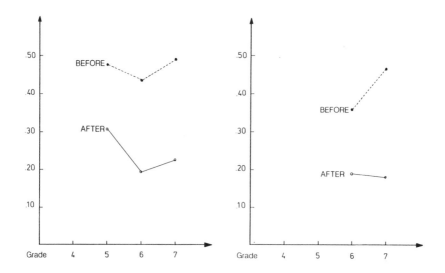

**Figure 21.2.** Effects of Intervention Program on "Being Exposed to Direct Bullying" for Boys

NOTE: Panel to the left shows effects after 8 months of intervention, and panel to the right displays results after 20 months of intervention. Upper curves (designated Before) show baseline data (Time 1), and lower curves (designated After) display data collected at Time 2 in the left-hand panel and at Time 3 in the right-hand panel.

panels, respectively. This is a consequence of the restriction of the analyses to subjects who had valid data at both time points; accordingly, these are not exactly the same subjects who entered the two sets of analyses.

The main findings of the analyses can be summarized as follows:

- There were marked reductions in the levels of bully/victim problems for the periods studied, after 8 and 20 months of intervention, respectively. By and large, reductions were obtained for both boys and girls and across all cohorts compared. For the longer time period the effects persisted in the case of "being exposed to direct bullying" and "being exposed to indirect bullying" and were strengthened for the variable "bullying others."

- Similar reductions were obtained for the aggregated "peer rating" variables "number of students being bullied in the class" and "number of students in the class bullying others." There was thus consensual agreement in the classes that bully/victim problems had decreased during the periods studied.

- In terms of percentages of students reporting being bullied or bullying others "now and then" or more frequently, the reductions amounted to approximately 50% or more in most comparisons (Time 1-Time 3 for "bullying others.")

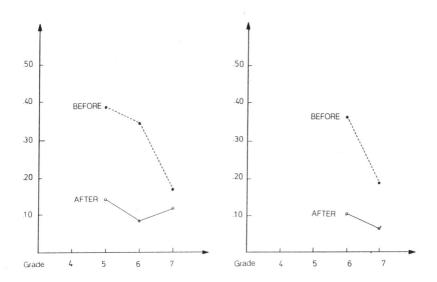

**Figure 21.3.** Effects of Intervention Program on "Being Exposed to Direct Bullying" for Girls

NOTE: See Figure 21.2 for an explanation of this figure.

- There was no displacement of bullying from the school to the way to and from school. There were reductions or no changes on the items measuring bully/victim problems on the way to and from school.
- There was also a reduction in general antisocial behavior such as vandalism, theft, and truancy. (For the grade 6 comparisons the effects were marginal for both time periods.)
- At the same time, there was an increase in student satisfaction with school life, as reflected in "liking recess time."
- There were weak and inconsistent changes for the questions concerning attitudes toward different aspects of bully/victim problems.

In the majority of comparisons for which reductions are reported above, the differences between baseline and intervention groups were highly significant or significant (in spite of the fact that many of them were based on single items).

## Prevention of New Cases of Victimization

By combining information from two questionnaire items ("How often have you been bullied in school [this spring term]?" and "Have you been bullied more or less this spring term compared with the spring term a year ago?"), it was possible, given certain reasonable assumptions, to estimate which victimized individuals at a certain time point were "new cases" and which were not. In this way, incidence rates (number and percentage of new cases; see Olweus, 1989) could be calculated for each cohort and time point, to be related to incidence data from the relevant comparison cohort.

At baseline (Time 1 in Figure 21.1)—before the intervention—the proportion of new victimization cases (out of the total number of subjects) was estimated at 2.6% for the boys and 1.7% for the girls. After the intervention program (Times 2 and 3 in Figure 21.1), corresponding figures were considerably lower, approximately .6% for the boys and .5% for the girls. These results indicate that the intervention program did not only affect already existing victimization problems but also reduced considerably the number of new cases. On the basis of these analyses it can be concluded that the intervention program had both primary and secondary prevention effects (Cowen, 1984). It should be noted that, at Time 1, the new cases estimated in this way constituted approximately 20% of the total number of victimized children.

### Quality of Data and
### Possible Alternative Interpretations

It is beyond the scope of this chapter to discuss in detail the quality of the data collected and the possibility of alternative interpretations of the findings. An extensive discussion of these matters can be found elsewhere (Olweus, 1990). Here I limit myself to summarizing the conclusions in the following statements:

- Self-reports, which were implicated in most of the analyses conducted so far, are in fact the best data source for the purposes of this study.
- It is very difficult to explain the results obtained as a consequence of (a) underreporting by the students, (b) gradual changes in the students' attitudes toward bully/victim problems, (c) repeated measurement, and (d) concomitant changes in other factors. All in all, it is concluded that the reductions in bully/victim and associated problems described above are likely to be mainly a consequence of the intervention program and not of some other "irrelevant" factor.

In addition, a clear "dosage-response" relationship has been established in preliminary analyses at the class level (which is the natural unit of analysis in this case): Those classes that showed larger reductions in bully/victim problems had implemented three presumably essential components of the intervention program (including establishment of class rules against bullying and use of class meetings) to a greater extent than those with smaller changes, $r = .51$, $n = 80$ (additional information on these analyses can be found in Olweus, in press). This finding certainly provides corroborating evidence for the effects of the intervention program. It will be followed up with more systematic and comprehensive analyses.

## Brief Comments

The reported effects of the intervention program must be considered quite positive, particularly because most previous attempts to reduce aggressive and antisocial behavior in preadolescents/adolescents systematically have been relatively unsuccessful (e.g., Dumas, 1989; Gottfredson, 1987; Kazdin, 1987). The importance of the results is also accentuated by the fact that there has occurred a highly disturbing increase in the prevalence of violence and other antisocial behavior in most industrialized societies in the last decades. In the Scandinavian countries, for instance, various forms of registered criminality have typically increased by 300-500% since the 1950s (and these increases cannot, or can only to a very small degree, be explained as a consequence of changes in risk of detection).

As mentioned above, we can estimate that approximately 80,000 students in Norwegian comprehensive schools were involved in bully/victim problems in 1983. On the basis of the results reported here, the following conclusion can be drawn: If all comprehensive schools in Norway used the intervention program in the way it was used in Bergen, the number of students involved in bully/victim problems would be reduced to 40,000 or less in a relatively short period. Effective use of the intervention program would also result in lower levels of theft, vandalism, and other antisocial behavior that would save society large amounts of money.

## Basic Principles

Having reported the main goals and components of the intervention program as well as some of its effects, it is now natural to present its underlying principles and major subgoals. The intervention program is built around a limited set of key principles derived chiefly from research on the development and modification of the implicated problem behaviors, in particular, aggressive behavior. It is considered important to try to create a school (and, ideally, home) environment characterized by warmth, positive interest, and involvement from adults on one hand and firm limits to unacceptable behavior on the other. In cases of violations of limits and rules, nonhostile, nonphysical sanctions should be consistently applied. Implied in the latter two principles is also a certain degree of monitoring and surveillance of the students' activities in and out of school (Patterson, 1986). Finally, adults are supposed to act as authorities, at least in some respects.

The first three of these principles largely represent the opposite of the child-rearing dimensions that I have found in my research to be important in the development of an aggressive personality pattern (Olweus, 1980): negativism on

**Table 21.1** Overview of Measures at School, Class, and Individual Levels

| | Components of the Program Package Against Bullying General Prerequisites: Awareness + Involvement | |
|---|---|---|
| *School Level* | *Class Level* | *Individual Level* |
| Better supervision of recess | Class rules against bullying: | Serious talks with bullies |
| More attractive school | clarification, praise, | and victims |
| playground | and sanctions | Serious talks with parents |
| Contact by telephone | Regular class meetings | of involved children |
| Meeting, staff-parents | Cooperative learning | Teacher use of imagination |
| Teacher groups for the | Meeting, teacher- | Help from "neutral" students |
| development of the | parents/children | Advice to parents |
| "school climate" | Common positive activities | (parent brochure) |
| Parent circles (study | Role playing | "Discussion" groups with |
| and discussion groups) | Literature | parents of bullies and victims |
| | | Change of class or school |

the part of the primary caretaker, permissiveness and lack of clear limits, and use of power-assertive methods. In a sense, the present intervention program is based on an authoritative adult-child interaction, or child-rearing model (see, e.g., Baumrind, 1967) applied to the school setting.

The principles listed above can be translated into a number of specific measures to be used at the school, class, and individual levels. It is considered important to work on all of these levels, if possible. Table 21.1 lists a number of such measures that were recommended in the intervention program (a few of the measures in Table 21.1, including cooperative learning, were not proposed in the original program). Space limitations prevent a detailed description of the various measures suggested, but such an account can be found in a small book designed for teachers and parents (Olweus, 1986; an English version of this book will soon be available—see Olweus, 1991).

With regard to implementation and execution, the program is mainly based on utilization of the existing social environment: teachers and other school personnel, students, and parents. Nonexperts thus play a major role in the desired restructuring of the social environment. Experts such as school psychologists and social workers may also serve important functions as planners and coordinators, in counseling teacher and parent groups, and in handling more serious cases.

## Additional Characteristics

Further understanding of the program and its way of working can be gained from a brief description of four major subgoals:

(1) *To increase awareness of the bully/victim problem and advance knowledge about it,* including to dispel some of the myths about it and its causes. Use of the questionnaire is an important step in obtaining more specific knowledge about the frequency and nature of the problems in a particular school.

(2) *To achieve active involvement on the part of teachers and parents,* which implies among other things that the adults must recognize that it is their responsibility to control to a certain degree what goes on among the children at school. One way of doing this is to provide adequate supervision during recess time. Further, teachers are encouraged to intervene in possible bullying situations and give a clear message to the students: Bullying is not accepted in our school. Teachers are also strongly advised to initiate serious talks with victims and bullies and their parents if a bully/victim problem has been identified in the class. Again, the basic message should be: We will not tolerate bullying in our school and will see to it that it comes to an end. Such an intervention on the part of the school must be regularly followed up and closely supervised, otherwise the situation may easily worsen following the intervention.

(3) *To develop clear rules against bullying behavior,* such as (a) we shall not bully others, (b) we shall try to help students who are bullied, and (c) we shall make it a point to include students who become easily left out. Such a set of rules may serve as a basis for class discussions about what is meant by bullying behavior in concrete situations and what kind of sanctions should be used for students who break the rules. The behavior of the students in the class should be regularly related to these rules in class meetings ("social hour"), and it is important that the teacher make consistent use of sanctions (some form of nonhostile, nonphysical punishment) in cases of rule violations and also give generous praise when the rules have been followed.

(4) *To provide support and protection for the victims.* If followed, class rules against bullying certainly support children who tend to be victimized. In addition, the teacher may enlist the help of "neutral" or well-adjusted students to alleviate the situation of the victims in various ways. Also, teachers are encouraged to use their imagination to help victimized students to assert themselves in class, to make them valuable in the eyes of their classmates. Parents of victims are exhorted to help their children develop new peer contacts and to teach them in detail how to make new acquaintances and to maintain friendship relations.

It may be added that the present intervention program has been evaluated by more than 1,000 Norwegian and Swedish teachers. In short, their reactions have generally been quite favorable, indicating among other things that the teachers see the proposed principles and measures as useful and realistic.

## Conclusion

Though what has been presented in this chapter about the effects of the intervention program represents only the first stages of analysis, the basic message of our findings is clear: It is definitely possible to reduce substantially bully/victim problems in school and related problem behaviors with a suitable intervention program. Thus whether these problems will be tackled or not no longer depends on whether we have the knowledge necessary to achieve desirable changes. It is much more a matter of our willingness to involve ourselves and to use existing knowledge to counteract these problems.

## Notes

1. There is now an (expanded) English version of this questionnaire (one version for grades 1-4, and another for grades 5-9 and higher grades). This questionnaire as well as other materials related to the intervention program (see note 2, below) are copyrighted, which implies certain restrictions on their use. For more details, please write to Dan Olweus, University of Bergen, Oysteinsgate 3, N-5007 Bergen, Norway.

2. The updated "package" related to the intervention program against bully/victim problems consists of the questionnaire for the measurement of bully/victim problems, a copy of a small book, *Bullying: What We Know and What We Can Do* (Olweus, 1986, 1991) aimed at teachers and parents, and a parent folder. (Additional materials are being developed.) These materials are copyrighted, which implies certain restrictions on their use. For more information, please write to the author at the address given in note 1.

## References

Baumrind, D. (1967). Child care practices anteceding three patterns of preschool behavior. *Genetic Psychology Monographs, 75*, 43-88.

Cook, T. D., & Campbell, D. T. (1979). *Quasi-experimentation.* Chicago: Rand McNally.

Cowen, E. L. (1984). A general structural model for primary program development in mental health. *Personnel and Guidance Journal, 62*, 485-490.

Dumas, J. E. (1989). Treating antisocial behavior in children: Child and family approaches. *Clinical Psychology Review, 9*, 197-222.

Gottfredson, G. D. (1987). Peer group interventions to reduce the risk of delinquent behavior: A selective review and a new evaluation. *Criminology, 25*, 187-203.

Kazdin, A. E. (1987). Treatment of antisocial behavior in children: Current status and future directions. *Psychological Bulletin, 102*, 187-203.

Lagerspetz, K. M., Björkqvist, K., Berts, M., & King, E. (1982). Group aggression among school children in three schools. *Scandinavian Journal of Psychology, 23*, 45-52.

Loeber, R., & Dishion, T. (1983). Early predictors of male delinquency: A review. *Psychological Bulletin, 94*, 69-99.

Magnusson, D., Stattin, H. & Dunér, A. (1983). Aggression and criminality in a longitudinal perspective. In K. T. Van Dusen & S. A. Mednick (Eds.), *Prospective studies of crime and delinquency* (pp. 111-122). Boston: Kluwer-Nijhoff.

Manger, T., & Olweus, D. (1985). Tilbakemelding til skulane. *Norsk Skoleblad* (Oslo), *35*, 20-22.

Olweus, D. (1973a). *Hackkycklingar och översittare: Forskning om skol-mobbning.* Stockholm: Almqvist & Wiksell.

Olweus, D. (1973b). Personality and aggression. In J. K. Cole & D. D. Jensen (Eds.), *Nebraska Symposium on Motivation* (Vol. 20, pp. 261-321). Lincoln: University of Nebraska Press.

Olweus, D. (1977). Aggression and peer acceptance in adolescent boys: Two short-term longitudinal studies of ratings. *Child Development, 48*, 1301-1313.

Olweus, D. (1978). *Aggression in the schools: Bullies and whipping boys.* Washington, DC: Hemisphere.

Olweus, D. (1979). Stability of aggressive reaction patterns in males: A review. *Psychological Bulletin, 86*, 852-875.

Olweus, D. (1980). Familial and temperamental determinants of aggressive behavior in adolescent boys: A causal analysis. *Developmental Psychology, 16*, 644-660.

Olweus, D. (1981). Bullying among school boys. In N. Cantwell (Ed.), *Children and violence* (pp. 97-131). Stockholm: Akademilitteratur.

Olweus, D. (1983). Low school achievement and aggressive behavior in adolescent boys. In D. Magnusson & V. Allen (Eds.), *Human development: An interactional perspective* (pp. 353-365). New York: Academic Press.

Olweus, D. (1984). Aggressors and their victims: Bullying at school. In N. Frude & H. Gault (Eds.), *Disruptive behavior in schools* (pp. 57-76). New York: John Wiley.

Olweus, D. (1985). 80 000 barn er innblandet i mobbing. *Norsk Skoleblad* (Oslo), *35*, 18-23.

Olweus, D. (1986). *Mobbning—vad vi vet och vad vi kan göra?* Stockholm: Liber.

Olweus, D. (1987). Bully/victim problems among schoolchildren. In J. P. Myklebust & R. Ommundsen (Eds.), *Psykologprofesjonen mot år 2000* (pp. 395-413). Oslo: Universitetsforlaget.

Olweus, D. (1989). Prevalence and incidence in the study of antisocial behavior: Definitions and measurement. In M. Klein (Ed.), *Cross-national research in self-reported crime and delinquency* (pp. 187-201). Dordrecht: Kluwer.

Olweus, D. (1990). Bully/victim problems among school children: Basic facts and effects of a school based intervention program. In K. Rubin & D. Pepler (Eds.), *The development and treatment of childhood aggression* (pp. 411-448). Hillsdale, NJ: Lawrence Erlbaum.

Olweus, D. (1991). *Bullying: What we know and what we can do.* Unpublished manuscript.

Olweus, D. (in press). Assessing change in a cohort longitudinal study with hierarchical data. In D. Magnusson, L. Bergman, G. Rudinger, & B. Törestad (Eds.), *Matching problems and methods in longitudinal research.* New York: Cambridge University Press.

Olweus, D., & Roland, E. (1983). *Mobbing—bakgrunn og tiltak.* Oslo: Kirke-og undevisningsdepartementet.

Patterson, G. R. (1986). Performance models for antisocial boys. *American Psychologist, 41*, 432-444.

Perry, D. G., Kusel, S. J., & Perry, L. C. (1988). Victims of peer aggression. *Developmental Psychology, 24*, 807-814.

Smith, P. (1989). *The silent nightmare: Bullying and victimization in school peer groups.* Paper presented at the annual meeting of the British Psychological Society, London.

**22**

# New Directions in Research in the Prevention of Conduct Disorder

**Doreen Spilton Koretz**
**Joyce Barham Lazar**

Persistent and serious conduct problems during childhood that extend into adolescence and early adulthood present a major and costly problem for society. Many children show antisocial behaviors at one time or another in their lives, but usually these are temporary behaviors that decline over time. To be classified as a conduct disorder, a pattern of behavior must be established that is persistent and in which social rules and the rights of others are violated at a high rate. Among younger children the behaviors typically include aggression and cruelty, lying, stealing, and destroying property; when the behaviors extend into adolescence and adulthood they often include alcohol and other drug abuse, delinquency, and crime. When severe antisocial behaviors persist and create interpersonal problems with the individual's family, peers, teachers, and community, they are clearly dysfunctional and have clinical and social significance.

These behavioral problems may have precursors in the preschool years, but they do not become fully apparent until later in childhood and adolescence (Institute of Medicine, 1989). While not all children with conduct disorder eventually come to the attention of the criminal justice system, many do. The persistence of these antisocial behaviors is such that about half of all clinically identified antisocial youngsters become antisocial adults (Robins, 1970).

### Significance of the Problem

The behaviors classified under the rubric of conduct disorder are frequent and widespread in the United States. A recent report on the mental health of American children notes that the estimated nationwide prevalence of conduct

AUTHORS' NOTE: The opinions expressed in this chapter are those of the authors and do not necessarily reflect the support or endorsement of the National Institute of Mental Health; the Alcohol, Drug Abuse, and Mental Health Administration; or the Public Health Service.

disorder ranges from 2% to 6%, or up to 1.8 million children (Institute of Medicine, 1989). While most of the children with behavior problems do not receive any treatment, about half of all children and youth who are referred to the mental health system manifest these antisocial behaviors. Longitudinal studies have shown that in adulthood, such children have much higher rates of alcohol and other drug abuse, criminal behaviors, poor marital and work adjustment, as well as other psychiatric disorders (Robins, 1978). The economic and emotional costs to the individual, the family, and the society are high.

The significance of the problem is intensified by the fact that available treatments have not been highly successful, thus increasing the importance of prevention (Kazdin, 1990). If the goal of preventing this (or any disorder) is to be attained, it is important to identify the factors that put people at risk for the disorder. Only then can preventive efforts be undertaken to deal with those risk factors that are modifiable.

**Who Are Those Most at Risk?**

A considerable body of research has focused on the characteristics of children and youth with antisocial behavior in community settings, in clinical settings, and within the criminal justice system (Ensminger, Kellam, & Rubin, 1981; Loeber, 1990; Robins, 1966). A large number of individual, family, and psychosocial factors have been identified as risk factors for conduct disorder (e.g., see review by Offord, 1989).

On an individual level, boys are more than twice as likely than girls to exhibit antisocial behavior, particularly at the younger ages (e.g., Offord, Adler, & Boyle, 1986). Children with chronic physical illness, brain damage, and learning disorders also have more than twice the risk of other children (e.g., Rutter, Tizzard, & Whitmore, 1970). While differences between racial groups have been found (e.g., Elliott & Ageton, 1980), it is unclear how much of these differences may be accounted for by variations in income, neighborhoods, and schools. Characteristics of the temperament of the child also have been associated with the emergence of antisocial behavior (e.g., Farrington, 1986), particularly since there is so much overlap between conduct disorder and hyperactivity.

Within the family both genetic and environmental factors are important influences on children's development. Genetic versus environmental effects are frequently studied, either by comparing identical twins with fraternal twins or by studying children who were separated from their biological parents at birth. Such studies have shown a greater concordance of criminal and antisocial behavior among identical twins than fraternal twins (e.g., Mednick, Moffit, Gabrielle, & Hutchings, 1986). Similarly, this research has found that children separated at birth from criminal and antisocial parents are more likely to exhibit such behaviors than are children whose biological parents do not. However, genetic factors alone are not sufficient to account for the emergence of antisocial behaviors.

In a review of the literature, Offord (1989) reports numerous findings on family environmental effects that manifest themselves in numerous and often interrelated ways. The factors he reviews include socioeconomic status of the family, marital status of the parents, number of children and others in the family, extent of crowding in the home, and child-rearing practices. All have been found to have influence on rates of conduct disorder. Rates are higher among children in lower socioeconomic groups, in particular neighborhoods, in families in which there is a high level of discord, where there is overcrowding in the home, and when the family size is large (e.g., Offord et al., 1986; Rutter et al., 1970). Criminal behavior, alcoholism, and other drug abuse by one or both parents are factors highly related to dysfunction in the children (Farrington, Osborn, & West, 1981; Lewis & Balla, 1976). Parental supervision, guidance, and punishment have been found consistently to be related to antisocial behavior (e.g., Patterson, 1982).

It has been known for many decades that conduct disorder and delinquency are far more frequent in certain communities, particularly in inner cities (e.g., Rutter, Cox, Tupling, Berger, & Yule, 1975). The conditions of poverty that prevail in inner cities overlap with factors in children's homes and peer groups. Many studies have found, however, that children in inner cities are no more at risk than other children when there is a stable, supporting family environment (e.g., see Offord, 1989).

The school setting is a major factor in children's lives and has been studied as contributing to the risk of conduct disorder. The physical condition of the school, teacher-pupil ratio, amount of time spent on academics, and teacher use of praise, as well as peer acceptance and rejection, all have been associated with rates of conduct problems (Rutter, Maughan, Mortimore, & Ouston, 1979; Wadsworth, 1979).

## Protective Factors

Given that not all at-risk children develop the disorder, it is important to examine the characteristics of those who appear to have a high level of resistance to negative influences (Masten & Garmezy, 1985; Rutter & Giller, 1983). While protective factors have not been studied as extensively as risk factors, a number of factors have been suggested that may serve to protect youngsters in high-risk environments. These include a positive relationship with a parent or other adult role model, nondelinquent peer group activities, a high level of cognitive achievement, and the acquisition of appropriate social skills (Jones & Offord, 1989; Spivack & Shure, 1974). Research has shown that it is possible to improve cognitive and behavioral skills (e.g., Dolan et al., 1990), and current research is examining whether such improved skills serve to improve children's psychosocial adjustment and prevent disorder.

## Intervention Strategies

In an effort to prevent conduct disorder, investigators have developed interventions aimed at reducing or eliminating malleable factors known (from the epidemiological and basic research literatures) to place individuals at risk. Child- and family-level risk factors have been the primary targets of these studies, with some efforts also aimed at community-level interventions (see Kazdin, 1990, for a review). Underlying all of these interventions has been the assumption that the targeted risk factor(s) plays some causal role in the development of conduct disorder, and that changing an individual's risk factor status will, in fact, reduce his or her probability of developing the full-blown disorder. In addition to providing a test of the efficacy of a particular intervention strategy, well-designed intervention studies also provide an experimental test of these causal assumptions. The testing of presumed causal mechanisms is an important and unique feature of prevention research that greatly enhances scientific knowledge about the etiology of disorders.

### Child-Focused Interventions

Child-focused interventions often are delivered within the school setting, and typically have been concerned with aggressive behavior or other aspects of poor peer relations, or with academic performance.

*Peer relations.* As noted by Bierman (1990) and Coie (1990), interventions concerned with the role of poor peer relations have focused on individual skills, dyadic interactions, or larger group processes. Increasingly, the field has moved toward integrating all three foci because of the difficulty in achieving real and sustained changes in peer group perceptions and acceptance of high-risk children through the use of a single intervention strategy (see, e.g., Coie, Underwood, & Lochman, 1989).

Skill-building interventions include those aimed at behaviors such as aggression (e.g., Bierman, 1989; Bierman, Miller, & Stabb, 1987; Dolan et al., 1990), at social cognitions such as social problem solving (e.g., Lochman, 1985; Shure & Spivack, 1982), and at emotional regulation such as anger control and self-control (e.g., Lochman & Curry, 1986). The goal of these interventions has been to compensate for deficits in social skills, or to foster prosocial competencies and cognitive strategies incompatible with antisocial behaviors associated with conduct disorder.

Although social skill interventions have been dominant in prevention research aimed at child-level risk factors, there has been increasing recognition that the social interaction patterns generated by these children need to be targeted as well. As noted by Bierman (1990), high-risk peer-rejected children not only engage in high rates of negative behaviors, but also create negative interaction patterns that often escalate over time (e.g., Dodge & Coie, 1987); recent studies suggest that these interaction patterns are generated not only with the existing peer group, but in new peer settings as well (e.g., Coie & Kupersmidt, 1983). As a result, a few intervention strategies have incorporated the use of contingency management approaches to prevent negative escalation in dyads or groups. As with social skills, these efforts, while sometimes successful in curtailing negative escalations (e.g., Bierman et al., 1987), may not result in changes in peer relations or peer perceptions of high-risk children because of generalized negative social expectations and attitudes that do not change easily, even in the face of changed behavior (e.g., Dodge & Frame, 1982; LaGreca & Santogrossi, 1980; Whitehall, Hersen, & Bellack, 1980).

Attempts to intervene with group processes affecting these attitudes and expectations are less well represented in current research efforts. Examples include manipulation of group composition to give low-risk peers opportunity to interact positively with high-risk children (Bierman, 1986; Bierman & Furman, 1984), as well as the use of games requiring ongoing peer cooperation to achieve superordinate goals (Dolan et al., 1990; Sherif, Harvey, White, Hood, & Sherif, 1961).

*Academic performance.* Poor academic performance has been correlated with aggressive behavior in many studies (e.g., Eron, Huesmann, Dubow, Romanoff, & Yarmel, 1987; Farrington, 1979; Hawkins & Lishner, 1987). Recent data suggest that deficits in cognitive functioning at age 7 may be causally related to conduct disorder at age 17 in black males (Schonfeld, Shaffer, O'Conner, & Portnoy, 1988). Because of these linkages, investigators have attempted to bolster the academic/cognitive functioning of young school-age children in an effort to improve later behavioral and psychiatric outcomes. As with the social skill area, a variety of intervention strategies have been studied, including variations on teacher-implemented mastery learning approaches (Dolan, 1986; Dolan et al., 1990) and tutoring (e.g., Coie & Krehbiel, 1984). Interestingly, investigators using both approaches have begun to incorporate more active parental involvement in order to consolidate academic gains through ongoing parental support and improved school-home communication and monitoring of child activities (Blechman, Kotanchik, & Taylor, 1981; Blechman, Taylor, & Schrader, 1981; Epstein, 1983; Stevenson & Baker, 1987).

### Family-Focused Interventions

As previously noted, a considerable body of evidence indicates that family structure and function are important in the development and maintenance of persistent behavior problems among children and adolescents. Some variables such as large family size and parental deviance (including criminality among fathers and mental illness among mothers) are found much more frequently among delinquent youth than among matched families, but these factors are difficult to affect through intervention efforts.

Other risks, including high marital discord and dysfunctional family interactional patterns, are pervasive among families of children with persistent behavior problems (Hetherington & Martin, 1986; Loeber & Dishion, 1983; Patterson, 1982, 1986) and may be more amenable to preventive interventions. Family therapy studies have helped identify some of the parent behaviors associated with oppositional behavior in children. In particular, poor parental supervision; harsh, inconsistent discipline; and extended coercive exchanges have been found to be parental behavioral variables most predictive of antisocial behavior (e.g., Reid & Patterson, 1989).

Programs to reduce severe conduct problems and delinquent behavior through effecting change in parental behavior are not new, though such efforts have peaked and diminished throughout the years. Teaching parenting skills has been a goal in many research projects as well as in social programs sponsored by the federal government, first by the Children's Bureau, later in the parent participation programs within Head Start, and most recently in the programs of the Office of Substance Abuse Prevention of the Alcohol, Drug Abuse and Mental Health Administration. A variety of preventive interventions have been attempted, some based on broad theoretical orientations and others atheoretical. While only a few have been well-controlled studies, a number of these do indicate progress, including prenatal education of young or economically disadvantaged mothers (Lally, Mangione, & Honig, 1988; Provence & Naylor, 1983), preschool educational programs involving parents (Weikart & Schweinhart, 1987), and family therapy (Alexander & Parsons, 1973). The diversity of interventions attempted could be expected given the diversity of risk factors for antisocial behavior.

In recent years a number of more rigorous attempts have been undertaken to prevent conduct disorder through family intervention. These include increased screening to identify those families at highest risk, the greater specificity of the particular parental behaviors to be changed, and expansion of family skills interventions into other domains. Family skills training programs have been developed and assessed by Patterson, Chamberlain, and Reid (1982), Webster-Stratton, Hollingsworth, and Kopacoff (1989), Miller and Prinz (in press), and Blechman (1985), among others.

A successful treatment intervention approach developed by Patterson and his associates (1982) at the Oregon Social Learning Center (OSLC) aimed at teaching family management skills to promote child social adjustment has been expanded to provide an integrated program aimed at families identified as being at very high risk. These family interventions are being linked with efforts to increase parental involvement in the children's schoolwork and activities. Both the theory and the prevention programs that are being evaluated are based on the central assumption that the early development of conduct disorder is embedded in the interaction between parent and child, particularly as it relates to oppositional and aggressive behavior and how the parents provide supervision and

support when the child makes the transition into school and peer groups. Further, once problem behaviors become established in the child, they are carried over into school and peer situations, so that even when the child moves to a new out-of-home situation, the problem behavior quickly reappears in the new setting. Interventions will be conducted with the target children and their parents, teachers, and peers. One set of interventions will take place in the first grade and another in the fifth grade. OSLC's current efforts are aimed at changing existing norms that may inhibit parental involvement in the schools and at increasing parental monitoring of home and out-of-home behavior of the children. For example, parents will be encouraged through a telephone hot line to get information about the daily school activities of their children and to ask their children specific questions about these activities. Outcome measures targeted for change include such parental behaviors as negative commands, disapproval, threatening, humiliating, yelling, hitting, and negativism; for the children, behaviors include crying, noncompliance, destructiveness, teasing, whining, and hitting.

Many other family interventions have been expanded to include efforts to change behavior in several domains. Blechman (1985) has used family skills training with classroom interventions using a "good behavior" game and a "home-note system" to modify classroom behavior, in separate studies and with different at-risk populations. Hawkins and his colleagues are also integrating interventions across family, child, and home domains in order to foster increased prosocial bonding (see, e.g., Hawkins & Lam, 1987). Their interventions have included classroom management of disruptive behavior, cooperative learning strategies, parent behavior management training, child social skills training, and community-based activities. Ongoing work by Kellam and his colleagues at Johns Hopkins University is now moving beyond classroom-based interventions aimed at poor academic performance and shy and aggressive behavior to include family-oriented strategies aimed at the same target behaviors and designed to support and integrate with the classroom-based interventions.

## NIMH Activities

Because of the individual and social costs associated with conduct disorder and related sequelae, the National Institute of Mental Health (NIMH) has supported an array of capacity-building and research activities aimed at the development of effective preventive interventions in this area. These activities include (a) identification of research on the prevention of conduct disorder as an area of high priority for the Prevention Research Branch, with sponsorship of a research working group concerned with the prevention of conduct disorder in high-risk populations; (b) solicitation and funding of a new Preventive Intervention Research Center aimed at conduct disorder; (c) commissioning of a state-of-the-art paper on the prevention of conduct disorder in order to stimulate the field and identify promising areas for future research; and (d) development of a request for applications in 1990 for Prevention Services Research Demonstration Grants for the prevention of serious and chronic conduct problems.

The ongoing research working group has involved a core of senior prevention researchers interested in conduct disorder who have met annually for several years in order to discuss existing models of the etiology and development of conduct disorder, as well as cross-cutting methodological and measurement issues. The goal of this effort has been to develop an integrated framework to help identify intervention strategies and appropriate settings for interventions during childhood and preadolescence. A secondary goal has been to encourage the use of common measures across research sites. The working group should help to move prevention research toward more of a chronic illness view of conduct disorder, and away from the current acute illness conceptualization that does not accurately reflect clinical understanding of the disorder (Kazdin, 1987).

The new Preventive Intervention Research Center (PIRC) aimed at conduct disorder is located at the Oregon Social Learning Center. This PIRC is based on 20 years of research and model development regarding the importance of how parents deal with their children's oppositional and aggressive behaviors and how they provide supervision and support during transitions into school and peer groups. Interventions will focus on multiple domains of risk, including parenting, school-home liaison, and child skills development (social and academic). (The work of this center is described above in the section on family interventions.)

As part of a broad examination of the state of prevention research, NIMH has commissioned a review by Alan Kazdin, Ph.D., an outstanding clinical researcher who has devoted his career to the area of conduct disorder. This state-of-the-art paper provides a description of conduct disorder, identifies risk and protective factors across a variety of ecological domains (child, family, school, and so on), reviews relevant theories about the development of conduct disorder, provides an assessment of the findings of preventive intervention studies, and discusses major issues and obstacles to prevention research in this area (Kazdin, 1990). In an effort to inform the field and stimulate a new generation of prevention studies in this area, NIMH intends to distribute this paper widely.

Finally, congressional action mandated that NIMH implement a new prevention demonstration program in fiscal year 1990. Because of the readiness of the field to undertake such work, the institute selected the prevention of serious and chronic conduct problems as a major initial focus for this research demonstration effort. As noted above, basic and epidemiological studies in this area suggest the existence of an etiological model involving a range of risk factors and mediators that persist over time and that span several domains—individual, family, peer, school, and community. Until recently, however, experimentally tested interventions have been aimed at single risk factors or developmental periods and, accordingly, have shown promising immediate effects that are only modest in size, and that often dissipate over time as intervention effects erode and new risk factors or conditions become salient. To overcome the limitations of these early efforts at prevention, the intervention packages implemented by the new research demonstrations begin early in childhood, take place over long periods of time, involve multiple components addressing multiple risk factors or mediators, and are intensive in nature. These characteristics should maximize the likelihood of long-term and significant preventive effects in these projects.

## References

Alexander, J., & Parsons, B. (1973). Short-term behavioral intervention with delinquent families: Impact on family process and recidivism. *Journal of Abnormal Psychology, 81*, 219-225.

Bierman, K. (1986). Process of change during social skills training with preadolescents and its relationship to treatment outcomes. *Child Development, 57*, 230-240.

Bierman, K. (1989). Improving the peer relationships of rejected children. In B. Lahey & A. Kazdin (Eds.), *Advances in clinical child psychology* (Vol. 12, pp. 53-84). New York: Plenum.

Bierman, K. (1990, June). *Social skills training with aggressive rejected children.* Paper presented at the Vermont Conference on the Primary Prevention of Psychopathology, Burlington.

Bierman, K., & Furman, W. (1984). The effects of social skills training and peer involvement on the social adjustment of preadolescents. *Child Development, 55*, 151-162.

Bierman, K., Miller, C., & Stabb, S. (1987). Improving the social behavior and peer acceptance of rejected boys: Effects of social skill training with instructions and prohibitions. *Journal of Consulting and Clinical Psychology, 55*, 194-200.

Blechman, E. (1985). *Solving childhood behavior problems at home and at school.* Champaign, IL: Research Press.

Blechman, E., Kotanchik, N., & Taylor, C. (1981). Families and schools together: Early behavioral intervention with high risk students. *Behavior Therapy, 12*, 308-319.

Blechman, E., Taylor, C., & Schrader, S. (1981). Family problem solving vs. home notes as early intervention with high risk children. *Journal of Consulting and Clinical Psychology, 49*, 919-926.

Coie, J. (1990, June). *Strategies for intervention with high risk aggressive children.* Paper presented at the Vermont Conference on the Primary Prevention of Psychopathology, Burlington.

Coie, J., & Krehbiel, G. (1984). Effects of academic tutoring on the social status of low-achieving, socially rejected children. *Child Development, 55*, 1465-1478.

Coie, J., & Kupersmidt, J. (1983). A behavioral analysis of emerging social status in boys' groups. *Child Development, 54*, 1400-1416.

Coie, J., Underwood, M., & Lochman, J. (1989). Programmatic intervention with aggressive children in the school setting. In D. Pepler & K. Rubin (Eds.), *The development and treatment of childhood aggression* (pp. 389-410). Toronto: Lawrence Erlbaum.

Dodge, K., & Coie, J. (1987). Social information processing factors in reactive and proactive aggression in children's peer groups. *Journal of Personality and Social Psychology, 53*, 1146-1158.

Dodge, K., & Frame, C. (1982). Social cognitive biases and deficits in aggressive boys. *Child Development, 53*, 620-635.

Dolan, L. (1986). Mastery learning as a preventive strategy. *Outcomes, 5*, 20-27.

Dolan, L., Kellam, S., Brown, C., Rebok, G., Mayer, L., Laudolff, J., Ford, C., & Wheeler, L. (1990). *Short term impact of a mastery learning preventive intervention on early risk behaviors.* Unpublished manuscript.

Elliott, D., & Ageton, S. (1980). Reconciling race and class differences in self-reported and official estimates of delinquency. *American Sociological Review, 45,* 95-110.

Ensminger, M., Kellam, S., & Rubin, B. (1981). School and family origins of delinquency: Comparisons by sex. In S. Mednick & K. Van Dusen (Eds.), *Antecedents of antisocial behavior* (pp. 75-97). Cambridge, MA: Nijhoff.

Epstein, J. (1983). Longitudinal effect of family-school-person interactions on students' outcomes. *Research in Sociology of Education and Socialization, 4,* 101-127.

Eron, L., Huesmann, L., Dubow, E., Romanoff, R., & Yarmel, P. (1987). Aggression and its correlates over 22 years. In D. Crowell, I. Evans, & C. O'Donnell (Eds.), *Childhood aggression and violence: Sources of influence, prevention, and control* (pp. 249-262). New York: Plenum.

Farrington, D. (1979). Longitudinal research on crime and delinquency. In N. Morris & M. Tonry (Eds.), *Crime and justice: An annual review of research* (pp. 289-348). Chicago: University of Chicago Press.

Farrington, D. (1986). Stepping stones to adult criminal careers. In D. Olweus, J. Block, & M. Yarrow (Eds.), *Development of antisocial and prosocial behavior* (pp. 359-384). New York: Academic Press.

Farrington, D., Osborn, S., & West, D. (1981). The Cambridge study in delinquent development (United Kingdom). In S. Mednick & A. Baert (Eds.), *Prospective longitudinal research: An empirical basis for the primary prevention of psychosocial disorders* (pp. 137-145). New York: Oxford University Press.

Hawkins, J., & Lam, T. (1987). Teacher practices, social development and delinquency. In J. Burchard & S. Burchard (Eds.), *The prevention of delinquent behavior* (pp. 241-274). Newbury Park, CA: Sage.

Hawkins, J., & Lishner, D. (1987). Etiology and prevention of antisocial behavior in children and adolescents. In D. Crowell, I. Evans, & C. O'Donnell (Eds.), *Childhood aggression and violence: Sources of influence, prevention, and control* (pp. 263-282). New York: Plenum.

Hetherington, E., & Martin, B. (1986). Family factors and psychopathology in children. In H. Quay & J. Werry (Eds.), *Psychopathological disorders of childhood* (3rd ed., pp. 332-390). New York: John Wiley.

Institute of Medicine. (1989). *Research on children and on adolescents with mental, behavioral and developmental disorders; Report by the Division of Mental and Behavioral Medicine.* Washington, DC: National Academy Press.

Jones, M., & Offord, D. (1989). *Prevention of antisocial behavior in poor children by nonschool skill development.* Unpublished manuscript.

Kazdin, A. (1987). *Conduct disorder in childhood and adolescence.* Newbury Park, CA: Sage.

Kazdin, A. (1990, June). *Prevention of conduct disorder.* Paper presented at the National Conference on Prevention Research, National Institute of Mental Health, Bethesda, MD.

LaGreca, A., & Santogrossi, D. (1980). Social skills training with elementary school students: A behavioral group approach. *Journal of Consulting and Clinical Psychology, 48,* 220-227.

Lally, R., Mangione, P., & Honig, A. (1988). The Syracuse University Development Research Program: Long-range impact on an early intervention with low-income children and their families. In D. Powell (Ed.), *Parent education as early childhood intervention: Emerging directions in theory, research, and practice* (pp. 79-104). Norwood, NJ: Ablex.

Lewis, D., & Balla, D. (1976). *Delinquency and psychopathology.* New York: Grune & Stratton.

Lochman, J. (1985). Effects of different treatment lengths in cognitive-behavioral interventions with aggressive boys. *Child Psychiatry and Human Development, 16,* 45-56.

Lochman, J., & Curry, J. (1986). Effects of social problem solving training and self instruction training with aggressive boys. *Journal of Clinical Child Psychology, 15*, 159-164.

Loeber, R. (1990). Development and risk factors of juvenile antisocial behavior and delinquency. *Clinical Psychology Review, 10*, 1-42.

Loeber, R., & Dishion, T. (1983). Early predictors of male delinquency: A review. *Psychological Bulletin, 94*, 68-99.

Masten, A., & Garmezy, N. (1985). Risk vulnerability and protective factors in developmental psychopathology. In B. Lahey & A. Kazdin (Eds.), *Advances in clinical child psychology* (Vol. 8, pp. 1-52). New York: Plenum.

Mednick, S., Moffitt, T., Gabrielle, W., Jr., & Hutchings, G. (1986). Genetic factors in criminal behavior: A review. In D. Olweus, J. Block, & M. Radke-Yarrow (Eds.), *Development of antisocial and prosocial behavior: Research theories and issues* (pp. 33-50). New York: Academic Press.

Miller, G., & Prinz, R. (in press). The enhancement of social learning family interventions for childhood conduct disorder. *Psychological Bulletin.*

Offord, D. (1989). Conduct disorder: Risk factors and prevention. In D. Shaffer, I. Philips, & N. Enzer (Eds.), *Prevention of mental disorders, alcohol and other drug use in children and adolescents* (OSAP Prevention Monograph No. 2) (pp. 273-307). Rockville, MD: National Institute of Mental Health.

Offord, D., Adler, R., & Boyle, M. (1986). Prevalence and sociodemographic correlates of conduct disorder. *American Journal of Social Psychiatry, 6*, 272-278.

Patterson, G. (1982). *Coercive family process.* Eugene, OR: Castalia.

Patterson, G. (1986). Performance models for antisocial boys. *American Psychologist, 41*, 432-444.

Patterson, G., Chamberlain, P., & Reid, J. (1982). A comparative evaluation of a parent-training program. *Behavior Therapy, 13*, 638-651.

Provence, S., & Naylor, A. (1983). *Working with disadvantaged parents and children: Scientific issues and practice.* New Haven, CT: Yale University Press.

Reid, J., & Patterson, G. (1989). The development of antisocial behavior patterns in childhood and adolescence. *European Journal of Personality, 3*, 107-119.

Robins, L. (1966). *Deviant children grown up.* Baltimore: Williams & Wilkins.

Robins, L. (1970). The adult development of the antisocial child. *Seminars in Psychiatry, 6*, 420-434.

Robins, L. (1978). Sturdy childhood predictors of adult anti-social behavior: Replications from longitudinal studies. *Psychological Medicine, 8*, 611-622.

Rutter, M., Cox, A., Tupling, C., Berger, M., & Yule, W. (1975). Attainment and adjustment in two geographical areas: 1. The prevalence of psychiatric disorder. *British Journal of Psychiatry, 126*, 493-509.

Rutter, M., & Giller, H. (1983). *Juvenile delinquency: Trends and prospectives.* New York: Penguin.

Rutter, M., Maughan, B., Mortimore, P., & Ouston, J. (1979). *Fifteen thousand hours: Secondary schools and their effect on children.* Cambridge, MA: Harvard University Press.

Rutter, M., Tizzard, J., & Whitmore, K. (1970). *Education, health and behavior.* London: Longman.

Schonfeld, I., Shaffer, D., O'Connor, P., & Portnoy, S. (1988). Conduct disorder and cognitive functioning: Testing three causal hypotheses. *Child Development, 59*, 993-1007.

Sherif, M., Harvey, O., White, B., Hood, W., & Sherif, C. (1961). *Intergroup conflict and cooperation.* Norman: University of Oklahoma Press.

Shure, M., & Spivack, G. (1982). Interpersonal problem solving in young children: A cognitive approach to prevention. *American Journal of Community Psychology, 10*, 341-356.

Spivack, G., & Shure, M. (1974). *Social adjustment of young children: A cognitive approach to solving real-life problems.* San Francisco: Jossey-Bass.

Stevenson, D., & Baker, D. (1987). The family-school relationship and the child's school performance. *Child Development, 58,* 1348-1357.

Wadsworth, M. (1979). *Roots of delinquency: Infancy, adolescence and crime.* Maryland: Barnes & Noble.

Webster-Stratton, C., Hollingsworth, T., & Kopacoff, M. (1989). The long-term effectiveness of three cost-effective training programs for families with conduct-problem children. *Journal of Consulting and Clinical Psychology, 57,* 550-553.

Weikart, D., & Schweinhart, L. (1987). The High/Scope cognitively oriented curriculum in early education. In J. Roopnarine & J. Johnson (Eds.), *Approaches to early childhood education* (pp. 253-268). Columbus, OH: Charles E. Merrill.

Whitehall, M., Hersen, M., & Bellack, A. (1980). Conversation skills training for socially isolated children. *Behavior Research and Therapy, 18,* 217-225.

# PART VI

# Reflections on Youth

The status of children's lives around the world can appear overwhelming in the urgency and complexity of the needs and challenges presented. Ambitious and creative efforts have been initiated to grapple with these issues. Yet we must continue to consider the broad conceptual, attitudinal, and organizational problems that underlie the current situation of youth. We invited a number of leading figures, scholars, and policymakers to reflect on some of the issues involved in current international problems affecting infants, children, and youth. These chapters take the form primarily of essays on broad topics affecting large numbers of children—reflections on youth.

George W. Albee is professor of psychology at the University of Vermont and president of the Vermont Conference on the Primary Prevention of Psychopathology. Chapter 23 is an expanded version of his Georgia Adams Memorial Lecture delivered in Halifax, Nova Scotia, Canada, June 3, 1989, and published as "Suffer the Little Children" in the *Journal of Primary Prevention* (1990, Vol. 11, pp. 69-82).

In Chapter 24, Kenneth B. Clark is critical of the educational system for not taking a strong stand on the epidemic of racism. Clark has been a lifelong opponent of every form of racism and discrimination and a strong supporter of integration. A distinguished professor emeritus of psychology at City College of the City University of New York, Clark helped formulate the social science evidence of the devastating consequences of racism on black children in a brief to the U.S. Supreme Court in the 1954 case *Brown v. Board of Education*. As a result of this case, the schools in the United States were ordered to develop and implement plans for desegregation. Now, some 37 years later, Clark shares his pessimistic view about the lack of major progress in racial integration. He faults the educational system, especially colleges and universities, and challenges educators to make major efforts to reduce racism and to teach tolerance and integration.

John A. Calhoun, M.P.A., M.Div., is a national figure in the area of child advocacy. He is the executive director of the U.S. National Crime Prevention Council, and has served as the commissioner of the Administration for Children, Youth and Families, and as chief of the Children's Bureau. In Chapter 25, he suggests a new paradigm be used in working with youth, one that considers youth as resources rather than as problems. He cites sobering statistics regarding teen substance abuse, murder, high school dropout, pregnancy, suicide, and victimization. By providing examples from the Minnesota Youth Poll (1985) and social policy regarding youth, he demonstrates that prevailing attitudes and policies toward teens in the United States are negative. Calhoun points out that if we are to affect the lives of youth we must shift our policies and perspectives, as an approach that relies only on a pathological model will not work. By considering youth as resources, he states, we can do something we do not usually do, which is to ask something of them in return. Calhoun believes, and presents a convincing case, that society must instill a sense of the value of service and obligation to others in youth, insisting on reciprocity rather than merely on punishment.

Michael Dorris is a well-known writer and novelist. He was, for a time, actively involved in the Native American Studies Program at Dartmouth College, where he continues to have a teaching appointment as adjunct professor of anthropology. His book *The Broken Cord* is an autobiographical account of his experience in adopting and raising a Native American child who, it turned out, had been severely damaged by fetal alcohol syndrome. Dorris is devoting significant efforts to warning others, through his writing and speaking, of the dangers of ingesting alcohol during pregnancy. Here he provides a personal and passionate essay regarding his experiences raising his children, three of whom are fetal alcohol affected, and the need for preventing fetal alcohol syndrome worldwide.

The final chapter of this section offers reflections on the status of adolescents in Mexico. Author Beatriz Rivera de Tarrab is director of, and authors Patricia Ortega-Andeane and Jorge Manuel Velasco-Alzaga are advisers to, the Division of Support to States of Mexico of the National System for the Comprehensive Development of the Family. They note that the problems of rapid population growth have led to increasing difficulty for Mexico in caring for its youth. In attempting to understand more fully the challenges of this situation, they have conducted a major survey designed to identify the needs, interests, and habits of Mexican adolescents. Data have been collected and analyzed from some 3,000 youths, including a substantial sample of adolescents living on the streets. While the results of their survey point to some of the distinctions between street youth and those who are living at home, the common needs for friendship, support, and help among both groups are clear.

# 23

# Saving Children
# Means Social Revolution

## George W. Albee

This year, and for many years in the past and many years in the future, some 14 million of the world's children will die before the age of 5. A very large proportion of these deaths are preventable. Approximately 3 million children die of dehydration due to diarrhea, and another 3 million die of preventable infectious diseases. Others starve or die of malnutrition-related infections. At a very modest cost, oral rehydration therapy could save the lives of the first group, and relatively inexpensive vaccination against the five major diseases of childhood could save many of the rest. Diarrhea could be eliminated or greatly reduced by ensuring safe water supplies throughout the world. This would require a modest investment by nations that care; unfortunately, too few care. A small part of the money the world has budgeted for military weapons could save the majority of these doomed children as well as their brothers and sisters who grow up undernourished with underdeveloped bodies and minds. But there is money to be made in manufacturing weapons—enormous sums of money. Contractor corporations—sometimes called Merchants of Death—make huge profits, as do their stockholders and managers. So millions of little children suffer and die, and other millions of little children suffer and live.

Many of the messages and actions that we display publicly about children are a kind of double bind—contrary and contradictory. We talk about how much we love children, about how much we hate child abuse and neglect. At the same time, we fail to fund schools adequately and we fail to enforce laws against child abuse. We defend the rights of parents to strike children; the U.S. Supreme Court upholds the right of teachers to spank school kids. We shed a tear at pictures of starving children in Central America, in Ethiopia or Bangladesh (or in

AUTHOR'S NOTE: This chapter was originally presented as the invited Georgia Adams Memorial Address to the International Council of Psychologists, in Halifax, Nova Scotia, Canada, June 3, 1989. A revised version titled "Suffer the Little Children" was published in the *Journal of Primary Prevention* (1990, Vol. 11, No. 1, pp. 69-82). This revised and expanded version is published by permission of Human Sciences Press.

Bedford-Stuyvesant, New York), and then we vote down or fail to support humanitarian aid for countries whose governments we disapprove.

We hear frightening statistics about the horror of children's lives and then we quickly forget or repress them. Looking ahead, the future for most of the world's children is bleak indeed. Some 40% of the population in developing nations (a term applied to "Third World" countries, most of which were, until recently, exploited colonies) are under the age of 15, which means that this huge mass of children is about to enter their most fertile childbearing years.

The world's population, right now, has passed 5 billion, but 30 years from now between 6 and 8 billion people will live in just Asia and Africa. Right now there are 100 million people living in Central America, most of them in poverty. Between the Rio Grande and the Isthmus of Panama this 100 million will grow to 225 million by the year 2025. The population of Africa will *triple* in the next 35 years. In country after country, outside the industrialized nations, population growth is massive, and the ones who suffer the most are women and children.

Some of us cherish the memory of Abraham Lincoln and as children learned many of his wise sayings. "A nation cannot exist half slave and half free," he said, but can a *world* exist half slave and half free? Where is the present-day Lincoln who will inspire us, not to save the Union this time, but to save the world? The wealthy nations are exploiting the poor nations, driving the affluent world farther and farther apart from the poor and the powerless. A large proportion of the poor and powerless are children.

Each year during the next decade, 10,000 unique species of plant life and animal life will disappear forever. Acute fuel shortages already affect hundreds of millions of people and will grow worse as the last vegetation is cut for cooking fires. Some 25 billion tons of topsoil disappear from the world's croplands every year because of erosion due to loss of vegetation. Timberland enough to cover the western half of North America will disappear from the world by the end of the century. Disposable chopsticks in Japan result in widespread loss of forests in the rest of Asia.

If we do not take action decisively and immediately, the lives of the majority of the world's children, and of their parents, will only get worse. If the rich and powerful nations do not reach out a hand to the powerless, we will all go down together. But before we go "gentle into that good night," let's make some noise. It was also Abraham Lincoln who said, "Everybody does the best they can—some sing, some shout, and all holler."

## A Major Prevention Strategy

As I considered ways of reaching out to help alleviate the problems of children around the world, I identified a few fundamental themes. The first of these derived from my experience working with the Commission on the Prevention of

Mental/Emotional Disabilities (1986) of the National Mental Health Association of the United States. That commission, chaired by Beverly Benson Long, reported its findings in 1986. It heard testimony from a wide range of experts in various fields, including genetics, family planning, infancy and early childhood experience, adolescence, marital relationships, nutrition, and aging.

One afternoon, as the members of the commission were sitting around a table, after listening to a full morning of testimony from experts, someone (I think it was psychiatrist George Tarjan) asked the question: "If we had just one prevention program we could put into place, and knew that it would succeed, which one would that be?" The question led to a couple of hours of discussion, at the end of which the members of the commission were agreed on an answer. We would opt for a program that would ensure that every baby born anywhere in the world would be a healthy, full-term infant weighing at least eight pounds and welcomed into the world by economically secure parents who wanted the child and had planned jointly for her or his conception and birth. (I would add the hope that the baby would be breast-fed by an adequately nourished mother who was not on drugs. I would also ask for good health care for expectant mother and child.) Such an arrival into the world would go a long way toward assuring later healthy relationships, reduced mother and child mortality, reduced retardation and reduced later mental disorders.

We know, from extensive research, the dangers of prematurity and associated low birth weight. We know, too, the dangers of inadequate maternal nutrition, such as lack of protein, iron, and iodine. We know the dangers of heavy consumption of alcohol during pregnancy, or heavy tobacco smoking, or the use of crack or heroin or other drugs that can damage the fetus and can lead to prematurity, low birth weight, an increased risk of mental retardation, and poor bonding between infant and parents. These conditions are associated, later, with continuing poor emotional relationships with parents and with a greatly increased risk of eventual emotional handicap.

Let me ask you to consider, for a moment, some of the exceptions to this ideal arrangement described by the commission. How many children are born into the world who are *not* planned for, *not* wanted, *not* welcome? A number of studies of the long-term consequences of being born an unwanted child show the devastating handicaps common to such children. Henry David and his colleagues have demonstrated in follow-up studies the long-term negative effects on children born to mothers who had twice sought permission to have an abortion and had been twice denied (see David, Dytrych, Matejcek, & Schüller, 1988). Dytrych reported on this research at the 1990 Vermont Conference on the Primary Prevention of Psychopathology (see Chapter 8 of this volume). Elsie Broussard (1976) has done compelling studies of the long-term damaging consequences for infants of being viewed by their mothers as "below average" at birth and a month after birth. (These infants were judged to be normal by pediatricians, but were seen as inferior by their mothers.) Even 10 and 15 years later most of these youngsters were emotional wrecks, incapable of meaningful relationships with others.

The epidemic of premature teenage pregnancy (in the United States, for example) results in dramatic increases in the number of high-risk infants who are born prematurely and with low birth weight, conditions that interfere with an already precarious relationship with their immature teenage mothers. The research of Gelles and Cornell (1983), Gelles and Straus (1988), and Finkelhor (1979), for example, shows the devastating emotional consequences of child abuse and neglect, and the long-term negative consequences of childhood sexual abuse. Many abused children grow up to be damaged adults who are incapable of mature interpersonal relationships. In the laboratory, the lifelong research of Harry Harlow and Margaret Harlow (1966) on the effects of damaging infant experiences in monkeys provides a model of the relationship between early trauma and later incapacity for mature relationships, including mature sexuality. (I must add that there are dramatic demonstrations that the long-term consequences of these early pathological relationships in both infant monkeys and humans are not irreversible, that effective interventions can and sometimes do help undo the damage. But I must remind us also that far more extensive damage is being done by uncaring, angry, thoughtless, and neglectful parents than can ever be undone by individual therapy or small group interventions. And a great many of these parents have been emotionally stunted or incapacitated by their own experience of being exploited and powerless.)

### Empathy

Another theme about which I have done a great deal of reading during the past several months is that of *empathy*. We are confronted almost daily with news accounts from around the world of the ways in which people hurt or kill each other, committing crimes shocking in their callousness and brutality. The impact of such damage is rivaled only by our mystification at the apparent absence of remorse or concern of the perpetrators. During the past couple of months we have seen, through the immediacy of the mass media, seemingly ordinary people who have committed brutal rapes, assaults, serial murders, and other forms of pathological aggression with no apparent resulting feelings of guilt, remorse, or regret. On a more global level, we continue to witness the exploitation and repression of the world's poor nations, lethal conflicts among and between religious groups, ethnic groups, and nationality groups, all frightening in their intensity and their devastation. I need not recite examples of what is apparent to anyone aware of world events.

What interests me, and calls for more research by mental health workers, is the role that empathy, or its absence, plays in determining the nature of interpersonal relationships. Exploiting other people for one's own personal or corporate advantage and gain must require the absence of empathic feeling for the victims. Concern for crime victims or for groups devastated by floods, mass starvation, war, and other calamities can occur only in persons with a fair amount of empathy. If empathy inhibits people from exploiting and damaging others, then the absence of empathy leads to cruelty and exploitation. We must determine the factors responsible for the development of empathy and take steps to foster its development in children throughout the world (see, for example, Eisenberg & Strayer, 1987; Goldstein & Michaels, 1985; Katz, 1963; Stotland, Mathews, Sherman, Hanson, & Richardson, 1978).

Let me attempt a very brief summary statement of the relevant literature. The ability to put oneself in the place of others is acquired in early childhood in what might be called emotional education. Understanding parents and understanding teachers can help children develop the capacity to put themselves emotionally in the place of others, to feel what others are feeling, to learn to imitate empathy in important mentors and role models. In psychodynamic terms this means the development of a social conscience. We know that conscience development occurs in loving families with clear values and often does not occur in cold, loveless social environments. A great many psychopaths grew up in orphanages and similar institutions, where physical needs were cared for but love was absent. Similarly, many problem children grow up unwanted or neglected in homes where parents are absent or disturbed, or lack the capacity to give love and discipline. So we know what is desirable; the next task for us is to find ways to ensure the best environmental circumstances for the development of what Alfred Adler has referred to as *social interest*—concern for the welfare of others. Alfred Adler was a major contributor to prevention theory and practice (see Ansbacher, 1989). He stressed a public health model and the importance of good parenting and schooling, and argued for women's rights, including the right to abortion. He was an impassioned advocate for social changes to abet the development of children's social interest.

Adler wrote extensively about widespread social conditions that interfered with the development of children's social interest, and he stressed the importance of changes in the social environment that would lead to better parenting and better schooling. For example:

The honest psychologist cannot shut his eyes to social conditions which prevent the child from becoming a part of the community and from feeling at home in the world, and which allow him to grow up as though he lived in enemy country. Thus the psychologist must work against nationalism when it is so poorly understood that it harms mankind as a whole; against wars of conquest, revenge, and prestige; against unemployment which plunges people into hopelessness; and against all other obstacles which interfere with the spreading of social interest in the family, the school, and society at large. (Adler, 1935/1956, p. 454)

So a third fundamental theme is concerned with psychology's own lack of commitment to the public interest. Public interest is not confined to our own individual nations and cultures, but to the whole world community. Psychologists often say they engage in "value-free" science or therapy, denying that people's behavior is influenced by such social forces as economic exploitation, sexism, racism, homophobia, and social injustice. We treat our individual clients as though their problems are all due to the repression of individual impulses and the expression of personal conflicts.

## Looking at the Social Structure

Several years ago Francis Macnab, executive director of the Cairnmillar Institute in Melbourne, Australia, invited me to give an address celebrating the twenty-first anniversary of the founding of that distinguished institution. In my talk I argued in some detail that psychology had to assume a role more actively useful in promoting a more humane world. Our social problems all begin as human problems, and human behavior is our focus of concern. I quoted my friend Kenneth B. Clark (1974), who told us:

> Psychology must be a value-laden science and the fundamental value which must sustain it is a concern with the welfare of man. A social scientist cannot be indifferent to the destiny and the predicament of man and society any more than medicine could have been indifferent to plagues and diseases. The social scientist must be committed to social change. There is no pure, indifferent, non-technologically oriented use of disciplined human intelligence in social science and there is room for none. (pp. 138-139)

Recently, as the external examiner, I read a very insightful dissertation related to this theme by Isaac Prilleltensky (1989a), submitted to the graduate faculty at the University of Manitoba, Winnepeg, Canada. He reviews carefully the failure of contemporary psychological schools to pay attention to the social origins of most psychopathology. He turns the spotlight of his critical scholarship on psychoanalysis, behavior therapy, humanistic psychology, and cognitive therapy, and shows how all of these approaches focus on within-the-individual causes. He shows how we have long defined psychology as the study of individual differences, but we have failed to look at the critical external social forces that are major factors in producing individual differences (see also Prilleltensky, 1989b).

Prilleltensky's (1989a) dissertation is titled *Psychology and the Status Quo*. I commend it to all of you. Let me simply quote from his abstract:

> The analysis would indicate that psychology is instrumental in upholding the status quo in a number of ways. First, by offering solutions to human predicaments, almost exclusively in terms of the *self*; leaving the social order conveniently unaffected. Such an approach derives from the widely held practice in psychology of studying the individual without satisfactorily considering socioeconomic and historical circumstances. Second, by endorsing and reflecting conservative social values such as individualism, male supremacy and political conformity. Third, by disseminating those values in the persuasive form of so called value-free scientific statements. In doing that psychology predisposes the public to accept its formulations as apolitical truisms rather than sociohistorically conditioned statements. As a result, many of psychology's prescriptive and proscriptive biases are erroneously interpreted as merely descriptive assertions about human behavior. (pp. 1-2)

In the latter part of his dissertation, Prilleltensky argues that psychologists must become aware of the sociocultural determinants of our practice and our theories in order to raise our consciousness to the point where we will be able to uncover the mechanisms involved in perpetuating the social system that breeds injustice and exploitation.

Psychologists consistently have focused their therapeutic efforts on restructuring or changing the internal dynamics or the behavioral responses of their clients. They have acted as if their clients exist in a sociocultural vacuum, affected only by internal traces of early childhood environmental experiences and/or intrapersonal and intrafamilial conflicts in the current world. We have almost totally neglected variables such as economic and sexual exploitation, and even feudalism—with resulting feelings of powerlessness, hopelessness, and apathy—and pathological parenting.

There are compelling reasons, of course, for the failure of mental health professionals to concern themselves with social systems that are based on the exploitation of people in the interest of maximizing profits and power. We are embedded in these systems and have been socialized in cultures that often paint laissez-faire capitalism as synonymous with democracy. As economist Joseph Schumpeter (1948/1962) pointed out a number of years ago, a socialist society can be democratic and a capitalist society can be authoritarian. But any social criticism of unbridled capitalism, and its dominant power motive that emphasizes profiteering at all costs, is attacked as unpatriotic and subversive, and while this may be an unjust accusation, it has succeeded in stilling voices of criticism; indeed, it has succeeded in papering over, with skilled and masterful propaganda, any awareness of the basic injustices of our economic system.

## Cokes and Smokes

We live in and tolerate "Cokes and smokes" societies. We export our soft drinks and cigarettes heartlessly and cynically to the Third World. Citizens of impoverished societies do not need to spend their limited personal income on tobacco and empty calories, but we spread these addictive substances with seductive propaganda and massive advertising. Why are psychologists so silent about this "cause of the causes" (Joffe, 1988) of poor health, poor nutrition, and poor parenting? Psychologists, and particularly psychotherapists, have clearly established the damage that overstressed, impoverished, and disturbed parents can inflict on their children. But no similar attention has been paid to the terrible damage that an exploitative society can, in turn, cause parents. We know, for example, that in American towns and cities where there has been sudden and mass involuntary unemployment, the rates of spouse abuse and child abuse go up very rapidly. Much is written about the psychodynamic causes of child abuse, but little about the role of inescapable economic stresses leading to the frustrations that result in abuse. When a steel mill closes there is a sharp increase among laid-off workers in alcohol consumption, drunken driving, physical acting out, and the whole range of people abuses. But few psychologists have spent time researching the causes of the mill closings, the decision making that leads to devastating impacts on family relationships. Similarly, when the police or the army in an authoritarian society acts in the interest of landowners to evict peasants, or to murder peasant leaders and priests, we need not search for psychodynamic causes of child neglect and hopelessness.

## Where Is the Power?

One of the major reasons that mental health professionals have not examined critically the exploitative power structure of laissez-faire capitalist societies is because we have to work for a living. Our salaries are paid by institutions that will not tolerate serious criticism of the social order. Community psychology has never really flourished because the economic Establishment is not inclined to provide training funds and economic support for programs that seek to correct injustices and to identify the exploitative causes of distress and disturbance. The Establishment is not so foolish as to encourage, or even tolerate, criticism and proposals for revolutionary reform. We are caught in a conflict between what is just and what is safe. French philosopher Blaise Pascal stated the dilemma well when he pointed out that because justice is not able to overcome power, we have settled for making what is powerful just.

During the last year I have visited four economically disadvantaged countries. In all of them there is a repetitive pattern—terribly overcrowded and polluted cities that are constantly growing as a result of migration of people from rural areas seeking employment, and population increase that is out of control. Illiteracy is generally the rule, and massive unemployment, hopelessness, and despair are pervasive. A family of eight or 10 people, including a married couple, a grandparent or two, and half a dozen children, are forced to live in one room constructed largely of discarded trash. Often there is no running water, and no toilets. Sewage is thrown into the streets and ditches, unsafe water is available only from a spigot two blocks or two miles away, and fuel for cooking is difficult or impossible to obtain because of the absence of firewood and the high cost of available fuel. Childhood mortality is high, infant diarrhea is rampant as a result of pollution (and effective treatment of this condition requires only clean water, salt, and sugar, none of which is available). Lack of iron produces childhood anemia and lack of iodine in the diet of the expectant mother produces mental retardation in hundreds of thousands of children. But Cokes and smokes are widely advertised and available everywhere.

In some countries I walked through endless slums, with a guide who was invariably a member of the privileged professional class (like me). It is not uncommon to hear professionals *blame the victims*—Why do they have so many children? Why do they marry so young? They have no ambition. And so on. Under such circumstances the mass of people have little choice but to adopt a fatalism that attributes their misery to the will of God. Their governments may be well-meaning, but they are largely powerless. Huge foreign debts prohibit further loans. In some countries corruption soaks up funds that could be used to help improve living conditions. While everyone suffers, it is the children who suffer the most. Poor nutrition, poor health, poor neighborhoods, and a poor future do little to enhance family life and meaningful relationships.

I do not intend to single out impoverished countries, expressing a kind of nouveau-colonial mentality. The slums of the United States—of Bedford-Stuyvesant, the South Bronx, Miami, Southeast Washington, and San Juan—are both real and close to home. The same hopelessness prevails. Poverty is also common in rural America (30% of poor children live in rural settings), and 44% of poor children are white. A large proportion of poor children in America have serious health and emotional problems. Former President Jimmy Carter and Rosalyn Carter send frequent appeals for money for Habitat for Humanity, a program to provide housing for the impoverished. Meanwhile, both Presidents Reagan and Bush have cut back billions of dollars of support for low-cost housing. What housing funds were available were diverted into profitable programs that were close to outright theft through fat contracts negotiated by "consultants" who were often conservative former government officials who earned huge fees with calls to cooperating senior political appointees. The Carters will never raise more than a small fraction of the money needed to replace what has been lost by the actions of the conservatives. Homelessness is growing. One-to-one assistance does not overcome the effects of massive social damage.

I suggest to you that it is difficult for meaningful, caring relationships to develop in the presence of hopelessness, powerlessness, low self-esteem, and exploitation. Abraham Maslow (1954) taught us, many years ago, that in the hierarchy of motivation, love, self-esteem, and self-actualization must rest on a secure foundation of security and safety—a base that is not riddled with hunger, danger, and hopelessness. How can children of poverty anywhere in the world develop a social conscience while living in despair?

### What Is to Be Done?

I commend to your reading the recent annual reports of UNICEF (Grant, 1987, 1988). In these reports, in easily readable and understandable form, are the statistics that detail the unnecessary deaths each year of 14 million children throughout the world. Others fail to thrive and die because their mothers die in childbirth.

What is required to prevent such tragic losses is a serious commitment by economically advantaged nations to divert modest amounts of their current expenditures (for weaponry, for example) to provide public health measures for the children in the deprived countries of the world. We often hear the excuse that we must wait for better economic times. The UNICEF report asks:

Can we really say that it is too difficult? Can we really say that we must wait for the return of economic growth when over 3 million children a year are dying of diarrheal dehydration which can be prevented by basic family health education and by oral therapies costing less than 1 dollar? And can we really say that it is too expensive, that we must wait for economic development, when 3.5 million children a year are dying of diseases which can be prevented by immunization at an additional yearly cost which is less than the price of five advanced fighter planes? (Grant, 1987, p. 9)

A frequent argument in discussions of the possibility of saving young children from needless death is that such efforts will only augment and increase the population explosion in countries that are already seriously overpopulated and growing at alarming rates. This is simply not true. Repeatedly the world has seen a dramatic drop in birthrates in countries where children have been saved from early and unnecessary death. When parents are convinced that their infants and young children will not die needlessly, they develop hope for the future and begin to reduce the number of conceptions and births. In many countries, a decline in unnecessary deaths of children has *preceded* an economic upturn, led to reduced family size, and improved lives. Demographers have shown that "there has never been a steep and sustained fall in child births which has not been preceded by a steep and sustained fall in child deaths" (Grant, 1988, p. 23). The reduction of infant mortality in Japan, for example, from 90 deaths per 1,000 births in 1940 to slightly over 5 per 1,000 births today, places Japan in a category with Finland and Sweden as having the lowest rate of infant deaths in the world. Similar reductions in the deaths of children have been occurring during this decade in China, Thailand, Singapore, Sri Lanka, and the Republic of Korea. All of these nations have invested heavily in the health of children and all have achieved dramatic reductions in child death rates and in birthrates (see Grant, 1988, p. 40).

As the UNICEF publications also remind us, families need to know about the importance of breast-feeding—that a baby in a poor family who is bottle-fed during the first six months of life is three times as likely to be ill and three times as likely to die as a baby who is breast-fed. Powdered baby formulas, pushed by international companies that give free "samples" to Third World mothers, result in increased death rates. This is a clear example, among many, of acts that are profitably perpetrated by companies without empathy. There is a need to teach families that after six months of breast-feeding the child must begin to get supplementary food, but that breast-feeding should continue well into the second year of life. One indirect benefit of long-term breast-feeding is that it makes conception less likely, so child spacing occurs naturally.

Each year about half a million mothers throughout the world die in pregnancy or childbirth. They leave behind more than a million motherless children. More than 5 million infants around the world are stillborn or die within the first week of life. A very large proportion of these deaths could be prevented with the wider availability of knowledge about safe pregnancy. As UNICEF points out, tetanus kills about a million newborn infants each year; most of these deaths could be prevented by immunizing the mother-to-be (Grant, 1988, p. 34).

Family planning information and contraceptive technology are also important in helping reduce the birthrates in a number of countries, yet during the 1980s help in the form of family planning information and contraception education and materials were drastically curtailed by conservative political administrations in the United States.

What can we do about these enormous human problems? Our first task is to make vocal what is now silent. It is to make conscious what is now unconscious. It is to resist being co-opted by an exploitative social system that pays us well with status, income, and upward social mobility in exchange for our remaining silent about injustice. We have watched the greed of the oil companies destroy the cultures of the native peoples of Alaska and more recently devastate the environment of everyone there. We are witnessing the rapid destruction of the Amazon rain forest so that more cattle can be grazed to satisfy the growing market for hamburgers. Some 30 million acres of irreplaceable rain forest are lost each year. At this rate, in 40 years there will be none left. Thousands of species of plants and animals will disappear forever. Why? Who benefits? What psychologists are concerned?

Once again, the question is whether the political will is strong enough to make modest changes in our national priorities. Are we willing to give up programs that largely benefit the rich for programs that can save the lives of millions of children and give hope to their parents for a better life and a better world?

President Bush announced in July 1989 a long-term space program to build a station on the moon, leading to the exploration of Mars. While it is possible to argue that many technological benefits will result from this effort, it still needs to be debated when set alongside the possibility of reducing poverty, hopelessness, and powerlessness throughout the world. The cost of exploring Mars will be hundreds of billions of dollars. Even a small portion of this expenditure could raise the hopes and aspirations of all the world's people. Unfortunately, the forces that control expenditures profit a great deal more from high-technology manufacturing than from public health programs and public health education. Only a widespread demand by informed and empathic citizens is likely to have any positive effect on diverting funds.

We have long shared and perpetuated the myth that the upper classes in the industrial nations enjoy a divine right to exploit the less fortunate peoples of the earth. Cecil Rhodes, when he set up the Rhodes Scholarships, opined that "2,000 to 3,000 Nordic Gentlemen" could rule the world. The latter-day version of his message is less overt but still the same—the leaders of world industry, the feudal landowners, the purveyors of high technology, and the princes of advertising, abetted by the powerful hierarchies of established religions, can rule the world for their own benefit, and do. More than 15 years ago, in a speech at a conference at Harvard organized by Marcia Guttentag, I said that the world would be a better place without laissez-faire capitalism and without organized patriarchal religions. I still believe this to be true. Both of these entrenched forces damage opportunities for meaningful family relations and for meaningful relationships generally.

## Who Is Responsible?

I believe there are three major contributing factors responsible for the social injustices that cause poverty, powerlessness, and despair. One is class conflict—the exploitation of the lower socioeconomic groups by the powerful elitist upper class; the second is the exploitation of females by males; the third is racism and ethnocentrism.

Sociologists have divided societies into five social classes. At the top, Class I is represented by a numerically small elite group with great wealth, usually inherited wealth. This group keeps to itself and usually intermarries, sending its children to private schools and elite universities, where they meet each other. Within the United States this group is composed largely of a white Protestant establishment. Members of this group, through ownership of international corporations, the banking industry, and communications media, control the society. With their power to hire and fire, they have a large measure of control of Classes II, III, and IV, thereby maintaining the existing social structure. Class II, the upper middle class, includes managers, most intellectuals, professionals, and highly educated technologists, all of whom are rewarded generously for supporting the system and are punished mercilessly if they try to change it. Class III, the white-collar workers, includes large groups of junior managers, junior technologists, and salaried lower-level professionals, such as nurses and schoolteachers. A great many of these are the children of blue-collar workers. Their jobs can be terminated with two weeks' notice, for the most part, and so they are a timorous group fearing the loss of their newly won white-collar status. Class IV, the blue-collar workers, ranges from skilled craftspeople through other industrial and service workers who hold regular jobs and who normally have weekly or biweekly paydays. Class V includes the great mass of unskilled and largely uneducated or poorly educated people, with high rates of unemployment and mobility, and a wide range of social pathologies. These are the day laborers, the landless farm workers, the unemployed or underemployed who live in miserable housing or are homeless, and who provide a large labor pool from which to recruit minimum-wage workers or laborers.

As a rule, it is this lowest social class that has the highest incidence and prevalence of most forms of mental disorders and the highest rates of physical illness, premature death, infant mortality, broken families headed by females, school dropouts, delinquency, and crime. In many countries this group constitutes a large majority of the population.

A few countries have attempted, with more or less success, to alter this class pattern. By heavy taxes on those earning high incomes coupled with major efforts at educating and improving the lot of the poor, countries such as the Netherlands, Finland, and those in Scandinavia have tried to blur class differences and distinctions.

A major difference between First World and Third World countries is in the size of the Class V group. Most of the "developing nations" have a huge Class V mass that is controlled and exploited by a small wealthy Class I elite. In these nations the middle classes are relatively small, with the exception of the police and the army, who serve the elite and who often are used to suppress any attempts at rebellion or social change that threaten the feudalistic structure.

This repressive control by the powerful elites makes it very difficult to see any way that land reform, peasant education, and expensive improved living conditions are to be achieved through peaceful efforts at equalization. If the elite controllers of most major industrial nations are unwilling to improve the lot of the impoverished Class V people in their own countries, how can we expect them to make major investments in relieving the poverty and powerlessness of impoverished underdeveloped countries? One suggestion would be for each ivantaged nation to focus its habilitative and rehabilitative efforts on a single disadvantaged country. One demonstrated success might be achieved, and this could lead to others. Large advantaged countries such as the United States, Germany, England, and Japan could take on a sizable impoverished country, while smaller advantaged nations such as Finland or Denmark could each work with a smaller disadvantaged country. It would be exciting to see this process undertaken by even one or two countries, with careful documentation of the results of efforts at improving public health, population control, education, and agriculture.

The second major factor causing wide despair is sexist repression and exploitation. The problems of women in male-dominated societies are so well documented as not to require any extensive discussion here. While the upper class exploits persons in all the classes below it, the exploitation of women by men is far more immediate, more stressful, and more inescapable, because all class levels are prone to such male domination and control. Sexist practices may be somewhat more subtle in some countries than others, but the practice of underpaying women workers in advanced industrial societies, the defeat of the Equal Rights Amendment in the United States, the vaginal mutilation of girls in the Middle East and Africa, the selling of female children into lives of slavery by impoverished families in South Asia, and the use of teenage girls as prostitutes (whether in New York City or in Bangkok) all show that the exploitation of women is nearly universal and more immediately painful than class discrimination, because it affects the immediate lives of most women, while economic exploitation by class level is not so clearly perceived in everyday life.

The forces responsible for sexism and the exploitation of women are, in significant measure, psychological. While members of the social classes exploited by the rich Establishment are threatened if they attempt to strike back at their bosses, at least all males, whatever their class, can achieve some sense of power by dominating and controlling "their" women. So wife abuse and child abuse, rape and sexual exploitation, prejudice and discrimination are socially sanctioned ways for males to pump up their sense of power even while they accept their own exploitation by the social system.

Racist practices (which often include ethnic and religious discrimination) serve essentially the same psychological purposes as sexist ones. The dominant majority race (or faith) can look down on members of the hated out-groups, a great many of whom are also in the lower classes, and augment their sense of power, authority, and importance. Racism, historically, has often been associated with colonialism. A country that exploits a colony needs to rationalize its heartless appropriation of wealth through the belief that the natives are an inferior race. While colonialism is no longer an acceptable form of exploitation, it has been replaced by a more subtle imperialism that also uses racism as psychological justification.

Galtung (1971), a Norwegian social scientist, has provided us with an insightful theory of imperialistic power between nations, a theory that also provides insight into power relationships within a society, among social classes, and between the sexes as well. Very briefly, Galtung accounts for the continuing inequality that exists among nations, and even among classes and between sexes of a particular nation, with the argument that imperialism is responsible. Powerful elites within a central industrial society form a community of self-interest that is deliberately tied into the self-interest of elites who are in power in a peripheral society (in an impoverished country, for example). This alliance results in the exploitation of a majority of people in the peripheral society. Military and religious leaders in the exploited society repress and control the mass of poor people in their own self-interest. Within the exploitative modern society a small elite maintains its authority and control by manipulating special groups (teachers and professors, for example) who themselves exploit (or justify the exploitation of) workers, women, minorities, and others. The mass media, and particularly television, owned and controlled by the power elite, constantly explain that this is the way things are and must be, and that anyway there are all kinds of ways to have fun through consumption and waste. Bread and circuses, Cokes and smokes. The tensions that result from exploitation can be relieved by headache remedies, antacids, laxatives, and/or the opposite—medicines that control diarrhea. I sometimes think that we are all crazy. In the United States we spend 25 hours a week sitting in front of an electronic gadget in our living rooms laughing at sitcoms, cheering our favorite gladiator team, or watching sanitized news that is dribbled out in 20-second snippets, all guaranteed to hold our attention so that we will watch the commercials that tell us how to be symptom free by eating our high-fiber oat sugarcoated breakfast flakes and through the frequent use of patented stress medicines as we drive our powerful cars at excessive speeds after drinking wine coolers and less filling beer that tastes great.

In a 10-year follow-up to his original lecture on exploitation, Galtung (1981) points to the fact that in many parts of the world we are exploiting both humans and nature beyond their regenerative capacity. Forests are being destroyed, topsoil is being washed away, the ozone layer is being depleted, the oceans are becoming cesspools, precious animal species that evolved over millions of years are disappearing—all faster than we can measure. And anyway, no one is measuring. We are busy with our sitcoms, our pro bowls, our Cokes and smokes.

Where are mental health professionals while all of this is happening? With our collective heads buried in the sand, that is where—focusing on "value-free" science and therapy designed to change the self through one-to-one treatment. How can we help to control people who have little or no conscience? Are powerful people and corporations, under the slogan of individual freedom, free to manipulate, exploit, and damage others? Many of us belong to Amnesty International because we empathize with those persons who are incarcerated without trial, tortured without hope of escape. But there is no Amnesty International for persons who are prisoners of social and economic circumstance, who are powerless and poverty-stricken because of manipulation by conscienceless international corporations and wealthy landowners. And there is no Amnesty International for children who are trapped and physically abused, for women in many parts of the world who are under the total domination of men because of patriarchal religious beliefs. Most of the world's major religions are patriarchal and sexist. Recently I spent a day in the library reading, in the *Encyclopedia Britannica*, about each of the world's major religions. The delusional content of most of the world's religions makes them technically pathological. Most major religions have beliefs that not only violate natural laws, but that also violate common decency and humanity. Most are patriarchal and insane.

Not all religions are authoritarian and blindly irrational, of course. The archbishop of Canterbury, Dr. Robert Runcie, recently spoke out against religious fundamentalism, which he calls "Ecclesiastical Apartheid":

> It is not merely individuals who practice Ecclesiastical Apartheid. Whole communities of fierce conviction remain vigorous. Where there is strife in our world, you do not have to look far to see the hand of various brands of fundamentalism— Islamic Fundamentalism in the Middle East, Christian Fundamentalism in Ulster, or Jewish Fundamentalism in Israel. The hands of such communities are stained with blood. Where toleration is in peril, persecution stalks not far behind. (quoted in *Manchester Guardian Weekly*, July 16, 1989, p. 4)

Why have we been unconcerned with the pernicious powers of authoritarian religions and their effects on human relationships? If we are students of individual differences, why do we not examine the effects of sexism, of homophobia, of class prejudice, of racist stereotypes in religious cultures around the world?

Let us go back to the Number One Priority Prevention Program. What can psychologists do to ensure that all the world's babies will be born wanted (this especially includes girl babies), that they are full term and healthy, and they are planned for in such a way as to control the currently out-of-control world population explosion?

What can we do to reduce and eliminate the exploitation of people by rich landowners and multinational corporations without consciences and without empathy? What can we do to reduce the power of patriarchal religions that foment sexist and homophobic persecution of a majority of the world's population? This is the *terra incognita* of mental health, the area in which an international group of mental health practitioners might be focusing its major attention.

### Discussion

If we are to improve the lives of children around the world, we must face the reality that the human infant and young child is incapable of autonomous self-protective behavior. As a result of millions of years of evolution, the human species gives birth to offspring that experience years of physical, emotional, and mental development almost entirely controlled and influenced by significant adults responsible for nurturance and care. While maturational processes are built into the developing organism, each of these processes requires a nutritious diet, physical care, social stimulation, and consistent parenting.

It is not difficult to describe a relatively ideal environment for the rearing of children with a high probability of successful, and effective, growth and development. Unfortunately, the conditions fostering such successful development are often absent or in short supply. As we have heard or read in papers delivered at the Vermont Conference, millions of children throughout the world are born unwanted or unplanned. Many of them are born to women who are physically debilitated. Many are born in households with inadequate resources for proper feeding and for meeting basic physical needs and support. Many are stunted due to lack of adequate nutrition and adequate loving care. We have heard that girl babies, and young girls, especially, are often neglected, are the last to be fed and most often receive inadequate health care in contrast to boy babies, who, in a great many cultures, are more highly valued.

Indeed, a theme constantly reiterated during the most recent Vermont Conference dealt with the devastating consequences of being born female, of growing up to be a woman, which so often leads to household drudgery, even household slavery, sexual exploitation, unremitting toil and despair, and early death. The low status of women appears to be partly a product of patriarchal religions, partly a result of widespread male chauvinism, and partly a result of the cultural myths perpetuated in the folkways and religious belief systems of the human species.

Patterns of child care that emphasize loving support, consistent and empathic interaction, and kindly guidance and discipline seem, in human history, to be relatively recent and relatively uncommon. While there are exceptions, especially in the world of the Class II professionals, the lot of the child throughout history, and across cultures, has not been a particularly happy one. In an earlier VCPPP volume, Bahr (1988) addresses the "mystique of the traditional family" and shows in compelling detail how the traditional family in the recent historical past, particularly in Europe and America, commonly resulted in child neglect and in the widespread exploitation of women, who were subordinate to their husbands. Bahr points out that there were incredibly high death rates among infants, in part because commonly mothers had to leave their small children alone for long periods while they engaged in work in the fields and around the farm, or in heavy cooking and laundry duties to support the men. He quotes John Locke, who reported that children in poor English families were put to work for at least part of the day when they reached the age of 3, and many of whom never lived to adulthood because of excessive demands for work. He points out the traditional American belief in female inferiority and male misogyny.

Women were prematurely disfigured from hard toil. Many of them preferred life in the factories and sweatshops to the backbreaking labor on the farm. Nostalgia for the traditional happy family is nostalgia for something that never existed for most people in any time or place, according to Bahr.

Let us face the problems squarely. If our goal is to try to organize societies to provide a more wholesome, nurturant, caring world for children (and especially for girls and women), we are setting an idealistic goal that has rarely been achieved anywhere at any time. As mental health workers we have seen compelling evidence that children who are properly reared in a healthy environment, with consistent love and nurturance, both psychological and physical, can be expected to grow up as responsible, autonomous, and competent adults. And so we react with shock and horror at accounts of unnecessary child deaths, disfigurement, sexual exploitation, and sweatshop and slave labor. But this is the way the world too often is, though not necessarily the way it has to be.

Standing directly in the path of reform is the chauvinistic, patriarchal male. This patriarch makes the rules, writes and interprets the scriptures, formulates the laws, prescribes the religious beliefs, enslaves women and children, and destroys the lives of uncounted millions. This patriarchal male may not understand what he is doing; he may simply be responding to what he has learned. He may be repeating the myths of his culture, the distorted and dangerous beliefs of his religion. He may react with religious fervor as the only source of solace in his own miserable, externally controlled life. He may have no one to look down on but his wife and children. So our task becomes one of finding ways to change the economic and religious forces that support patriarchy, if our goal is to improve children's lives around the world.

## References

Adler, A. (1956). *The individual psychology of Alfred Adler* (H. L. Ansbacher & R. R. Ansbacher, Eds.). New York: Basic Books. (Original work published 1935.)

Ansbacher, H. (1989). Alfred Adler, pioneer in prevention of mental disorders. *Journal of Primary Prevention.*

Bahr, H. M. (1988). Family change and the mystique of the traditional family. In L. A. Bond & B. M. Wagner (Eds.), *Families in transition: Primary prevention programs that work* (pp. 11-30). Newbury Park, CA: Sage.

Broussard, E. (1976). Neonatal prediction and outcome at 10/11 years. *Child Psychiatry and Human Development, 7,* 85-93.

Clark, K. B. (1974). *The pathos of power.* New York: Dryden.

Commission on the Prevention of Mental/Emotional Disabilities. (1986). *Report of the commission.* Alexandria, VA: National Mental Health Association.

David, H., Dytrych, Z., Matejcek, Z., & Schüller (Eds.). (1988). *Born unwanted.* New York: Springer.

Eisenberg, N., & Strayer, J. (Eds.). (1987). *Empathy and its development.* New York: Cambridge University Press.

Finkelhor, D. (1979). *Sexually victimized children.* New York: Free Press.

Galtung, J. (1971). A structural theory of imperialism. *Journal of Peace Research, 13*(2), 81-94.

Galtung, J. (1981). *Fourth Annual Chase Millennium Lecture.* London: London School of Economics.

Gelles, R. J., & Cornell, C. P. (Eds.). (1983). *International perspectives on family violence.* Lexington, MA: Lexington.

Gelles, R. J., & Straus, M. A. (1988). *Intimate violence.* New York: Simon & Schuster.

Goldstein, A. P., & Michaels, G. Y. (1985). *Empathy: Development, training and consequences.* Hillside, NJ: Lawrence Erlbaum.

Grant, J. P. (1987). *The state of the world's children, 1987* (published for UNICEF). New York: Oxford University Press.

Grant, J. P. (1988). *The state of the world's children, 1988* (published for UNICEF). New York: Oxford University Press.

Harlow, H., & Harlow, M. (1966). Learning to love. *American Scientist, 54,* 244-272.

Joffe, J. (1988). The cause of the causes. In G. Albee, J. Joffe, & L. Dusenbury (Eds.), *Prevention, powerlessness, and politics: Reading on social change* (pp. 57-79). Newbury Park, CA: Sage.

Katz, R. L. (1963). *Empathy: Its nature and uses.* Glencoe, IL: Free Press.

Maslow, A. (1954). *Motivation and personality.* New York: Harper.

Prilleltensky, J. (1989a). *Psychology and the status quo.* Unpublished doctoral dissertation, University of Manitoba, Department of Psychology.

Prilleltensky, J. (1989b). Psychology and the status quo. *American Psychologist, 44,* 795-802.

Schumpeter, J. (1962). *Capitalism, socialism and democracy* (3rd ed.). New York: Harper. (Original work published 1948.)

Stotland, E., Mathews, K., Jr., Sherman, S., Hanson, R., & Richardson, B. (1978). *Empathy, fantasy and helping.* Beverly Hills, CA: Sage.

# Inj.. :ting Our Children With Hostility

## Kenneth B. Clark

A number of years ago I saw on television a group of white students marching toward a public school in South Boston. They were protesting the assignment of black students to "their school." Their faces were contorted with hatred and hostility. Some were carrying American flags attached to sticks and clubs. They were shouting racial epithets.

As I looked at those distorted faces, I felt deep sorrow for those dehumanized young human beings. I was deeply disturbed that our society and our educational system could have permitted this disease of violence to infect those young people. How had this come about? Had their families abandoned them? Had they been directly or indirectly infected with hatred toward their fellow human beings by those who were supposed to guide them? Had religion and the church remained indifferent to, or were they so intimidated by, the pervasive prejudices of their parishioners that they remained silent in the face of evidence of cruelty and symptoms of immorality? Had the educational system so neglected its pupils that it would leave them to wallow in the cesspool of moral illiteracy? Whatever the cause, the behavior of those children was symptomatic of a corrosive hostility injection causing an epidemic, as an embarrassingly large percentage of children, who had been socialized in American democratic society, joined the rabble.

As one observes these tragic symptoms of human ignorance, violence, and hostility, one attempts to contain one's sorrow by wishing for limited boundaries. One would hope that the personality distortions could be contained, that through appropriate social remedies and educational methods, these young people could be brought around to a more constructive perspective and positive relationships with their fellow human beings.

We want to be reassured. We want to believe that these serious symptoms and cruel cases of social and psychological disease can be cured or prevented. However, the evidence we have gathered in the last decade has made it more and more evident that the boundaries of this epidemic are not limited to the victims of South Boston. There have been many outbursts by gangs of youths who have inflicted violence on others who differ from them in race, color, or religion.

330

Lately we have seen upwardly mobile youths in colleges and universities who have been aggressive in their expression of racial hostility. It is curious that the faculties and administrators of these colleges and universities—even in the more prestigious institutions—have been helpless, hopeless, or unconcerned, and unable to block racism and its manifestations. These college students who consistently express racial and religious intolerance in campus newspapers, or on the walls of academic halls and dormitories, are clearly morally illiterate and ethically sick. They need help. Before the educational institutions can bestow academic credentials, these students should be psychologically and educationally worthy of being described as healthy, educated human beings.

At this point, our educational system and educational institutions must be seen as morally deficient. It is incompatible to permit racism and hostility among human beings to coexist as part of a total pattern of education. Yet, from the earliest school years, parents and teachers encourage and stress a competitive approach to grades. Even at this early stage, education is seen and defined in terms of competitive upward mobility, where success or failure is of paramount importance. It is difficult to find an educational atmosphere where the ability of an individual is measured by the ability to help, rather than to dominate, others.

Personal—and some personality—problems of individuals may reflect aspects of the social complexities accepted in the larger society. In the normal inescapable socialization process, the conflict between the democratic ideals transmitted by the family, the church, and the school on the one hand and the realities of status aspirations, differences, and hostilities propagated on young people by parents, religion, and education on the other results in the internalization of ideational inconsistencies and behavioral conflicts. A pattern of moral schizophrenia becomes the foundation for personal, social, and ethical instability that varies in degree of expressed hostility among individuals. In the Social Science Statement submitted to the U.S. Supreme Court in the 1954 *Brown* decision, it was stated that the inconsistencies inherent in the existence of racism in a democratic society "are psychologically detrimental to the majority group members."

In addressing itself specifically to the problem of institutionalized racism in the social and personal problems of members of the *majority* group, the Mid-century White House Conference on Children and Youth asserts:

> Those children who learn the prejudices of our society are also being taught to gain personal status in an unrealistic and non-adaptive way. . . . they are not required to evaluate themselves in terms of the more basic standards of actual personal ability and achievement. *The culture permits and at times, encourages them to direct their feelings of hostility and aggression against whole groups of people* the members of which are perceived as weaker than themselves. They often develop patterns of guilt feelings, rationalizations and other mechanisms which they must use in an attempt to protect themselves from

recognizing the essential injustice of their unrealistic fears and hatred of minority groups. (Clark, 1963, p. 170; emphasis added)

As if prophetically sketching the end of the century, the report describes how that "confusion, conflict, moral cynicism, and disrespect for authority may arise in majority group children as a consequence of being taught the moral, religious, and democratic principles of the brotherhood of man and the importance of justice and fair play by the same persons and institutions who . . . seem to be acting in a prejudiced and discriminatory manner" (p. 170). While the reactions of individuals to this confusion vary, with some the conflict is resolved by intensifying their hostility toward the minority group, while others will internalize this and have guilt feelings that "are not necessarily reflected in more humane attitudes toward the minority group" (p. 170).

Furthermore, by permitting rejection, abandonment, and abuse of individuals and groups, we allow the seeds of hostility to be sown. Society establishes the basis for the victims to develop deep feelings of personal unworthiness; an inability to cope constructively with positive values and with social goals. Social destructiveness directed toward themselves and toward others with whom they are identified results in their being destructive toward the society that they perceive as hostile to them. As a matter of fact, they tend to see hostility as the only value that supports personal survival. They, too, become hostile, not only toward society in general, but also toward individuals. Not infrequently, they turn their hostility inward and become self-destructive. Suicide tends to take the form of homicide. Oppressed individuals perpetrate violence toward others. They are important components of the cycle of personal and social hostilities. The potential for kindness atrophies.

Inferior education—the self-fulfilling prophecy that children who are the products of poverty are unable to learn—is an insidious form of rejection. Lack of academic achievement results in feelings of inferiority and lack of self-esteem. Those so rejected are blocked from a constructive role in society. They are, therefore, relegated to destructive patterns of behavior as they seek some modicum of ego gratification. Often, various patterns of individual and group hostility become a way of life.

Empathy and kindness are suppressed in persistent forms of sociopathy. Regard for others is misunderstood. By generating and reinforcing the negative within human beings, society effectively shackles many within the boundaries of hostility.

How does the society prevent the continuing infection of our youth with social group violence and hostilities? How can society correct the distortion of their personalities and remove the block to positive expression to their lives? The acceptance of uncontrolled hostilities and violence directed toward groups of human beings who differ must be understood as a form of social psychopathology. Once this is understood, we must seek to remedy and prevent it. As we have seen, failure to do so makes this social and moral psychosis contagious.

These antidotes to the infection of racial and social hostility are available and can be applied:

- We must have a clear recognition of the scope of the disease.

- We can teach children to cooperate with others so that they can be helped even as they are helping others.

- We can introduce kindness and empathy as social moralities essential to our well-being.

- We can establish that a truly educated person functions with empathy, compassion, and humility. We can teach children that cruelty, violence, and subtle or flagrant forms of hostility are the gross behavior of the ignorant.

- We can set the premise for educational, religious, and social leaders that their behavior, rather than their rationale, is *prima facie* true.

The inescapable responsibility for the solidification of civilization is for the society as a whole to undertake an effective therapy for the moral ills of our youth. This infectious violence and hostility can be corrected.

## Reference

Clark, K. B. (1963). Appendix III: Effect of prejudice and discrimination personality develop-ment. In Midcentury White House Conference on Children and Youth, *Prejudice and your child* (Fact-Finding Report, Federal Security Agency, 1950). Middletown, CT: Wesleyan University Press.

# 25

# Youth as Resources:
# A New Paradigm in
# Social Policy for Youth

**John A. Calhoun**

It is not news to the youth-serving community that something new is afoot regarding how we think about and work with youth. Well known is the youth-in-service movement on the national level: President Bush's YES (Youth Entering Service) program, a White House initiative that encourages youth voluntarism; numerous pieces of congressional legislation with proposals that range from school-based programs through conservation and urban corps to mandated national service. At the local level, projects are being implemented in schools, youth-serving agencies, and other organizations whose functions affect youth. A key notion that is often lost in these projects is that youth service is not simply a program but rather a perspective that must be embraced by all agencies working with youth. This perspective involves viewing youth as potential resources rather than as potential problems. The "youth as resources" dimension, then, becomes program, perspective, and policy.

Our methods of identifying and diagnosing the pathologies of youth are finely honed—a good thing, for many adolescents need the best in services. However, our tools for eliciting and channeling the strengths and talents of youth are either blunt or nonexistent. Our approach to youth must be rethought, because our current practices are not working. Statistics regarding teen pregnancy, high school dropout, teen suicide, and victimization are sobering. The incidence of births to unmarried teens nearly doubled between 1965 and 1985; more than a million adolescents (almost 1 in 10) get pregnant each year; the incidence of gonorrhea among teens tripled between 1965 and 1985; the Centers for Disease Control estimate that 2.5 million adolescents contract a sexually transmitted disease each year (and one of those diseases, AIDS, has no cure); 39% of high school seniors reported getting drunk within the previous two weeks; the teen suicide rate has doubled since 1968. Some 10% of adolescent boys and 18% of girls have attempted suicide; every day in the United States

135,000 students bring guns to school; homicide is the leading cause of death among 15- to 19-year-old minority youth; 20% of 6- to 17-year-olds live in poverty (almost 25% of those under age 6 live in poverty); four of five 12-year-olds now alive will experience a violent personal crime during their lifetimes (robbery, rape, or assault); in 1955, there were eight murders in Oakland, and in 1988 there were 145; in Los Angeles a 10-foot-high concrete wall was built around a junior high school in order to keep stray bullets from hitting children on the playground—this is not a "war zone," but Los Angeles, California. No Little League team can be fielded in Detroit, not for lack of money or uniforms, but for lack of kids and coaches, the drug trade having claimed them; the nation's capital experiences more than one murder per day. Our acceptance of violence is so high that murders of 16-year-olds no longer appear on the front page, but in the back pages of the local news section; crack is so pernicious that it is sundering even the most elemental of bonds, that between mother and child; we witness legions of unparented, unmentored 10-year-olds; a young boy in one of our community programs worries not *how* he will live, but *whether* he will live, saying, "I want to live long enough to be an adult."

One could say that we will muddle through. People have always had trouble with teens. There has been an age-old tendency to see the problem with teens as being "worse than ever." A seemingly despondent Egyptian priest said, almost 4,000 years ago:

> Youth are disintegrating. The youngsters of the land have a disrespect for their elders and a contempt for authority in every form. Vandalism is rife and crime of all kinds is rampant among our young people. The nation is in peril. (cited in Burgess & Richardson, 1984, p. 123)

And the beloved and tolerant Socrates said:

> Children today love luxury. They have bad manners, a contempt for authority, a disrespect for their elders, and they like to talk instead of work. They contradict their parents, chatter before company, gobble up the best of the table and tyrannize over their teachers. (cited in Burgess & Richardson, 1984, p. 123)

The word *teen* comes from the Anglo-Saxon word *tenoa*, which means vexation. Those working with youth must not be lulled into complacency by relegating our teen issue to historic inevitably, for have we ever before witnessed children fearing to go to school, such a breakdown of families, and such a collapse of sustaining communities and resultant isolation?

There is even some evidence to suggest that we may not like kids. In the Minnesota Youth Poll, nearly 1,600 youth ages 10-18 were interviewed (Hedin, Hannes, & Saito, 1985). Those polled were male and female, rich and poor, black and white, and lived in urban, rural, and suburban settings. Two thirds of the participants indicated that they believed they were negatively perceived by adults. The participants reported that adults see them as "troublemakers, druggies, delinquents, thieves, losers, and vandals" (Hedin et al., 1985, p. 4). Only 25% of the participants offered positive images, saying that adults saw them as "wonderful, special, great, sweet, cute, mature, smart, etc." (Hedin et al., 1985, p. 4). Unfortunately, this problem begins at a young age. Elementary students, in most cases, used relatively mild terms such as "mischievous, pest, noisy, sassy and clumsy" (Hedin et al., 1985, p. 5), but by the time they moved to junior and senior high school, the views of negative adult attitudes seemed more extreme, tending to emphasize images like "druggies, sex maniacs, rowdies, delinquents, hateful, no good, worthless" (Hedin et al., 1985, p. 5). Interestingly, teens do not have this view of themselves. They say they are "more responsible than adults give us credit for. . . . We can be responsible but we want to have fun. . . . We're more good than bad" (Hedin et al., 1985, p. 5). This is not representative of a normal generation in transition; the country's social policy for youth needs to be rethought.

Policy responding to youth clusters into roughly five areas. The first concerns family and child welfare policies. These include teen pregnancy, family preservation programs, child abuse prevention strategies, child protection, child support enforcement, aid to families with dependent children, and programs that reduce unnecessary out-of-home placement. The second concerns education, especially early childhood education (e.g., Head Start, an enrichment program for poor children). Also included in this category are special tutoring programs and dropout prevention initiatives. The third policy area includes job training, retraining, and apprenticeship programs, and work to establish an adequate minimum wage. A fourth category concerns health: immunization, expanded health coverage, mental health care, and so on. Finally, a fifth area includes juvenile crime, delinquency, and drug abuse prevention. I would like to propose a sixth policy area, "youth as resources" (YAR). Because so many teens today feel alone and unwanted, we need to claim our youth as resources. This policy area is separate from the others yet can be infused into those policy clusters because it is both a program and a perspective.

Library shelves are filled with books describing adolescents in critical and pathological terms. Ironically, one of the few individuals writing positively about youth is a Holocaust survivor, Gisala Konopka (1973), who writes:

Adolescence is . . . an age of commitment, a move into true independence. . . . Commitment includes a search for one's identity but also points to the emotional, intellectual, and sometimes physical reach for other people as well as ideas, ideologies, causes, and work choices. (p. 301)

According to Konopka (1973), to acknowledge adolescence as an age of commitment is to elevate it from a stage to "be endured and passed through as rapidly as possible to a stage of earnest and significant human development" (p. 303). She points out that the only opportunities we give adolescents for displaying their competencies are through academics and athletics. It is her contention that because we fail to involve youth in community activities and services, many adolescents do not receive adult recognition.

If we are to affect the lives of youth with whom we work, and the communities in which they grow, we must shift our policies and perspectives. An approach that rests solely on a pathological model will not work. While we need the best in healers, those who counsel, mentor, provide job training, and so on, we also need to make youth feel connected and needed and that they have something of value to give to others.

It is critical that we take this "youth as resources" position with all youth, including the delinquent, the addicted, the runaway, the suicidal, those who make trouble, and those who are troubled. As we work with these youth from the YAR perspective, we can do something we normally do not do, namely, ask something of them in return. This is the concept of reciprocity. By demanding reciprocity, we imply that even the most difficult and wounded of them have something of worth that the larger society needs. By making demands, we acknowledge worth. If there is one common element among those who enter our various treatment systems, it is that they feel they have nothing of worth to contribute to anyone. By asking something in return, we begin the process of rebinding and reconnecting the individual to community.

When working with delinquent youth in Boston, I was struck by how many of them would say, "Yes, I hurt somebody, but I had a lousy lawyer," or "Yes, I robbed the house, but the judge doesn't understand me." There was a curious mixture of admission of guilt and denial of human connectedness. In order to establish a program where responsibility would be fixed, not just in legal but in human terms, I helped set up a mediation and sentencing project in which youth met their victims, with community people as mediators. The youth saw the implications of their acts in human terms, and were asked to give something back. The purpose was dual; the youth were told they were responsible for their actions, but they were also told they were needed by the community.

Three years ago the National Crime Prevention Council, with funding from the Lilly Endowment, established a YAR program. The goals of the program are as follows: to change society's view of teens from a source of problems to a rich source of solutions; to harness the skills, ideas, and energy of all teens to improve communities through youth-led service projects; to acknowledge the mutual obligation of society to youth and youth to society; and to give youth a stake in the community.

In three Indiana cities, YAR is guided by a board consisting of local leaders (including youth themselves) in community service, business, education, justice, youth affairs, social and employment services, and communications. Groups apply to the board who then funds projects in which youth work in their community and contribute to its vitality and improvement. Projects emphasize delivery of services by youth as opposed to delivery of services by adults to youth. Youth participate in developing and governing the projects. Grants range from $100 to $5,000, with most falling in the $1,500-$3,000 range. The board and staff of YAR are actively involved in encouraging applications for grants; screening, selecting, and monitoring grantees; and training both youth and agencies that serve youth. Projects reflect a marvelous diversity in the youth involved, the social issues confronted, and the recipients. The youth are scouts, dropouts, probationers, teen mothers, 4-H junior leaders, teens linked to schools and church groups, and honor society students. All youth can serve.

YAR youth confront social issues through presenting plays about drug abuse prevention, organizing outings for children living in shelters for battered women, helping in construction of quality low-income housing, providing services for shut-ins, serving as "buddies" for children in foster care, taking on community beautification projects, and growing vegetables for a food bank. Youth are partnered with adults to tackle every social issue of community concern. Among the many recipients of program services are children, the elderly, parks, schools, a housing authority, and youth in foster care and detention. All individuals and agencies can benefit from the caring and talent of youth.

All types of organizations in the community can participate, and many have changed substantively. Youth now serve on boards of many community organizations. Youth-generated projects are so valued that some host agencies contribute their own resources to sustain them. Adults operating a shelter for the homeless see teens as a source of sorely needed human resources; parents find their young children read better and enjoy it more; counselors discover that young people can deliver messages to one another that adults cannot seem to convey. It is an easy model to integrate into any program for youth.

The reactions of participants illustrate the effectiveness of the program. Earl, a probationer who was involved in a program doing cleanup for the elderly and reading to them, said of the program, "This is the first time in my life that I have ever been thanked." A young black woman, a brilliant student, wanting to become a lawyer in order "to make all the money I could possibly make to get away from my background," said of her experience after one year in this project, that the response from kids in a battered women's shelter for which she volunteered was so powerful she now wants to devote her life to medicine. An adult said, "This project and its success have stimulated interest from various community organizations as we have received several requests of a need for youth to serve in community projects."

Youth are tackling issues of importance now, not when they turn 21 and not never. The act of taking on responsibility, far from confounding adolescence, helps sustain youth through it.

Why is this social policy so important? We will have a shortage of workers who can meet the needs of a postindustrial, high-tech society by the year 2000. We need the talent. We must understand and relearn what we have always known, namely that there is experiential learning as well as formal school learning. Youth service represents part of the dues we all should pay as part of a democratic society. There are critical tasks in each community that must be completed. When we look for volunteers, do we even look to teens? Kids are often told that they are loved, but given fragmented families and anonymous neighborhoods, they do not feel a sense of their place; they do not feel needed or connected in a vital way. Youth spend less time with adults than in the past, and such projects can bring them into partnership with adults. Service encourages a sense of stake and belonging. So often we talk about "alienated" youth, and our response is to "rehabilitate." Rehabilitation is not the opposite of alienation. Inclusion and engagement are the opposites of alienation. We must broaden our definition of *good* to include not only "being good" (which we usually tell youth) but to "doing good" as well.

Finally, there is the social justice dimension of voluntarism. Youth will experience the fact that volunteers cannot do all things. We all can do more to build community and to help others. But who will inoculate? Who will fund research for AIDS? Who will help repair collapsing bridges? Who will help guarantee that a welfare mother taking her first tentative steps off of state support will have medical coverage for herself and for her children? And can charity compensate for the fact that 25% of America's children live in poverty? This suggests that we must have a government that provides more help and caring, and at the same time individuals who are willing to give more, to be citizens. It is reciprocal.

American historian Arthur Schlesinger (1986) asserts that U.S. history moves in 30-year cycles. In between periods of intense government activity, he claims, we seem to take a national breather, a time-out as we focus less on government and more on self. On one level he is right. John F. Kennedy was elected president 30 years ago. Following his tragic death and the ascendancy of Lyndon Johnson, one of the most activist governments in recent memory launched the War on Poverty and landmark civil rights legislation. And 30 years before that, Franklin D. Roosevelt launched a flurry of government programs to help pull the United States out of its paralyzing depression. Now, after almost 30 years of government cutbacks, and a government that has talked about "getting government off our backs," we hear stirrings for a more active government, especially in the areas of education, health, the environment, and the economy. But the problem with Schlesinger's assertion is that he views it as an either/or proposition—a strong government thrust *or* an individual thrust. Our challenge is to demand both, more of our government and more of each other. The cause of compassion, of helping others, should not be antithetical to asking for something in return. Usually, in working with kids, especially troubled kids, we want to help them. This is entirely legitimate. But why do words like *duty* and *obligation* to others and community stick in our throats? Why are these words not part of our lexicon?

The reciprocity model may, however, have a tough time politically. When testifying before Congress (the Select Committee on Children, Youth, and Families) on "Violence, Youth and a Way Out," I outlined an ambitious, expanded federal agenda including programs addressing health, child care, job training, and so on. During that part of my testimony, the liberal Democrat from California, Representative George Miller, nodded in agreement while the Republican from Indiana, Senator Dan Coates, sat back with his arms folded. During the second part of my testimony, I talked about citizenship. I referenced my work with youth in the early 1960s in an impoverished section of Philadelphia. One block stood out as a beacon, because of two concerned residents, Mrs. Thomas and Mr. Collins, who cherished, admonished, worried over, and knew every child on their block. Mr. Collins would station himself in a lawn chair on the sidewalk with a whistle hung around his neck to get the kids' attention. No child could go to school without going by Mr. Collins—"Where's your history book?" "Why is your braid untied?" Mrs. Thomas was the sage adviser and no less determined to find out how each child was, or how school was that day. Together they formed a foundation of support, attention, and affection that nurtured every child who passed by them.

What would happen, I asked, if Mr. Collins and Mrs. Thomas stood before the Congress today? Would they be welcomed or scorned, shot or applauded? The government must provide tools to enable its people to be fully functioning citizens, I asserted, but the government cannot create citizens. The community, through its Mr. Collinses and Mrs. Thomases, must do that. The burden is on each of us. Unless we help our young people develop a sense of stake in our communities and in their futures, there may be neither communities nor a future. During this part of my testimony Democrat George Miller leaned back away from me, wondering what planet I had been transported to, and his Republican counterpart leaned forward, nodding vigorously. I think I satisfied neither.

It will not be easy. The challenge is to establish a new framework through which to view and work with youth. I suggest that the framework be the concept of reciprocity. I agree with Leonard Duhl (1987), who points out in his article "The Health of Cities":

Intrinsic to the social ecology model is the concept of reciprocal maintenance: If I take something out of the system, I must put something back. In *Lives of a Cell* (1974), Lewis Thomas observed that, "we do not have solitary beings. Every creature is, in some sense, connected to and dependent on the rest."

Aristotle believed that no city should be larger than one in which a cry for help could be heard on all of the city's walls. This observation probably was not meant as a comment on the logistical consideration but on an organic one. In such a city, people would reasonably be expected to know and assist one another, making the city functional as a social entity. (pp. 60-61)

I believe that if we do not start to understand the value of service, of obligation to others, we will die as a society: no more Mr. Collinses, no more Mrs. Thomases.

I will let George Bernard Shaw have the final word:

This is the true joy in life, the being used for a purpose, recognized by yourself as a mighty one; . . . the being a force of nature instead of a feverish, selfish little clod of ailments and grievances complaining that the world will not devote itself to making you happy. . . . I am of the opinion that my life belongs to the community, and as long as I live, it is my privilege to do for it whatever I can. I want to be thoroughly used up when I die for the harder I work the more I live. I rejoice in life for its own sake. Life is no brief candle for me. It's sort of a splendid torch which I have got hold of for a moment, and I want to make it burn as brightly as possible before handing it on to future generations. (From the epistle dedicatory to *Man and Superman*)

## References

Burgess, R. L., & Richardson, R. A. (1984). Child abuse during adolescence. In R. M. Lerner & N. L. Golombos (Eds.), *Experiencing adolescence: A sourcebook for parents, teachers and teens* (pp. 119-151). New York: Garland.

Duhl, L. (1987). The health of cities. In R. J. Carlson & B. Newman (Eds.), *Issues and trends in health* (pp. 58-62). St. Louis, MO: C. V. Mosby.

Hedin, D., Hannes, K., & Saito, R. (1985). *Minnesota Youth Poll: Youth look at themselves and the world.* Minneapolis: University of Minnesota, Center for Youth Development and Research.

Konopka, G. (1973). Requirements for healthy development of adolescent youth. *Adolescence,* 8(31), 291-316.

Schlesinger, A. M. (1986). *The cycles of American history.* Boston: Houghton Mifflin.

Thomas, L. (1974). *The lives of a cell: Notes of a biology watcher.* New York: Viking.

# 26

# Fetal Alcohol Syndrome:
# A Parent's Perspective

## Michael Dorris

Unlike the many scientists, social workers, and politicians who have chosen, out of the kindness of their hearts and the dictates of their social consciences, to become knowledgeable about fetal alcohol syndrome and fetal alcohol effect, to work with its victims, and to demand its prevention, I was dragged to the subject blindfolded, kicking and screaming. I'm the worst kind of expert, a grudging, reluctant witness, an embittered amateur—above all else, a failure. A parent.

I'm a living, breathing encyclopedia of what hasn't worked in curing or reversing the damage to one child prenatally exposed to too much alcohol. Certain drugs temporarily curbed his seizures and hyperactivity, but their dampening effects on his learning ability and personality development are unknown. Fifteen years of special education—isolation in a classroom, repetitive instruction, hands-on learning—maximized his potential, but they didn't add up to a normal IQ. Psychological counseling—introspective techniques, group therapy—had no positive results, and may even have encouraged his ongoing confusion between what is real and what's imagined.

Brain surgery hasn't worked.

Anger hasn't worked.

Patience hasn't worked.

Love hasn't worked.

When you're the parent of a fetal alcohol syndrome (FAS) or fetal alcohol effect (FAE) child, your goals change with the passing years. At first you start with seeking solutions: ideas and regimens to penetrate the fog that blocks your son's or daughter's ability to comprehend rules, retain information, or even be curious. You firmly believe—because it has to be true—that the answers are "out there." It's just a matter of locating them. You go through teachers and their various learning theories like so many Christmas catalogs received in the mail, determined to find the perfect gift, the right combination of toughness and compassion, optimism and realism, training and intuition. Once you find a likely prospect, you badger her (and most teachers working with learning disabled children seem to be women),

342

demand results, attempt to coerce with praise or threat. You become first an ally, then increasingly a pain in the neck, a judgmental critic, an occasionally hysterical, ever-persistent nuisance. When the teacher, worn out and frustrated, eventually gives up on your child, decides he's beyond her ability or resources to help, she's as glad to see you go as she's relieved that your son won't be back to remind her of her limitations. "With a crazy, irrational parent like that," you imagine her saying to her colleagues, "no wonder the kid has problems."

Do I sound paranoid, cynical? I didn't used to be this way, but I'm the product of a combined total of 50 years of dealing with alcohol-damaged children—for not only does the son I wrote about in *The Broken Cord* (1989) suffer from fetal alcohol syndrome, but his adopted brother and sister are, to a lesser extent, victims of fetal alcohol effect.

My wife and I and our extended families have had no choice but to become a kind of full-time social service agency specializing in referrals, the admissions policies of various institutions, the penalties meted out under the juvenile justice system, the nightmares of dealing with uninformed, often smug, bureaucrats given by default responsibility for people who can't make it on their own in contemporary America. We were forced to progress from attending increasingly sour PTA meetings to learning the intricacies of intelligence testing—hoping that the score will come in below 70 and thus qualify the child for legal disability. We've had to become acquainted with the admissions policies and maximum lengths of stays at institutions such as Covenant House, Boys Town, and the Salvation Army. We've paid out well over $150,000, not counting what insurance has covered, for our children's primary and secondary special school tuitions, counseling, doctors of every sort, experimental medical procedures, Outward Bound for Troubled Youth, and private camps for the learning disabled. We have managed to try every single avenue that has been suggested to us by well-meaning people who should know what might benefit our sons and daughter, and nothing—nothing—has consistently worked for more than a few months.

Our older children, now all adults or nearly so, cannot function independently, cannot hold jobs, tell the truth, manage money, plan a future. They have all, at one time or another, been arrested or otherwise detained for shoplifting, inappropriate sexual conduct, or violent behavior. Despite all our efforts to protect them, they have periodically come under the influence of people who, for instance, worship Satan, or who take advantage of them physically, mentally, and/or financially. They maintain no enduring friendships, set for themselves no realistic goals, can call upon no inner voice to distinguish right from wrong or the safe from the dangerous.

Okay—maybe it's us. Maybe we're incredibly dysfunctional parents. Believe me, we've spent years feeling guilty and inadequate, holding on to the belief that if only we could become better, more resourceful, more sympathetic, more enlightened in our expectations and requirements, we could alter the bleak future that seems to lie in store or has already arrived for them. Like every self-reflective father and mother, we can recall our failures, our lapses, our losses of temper, and time after time we have added up these shortcomings to see if they balance the devastating total of our children's current situations. *The Broken Cord* was written, at least in part, to further this process, to assign guilt—if not wholly to us, then to somebody, something—to make not just sense of a senseless waste, but a difference. If every stone were overturned maybe something would be discovered that could reverse the fate of not just any anonymous afflicted fetus, child, or adult, but of our children.

But what the book yielded was worse than the least I had expected. Not only was there no magic trick, no scientific breakthrough that could "cure" our sons and daughter, but from the thousands of letters that have come from around the country it is clear that our family's private sorrow is far from unusual. In the year and a half since *The Broken Cord* was published, we have heard from parents rich and poor, religious and agnostic, and of all ethnic groups. Some live in cities, some in small towns, some on reservations. Some are adoptive parents like us, others are the biological parents. All love their children, and almost none has given up hope. But none of them knows what to do next.

The hardest group to answer are the parents of very young children, children who seem from the symptoms described to be clearly fetal alcohol affected. I recognize these parents: in the early stages of denial, full of the surety that answers exist. They want practical advice, experts to consult, books to read, effective doctors to visit. They want to head off the unpleasant disappointments described in my book, to save their child—and themselves—from such a miserable chain of events. If *The Broken Cord* had been written by somebody else, I would have written just such a letter to its author. I would have been skeptical of his pessimism, sure that I could do better, last longer, be smarter, succeed where he had failed, so when I answer those letters, I root for those parents, applaud their confidence, ask them to write back and tell me when things improve. So far, there have been no replies.

Almost equally difficult to absorb is the mail I receive from parents whose FAS or FAE children are older than ours. They write with the weary echo of experience, the products of many cycles of raised expectations followed by dejection. They tell of their "52-year-old child", their FAE adult daughter who's just given birth to her third FAS baby and is pregnant again and still drinking. They tell of children serving 20 year prison terms or, in one case, of a "sweet" son sentenced to the death penalty for an impulsive murder for which he has never shown the slightest remorse. They tell of children raised in privilege who are now lost among the homeless on a distant city's streets, of children, once so loving and gentle, who have been maimed from drug use or knife fights, or, as is so often the case, who have been raped. They tell of innocents becoming prostitutes, of inexplicable suicide attempts, and always, always, of chemical dependency. They tell of children whose whereabouts are unknown, or who are dead at 25. This is not the way it was supposed to happen, these parents cry. It's not fair. It's not right.

We read these letters and wonder: Is this in store for our children?

I've even heard from adults diagnosed with fetal alcohol effect—one of them with a Ph.D. from Harvard and several others with master's degrees. These are highly intelligent people, the Jackie Robinsons of FAE, who have had to become specialists on themselves. Through years of observing their own trials and errors, of watching how "normal" people behave in a given context and analyzing how that contrasts with their own uncertain reactions, some of them have worked out complicated formulae to simulate a greater connection with the world than they in fact possess. One woman carries in her purse a card on which is typed a series of questions she explicitly asks herself in an attempt to gauge the consequences of her possible responses to an unprecedented situation: What would so-and-so do in this instance? What will people think if I do x, y, or z? She's compensating for life in a universe that's slightly, almost imperceptibly, alien, and speaks a language whose idiom and nuance are forever just beyond her automatic reach.

The correspondence we've received from around this country, and lately from around the world, has magnified exponentially our particular family experience, but hasn't contradicted it. The letter I've waited for, but that has yet to arrive, is the one that begins, "I've read your book and you're dead wrong," or "My child was diagnosed as having FAS but we fixed it by doing the following things and now, five years later, he's perfectly fine."

To what extent does this preventable scourge affect American Indian people? The answer, like so much about FAS, is ambiguous. On the one hand, prenatal exposure to ethanol impairs the individual fetus in exactly the same ways whether its mother is a member of a country club in Greenwich, Connecticut, or a mother receiving aid to dependent children on the White Earth reservation. Every human being is vulnerable, fragile, and easy to poison during the developmental stages; ethnicity acts as neither a shield nor a magnet. Yes, "drinking age" matters, diet counts, and smoking or other drug use will exacerbate the damage done by alcohol, but all things considered, *no* woman needs to give birth to an FAS baby; both FAS and FAE are preventable problems.

The factors that really make a difference in preventing FAS and FAE have to do with things like strong family and community support for abstinence, access to good prenatal care and chemical dependency treatment, and clear and widespread information on the dangers of drinking during pregnancy. And it's here that Native American women are at a severe disadvantage. Health programs on reservations have been among the first things cut when the federal budget gets tight: Clinics are shut down, counselors laid off, preventive educational campaigns scrapped. Access to organizations such as Planned Parenthood is, in many tribal communities, impossible. Poverty, unemployment, despair—familiar elements in the daily lives of too many Indian people—lead to alcohol and other drug abuse. The long-range roots of the problem, and their solution, are so much bigger and more complex than "just saying no."

When you factor into the statistics on FAS and FAE those having to do with pre-natal exposure to crack cocaine—which seems to produce in children many of the same learning disabilities as too much alcohol—we are looking at something like 300,000 impaired babies born in this country annually. In 10 years that's 3 million people. By the time the first generation counted is 20, it's 6 million, and that's assuming a stable rate—not the current exponentially accelerating one. How does our society handle this onslaught, on either a local or a national level? How do we make laws that apply equally to those of us who can understand the rules and to a significant minority who, through no fault of their own, can't? How do we preserve individual liberty, free choice, safe streets, and mutual trust, when some members of society have only a minimal grasp of moral responsibility? How do we cope with the growing crime rate among young people and with violence such as "wilding" when we are faced with teaching rules and morals to individuals who are unable to comprehend our lessons?

The thorny ethical issue that has troubled me most in thinking about the social impact of FAS and other such lifelong but preventable afflictions concerns responsibility. When, if ever, are we, one on one or collectively, obliged to intervene? It's becoming increasingly clear FAS victims beget more FAS victims: A pregnant woman who can't calculate the long-term consequences of her decisions is not likely to respond to prenatal counseling. It is difficult, if not impossible, to convince her to defer an immediate gratification because nine months or nine years later her hypothetical child might suffer from it. That child is an abstraction, a hazy shadow at best, and its argument is a great deal less compelling than the draw of another drink or fix.

Some studies have suggested that compared to the "average" woman, female FAS and FAE victims start having children younger, continue having them longer, and ultimately conceive and bring to term more offspring. They are less likely to seek prenatal care, to abstain from dangerous activities during their pregnancies, or to keep custody of their babies. Statistically, a woman who has given birth to an FAS baby has almost an 8 out of 10 chance to do so again in her next pregnancy, if she continues drinking, and subsequent siblings are likely to be even more impaired than the first.

These often abandoned or removed children, whether adopted or institutionalized, are ultimately our culture's victims and therefore are its responsibility. How do we cope? At the absolute minimum, how do we—especially in a recession economy—pay the medical bills, build the prisons, construct the homeless shelters? How do we train special education teachers to function indefinitely with no hope of success, or ordinary citizens to forgive behaviors that are irritating at best, dangerous or fatal at worst? How do we teach compassion for a growing class of people who are likely to exhibit neither pity nor gratitude, who take everything society has to offer and have almost nothing constructive to give back? How do we maintain the universal franchise to vote, the cornerstone of our political system? How do we redefine "not guilty by reason of insanity" to apply to heartless acts committed by people who are fundamentally incapable of comprehending the law?

To me these questions boil down to a simple analogy: Imagine we saw a blind woman holding a child by the hand attempt to cross a busy street. The traffic was moving fast, she started to cross the street, and before our eyes her child was struck by a car and killed; a tragedy we would never forget. Then a year later we come by the same intersection again, and there's the same woman with another child. The light is against her but she doesn't see and tries to cross the street. Again, the child is hit by a car and severely injured as we stand by helplessly and watch. The next year it happens again, and the next, and the next. How many times must it happen before we become involved and take the woman's arm or hold up our hand to stop the cars or carry her child safely across the street or at least tell her when the signal is green? How many deaths or injuries are too many? When do the rights of children to safe passage assert themselves? And how long before the mother herself is killed?—for remember, she's a victim and at grave risk, too. It does no good to blame the mother, to punish her in retrospect for her blindness. Once the street is crossed, the child is dead. She needs help and we need to find a way to provide it. If we turn our backs and walk away, we stop being innocent bystanders and become accomplices in the inevitable accident.

Let us make no mistake about one point: We're not facing a crisis, we're in one, though official statistics can be deceiving. A couple of years ago South Dakota, a state with no resident dysmorphologist at the time, reported a grand total of two FAS births—during the same period in which my friend Jeaneen Grey Eagle, director of Project Recovery in Pine Ridge, estimated that somewhere between one-third and one-half of the infants born in certain communities of her reservation were at high risk due to heavy maternal drinking. Underdiagnosis, unfortunately, does not mean small numbers.

But what can we do about it? Each person must provide his or her own answers. Some of us—the scientists—can study the biochemistry involved in fetal damage from drugs, learn to predict which women are most at risk and then, figure out how much ethanol, if any, is tolerable. Others—advocates and politicians—can address the issue of prevention: get out the word, make pests of ourselves, speak up even when it makes our friends uncomfortable, fight for the future of a child not yet even conceived. Still others—social workers, psychologists, and educators—can tackle the needs of the here-and-now, of the tens of thousands of FAS and FAE men, women, and children who exist on the margins of society. We can devise effective curricula, learning regimens, humane models for dependent care.

If we put our minds to it, if we do our part, we might not obliterate fetal alcohol syndrome on a global level, but, in all candor, we could save many lives, many mothers, many babies. All it takes is nine months of abstinence, a bit longer if a mother breast-feeds—300,000 separate and discrete solutions, 300,000 miracles, and it's a clean year.

And finally, some of us, the parents into whose care these children have been given, whether by birth or adoption, can try to get through another day, to survive the next unexpected catastrophe, to preserve a sense of humor. We laugh at things that really aren't funny—quite the contrary—but we laugh, without malice, for relief. When our oldest son, "Adam" in *The Broken Cord*, went with me last fall to his annual case management meeting, he was asked to list all the accomplishments in the last 12 months about which he felt especially proud. He drew a blank.

"Then, tell us what you've been doing since we met here last year," the man directed—and Adam complied.

"Well, I went down the stairs and I opened the door," he began. "Then I got into the car and my father took me home. For supper we had . . . " Adam tried to remember that anonymous meal he polished off some 365 days before, stalled, and looked to me for help.

"Next question," I suggested, and the social worker consulted his list.

"Tell me what things you really *don't* like to do," he invited.

Adam's eyes lit. This was an easy one. "I don't like to dig up burdocks," he stated.

I blinked in surprise. Adam hadn't dug up burdocks in three years. He was simply using a response that had worked in the past.

"Wait a minute," I said. "Adam, thousands of people all over the country have read your chapter at the end of the book about how you dug up those burdocks to help us. People liked that part so much I think that's why they gave our book that prize you have sitting on your dresser. People are very proud of you for what you did. I know it wasn't fun to dig up those plants, but you should feel good that you did it."

Adam was having an especially polite day. He smiled at me, cocked his head, and asked: "What book would that be?"

The grind doesn't get easier and it doesn't go away. FAS victims do not learn from experience, do not get well. My wife, Louise, keeps a diary, and a while back she glanced back over the last four years. That can be dangerous, because there are some things you don't notice until you take the long view. It turned out that as a family we hadn't had a single period longer than three consecutive days in all that time when one of our alcohol-impaired children was *not* in a crisis—health, home, school—that demanded our undivided attention. It often seems to us that their problems define our existence as well as their own, and in that respect perhaps we are in a small way the forecast of things to come for this country. FAS is not a problem whose impact is restricted to its victims. It is not just a woman's issue, and not just a man's issue. No one is exempt. These are everybody's children.

## Reference

Dorris, M. (1989). *The broken cord.* New York: Harper & Row.

27

# Mexico's Challenge:
# Facing a Growing Youth Population

**Beatriz Rivera de Tarrab**
**Patricia Ortega-Andeane**
**Jorge Manuel Velasco-Alzaga**

This chapter gives us an opportunity to present some basic observations about the prevention of human distress, the distribution of major suffering, and the anguish of those who are disturbed, and their families and communities as well. Such disturbances represent a very high financial and social cost.

We are aware that primary prevention is a mode of achieving, in a very broad and idealistic way, the attainment of health as it is defined by the World Health Organization (WHO), namely, an integral state of well-being, physical, mental, and social, rather than simply the absence of disease. Mexico has been associated with the WHO ever since this organization was established as a specialized agency concerned with health within the organization of the United Nations. Our country has a long history of struggle for these ideals. We share with other countries this aspiration for health because of its humanistic content and because of the universal nature of these longings; this motivation is shared by every human being on this planet.

## A Little History

Even before the arrival of the Spaniards in 1492 there existed two very widely developed civilizations in the territories that are now Mexico and Peru. After almost half a millennium, there are many cultural and social values remaining among the present populations that are reasons for pride and identification.

EDITORS' NOTE: The VCPPP presentation by the Mexican participants was largely in the form of charts and tables. They presented 13 tables and 17 graphs, with brief discussion and commentary about each. This chapter has been adapted from their presentation to give a reasonable summary of their report. For additional information, write to Patricia Ortega-Andeane, director, Division of Support to States of Mexico of the National System for the Comprehensive Development of the Family, Mexico City, Mexico.

349

This is why, in spite of the submission forced upon the people since the conquest of Mexico and Peru, and the unequal and cruel battles that followed from 1521 to 1821, Mexico finally reached political independence. Since then there has been a persistent need, deeply rooted in the population, for freedom and independence. This need was reactivated in 1910 when the first social revolution of this century led to the present Mexico and its culture. The growth of the country has not been easy, as it has had to survive many conquests, invasions, and abuses. For many reasons the present country is a young nation. It is growing rapidly, as indicated by a population of young people who are in a significant majority. Mexico has a very high rate of growth from the demographic point of view. Since the beginning of this century the nation has grown from 13.5 million to slightly more than 86 million persons. By the year 2000 it is anticipated that the population will be more than 100 million. In this respect Mexico follows a phenomenon observed in many other countries of the world, particularly in the so-called less developed regions.

Early in the 1970s the president of the Republic of Mexico sent to the Legislative Congress of the Union an initiative for a new law that was approved on December 11, 1973. The law involved the adoption of population policies concerned with the reduction of infant mortality, the promotion of services for family planning, and efforts at motivating the public to make use of family planning methods.

On February 6, 1990, the president of the Republic of Mexico, Licenciado Carlos Salinas de Gortari, on the occasion of the presentation of the national program of population, stated that the economic crisis of the decade of the 1980s seems to have slowed the speed of the important trend achieved in demographic control. President Salinas indicated further that with a simultaneous action to reduce the rate of growth of the population there should be efforts at promoting the well-being of inhabitants and increasing life expectancy at birth.

We cannot forget that there are infants and children who do not find satisfactory responses to their basic needs, from either their families or their social milieu. Therefore, they seek in the streets what they need and hope to find. But they encounter a real social risk. Many times what they find is indifference, violence, and lack of genuine affection. Because of this, the National System for the Comprehensive Development of the Family (Spanish acronym, DIF) has conceptualized policies to develop programs to attend to youth through two main action lines: first, for young people who live in the streets, the DIF has developed the Program for Youngsters in Special Situations; second, with a preventive focus, is the Program for the Comprehensive Development of Adolescents (which actually is the main program of the DIF).

### Program for Youngsters in Special Situations

The Program for Youngsters in Special Situations began three years ago across the whole country. Today we know, based on data, that these adolescents actually do have families, and in general are neither delinquents nor addicted to drugs. Some 89% are between the ages of 10 and 18, and 90% are living in family situations. They work in the streets in order to assist their families financially. However, many social agencies confuse children who work in the streets with children who live in the streets.

Street life represents a high social risk for all the children who spend parts of their day living and working there. One of the objectives of our programs is to help youths to engage in satisfactory activities and prevent their detachment from the family and the school. Therefore, this program is basically preventive because it attempts to give support to the comprehensive development to which every youngster is entitled.

### Program for the Comprehensive Development of Adolescents

Mexico is a country of young people who require adequate challenges to their energies and potentialities. It has been estimated that in 1990 there were more than 15 million Mexican youth between the ages of 12 and 19.

The Program for the Comprehensive Development of Adolescents is an alternative program that promotes the adequate development of all areas of teenage life within the framework of Mexican cultural richness and with the aim of recovering and asserting our national values. It is assumed that adolescence is a stage of transition, in which the individual undergoes profound transformation in biological, psychological, and social spheres that contribute to the process of self-assertion.

### Survey of the National System for the Comprehensive Development of the Family

Young people are the products of the society to which they belong. Their opportunities for development are often restricted, and that is why they represent a high-risk group. One of the most important tasks of society is to promote in youth a sense of responsibility for their nation and their culture. Therefore, the National System for the Comprehensive Development of the Family has prepared a program to promote the development of adolescents as an institutional responsibility based on the law for a national system for social welfare. This program attends the needs of adolescents, using a preventive approach. It is based on knowledge of the specific situations and factors that affect the quality and the development of youth.

In order to identify the needs, interests, and habits of adolescence we have carried out a survey to understand the characteristics, situations, and opinions of the youth population. This has been developed as the Inventory of Needs, Interests, and Habits of Adolescents. Two preliminary versions of the inventory have been developed in order to make necessary adjustments by applying it to public school junior high and high school samples in Mexico City. A third version of the instrument consists of 10 general demographic questions and 99 items (with a Likert-type response scale). The general areas evaluated are health, personal development, family and social relationships, school, and work.

A large random sample was surveyed using the instruments in the five most important regions in Mexico: North, South, Central, Gulf of Mexico, and Pacific Coast. The sample included an open population of adolescents. A second, smaller sample consisted of young people on the streets. Altogether, close to 3,000 adolescents were sampled.

A factor analysis of the results was carried out using the principal component method. This resulted in an explained variance of 82.5% with 12 valid factors. Listed in order of explained variance, the factors are as follows:

(1) Family relationships
(2) Work
(3) Delinquency and drug abuse
(4) School
(5) Sex
(6) Social welfare
(7) Sex education
(8) Work orientation
(9) Modern life-styles
(10) Friendship
(11) Personal development
(12) Attitudes toward addiction

A reliability analysis resulted in very high reliability quotients of .94 and .95.

Detailed results are available from the authors. Briefly, it is clear that the families of the open sample group had a very positive outlook in terms of support, communication, and concern for family members, thus demonstrating no need for help in this area. On the other hand, the street youth were different enough to demonstrate a need for support.

The second factor, which measures work, showed that in the open sample nearly one-fourth had never worked, 30% had worked sometimes, and 45.6% had always worked. By way of contrast, the street sample showed that only

11.5% had never worked, 27.4% had worked sometimes, and 61.1% had always worked.

With regard to delinquency and drug abuse, the overwhelming majority of the open sample (84.5%) rejected gangs and drug abuse. In the street sample only 62% always reported such rejection. It was concluded that because in the latter group a significant proportion did not reject delinquency and drug abuse there was cause for alarm and a demonstrated need for drug education.

Other findings showed fairly consistently that the open sample was more interested in school, had received more information about sex, and felt more secure than the street sample. Both groups had negative perceptions about social services and social welfare, demonstrating a need for more information and more support. There was clearly a greater need for sex education in the street youth. On the other hand, street youth knew a lot more about how and where to get jobs, in contrast to the random group. In general, both groups reacted in similar ways to adapting to modern life. There was need for friendship, support, and help in both groups.

## Conclusion

From the overall analysis of our sampling of Mexican youth we conclude that there are significant differences between the open sample and the street youth sample. Considering that the open sample adolescents showed very close family relationships, the street youth did not have as stable family lives and yet they still preserved family links. The street youth go into the streets driven by economic needs, looking for jobs, not because of critical family situations. On the other hand, the open sample shows that apart from having a stable family this group feels relatively satisfied with school activities and is interested in becoming acquainted with future work possibilities.

However, there are factors that should be addressed in both the open and street youth samples. These are reflected in attitudes toward sexuality and friendship. There is a need for greater information about these areas, so that fear and insecurity can be overcome and the emotions and actions of young people can be channeled in a positive way. Attitudes toward drug addiction can become a very important risk, particularly for the street youth, since they do not show consistent rejection in their attitudes toward drug use.

Finally, we believe we have created an instrument for the evaluation of the principal needs, interests, and habits of adolescents that is a valid and reliable measurement tool. The instrument will be applied in a national survey in the near future.

# PART VII
# Looking Ahead

On the final morning of the 1990 Vermont Conference, participants gathered to consider a vision for future worldwide collaborations in improving children's lives. A panel including George Albee and Lynne Bond from the VCPPP; Max Abbott, president elect of the World Federation for Mental Health (WFMH); Beverly Benson Long, vice president for North America of the WFMH; and Hilda Robbins, board member at large for the WFMH, briefly discussed strategies for developing a more powerful international prevention network around supporting our youth. After spirited discussion among conference attendees, Dr. Abbott announced that at the upcoming board meeting of the WFMH he would propose the establishment of an international committee on primary prevention. This committee was subsequently appointed, with Beverly Benson Long as chair.

Dr. Abbott also indicated that he was going to recommend to the WFMH the establishment of a Committee Investigating the Commercial Sexual Exploitation of Children. With the approval of the board of the WFMH, this committee was subsequently established, with Drs. Mawaheb El-Mouelhy and Arshad Husain, two of the conference speakers and authors in this volume, named as cochairs.

Conference participants were also informed of the existence of other committees concerned with primary prevention efforts. These committees include the International Committee for Primary Prevention, World Federation for Mental Health (c/o Beverly Long, vice president for North America, 1036 Somerset Drive, N.W., Atlanta, GA 30327, USA); International Network of Community Research and Action (c/o Wolfgang Stark, Selbsthilfezentrum, Munchen Bayenstr. 77a, D-800 Munchen 2, Germany); and Prevention Clearinghouse, National Mental Health Association (1021 Prince Street, Alexandria, VA 22314-2971, USA).

Finally, the conference participants unanimously endorsed the subsequently enacted U.N. Convention on the Rights of the Child. With permission from the American Psychological Association, we reprint a summary of these rights from the January 1991 issue of the *American Psychologist* (Vol. 46, No. 1, pp. 50-52), together with a descriptive article by Brian L. Wilcox and Hedwin Naimark.

# 28

# The Rights of the Child: Progress Toward Human Dignity

Brian L. Wilcox
Hedwin Naimark

The United Nations (U.N.) Convention on the Rights of the Child was adopted by the 159 Member States of the U.N. General Assembly on November 20, 1989. The Convention, which is in fact a treaty, went into force less than a year later, on September 2, 1990, after ratification by more than 20 member nations. Never before in the history of the U.N. has an international human rights treaty so quickly come into force. To date, 54 nations, not including the United States, have ratified the Convention.

Although the Convention is legally binding only on those nations that have ratified it, its ramifications extend beyond the legal aspects. The adoption, rapid ratification, and very existence of this Convention exert a moral pressure on all nations—including those that have not yet ratified it—to examine their current attitudes toward and treatment of children.

For psychologists, the implications also extend beyond the obvious ones for the world's children. The existence of such a comprehensive document defining the rights of children can serve as a stimulus or tool for the work of psychologists in all their professional settings. The rights detailed in the Convention, and the developmental model of the child they imply, can stimulate a rethinking of the ways in which psychologists interact with children in therapeutic, research, education,and public policy settings. Likewise, implementation of the rights defined in the Convention can provide opportunities for psychologists to contribute to a better understanding of the developmental and social effects of these rights on the lives of children and adults.

AUTHORS' NOTE: This article appeared originally in *American Psychologist*, Vol. 46, No. 1, p. 49. Copyright 1991 by the American Psychological Association. Reprinted by permission. Correspondence concerning this article should be addressed to Brian Wilcox, Public Interest Directorate, American Psychological Association, 1200 Seventeenth Street, N. W., Washington, DC 20036.

The articles from this Convention are not the first ones on the subject of the rights of children that have appeared in the *American Psychologist*. A number of authors have analyzed various aspects of children's rights (e.g., Hart & Brassard, 1987; Horowitz, 1989; Melton, 1983; Melton & Davidson, 1987); however, the authors here focus on the rights of children from psychological and legal perspectives in an international context. Each article examines the interrelationships among child, family, and the state; the reshaping of these interrelationships represents one of the primary goals of the Convention. The principles contained in the Convention express a powerful view of the child not only as a member of a family but as a unique individual. The combining of the political and civil rights of children with economic, social, and cultural rights makes this Convention unique. The drafters of the Convention realized that unless economic or nurturance rights that serve as the basis for survival and healthy development are recognized, civil and political freedoms might well be irrelevant.

Although the U.N. Convention on the Rights of the Child offers new hope in the effort to foster children's health and development, it is not a panacea for all of the ills afflicting the world's children. By and large, human rights treaties, as legal documents, are only as powerful as the developing international consensus on the rights defined. The moral consensus that is expressed in the Convention is a tool that can be used to help not only governments but all interested parties enhance their understanding of children's needs and make the financial commitment required to meet those needs. It is incumbent upon professionals to acknowledge that children represent the future and that the future must be protected by recognizing the rights of every child. Psychologists can help in this process through their teaching, practice, research, and advocacy.

Although only a small number of social scientists participated in the development of the Convention, psychologists now have the opportunity to use their expertise to enhance the process of interpreting and implementing it. One goal of the articles in this Convention is to stimulate the interest and involvement of psychologists in this process.

## References

Hart, S. N., & Brassard, M. R. (1987). A major threat to children's mental health: Psychological maltreatment. *American Psychologist, 42,* 160-165.

Horowitz, F. D. (Ed.). (1989). Children and their development: Knowledge base, research agenda, and social policy application [Special issue]. *American Psychologist, 44* 95-490.

Melton, G. (1983). Toward "personhood" for adolescents: Autonomy and privacy as values in public policy. *American Psychologist, 38,* 99-103.

Melton, G., & Davidson, H. A. (1987). Child protection and society: When should the state intervene? *American Psychologist, 42,* 172-175.

**29**

# U.N. Convention on
# the Rights of the Child:
# Unofficial Summary of Articles

### Foreword

This is a summary of the contents of the 54 articles contained in the United Nations Convention on the Rights of the Child. It is meant to be used as a guide for those who want to study or locate certain parts of the actual text or for those who want to gain a sense of the content of the U.N. Convention without reading each article in its original form. As such, there are many omissions, as well as language that differs from the original text. Therefore, this should not be considered an official abbreviated version of the Convention. It was adapted with permission from publications of Defense for Children International-USA.

### Article 1—Definition of Child

Every person under 18, unless national law grants majority at an earlier age.

### Article 2—Freedom From Discrimination

Rights in the Convention to apply to all children without exception; the State to protect children from any form of discrimination or punishment based on family's status, activities, or beliefs.

---

EDITORS' NOTE: This summary appeared originally in *American Psychologist*, Vol. 46, No. 1, pp. 40-52. Copyright 1991 by the American Psychological Association. Reprinted by permission. Correspondence concerning this article should be addressed to Stuart Hart, Office for the Study of the Psychological Rights of the Child, School of Education, Indiana University-Purdue University at Indianapolis, 902 West New York Street, Indianapolis, IN 46202-5155.

### Article 3—Best Interests of Child

The best interests of the child to prevail in all legal and administrative decisions; the State to ensure the establishment of institutional standards for the care and protection of children.

### Article 4—Implementation of Rights

The State to translate the rights in the Convention into actuality.

### Article 5—Respect for Parental Responsibility

The State to respect the rights of parents or guardians to provide direction to the child in the exercise of the rights in the Convention in a manner consistent with the child's evolving capacities.

### Article 6—Survival and Development

The child's right to life; the State to ensure the survival and maximum development of the child.

### Article 7—Name and Nationality

The right to a name and to acquire a nationality; the right to know and be cared for by parents.

### Article 8—Preservation of Identity

The right to preserve or reestablish the child's identity (name, nationality,and family ties).

### Article 9—Parental Care and Nonseparation

The right to live with parents unless this is deemed incompatible with the child's best interests; the right to maintain contact with both parents; the State to provide information when separation results from State action.

## Article 10—Family Reunification

The right to leave or enter any country for family reunification and to maintain contact with both parents.

## Article 11—Illicit Transfer and Nonreturn

The State to combat the illicit transfer and nonreturn of children abroad.

## Article 12—Free Expression of Opinion

The child's right to express an opinion in matters affecting the child and to have that opinion heard.

## Article 13—Freedom of Information

The right to seek, receive, and impart information through the medium of choice.

## Article 14—Freedom of Thought, Conscience, and Religion

The right to determine and practice any belief; the State to respect the rights of parents or guardians to provide direction in the exercise of this right in a manner consistent with the child's evolving capacities.

## Article 15—Freedom of Association

The right to freedom of association and freedom of peaceful assembly.

## Article 16—Protection of Privacy

The right to legal protection against arbitrary or unlawful interference with privacy, family, home, or correspondence, or attacks on honor and reputation.

## Article 17—Media and Information

The State to ensure access to information and material from a diversity of national and international sources.

## Article 18—Parental Responsibilities

The State to recognize the principle that both parents are responsible for the upbringing of their children; the State to assist parents or guardians in this responsibility and to ensure the provision of child care for eligible working parents.

## Article 19—Abuse and Neglect

The State to protect children from all forms of physical or mental injury or abuse, neglect, and exploitation by parents or others, and to undertake preventive and treatment programs in this regard.

## Article 20—Children Without Families

The right to receive special protection and assistance from the State when deprived of family environment and to be provided with alternative care, such as foster placements or Kafala of Islamic Law, adoption, or institutional placement.

## Article 21—Adoption

The State to regulate the process of adoption (including intercountry adoption), where it is permitted.

## Article 22—Refugee Children

The State to ensure protection and assistance to children who are refugees or are seeking refugee status, and to cooperate with competent organizations providing such protection and assistance, including assistance in locating missing family members.

## Article 23—Disabled Children

The right of disabled children to special care and training designed to help achieve self-reliance and a full and active life in society; the State to promote international cooperation in the exchange and dissemination of information on preventive health care, treatment of disabled children, and methods of rehabilitation.

## Article 24—Health Care

The right to the highest attainable standard of health and access to medical services; the State to attempt to diminish infant and child mortality, combat disease and malnutrition, ensure health care for expectant mothers, provide access to health education, including the advantages of breast-feeding, develop preventive health care, abolish harmful traditional practices, and promote international cooperation to achieve this right.

## Article 25—Periodic Review

The right of children placed by the State for reasons of care, protection, or treatment, to have all aspects of that placement reviewed regularly.

## Article 26—Social Security

The right, where appropriate, to benefit from social security or insurance.

## Article 27—Standard of Living

The right to an adequate standard of living; the State to assist parents who cannot meet this responsibility and to try to recover maintenance for the child from persons having financial responsibility, both within the State and abroad.

## Article 28—Education

The right to education; the State to provide free and compulsory primary education, to ensure equal access to secondary and higher education, and to ensure that school discipline reflects the child's human dignity.

## Article 29—Aims of Education

The States Parties' agreement that education be directed at developing the child's personality and talents to their fullest potential; preparing the child for active life as an adult; developing respect for the child's parents, basic human rights, the natural environment, and the child's own cultural and national values and those of others.

### Article 30—Children of Minorities

The right of children of minority communities and indigenous populations to enjoy their own culture, to practice their own religion, and to use their own language.

### Article 31—Leisure and Recreation

The right to leisure, play, and participation in cultural and artistic activities.

### Article 32—Child Labor

The right to be protected from economic exploitation and from engaging in work that constitutes a threat to health, education, and development; the State to set minimum ages for employment, regulate conditions of employment, and provide sanctions for effective enforcement.

### Article 33—Narcotics

The State to protect children from illegal narcotic and psychotropic drugs and from involvement in their production or distribution.

### Article 34—Sexual Exploitation

The State to protect children from sexual exploitation and abuse, including prostitution and involvement in pornography.

### Article 35—Sale and Trafficking

The State to prevent the sale, trafficking, and abduction of children.

### Article 36—Other Exploitation

The State to protect children from all other forms of exploitation.

## Article 37—Torture, Capital Punishment, and Deprivation of Liberty

The State to protect children from torture or other cruel, inhuman, or degrading treatment or punishment; capital punishment or life imprisonment for offenses committed by persons below the age of 18; and unlawful or arbitrary deprivation of liberty. The right of children deprived of liberty to be treated with humanity and respect, to be separated from adults, to maintain contact with family members, and to have prompt access to legal assistance.

## Article 38—Armed Conflict

The State to respect international humanitarian law, to ensure that no child under 15 takes a direct part in hostilities, to refrain from recruiting any child under 15 into the armed forces, and to ensure that all children affected by armed conflict benefit from protection and care.

## Article 39—Rehabilitative Care

The State to ensure the physical and psychological recovery and social reintegration of child victims of abuse, neglect, exploitation, torture, or armed conflicts.

## Article 40—Juvenile Justice

The right of accused children to be treated with dignity. The State to ensure that no child is accused by reason of acts or omissions not prohibited by law at the time committed; every accused child is informed promptly of the charges, presumed innocent until proven guilty in a prompt and fair trial, receives legal assistance, and is not compelled to give testimony or confess guilt; and alternatives to institutional care are available.

## Article 41—Supremacy of Higher Standards

The standards contained in this Convention not to supersede higher standards contained in national law or other international instruments.

### Article 42—Public Awareness

States to make the rights contained in this Convention widely known to both adults and children.

### Article 43—Committee on the Rights of the Child

Election of a Committee on the Rights of the Child to examine the progress made by States Parties in achieving their obligations under the Convention and establishment of rules of procedure.

### Article 44—Reports by States

States to submit to the Committee reports on measures adopted that give effect to rights in the Convention and on progress made in the enjoyment of those rights, and to make the reports widely available to the public in their own countries.

### Article 45—Implementation

The right of the specialized agencies and UNICEF to be represented at Committee proceedings; the prerogative of the Committee to invite competent bodies to provide expert advice, to request the Secretary-General to undertake studies and to make recommendations.

### Article 46—Signature

The Convention to be open for signature by all States.

### Article 47—Ratification

The Convention to be subject to ratification.

### Article 48—Accession

The Convention to be open to accession by any State.

## Article 49—Entry into Force

The Convention to enter into force on the 30th day after the 20th instrument of ratification or accession deposited with the Secretary-General.

## Article 50—Amendments

Provision for amending the Convention if approved by the General Assembly of the U.N. and accepted by a two-thirds majority of States Parties; binding on those States Parties that have accepted it.

## Article 51—Reservations

Provisions for States to make certain permitted reservations, so long as they do not conflict with the object and purpose of the Convention.

## Article 52—Denunciation

Provision for denunciation of the Convention by a State Party to become effective one year after date of receipt.

## Article 53—Depositary

Designation of Secretary-General of the U.N. as the depositary of the Convention.

## Article 54—Authentic Text

Arabic, Chinese, English, French, Russian, and Spanish texts of the Convention to be equally authentic.

# Name Index

368

# Subject Index

# About the Contributors

**Max W. Abbott**, Ph.D., is the Director of the Mental Health Foundation of New Zealand and President Elect of the World Federation of Mental Health. Last year he coordinated the biennial meeting of the WFMH in Auckland. He has been active in research on primary prevention, including sexual abuse, media violence, and health promotion.

**George W. Albee**, Ph.D., is Professor of Psychology at the University of Vermont and President of the Vermont Conference on Primary Prevention of Psychopathology, Inc. He is past president of the American Psychological Association (1969-1970), and he has been Chair of the Board of Social and Ethical Responsibility in Psychology. He chaired the Task Panel on Prevention for President Carter's Commission on Mental Health, and served as a member of the Commission on Prevention of the National Mental Health Association.

**Victor A. Battistich**, Ph.D., is Senior Research Associate at the Developmental Studies Center in San Ramon, California. He has been conducting research on the Child Development Project since its inception in 1981, and has published widely on the project and its effects on children's social and moral development. His current interests include the relationships between school practices and children's cognitive, affective, and social development, and the promotion of healthy development through school-based primary prevention.

**Olga V. Bazhenova**, Ph.D., is a Senior Researcher in the Department for Child Preventive Psychiatry at All-Union Research Center for Mental Health in Moscow. She is a principal investigator in a project investigating circular dependencies between mother's behavior and infant mental health. She is also interested in the development of primary prevention programs for infants and toddlers in all-day child-care centers. She is the author of the Soviet Infant Mental Development Assessment Scales, and has published 12 articles and a monograph.

**Agnieszka Bleja**, M.A., is Assistant in Preventive Psychology at the Adam Mickiewicz University in Poznan, Poland. Her research and teaching interests are focused on risk factors in psychopathology, the role of competence in art, and music in health promotion.

**Lynne A. Bond**, Ph.D., is Professor of Psychology and Dean of the Graduate College at the University of Vermont. Her research has focused on early child development, family interaction, and strategies for optimizing early childhood development. She is Co-Principal Investigator of Listening Partners, a preventive/promotive intervention to foster the cognitive and socioemotional development of isolated rural mothers and their children. She has chaired a number of the Vermont Conferences on the Primary Prevention of Psychopathology.

**Leslie R. Branden-Muller**, M.S., is a doctoral student in clinical psychology at Rutgers University, where her principal clinical interests are in children and families. Her research has focused on the interrelationship and development of cognitive, affective, and social-cognitive skills in children. She also works as a consultant for the Improving Social Awareness-Social Problem Solving Project.

**John A. Calhoun**, M.P.A., M.Div., is Executive Director of the U.S. National Crime Prevention Council. During his tenure as the Commissioner of the Administration for Children, Youth and Families and Chief of the Children's Bureau, the landmark Adoption and Child Welfare Act of 1980 was passed. He currently serves on several national boards: National Committee for the Prevention of Child Abuse, Youth Service America, National Center for Early Adolescence, National Parent Aide Association, and the Center for International Leadership.

**Kenneth B. Clark**, Ph.D., is Distinguished Professor of Psychology Emeritus of the City College of the City University of New York, and one of the best-known architects of the U.S. Supreme Court's decision on school integration (*Brown v. Board of Education*, 1954). He is President of Kenneth B. Clark and Associates, Inc., a consultation firm working with educational institutions, private corporations, and government agencies on personnel matters, with particular emphasis on human relations, race relations, and affirmative action programs. He is the author of numerous articles and several books, including *Prejudice and Your Child* (1955) and the prize-winning *Dark Ghetto* (1965). He is past president of the American Psychological Association and of the Society for the Psychological Study of Social Issues.

**Mark R. Connolly**, M.P.H., is Principal Adviser of CHILDHOPE in Guatemala and is active in several programs to support children and war victims in Central America. He is also a Program Consultant for Street Kids International in Toronto, Canada, and a Health Education Consultant for the Division of Community Affairs at the H.B. Fuller Company in Saint Paul, Minnesota. His recent publications include a book he coauthored with David Werner titled *The Karate Kid Book: What We Need to Know About AIDS*; *Street Kids International*; and

*Adrift in the City: A Comparative Study of Street Children in Bogota, Colombia and Guatemala City.*

**Michael Dorris** is Adjunct Professor of Anthropology at Dartmouth College, where he has taught in the Native American Studies Program. Now a full-time writer, he is author of two novels, *A Yellow Raft in Blue Water* and *The Crown of Columbus*, the latter coauthored by Louise Erdrich. In addition, he wrote *The Broken Cord*, a work of nonfiction that has been translated into many languages. He is active in efforts to prevent damaging effects on infants of maternal use of alcohol, crack, and other toxic substances.

**Alan Durning** is Senior Researcher at the Worldwatch Institute. His writing and thinking have focused, in particular, upon the relationship between poverty and ecological degradation. He is also the author of *Poverty and the Environment: Reversing the Downward Spiral* (Worldwatch Paper 92).

**Zdenek Dytrych**, M.D., is Associate Professor and Head of the Department of Social Psychiatry at the Psychiatric Research Institute in Prague, Czechoslovakia. He has collaborated extensively with Henry David, director of the Transnational Family Research Institute, on investigations of the long-term effects on children of being born from an unwanted pregnancy. His research has been funded by the Center for Population Research, the U.S. National Institute for Child Health and Human Development, the Ford Foundation, the World Health Organization, and the Czechoslovak State Research Plan.

**Maurice J. Elias**, Ph.D., is Associate Professor of Psychology at Rutgers University and is Co-Director of the William T. Grant Foundation-supported Improving Social Awareness-Social Problem Solving Project. This project received the 1988 Lela Rowland Prevention Award from the National Mental Health Association and, most recently, was approved by the Program Effectiveness Panel of the National Diffusion Network as a federally validated substance abuse prevention program. He is also Co-Chair of the Consortium on the School-Based Promotion of Social Competence. He specializes in clinical/community psychology and child, adolescent, and family development.

**Mawaheb El-Mouelhy**, M.D., trained and practiced obstetrics and gynecology in Cairo, and then worked in Saudi Arabia and the United Arab Emirates. She has focused on the field of family planning and women's health for the last four years. She is currently the Director of the Model Centre Affiliated with the Cairo Family Planning Association and is involved in research on women's reproductive health, status, and development. She is a member of the Arab Women Solidarity Association and the Association of African Women for

Research and Development, and was recently named Co-Chair of the World Federation of Mental Health's Committee to Investigate the Commercial Sexual Exploitation of Children.

**Anna V. Gorunova,** M.D., is a Senior Researcher in the Department for Child Preventive Psychiatry at All-Union Research Center for Mental Health in Moscow. Her research interests focus on neurological markers of child mental disorders. She has authored 25 articles.

**Chok C. Hiew,** Ph.D., born in Malaysia, is Professor of Psychology at the University of New Brunswick in Canada. He received his Ph.D. from the University of Colorado in Boulder in 1973. He has lived and worked in Malaysia, Singapore, Thailand, and Japan. His teaching interests include community and health psychology. Currently he is working on a preventive intervention with adolescents as well as projects concerned with stress management and health promotion in the workplace, and work life and family life linkages.

**Cees Hoefnagels,** M.Sc., has 10 years of experience in the field of prevention, having held several positions in outpatient mental health services and in the field of education in the Netherlands. His work has focused on child sexual abuse, and he has written about perpetrators of sexual violence. Recently he has been working on a nationwide community awareness program on child abuse in the Netherlands. He is a psychologist and a project manager, and is Chief of the Prevention Team of the Institute for Outpatient Mental Health Care in Utrecht.

**Clemens M. H. Hosman,** Ph.D., is Associate Professor in Preventive Psychology at the University of Nijmegen in the Netherlands. His main research focus is on the systematic development and evaluation of prevention programs. At the Nijmegen Postgraduate School for Mental Health, he is participating in the development of a National Postgraduate Program on Prevention of Mental Disorders and Mental Health Promotion. He is a prevention consultant for the World Health Organization in Europe and member of the WHO Task Force on Mental Health Education and Mental Health Promotion, as well as the initiator of a European WHO Task Force for Prevention of Mental Disorders.

**Syed Arshad Husain,** M.D., is Professor of Child Psychiatry and Chief of the Section, and Professor of Child Health at the University of Missouri School of Medicine. Born in Delhi, India, and trained at Dow Medical College, Karachi, Pakistan, he has been active in cross-cultural psychiatric groups and recently served as President of the Asian American Caucus of Psychiatrists. He is Vice President for North America of the World Islamic Mental Health Association. A frequent visitor to Pakistan, where he continues an active cross-cultural research program, he has written extensively about sexual abuse of children and about suicide and depression in children and adolescents.

**Hans Janssen** is a social educationalist with 20 years of experience in producing television programs, magazines, and books for parents, as well as providing educational guidance to parent groups. He is currently working as a Youth Preventive Worker at a Regional Institute for Outpatient Mental Health Care (RIAGG Zuidhage) in the Hague. His prevention work has focused on child sexual abuse, social skills, bullying, children of parents with mental disorders, and play guidance at home.

**K. V. Kaliappan**, Ph.D., is Professor of Clinical Psychology at the University of Madras, India. He is coordinating the National Service Scheme activities for 21,000 volunteers/college students concerned with development camps that are considered as models in India. In addition to training teachers in India, he has been a visiting professor at ten different Indian universities. Widely published, he has developed training programs in behavior modification, stress management, and personality development.

**Doreen Spilton Koretz**, Ph.D., is Assistant Chief of the Prevention Research Branch, Division of Clinical Research, National Institute of Mental Health. For the last 10 years she has worked in a variety of applied research settings, performing program evaluations and policy studies related to the physical and mental health of children and families. She has special interests in developmental psychopathology and preventive research methods, and has been responsible for developing the Prevention Research Branch portfolio on the prevention of conduct disorders.

**Galina V. Kozlovskaya**, M.D., is Head of the Department for Child Preventive Psychiatry at All-Union Research Center for Mental Health in Moscow. Her research interests include mental development disorders in early childhood, their frequency in the child population, and schizophrenia risk factors. She has authored 50 articles.

**Morton Kramer**, Sc.D., is Professor Emeritus in the Department of Mental Hygiene at the School of Hygiene and Public Health, Johns Hopkins University. He has had a long and productive research career. For many years he was Head of the Biometrics Branch at the National Institute of Mental Health and subsequently at Johns Hopkins University. He has published extensively on demographic and epidemiological factors in the field; his reports have long influenced government policy as well as more specific state programs.

**Joyce Barham Lazar**, M.A., has taught at the Universities of Pittsburgh, Southern Nevada, and Southern California. At the National Institute of Mental Health she has served as Chief of the Epidemiology Training Section, of the Social Sciences Research Section, of the Research Planning and Evaluation Branch, and of the Prevention Research Branch. Her consultancies include the national Head Start program, the Parent-Child Centers, the Job Corps, the YWCA, and the Mental Health Association. She has served on the Public Health Service Task Force on Women's Health, the Task Panel on Women of the President's Commission on Mental Health, and the Public Health Service Year 2000 Health Objectives for the Nation.

**Toni V. Cook Monsey**, M.A., is a doctoral candidate in developmental psychology at the University of Vermont. Her research has focused on the relationship between mothers' epistemologies and their communication strategies with their children. She is currently working on a project to prevent school failure and school-age pregnancy in middle school and high school girls.

**Hedwin Naimark**, Ph.D., is a licensed psychologist serving as a trainer and organizational consultant to not-for-profit organizations, and a Fellow of the Institute for Rational-Emotive Therapy. Trained originally in social and developmental psychology, she represents the Society for the Psychological Study of Social Issues at the United Nations, where she worked closely with UNICEF and other nongovernment organizations to promote the U.N. Convention on the Rights of the Child and to develop materials to educate children and adults about human rights.

**Irena Obuchowska**, Ph.D., is Professor and Head of the Department of Child Psychopathology and Special Education at Adam Mickiewicz University in Poznan, Poland. She is a member of the Polish Psychological Association and the International Society for the Study of Behavioral Development. She has published several books in Polish as well as numerous journal articles in Polish, German, and English.

**Michael Obuchowski**, M.A., is a doctoral student in clinical psychology at the New School for Social Research, New York, and a Research Scientist in the Department of Medical Genetics at the New York Psychiatric Institute. He specializes in experimental psychopathology, especially cognitive dysfunctions in psychosis. He is a member of the American Psychological Society, the International Neural Network Society, and the New York Neuropsychology Group.

**Dan Olweus**, Ph.D., is Professor of Personality Psychology at the University of Bergen, Norway. He has taught at the Universities of Stockholm and Umea. His research interests include aggression, developmental psychopathology, and bully/victim problems. He is past Vice President of the Swedish Psychological Association. He has published numerous works in Swedish, Norwegian, and English, and has received several awards for his research on aggression. He has lectured in England, the United States, and throughout Europe.

**Patricia Ortega-Andeane**, M.Sc., has training in general and experimental psychology. She is Head of the Environmental Psychology Department in the Graduate Division of the School of Psychology at the National Autonomous University of Mexico. She is responsible for designing and analyzing data for the national survey of the needs, interests, and habits of Mexican adolescents. She has also been active in designing the graduate curriculum in environmental psychology and has published many papers in the general areas of curriculum evaluation, environmental stressors, and related fields.

**Marion Rikken** works in the Prevention Section of the Regional Institute for Outpatient Mental Health Care (RIAGG Oost-Veluwe) in Apeldoorn. Her main areas of interest include children of parents with mental disorders, women and depression, sexual violence, social functioning, and school programs. She is a Lecturer in Prevention at the Hogeschool Nijmegen, a Visiting Lecturer at the University of Nijmegen, and a supervisor for prevention workers, and has published several prevention articles in Dutch journals.

**Milton Schwebel**, Ph.D., is Professor Emeritus at Rutgers University, where he still teaches and supervises doctoral research part-time. He is Senior Research Scholar at the Center for Psychological Studies in the Nuclear Age at the Harvard Medical School and a Visiting Professor at the Universities of Hawaii and Southern California. His research interests include assessment of educability, facilitation of cognitive development, the psychological effects of nuclear war threat, and the construction of nuclear reality in the developmental process. He is author or coauthor/editor of 13 books and more than 100 journal articles and book chapters. His recent books include *Research on Cognitive Development and Its Facilitation: A State of the Art Report*; *Facilitating Cognitive Development*; and *Promoting Cognitive Growth Over the Life Span* (in press).

**Araba Sefa-Dedeh**, Ph.D., is a Clinical Psychologist in the Department of Psychiatry at the Ghana Medical School in Ghana, West Africa. She earned her Ph.D. from Washington University in St. Louis, Missouri. She has been a Fulbright scholar, and at the time of authoring her chapter in this volume, she was an African-American Institute postgraduate student at the University of Vermont.

**Helena Sek, Ph.D.**, is Professor of Psychology at Adam Mickiewicz University in Poznan, Poland. She is involved extensively in research dealing with stress and coping in school-aged children. Recently, she has related these measures in children to certain behaviors in their parents, emphasizing the contribution of parental competence. She is the leading advocate in Poland of primary prevention research and programs.

**Galina V. Skoblo, M.D.**, is Senior Researcher in the Department for Child Preventive Psychiatry at All-Union Research Center for Mental Health in Moscow. Her interests include social and biological risk factors for child mental disorders and methods of preventive intervention. She has authored 35 articles.

**Aleksandra Sommerfeld, M.A.**, is a Clinical Psychologist and Assistant in Preventive Psychology at the Adam Mickiewicz University in Poznan, Poland. She is trained in family counseling and therapy. Her doctoral research program concerns creative activity in parent-child interactions.

**Nomita Sonty, Ph.D.**, is a postdoctoral fellow in behavioral medicine at the St. Louis University Medical Center, Missouri. Her doctoral research examined life stresses, social supports, and coping in rural women with psychological distress. While on the faculty of the National Institute of Mental Health and Neurosciences in India, she worked in community mental health, with a special interest in mental handicaps and the role of Anganwadi workers in working with mentally handicapped persons.

**Wolfgang Stark, Dipl. Psych.**, is Director of the Munich Self-Help Resource Center in West Germany. His project on health promotion for children is part of the World Health Organization's networking of 30 cities in Europe to develop health promotion strategies and healthy public policy in the urban context. He is developing a survey of international aspects of primary prevention.

**Beatriz Rivera de Tarrab, Ph.D.**, is General Director of Support to State Programs in the Comprehensive National System for the Development of the Family in Mexico. She has represented Mexico before the Executive Council of UNICEF and was Coordinator of the Psychopedagogic Unit of the National Institute of Mental Health in Mexico. Her degrees are in psychology, primary education, and public administration. She has done research on the normal development of children, psychodiagnosis, learning processes, and public health.

**Anthony Tommasello, M.S.**, is active in the addictions field. Holding master's degrees in both pharmacology and epidemiology, he is Associate Professor of Clinical Pharmacy and the Director of the Office of Substance Abuse Studies in the Pharmacy School at the University of Maryland, conducting clinical service, student education, and research in the addictions field. His research interests include alcoholism treatment, methadone maintenance treatment, and the epidemiology and prevention of drug abuse and addiction.

**Forrest B. Tyler**, Ph.D., is Professor of Psychology at the University of Maryland. Throughout his career in clinical and community psychology he has focused on work with underserved populations, ranging from preschool children to the elderly. He spent five years at the National Institute of Mental Health working in support of psychological training in innovative and community outreach directions. For the last 20 years he has been at the University of Maryland, where he has served as Director of the Clinical/Community Psychology Program and has worked to develop community-oriented programs with emphases on multicultural perspectives. At the same time, he has been teaching and conducting research in Colombia, India, and China.

**Sandra L. Tyler**, R.N., M.S., M.A., is Coordinator of the Children's Outreach and Program Evaluation Project at the University of Maryland. Her nursing career experiences range from work with impoverished populations in Appalachia to work in inner-city hospitals in Chicago, Detroit, and Washington, D.C. She taught nursing at the University of Maryland School of Nursing, Prince George's Community College, and the Johns Hopkins University International Nurse Education Program. With her cross-cultural interests, she completed a master's degree in applied anthropology and has combined her interests in work involving health care and street youth.

**Elsa M. van Willenswaard** has worked for more than 12 years as a social worker/psychotherapist in a variety of institutes of mental health care. An expert in feminist therapy and child sexual abuse, she works as a Prevention Staff Member for the RNO Institute for Outpatient Mental Health Care in Rotterdam. As a project manager she is responsible for the new prevention project, "Treatment of Incest Offenders Rotterdam." She is one of the founders of the first Women's Help and Health Centres in Rotterdam.

**Jorge Manuel Velasco-Alzaga**, M.D., has training in both medicine and public health in Mexico, with postgraduate studies at Fort Sam Houston in Texas and Johns Hopkins University, as well as training as a psychoanalyst. He organized the first program on mental health for the World Health Organization in the Americas during 1960-1965 and has been Consultant for the Pan American Health Organization and the American Regional Office of the World Health Organization. He has held a wide variety of offices in the American Psychiatric Association, particularly on task forces and in programs stressing international

affairs and transcultural projects. He is one of the most experienced and distinguished psychiatrists/psychoanalysts in Mexico.

**Henk Verburg** has studied chemistry and sociology/adult education. From 1974
through 1984 he worked as a Prevention Worker at a Regional Institute for Outpatient Mental Health Care, after which he became National Prevention Coordinator at the Dutch Union for Outpatient Mental Health Care. In this function he
has published the *Second Policy Paper on Mental Health Prevention.* Currently
he is working at the Dutch Union for Outpatient Mental Health Care as National
Coordinator for Outpatient Mental Health Care in the Netherlands.

**Brian L. Wilcox,** Ph.D., is Director of Legislative Affairs and Policy Studies
for the Public Interest Directorate of the American Psychological Association.
His principal research focus is child and family policy. Prior to working at
APA, he was a Congressional Science Fellow in the office of U.S. Senator Bill
Bradley (D-NJ) and a member of the Psychology Department faculty at the University of Virginia. He received his Ph.D. in community psychology at the University of Texas. His recent research and writing have focused on adolescent
health issues.

ACG - 9433